NEW RESEARCH ON THE PSYCHOLOGY OF FEAR

New Research on the Psychology of Fear

Paul L. Gower
Editor

Nova Science Publishers, Inc.
New York

For permission to use material from this book please contact us:
Telephone 631-231-7269; Fax 631-231-8175
Web Site: http://www.novapublishers.com

NOTICE TO THE READER

The Publisher has taken reasonable care in the preparation of this book, but makes no expressed or implied warranty of any kind and assumes no responsibility for any errors or omissions. No liability is assumed for incidental or consequential damages in connection with or arising out of information contained in this book. The Publisher shall not be liable for any special, consequential, or exemplary damages resulting, in whole or in part, from the readers' use of, or reliance upon, this material.

This publication is designed to provide accurate and authoritative information with regard to the subject matter covered herein. It is sold with the clear understanding that the Publisher is not engaged in rendering legal or any other professional services. If legal or any other expert assistance is required, the services of a competent person should be sought. FROM A DECLARATION OF PARTICIPANTS JOINTLY ADOPTED BY A COMMITTEE OF THE AMERICAN BAR ASSOCIATION AND A COMMITTEE OF PUBLISHERS.

LIBRARY OF CONGRESS CATALOGING-IN-PUBLICATION DATA

New research on the psychology of fear / Paul L. Gower, editor.
     p. cm.
Includes bibliographical references and index.
ISBN 1-59454-334-8
1. Fear. I. Gower, Paul L.
BF575.F2N49   2005
152.4'6--dc22   2005011326

Published by Nova Science Publishers, Inc. ✣New York

CONTENTS

Preface   vii

Chapter 1   Cognitive Biases Associated with Social
                 Interaction Fears and Anxiety   1
                 Amy Wenzel and Nicholas Finstrom

Chapter 2   Focus of Attention and Causal Attributions in Social Anxiety   25
                 Bethany A. Teachman, Sheila R. Woody and Michael A. Friedman

Chapter 3   Fear and Learning   43
                 Jacklin Fisher and Jan Horsfall

Chapter 4   Fear of Death   59
                 Shulamith Kreitler

Chapter 5   Oral Surgery Appointment Attendance:
                 Effects from Fears of Dentistry and Pain   91
                 Kevin E. Vowles, Daniel W. McNeil, John T. Sorrell,
                 Deborah Rettig McKee, Michael J. Zvolensky,
                 Robert W. Graves, Bryan D. Weaver and James R. Riel

Chapter 6   The Treatment of Dental Fear in Children and
                 Adolescents – A Cognitive-Behavioural Approach
                 to the Development of Coping Skills and their Clinical Application   105
                 Helen R. Chapman and Nick C. Kirby-Turner

Chapter 7   The Impact of Behavioural and Emotional Problems in
                 Children's Dental Fear Development   141
                 Maaike Ten Berge and Jaap S.J. Veerkamp

Chapter 8   Dental Phobia: An Overview of Cognitive Behavioural
                 Theory, Models and Treatment   153
                 Ad de Jongh and Marieke Meyerink-Anderson

Chapter 9   Variations on a Theme: The Spectrum of Anxiety Disorders
                  and Problems with DSM Classification in Primary Care Settings   **181**
                  David Katerndahl

Index   **223**

PREFACE

Fear is a normal human emotional reaction - it is a built-in survival mechanism with which we are all equipped. Fear is a reaction to danger that involves both the mind and body. It serves a protective purpose - signaling us of danger and preparing us to deal with it. The major components of fear are sensations, feelings, cognitions and behaviors. Fear can be individual or collective such as expressed in the national fear in the United States related to terrorism. The Washington DC sniper attacks caused widespread fear in a large geographic region far out of proportion to the real danger. Individuals must cope with fear on a daily basis in a myriad of forms: financial fears, health fears, relationship conflict fears, dental appointments, fears about the future etc. This new book collects important research which helps shed light on important issues in this field which touches all of us each day.

Cognitive models of social anxiety suggest that maladaptive schemata cause attentional biases toward threat, memory biases toward threat, and the tendency to interpret ambiguous information in social or evaluative situations as threatening. Chapter 1 reviews results from a series of studies designed to validate the existence of these cognitive biases and determine their relation to the activation of maladaptive schema content. Studies using the script methodology indicate that threat-relevant schemata of socially anxious individuals contain both adaptive and maladaptive elements. Although the literature confirms that socially anxious individuals indeed exhibit attentional biases toward threat, there is no evidence to suggest that these biases are driven by the activation of maladaptive schemata. Contrary to predictions made by cognitive theories of social anxiety, there is little evidence to support the notion that socially anxious individuals are characterized by memory biases toward threat. Instead, it is speculated that the few observed memory biases documented in the literature might have arisen because accurately recalled threat-relevant material is interpreted in a negative manner. Implications for cognitive theories of social anxiety are discussed, and future directions for research on cognition and social anxiety are proposed.

As reported in chapter 2, the association between self-focused attention and social anxiety is well documented, but the mediators of this relation are unknown. This experiment manipulated attentional focus from the self to a conversation partner in order to observe causal attributions of performance in an experimental social situation. Change in attentional focus was expected to evoke shifts in attributions, mirroring those documented in the actor-observer effect. Forty-two college students participated in self- and other-focused mock job interviews, and then rated the degree to which their performance had been due to themselves or to the situation. Participants attributed their behavior primarily to situational causes across all conditions. However, when self-focused, participants demonstrated an attenuation of the self-serving bias. Given that socially phobic persons typically show a reversed self-serving bias, this finding may have implications for understanding cognitive processing in social phobia.

Chapter 3 explores the consequence of fear and anxiety on student learning in clinical settings. Student identified clinical incidents and their emotional corollary, particularly the emotions of fear and anxiety, provide the focus of the study. Mental health settings were selected because community attitudes towards the mentally ill frequently equate mental illness with the potential for violence, criminality and even homicide. It can be anticipated therefore that health care students undertaking clinical education in mental health settings are likely to be apprehensive and fearful and may confront considerable difficulty attempting to assimilate theory into practice in these learning environments. Data were gathered from one hundred and thirty students undertaking clinical experience in mental health settings. Two hundred and sixty critical incident reports were read and their content analyzed within three broad categories: description of incident, affect produced and effect on student learning. Immediate emotional and cognitive responses and perceived levels of fear and anxiety triggered in the students by the critical incident are reported. The impact of these emotions and cognitions was ascertained through small group debriefing and reflection exercises with the students. The findings from the study demonstrate the need for educators to integrate into the clinical curriculum learning activities aimed at assisting students manage fear and anxiety.

In chapter 4, there may be nothing more human and ubiquitous than the fear of death. It would probably be correct to state that there is no human being who has never in his or her life experienced the fear of death, in some form, for a *given* duration of time. This statement would not be complete without the sequel which is that whatever else death may be it is first and foremost an integral part of life. These two assumptions provide a good starting point for dealing psychologically with the fear of death.

Chapter 5 focuses on, dental fears are prevalent in the general population and can have detrimental effects on dental care utilization, and subsequent oral health status. Fear of pain is an integral component in many individuals with high dental fear. The present investigation assessed how oral surgery appointment attendance rates were related to fears of dentistry and pain. Participants completed the Dental Fear Survey and Fear of Pain Questionnaire-III prior to scheduled or emergency oral surgery appointments. An oral surgery appointment attendance ratio was calculated retrospectively with data from a six-year period. Findings indicated that attendance rates were directly and negatively related to both dental fear and fear of pain. Further analyses investigated differences among three groups of patients: appointment attenders, appointment nonattenders, and individuals with emergency appointments. In general, nonattenders were more fearful than attenders; emergency patients also reported more dental fear and were older than attenders. These data indicate the importance of dental fear and fear of pain in understanding attendance behavior, and suggest that assessing these variables prospectively may aid in the identification of avoidant individuals.

In chapter 6, dental fear in children is a widespread and acknowledged problem. Much research has been conducted into aspects of dental fear such as aetiology, measurement of severity and treatment delivery, with the aim of dental fitness, rather than psychological well-being. In this very practically orientated article we hope to expound our cognitive-behavioural approach to the treatment of child dental fear which aims both to achieve dental fitness, and facilitate the development of coping strategies, thus enabling long term access to dental treatment.

As reported in chapter 7, this study was undertaken to assess the role of emotional and behavioural problems, as measured by the Child Behaviour Checklist (CBCL), in a child's dental fear development. The parents of 178 children (85 girls) referred to the Centre for Special Dental Care were asked to complete the Dental Subscale of the Children's Fear Survey Schedule (CFSS-DS) on behalf of their child, after the child's treatment at the Centre had finished. The results showed that the children's level of fear has decreased substantially after treatment at the Centre (mean 39.1 vs. 31.5, t=8.09, p=.000), but was still relatively high in comparison with children from the general Dutch child population. Fear reduction was found in all subgroups of children, with and without other problems, indicating that a structured behavioural management approach can be sufficient in reducing children's dental fear to a more controllable level. However, it was suggested that fearful children with a more complex problematic nature, in particular with internalising problems such as withdrawal and somatic complaints, might still form a risk group in daily practice. Extra attention is still needed for these children.

Anxiety about dental treatment is a worldwide health problem of considerable significance. While 20 per cent of the population dislikes visiting the dentist to such an extent that they use dental services only when it is really necessary, approximately 5% of the population in Western countries demonstrate such an excessive and 'unreasonable' fear of dental appointments that these situations are entirely avoided.

Chapter 8 considers the current knowledge concerning onset, theories, presentation and maintenance of the pathological form of dental anxiety, dental phobia. Particular attention is given to the behavioural model and to meaning and role of cognitive phenomena in the aetiology and maintenance of this condition. Furthermore, it includes a brief overview of effective methods and techniques that can be used for the treatment of dental phobia.

In chapter 9, although the psychiatric literature can support the splintered model of a DSM world, considerable evidence also exists in support of commonality among depressive disorders. Does this commonality of disorders also apply to the anxiety disorders? Not only do people with anxiety disorders display similar backgrounds, comorbidity, and treatment response, but similarities at both the micro- and macro- levels of the brain lead to similarities in phenomenology. Thus, the majority of anxiety disorders may represent different aspects of the same disorder. In fact, there is growing evidence for commonality between depressive and anxiety disorders. Not only do anxiety and depressive disorders frequently co-occur and their symptoms suggest a continuum, but some of these disorders have similar genetics and neurochemistry. The overlap between anxiety and depression suggests a common underlying diathesis. The unification of anxiety disorders and anxiety with depressive disorders would raise new concerns about the appropriateness of the DSM system to primary care. Not only would the appropriateness of the DSM system be compromised in primary care by patients with transient, subthreshold disorders, and distress not meeting diagnostic criteria, but if disorders are clinically indistinguishable from each other, then the DSM system would lose all relevance to primary care settings. If true, two primary clinical implications arise. First, mental health treatment is far more important than diagnosis; categorization becomes an academic exercise. Second, a new classification system for mental illness in primary care, which is dimensional, multi-axial, reliable, and reflective of the spectrum of mental disorders seen in primary care, is needed if we are to promote a common language and conduct relevant research on mental illness in primary care settings.

In: New Research on the Psychology of Fear
Editor: Paul L. Gower, pp. 1-23

ISBN 1-59454-334-8
© 2005 Nova Science Publishers, Inc.

Chapter 1

COGNITIVE BIASES ASSOCIATED WITH SOCIAL INTERACTION FEARS AND ANXIETY

Amy Wenzel and Nicholas Finstrom
University of North Dakota

ABSTRACT

Cognitive models of social anxiety suggest that maladaptive schemata cause attentional biases toward threat, memory biases toward threat, and the tendency to interpret ambiguous information in social or evaluative situations as threatening. This chapter reviews results from a series of studies designed to validate the existence of these cognitive biases and determine their relation to the activation of maladaptive schema content. Studies using the script methodology indicate that threat-relevant schemata of socially anxious individuals contain both adaptive and maladaptive elements. Although the literature confirms that socially anxious individuals indeed exhibit attentional biases toward threat, there is no evidence to suggest that these biases are driven by the activation of maladaptive schemata. Contrary to predictions made by cognitive theories of social anxiety, there is little evidence to support the notion that socially anxious individuals are characterized by memory biases toward threat. Instead, it is speculated that the few observed memory biases documented in the literature might have arisen because accurately recalled threat-relevant material is interpreted in a negative manner. Implications for cognitive theories of social anxiety are discussed, and future directions for research on cognition and social anxiety are proposed.

Most people experience some degree of fear and apprehension in certain social or evaluative situations, such as not knowing anyone at a large party, presenting a speech in front of an instructor and classmates, or participating in a job interview. However, a substantial percentage of the population experiences social/evaluative fears and anxiety to the degree that it causes significant life interference or personal distress. In their National Comorbidity Study, Kessler et al. (1994) estimated that 13% of the American public meets criteria for social phobia according to the *Diagnostic and Statistical Manual, Fourth Edition* (DSM-IV; APA, 1994) at some point in their lives, making it one of the most prevalent mental disorders. Nevertheless, it has only been over the past two decades that social phobia has received systematic attention in the clinical psychiatry and psychology literatures (cf. Liebowitz, Gorman, Fyer, & Klein, 1985). Moreover, only recently have mental health professionals fully grasped the profound impact that social interaction fears have on people's lives, often limiting these individuals' occupational success, recreational choices, and dating frequency (Whittchen & Beloch, 1996).

The purpose of this chapter is to describe and critically evaluate current research on social interaction fears and anxiety from a cognitive perspective. Several cognitive theories of social anxiety (e.g., Clark & Wells, 1995; Rapee & Heimberg, 1997) have described the mechanism by which social interaction fears cause performance deficits and personal distress, and these theories provide the rationale for cognitive behavioral therapy (CBT) for social phobia (e.g., Heimberg, Dodge, Hope, Kennedy, Zollo, & Becker, 1990). This chapter exemplifies the study of social interaction fears and anxiety using data from one specific laboratory that is dedicated to the study of cognition and emotion by using innovative methodologies from cognitive psychology to elucidate cognitive and behavioral sequelae of clinical and sub-clinical instances of anxiety. It should be noted that experiments from this laboratory involve either socially anxious or social phobic individuals. We define socially anxious individuals as individuals, usually undergraduate students, who score high on self-report inventories of fear of negative evaluation and social avoidance and distress. Social phobic individuals, in contrast, are those who meet DSM-IV criteria for social phobia using the *Structured Clinical Interview for DSM-IV Disorders* (SCID; First, Spitzer, Gibbon, & Williams, 1994).

Before embarking on this discussion, we wish to acknowledge the different connotations associated with the constructs of anxiety and fear. Barlow (2002) argued that fear and anxiety are two separate experiences, with fear being an innate response to imminent danger, and anxiety being a more complex interplay of emotions resulting in worry and a sense of uncontrollability. He suggested that the clinical manifestation of fear is panic and that the clinical manifestation of anxiety is apprehension about potential encounters with danger. We believe that both fear and anxiety play important roles in the experience of social anxiety and phobia. It is not uncommon for socially anxious individuals to have panic attacks when confronted with a situation involving performance in front of others. However, socially anxious individuals also ruminate over future social and performance obligations, worry about potential social errors, and arrange their lives to that they can avoid uncomfortable social and evaluative situations. In fact, in their etiological model of social phobia, Hofmann and Barlow (2002) include true alarms and false alarms (i.e., factors also important in the development of panic) as well as anxious apprehension as factors that interact with a biological vulnerability and environmental stressors to produce social anxiety. Moreover, Epstein (1972) proposed a relationship between fear and anxiety, such that "anxiety can be defined as unresolved fear, or, alternatively, as a state of undirected arousal following the perception of threat" (p. 311). For the purpose of this chapter we will regard social anxiety as an unresolved fear of social interactions resulting in apprehension about others' evaluations.

COGNITION AND SOCIAL INTERACTION FEARS

According to cognitive models of social anxiety (e.g., Beck & Emery, 1985; Clark & Wells, 1995; Rapee & Heimberg, 1997; Stopa & Clark, 1993), socially anxious individuals believe that they are in imminent danger of negative evaluation by others. Rapee and Heimberg (1997) indicated that socially anxious individuals construct a negative mental image of their external appearance and social performance as would be perceived by an audience. All of these models suggest that socially anxious individuals preferentially allocate their cognitive resources in the direction of threat, although they differ in conceptualizing exact where the threat lies. Clark and Wells (1995) proposed that when socially anxious individuals detect the possibility of negative evaluation, they shift their attention to monitoring their own behavior rather than attending fully to the interaction at hand, which paradoxically results in awkward, unskilled behavior. On the other hand, Rapee and Heimberg (1997) suggested that socially anxious individuals allocate attentional resources to monitoring the reactions of others, and when encountered with ambiguous information (e.g., an interaction partner glancing at his or her watch), they interpret such gestures as disapproval or criticism.

Thus, these models assume that a number of cognitive biases characterize socially anxious individuals. First, they posit that socially anxious individuals exhibit attentional biases toward threat, such that they quickly detect clues about others' negative evaluation of them as well as internal bodily cues that they appear anxious or are otherwise performing inadequately. Second, these models suggest that socially anxious individuals interpret ambiguous information in a negative manner, such that they mistakenly conclude that others are interpreting them negatively, they equate mild signs of anxiety as indicators of a failed performance, and they judge that they are performing worse than others with the same behavioral repertoire. Third, Beck and Emery (1985) and Rapee and Heimberg (1997) indicate that socially anxious individuals are characterized by dysfunctional beliefs or maladaptive mental representations concerning their performance. In other words, these models purport that overarching cognitive structures, such as *schemata*, create a cognitive orientation in which socially anxious individuals expect to encounter danger and process information accordingly. Finally, one model (i.e., Rapee & Heimberg, 1997) raises the possibility that socially anxious individuals are characterized by a memory bias for threat-relevant information, as it indicates that long-term memories, in part, form the mental representations that in turn facilitate attention and interpretation biases.

These models justify the use of CBT for social anxiety, and in fact there exists evidence that CBT reduces dysfunctional interpretations in ambiguous social situations (see Cohn & Hope, 2001, for a review). However, clinical scientists strive to provide empirical data that validate models of psychopathology in order to confirm that theoretical accounts are indeed accurate. For the past decade, research in our laboratory has been conducted to empirically validate aspects of these cognitive theories of anxiety. The following is a review of empirical studies from our laboratory designed to examine schema content associated with social anxiety, attentional biases toward socially-relevant threat, memory biases for socially-relevant threat, and interpretations of ambiguous stimuli in the context of social situations.

Threat-Relevant Schemata

We begin with a discussion of empirical studies designed to elucidate schema content associated with social interaction fears because cognitive models of anxiety suggest that the presence of such cognitive structures set the context for specific cognitive biases toward threat to emerge. According to many clinical scientists, threat-relevant schemata are defined as dysfunctional attitudes and beliefs, such as "Something terrible is going to happen" or "If something terrible happens, I won't be able to cope" (Beck & Emery, 1985). Typically, such beliefs and attitudes are assessed by administering self-report inventories to participants and asking them to rate the extent to which they endorse thoughts that reflect such beliefs (e.g., Glass, Merluzzi, Biever, & Larsen, 1982; Kendall & Hollon, 1989). However, many cognitive psychopathologists question the usefulness of the information obtained from these inventories (e.g., Eysenck, 1997; MacLeod, 1993), as by its nature, pathology distorts individuals' self-reports and inhibits self-awareness. Moreover, self-reports are often biased by demand characteristics, distorted memory, and inaccurate reporting due to social desirability concerns.

In order to examine schema content from a different perspective, we shifted our attention to the cognitive psychology literature and uncovered a sound methodology to examine scripts, or schemata composed of events that typically occur in common events or situation s (cf. Schank & Abelson, 1977). In the typical script study (e.g., Bower, Black, & Turner, 1979), participants are instructed to list 20 events that most people experience in common situations, such as going to a restaurant or making breakfast. Events listed by at least 25% of the participants are aggregated into a group script and are assumed to be reflective of schema content for those situations. We reasoned that event-based scripts could be compared between socially anxious and nonanxious individuals for common situations that involve social interaction or evaluation, such as going to a party or giving a speech (cf. Wenzel & Holt, 2003a).

To investigate this possibility, socially anxious ($\underline{n}$ = 46) and nonanxious ($\underline{n}$ = 45) participants were instructed to list the typical events that most people experience in six social or evaluative situations: (a) going to a party, (b) going on a date, (c) presenting a speech, (d) eating at a restaurant with acquaintances, (e) presenting a new idea to a supervisor, and (f) complaining to a store manager about a product. Participants were screened in mass testing sessions and invited to participate in the experiment if they scored in the upper and lower quartiles on both the Fear of Negative Evaluation Scale (FNE; Watson & Friend, 1969) and the Social Avoidance and Distress Scale (SAD; Watson & Friend, 1969). The same instructions were used as those described in Bower et al. (1979), with the exception that participants were explicitly told to in clued concrete events, emotions, and thoughts into their sequences. Aggregate scripts for the socially anxious and nonanxious groups were compiled with events listed by at least 25% of the participants in the respective groups.

It was predicted that the scripts of socially anxious participants would comprise different, and presumably more maladaptive, events than the scripts of the nonanxious participants. In the party script, for example, it was expected that the nonanxious participants would list enjoyable, relaxed events, whereas the socially anxious participants would list events reflecting the experience of anxiety, such as "Sit in the corner of the room", "Spill food on clothes", and so on. Contrary to expectation, the aggregate scripts of the socially anxious and nonanxious groups contained nearly identical events. Events included in the socially anxious participants' aggregates that were not included in the nonanxious participants' aggregates were mundane and fit logically with the sequences. Moreover, some events included in the aggregates of both the socially anxious and nonanxious participants reflected the experience of anxiety, such as "Feel nervous" in the party, speech, and date scenarios. Thus, results did not support the notion put forth by cognitive theories of anxiety that socially anxious individuals would be characterized by threat-relevant schemata.

However, one criticism of this study was that it examined general schema content, or knowledge that would pertain to most people in these threatening situations. This decision was made in order to align the methodology as closely as possible with that which was standard in the cognitive psychology literature. However, we acknowledge that cognitive theories of anxiety suggest that cognitive biases are most pronounced in conditions in which anxious individuals perceive themselves in direct contact with threat, but that they show no biases when they imagine others in the same situations (e.g., Butler & Mathews, 1983). Thus, Wenzel and Holt (2003a) reported a second study in which socially anxious ($\underline{n}$ = 40) and nonanxious ($\underline{n}$ = 40) participants listed events for the same situations, but this time they were instructed to list events that they personally typically experience rather than the events that most people experience. Results were largely consistent with those found in Study 1, such that the sequences of events generated by the two groups comprised similar events. Wenzel and Holt (2003a) concluded that there is no evidence to support the notion that socially anxious individuals are characterized by maladaptive schemata for threat.

Although the Wenzel and Holt (2003a) study was an important first step in elucidating schema content associated with anxiety, the extent to which their findings generalize to clinical samples is unclear, as participants were socially anxious individuals who scored high on two self-report measures rather than individuals who were seeking treatment for social/evaluative fears. To examine this issue in a clinical sample, Wenzel (in press, a) recruited participants diagnosed with social phobia using DSM-IV criteria ($\underline{n}$ = 16) and nonanxious participants ($\underline{n}$ = 17) and adopted the instructions from Wenzel and Holt's (2003a) Study 2 for two scenarios: going to a party and presenting a speech. In addition to comparing the group aggregates descriptively, Wenzel trained coders to rate the emotional tone of participants' sequences on the broad dimensions of positive and negative affect, which were analyzed using inferential statistics. Although both group aggregates followed a similar macrostructure, the group aggregates of the social phobic participants contained more references to the experience of anxiety than the group aggregates of the nonanxious participants, such as "Feel relieved" in the party scenario after they had found people they knew, and "Hands shake" in the presenting a speech scenario. Moreover, social phobic participants generated sequences that reflected more negative affect than the sequences generated by nonanxious participants. Taking into account these results as well as the results from Wenzel and Holt (2003a), Wenzel raised the possibility that the schemata of socially anxious individuals contain both adaptive and maladaptive elements. Specifically, it was speculated that socially anxious individuals have accurate knowledge for the events that transpire in social and evaluative situations, but that these events are associated with elevated levels of negative affect.

This line of research increased awareness of the necessity of empirically validating accepted constructs in theoretical accounts of pathology; however, methodological confounds limit the degree to which one can have confidence in these findings. First, analyses were descriptive in nature, making it difficult to draw definitive conclusions in the nature of subtle differences between scripts. Events listed by each participant were coded for their main idea, such that associated descriptors were averaged out. For example, in the date scenario, it is possible that a socially anxious participant could have listed the event, "Call date reluctantly", whereas a nonanxious participant could have listed the event, "Call date excitedly". Both of these entries would have been categorized as "Call date", although there are clearly differences in the emotional tone associated with carrying out this action. Second, the guidelines from Bower et al. (1979) were adopted in creating group aggregates, such that events were included if at least 25% of participants in each group included it into their sequences. Although this cutoff was determined objectively by the distribution of events generated by participants in Bower et al.'s study, the possibility remains that events listed by, for example, between 20 and 24% of participants in each group would not have been included in aggregates, but would have similar psychological significance as events listed by 25% of participants. Third, ratings of emotional tone in the Wenzel (in press, a) study were made on two broad dimensions of affect, and it is likely that more specific ratings of anxiety-related constructs might differentiate more effectively between socially anxious and nonanxious groups.

To address these methodological limitations, Wenzel, Kerr, Finstrom, Jordan, and Lystad (submitted) undertook a re-analysis of the Wenzel and Holt (2003a) data. They developed two coding schemes to characterize each event included in participants' sequences. The first coding scheme quantified instances of affective tone, and the number of anxiety-related, anger-related, and positive events were tabulated. They chose to include anger-related events because of Barlow's (2002) recent observation that many anxious individuals also have anger difficulties and that these emotional expressions share similar a similar underlying vulnerability (e.g., autonomic lability). The second coding scheme quantified instances of deviant responding, which was operationalized as script errors described in Bower et al. (1979) and included *obstacles* (i.e., anything that prevents a script-relevant goal from being accomplished), *errors* (i.e., an unexpected outcome to an action or behavior), and *distractions* (i.e., any action, thought, or behavior that results in a new irrelevant temporary goal being set). They viewed these coding schemes as more rigorous than those used in Wenzel and Holt (2003a) and Wenzel (in press, a), as they yielded a quantitative estimate of the number of pathology-relevant events included in participants' scripts. Results indicated that socially anxious participants included more anxious and deviant events in their scripts, but not more angry and fewer positive events, and only when they generated scripts that were personally relevant. Thus, this study provided evidence indicating that the *self*-schemata associated with threat are disturbed in socially anxious individuals, but not necessarily their *general* schemata for threat.

In all, this line of research demonstrates that socially anxious and social phobic individuals have the knowledge of the events that are expected to occur in social and evaluative situations. However, when they consider their own performance in these situations, their scripts contain some maladaptive characteristics relative to the scripts of nonanxious individuals. If socially anxious individuals expect threatening and deviant events to occur in these situations, it is likely that they will quickly detect any indication that these are occurring and interpret ambiguous cues as signaling possible danger. Thus, activating, challenging, and modifying the scripts of socially anxious individuals might be a useful technique to include in CBT in order to address the underlying schema that is driving information processing biases. Indeed, Holt and Wenzel (1997) reported preliminary evidence that such an exercise was useful in reducing fears of public speaking and flying in two individuals receiving CBT in a psychiatric outpatient setting.

Attentional Biases

The study of attentional biases associated with fear and anxiety commenced in 1985 with a landmark study by Mathews and MacLeod, who used a modified Stroop color naming task to examine anxious and nonanxious participants' latencies to name the colors of threat-relevant and neutral single word stimuli. Not only did Mathews and MacLeod (1985) find that anxious participants named the colors of threat-relevant words more slowly than nonanxious participants, they also determined that individuals with primarily physical concerns were slowed most on the physical threat stimuli, whereas individuals with primarily social concerns were slowed only on the social threat stimuli. In addition, other groups of researchers (e.g., Hope, Rapee, Heimberg & Dombeck, 1990; Maidenberg, Chen, Craske, & Bytrisky, 1996) found that participants with social phobia exhibited slower color naming latencies relative to nonanxious participants when presented with social threat stimuli, and Mattia, Heimberg, and Hope (1993) reported that such color naming interference attenuates after successful treatment for social phobia.

Although these studies clearly demonstrate that individuals with social phobia are characterized by a distinct cognitive bias, the particular stage of information processing to which Stroop performance corresponds is unclear. This pattern of results could very well reflect an attentional bias toward threat, such that the attentional resources of social phobic individuals are consumed by threat-relevant stimuli, preventing them from directing their attention to the color naming task at hand. However, an alternative explanation is that social phobic individuals are demonstrating cognitive avoidance when they are slow to name the ink colors of these stimuli, such that they are actually directing their attention away from these words instead of being consumed by their meaning (cf. de Ruiter & Brosschot, 1994). A third explanation has nothing to do with attentional biases, but instead suggests that this pattern of results implies a response bias, in that social phobic individuals have more difficulty than nonanxious individuals in responding to a characteristic of threat-relevant stimuli.

Due to the nature of these methodological confounds, cognitive psychopathologists adopted the probe detection task to isolate attentional processes in a more specific manner. In the original version of this task (MacLeod, Mathews, & Tata, 1986), participants were presented with two words, one about the other, and were instructed to read the first word aloud in order to focus their attention on that location. On one third of the trials, a small dot replaced one of the words, and participants were required to press a key as quickly as possible when they detected its presence. The critical trials were the ones in which a probe replaced a threat-relevant word in the lower position, as participants were not already directing their attention to that location. It was reasoned that an attentional bias toward threat would be demonstrated if anxious and fearful individuals respond to probes that replace threat-relevant stimuli in the lower position more quickly than nonanxious individuals, as it was assumed that the contents of the stimulus would have already drawn their attention to that location, making it particularly easy to detect a probe that would replace it. This elegant design eliminates the possibility of a response bias because participants respond to a neutral stimulus (i.e., the dot probe) rather than a property of the threat stimulus itself. Using this design,

Mogg, Mathews, and Weinman (1989) demonstrated that individuals with social phobia indeed exhibit facilitated probe detection when the probes replace social threat stimuli, although Asmundson and Stein (1994) found that this pattern only held for probes that replaced social threat stimuli in the upper, but not the lower position.

More recently, cognitive psychopathologists have used this task to examine attentional biases toward various facial expressions, with the reasoning that threatening facial expressions would more readily activate threat-relevant fear structures than threatening single words in socially anxious individuals. Many of these studies adopted a variant of the probe detection task described above, in which participants are presented with two faces simultaneously, followed by a probe replacing the face in one of two locations. The probe requires participants to make one of two responses (e.g., an up or down arrow), and participants are instructed to make the appropriate responses as quickly and as accurately as possible. Using this task, Mogg and her colleagues (Mogg & Bradley, 2002; Mogg, Philippot, & Bradley, 2004) found that socially anxious individuals demonstrate attentional biases toward threatening faces but not happy and neutral faces. These results were evident in masked conditions and unmasked conditions in which stimuli were presented for 500 ms., but not when stimuli were presented for 1,250 ms. Mogg et al. (2004) suggested that attentional biases toward threatening are best captured as an initial orienting response rather than as a response that involves sustained attention. In contrast, using a similar task, Mansell and his colleagues (e.g., Chen, Ehlers, Clark, & Mansell, 2002; Mansell, Clark, Ehlers, & Chen, 1999) demonstrated that socially anxious individuals direct their attention *away* from emotional faces. To reconcile these discrepant findings, Mogg et al. (2004) pointed out that Mansell's studies also included neutral, non-facial stimuli (i.e., household items) and speculated that the vigilance response is inhibited when socially anxious individuals have a choice of where to direct their attention.

Many researchers who find attentional biases toward threat attribute their findings to the activation of maladaptive schemata (e.g., Hope et al., 1990). That is, they suggest that the threat included in their experiments activate maladaptive schemata, which in turn make anxious individuals more likely to exhibit cognitive biases. Although this mechanism is consistent with cognitive theories of anxiety (e.g., Rapee & Heimberg, 1997), no empirical evidence exists to suggest that maladaptive schemata play a causal role in cognitive biases that are observed in anxious individuals. Moreover, it seems questionable that experiments relying on single words to disrupt performance are adequately accessing the maladaptive elements of schema content in anxious individuals. Inclusion of threat-relevant faces as stimuli in these experiments enhances their ecological validity, but the degree to which faces activate threat-relevant cognitive structures is unknown.

Wenzel (submitted) attempted to examine attentional biases in individuals diagnosed with social phobia using stimuli more representative of schema content than single words. She included automatic thoughts relevant to social interaction fears and anxiety (e.g., "I feel awkward and dumb", "They'll think I'm inept"), reasoning that these statements are activated in specific social and evaluative situations and are reflective of underlying schema content (cf. Kendall & Hollon, 1989). Because the task involved the processing of full sentences, the modified Stroop task was inappropriate because participants can respond to the ink color without reading and entire sentence, as was the probe detection task because most versions of this experiment involve the presentation of stimuli for less than one second (cf. Yiend & Mathews, in press). Instead, Wenzel used a dichotic listening shadowing task (cf. Mathews &

MacLeod, 1986), in which participants were presented with ambiguous but potentially threatening stories in their dominant ear and were instructed to repeat what they heard. In addition, they were presented with lists of threat-relevant and neutral automatic thoughts in their non-dominant ear, which they were instructed to ignore. Simultaneously, participants completed a simple reaction time task, in which they were instructed to click the computer mouse as soon as they detected a probe on the computer screen. There were two dependent variables of interest: (a) shadowing errors committed in the presence of threat-relevant and neutral automatic thoughts presented in the non-dominant ear, and (b) reaction time in the presence of threat-relevant and neutral automatic thoughts presented in the non-dominant ear. It was predicted that social phobic participants would make more shadowing errors and exhibit slower reaction times than nonanxious participants when threat-relevant automatic thoughts were presented.

Social phobic participants exhibited poorer shadowing performance than nonanxious participants, but their performance did not vary as a function of type of automatic thought that was presented in their non-dominant ear. Moreover, social phobic and nonanxious participants had similar reaction times, again regardless of the type of automatic thought that was presented. Anecdotally, social phobic participants often made the comment that the shadowing task was difficult and that the task was quite stressful. Thus, although they exhibited overall attentional disruption, there were no biases that could be attributed to their attention being consumed by the social threat automatic thoughts being presented. Their impaired shadowing performance could easily be attributed to general features of the impairment associated with their pathology. There was a great deal of evidence that social phobic participants were generally more impaired than nonanxious participants, as they had higher Beck Depression Inventory scores (though not in the clinically significant range), and a higher percentage of them were seeking treatment.

Wenzel's (submitted) study refutes the theoretical notion that maladaptive schemata cause attentional biases toward threat. However, it is consistent with Beck and Clark's (1997) revised theory of cognitive biases associated with anxiety. These authors suggest that attentional biases occur in the first stage of information processing, *initial registration*. This orienting mode is an automatic process that occurs outside of conscious awareness, consistent with an *early warning detection system* whose purpose is to identify potentially threatening stimuli in the environment and assign their priority for the allocation of cognitive resources. Stimuli are assessed in a global manner in this stage, and the details and associated meanings are not processed. Instead, Beck and Clark suggest that the influence of schemata begins to be observed in the second stage of information processing, *immediate preparation*, which is a mixture of automatic and controlled processes that prepare the individual for dealing with the threat. Moreover, schemata are fully activated in the third stage of information processing, *secondary elaboration*, which involves controlled processing that links threat-relevant information to current concerns and personal issues affecting the individual. In other words, automatic attentional biases toward threat are *not* due to the influence of maladaptive schemata, but Beck and Clark raise the possibility that cognitive tasks involving controlled processing, such as memory and interpretation tasks, would indeed be influenced by these cognitive structures.

Memory Biases

Contrary to the literature on attentional biases associated with social anxiety, the literature on memory biases associated with social anxiety has yielded equivocal results. Several studies examining explicit memory have failed to uncovered enhanced memory for threat-relevant single words (e.g., Becker, Roth, Andrich, & Margraf, 1999; Cloitre, Cancienne, Heimberg, Holt, & Liebowitz, 1995; Rapee, McCallum, Ravenscroft, & Rodney, 1994). That is, these studies show that socially anxious individuals are no more likely than nonanxious individuals to recall single words relating to social or evaluative experiences to a greater degree than neutral single words. On the other hand, several groups of researchers (e.g., Coles & Heimberg, in press; Foa, Gilboa-Schechtman, Amir, & Freshman, 2000; Lundh & Öst, 1996) reported that socially anxious individuals were more likely to recognize critical faces than accepting faces, raising the possibility that socially anxious individuals demonstrate explicit memory biases toward threat only when stimuli are more ecologically valid than single words.

Findings from studies examining implicit memory associated with social anxiety are similarly unclear. Amir, Foa, and Coles (2000) demonstrated an implicit memory bias toward threat in individuals with social phobia using a white noise task. In this procedure, participants heard a series of threat-relevant and neutral sentences mixed with one of three volumes of white noise. Subsequently, they were presented with a combination of old and new sentences against a background of the three levels of white noise and were asked to rate the level of white noise associated with each sentence. It was assumed that implicit memory would be demonstrated if participants rate the level of white noise as softer for the old sentences than the new sentences, and that memory biases would be demonstrated if the noise is rated especially softer for previously presented threat-relevant sentences. Results suggested that individuals with social phobia indeed rated threat-relevant sentences softer than nonanxious individuals. In contrast, Lundh and Öst (1997) examined implicit memory associated with social phobia using a word-stem completion task. Although their main analyses detected no implicit memory bias in their participants with social phobia, they found an interesting dichotomy in implicit memory performance when their social phobia group was divided post-hoc into those with generalized social phobia and those with non-generalized social phobia. Specifically, individuals with generalized social phobia demonstrated a baseline bias, such that they were more likely than nonanxious individuals to complete unprimed word stems with threat-relevant words. In contrast, individuals with non-generalized social phobia were more likely than nonanxious individuals to demonstrate the expected priming effect, such that they completed the primed word stems with the previously-presented threat relevant words. However, Lundh and Öst admitted that this distinction was uncovered in post-hoc, exploratory analyses and that it is unlikely that implicit memory biases are associated with social anxiety above and beyond baseline biases.

A series of studies has been conducted in our laboratory that applies other methodologies to examine memory biases associated with social anxiety. First, Wenzel and Holt (2002) examined explicit memory for threat-relevant and neutral prose passages in participants with social phobia ($\underline{n} = 16$) and nonanxious participants ($\underline{n} = 17$). Previous studies examining recall for prose passages found that individuals with agoraphobia (Nunn, Stevenson, & Whalen, 1984) and individuals with spider phobia (Rusted & Dighton, 1991) recalled a greater percentage of threatening passages than nonanxious individuals and a greater percentage of this material than neutral material. Based on these investigations, it was expected that social phobic participants would recall a greater percentage of evaluative threat passages than nonanxious participants and a greater percentage of this material than neutral material. Two neutral prose passages were adopted from the Wechsler Memory Scales-Revised (WMS-R) *Logical Memory* subtest (Wechsler, 1987), and two evaluative threat passages were constructed to be parallel in sentence structure and number of words as the passages from the WMS-R. Contrary to expectation, social phobic participants recalled fewer units of material from the evaluative threat prose passages than nonanxious participants.

Results were interpreted in light of the *vigilance-avoidance hypothesis*, first proposed by Mogg, Mathews, and Weinman (1987). In this study, Mogg et al. detected a nonsignificant trend for generally anxious participants to recall fewer threat-relevant words than nonanxious participants—a pattern similar to that reported by Wenzel and Holt (2002). The authors raised the intriguing possibility that some anxiety disorders, such as generalized anxiety disorder, are characterized by a tendency to quickly detect threat in the environment (i.e., attentional bias) but then avoid elaborate processing of that material, perhaps because it is too threatening to tolerate prolonged exposure. Mogg et al. speculated that this cognitive bias serves to maintain pathology because anxious individuals are unable to accurately retrieve this material in order to make a more realistic appraisal of it. Wenzel and Holt speculated that this mechanism indeed may be at work in individuals with social phobia, as a key diagnostic feature of social phobia is the avoidance of encounters with social or evaluative situations (APA, 1994).

To further examine whether the vigilance-avoidance pattern is associated with information processing social anxious individuals, Wenzel, Jostad, Brendle, Ferraro, and Lystad (in press) examined the occurrence of false memories in socially anxious and nonanxious individuals. According to Roediger and McDermott (1995), false memories are experimentally induced instances in which participants recalled or recognized that a particular stimulus was presented, when in fact, it was not. To examine false memories, participants are presented with a list of single words, all of which are associated with an unpresented target word (e.g., 15 words associated with "party" are presented, but the word "party" is not). Rather than the number of words associated with each list that participants recall, the variable of interest is the percentage of time participants recall and recognize target words that were never presented. It was reasoned that the false memory paradigm has the potential to uncover the explanation for why socially anxious individuals are not characterized by a memory bias for threat. Specifically, it is possible that anxious individuals accurately recall threat-relevant material that is *actually present* in their environment because they closely monitor it and direct a substantial amount of cognitive resources toward it (cf. Wessel & Merckelbach, 1997, 1998 for examples of this phenomenon with specific phobic individuals). However, because anxious individuals often catastrophize the implications of and exaggerate the distress associated with encounters with threat (Marks & Hemsley, 1999), it also is likely that they would be prone to recalling some aspects of threat that were *never present*. Straightforward list-learning procedures to study explicit memory would not capture the latter type of memory bias because the primary dependent measure would be number of previously presented words recalled, which is limited to the stimuli to which participants had been exposed.

To investigate this possibility, socially anxious ($\underline{n}$ = 48) and nonanxious ($\underline{n}$ = 51) participants were presented with four social threat lists of single words relating to the target words *party*, *interview*, *date*, and *speech*, and four neutral list of single words relating to the target words *music, river, fruit,* and *window.* Prior to beginning the session, participants were told that they would be asked to stand up and present a two-minute introduction of their name and interests after completing the task. Although participants were not asked to follow through with this request, it was included in the experimental design in order to create a state of mild anxious apprehension. Words were presented by a recorded male voice at a rate of one word every 1.5 seconds. After each list presentation, participants were given two minutes to perform either an immediate free recall test or a word search distracter task. After all of the lists were presented, participants completed a recognition test that included the unpresented target words, stimuli presented in the first, second, eighth, fourteenth, and fifteenth serial positions of each list, and forty-eight words from the same serial positions in eight of Roediger and McDermott's (1995) lists that were not presented in this study.

It was predicted that socially anxious participants would demonstrate higher rates of false memories for *unpresented* threat-relevant target words than nonanxious participants. However, consistent with the lack of compelling results found in the literature on explicit memory biases toward single threat-relevant stimuli, it was expected that socially anxious participants would not recall more *presented* threat-relevant words than nonanxious and nonfearful participants. Consistent with expectation, groups performed similarly in their memory for words actually presented, but contrary to expectation, the groups had similar rates of threat-relevant false memories. However, socially anxious participants recalled fewer targets and more words in serial positions 4-11 than nonanxious individuals, which provides some evidence that socially anxious participants performed more accurately than nonanxious participants. This finding does not provide evidence that sheds light on whether socially anxious individuals are characterized by a content-specific memory bias, but it raises the possibility that being in a state of anxious activation, prompted by the expectation of having to give a formal introduction, narrowed their attention on the task at hand and facilitated performance (cf. Christianson, 1992; Wessel & Merckelbach, 1997, 1998).

All of the studies reviewed to this point incorporated linguistic stimuli, mainly single words, into their memory task. Another possibility for the mixed pattern of results in this literature is that most studies do not use stimuli that are particularly ecologically valid (e.g., single words). This methodological limitation might not attenuate attentional biases toward threat, as detection of threat occurs quickly in response to general indications of danger. However, memory retrieval involves elaborate processing, and it is possible that socially anxious individuals do not assign single words high processing priority during the encoding process because they realize that single words do not pose a high level of danger. In order to examine more ecologically valid memories, we embarked on a series of studies examining threat-relevant and neutral autobiographical memories. Autobiographical memory is the recollection of one's personal experiences that incorporates verbal description, mental imagery, and often emotional experiencing (Rubin, 1998). In typical autobiographical memory studies, participants are cued with a stimulus, often a single word, and instructed to retrieve the first specific memory that comes to mind (Crovitz & Schiffman, 1974; Rubin, 1982). Because performance is evaluated on the recall of ideographic personal experiences rather than on artificial stimuli learned in the laboratory, results from autobiographical memory studies are thought to reflect memory that occurs in everyday life (Neisser, 1978).

Wenzel, Jackson, and Holt (2002) cued participants with social phobia ($n = 16$) and nonanxious participants ($n = 17$) with 15 social threat single cue words and 15 neutral cues. Participants were instructed to record the first specific memory that came to mind. Memories were coded on two dimensions—affective tone and specificity. It was predicted that social phobic participants would recall memories when cued with social threat words that contained more negative affect and that were more specific than the social threat memories of nonanxious participants. Although there were no between groups differences in the percentage of specific memories retrieved, social phobic participants indeed made more frequent references to negative affect when retrieving social threat memories relative to nonanxious participants. However, examination of the means suggested that 8% of the social threat memories of social phobic participants contained references to negative affect, compared to 3% of the social threat memories of nonanxious participants, so the practical significance of the results are questionable.

Strengths of the Wenzel et al. (2002) study were that participants were experiencing clinically significant levels of social phobia and that coding schemes were implemented rigorously with precise operational definitions for constructs and high levels of interrater reliability. However, the autobiographical memory cueing task was implemented differently than similar tasks in the clinical science literature. Most studies examining autobiographical memory associated with pathology use oral, rather than written procedures, such that participants are presented with a cue word and instructed to verbalize the first specific memory that comes to mind (see Wenzel, in press, for a methodological review). Thus, it is difficult to compare the Wenzel et al. (2002) study with studies examining autobiographical memories associated with other pathologies (e.g., McNally, Lasko, Macklin, & Pitman, 1995; McNally, Litz, Prassas, Shin, & Weathers, 1994; Williams & Broadbent, 1986) because the procedures used were significantly different. Wenzel, Werner, Cochran, and Holt (2004) adopted the oral autobiographical memory test in a sample of 15 individuals with mild levels of social phobia and 17 nonanxious individuals. Affective tone and specificity were again quantified, and the oral format allowed the authors to examine the latency to retrieve the first memory. A complex pattern of results emerged. Although there were no straightforward between-groups differences, within-group analyses revealed that nonanxious participants, rather than social phobic participants, retrieved memories cued by social threat words more quickly, with more specificity, and with more negative affect than memories cued by neutral words. Thus, memories cued by social threat words were more salient for nonanxious individuals than for social phobic individuals.

Despite the fact that autobiographical memories are more ecologically valid than memories of single words, these studies suggest that autobiographical memories are not distorted in individuals with social phobia. However, if schemata indeed influence elaborate processing in later stages of cognition, then it is possible that the single word cues were not potent enough to activate these relevant cognitive structures. Consistent with the vigilance-avoidance hypothesis, perhaps the single words were general and impersonal enough that social phobic participants avoided retrieving the most painful or threatening memories. To overcome this limitation Wenzel and Cochran (submitted) conducted an autobiographical memory test in which the stimuli used to cue memories were automatic thoughts relevant to the pathology of social phobia rather than single words (cf. Wenzel, submitted). Participants were presented with social threat-relevant and control automatic thoughts via a computer voice with the experimenter outside the room, and they were instructed to verbalize the first personal memory that came to mind. Results indicated that participants with social phobia retrieved memories cued by social thrat-relevant automatic thoughts more quickly than nonanxious participants. There were no between-groups differences in the number of specific memories retrieved. Compared to nonanxious participants, social phobic participants retrieved more memories characterized by higher levels of anxious/worried and fearful affect when cued by both social threat-relevant and control automatic thoughts. Thus, participants with social phobia demonstrated a general bias toward the retrieval of anxiety-laden memories, but the activation of threat-relevant automatic thoughts did not bias memory performance as much as had been expected.

It could be argued that automatic thoughts are idiosyncratic and that there is no evidence that generic pathology-relevant automatic thoughts activate threat-relevant schemata in each individual. Thus, the effect of schema content upon memory performance was examined from a different perspective by Wenzel, Haugen, and Schmutzer (2003). The authors used scripts as stimuli to examine short- and long-term memory for schematic, non-schematic but positive, and non-schematic but negative material. They based their study on a small series of studies from the cognitive psychology literature, in which cognitive researchers constructed short prose passages containing both scripted actions as well as atypical actions that were not included in aggregate scripts (Bower et al., 1979; Graesser, Woll, Kowalski, & Smith, 1980). After a 20-minute delay, participants in these cognitive psychology studies recalled the atypical events at a higher rate than scripted events, presumably because the atypical events were more salient than scripted events and were assigned a higher value during encoding. As retention intervals increased, participants recalled scripted actions at a higher rate than atypical actions, perhaps because they relied on their schemata to guide their recollection.

It was predicted that nonanxious participants would perform in a similar manner as participants from the cognitive psychology studies, such that they would recall more atypical than scripted material in the short-term, but that they would recall more scripted material than atypical material in the long-term. In contrast, it was expected that, relative to nonanxious individuals, socially anxious individuals would recall a higher percentage of negative atypical information than scripted information in both immediate and delayed recall conditions. Moreover, it was predicted that, relative to nonanxious individuals, socially anxious individuals would recall a smaller percentage of positive atypical information than scripted information in both immediate and delayed recall conditions. That is, Wenzel et al. (2003) expected to obtain a memory bias *toward* the recall of negative atypical information compared to scripted and neutral atypical information as well as a memory bias *against* the recall of positive atypical information in the sample of socially anxious individuals.

Participants were 24 socially anxious individuals who scored one standard deviation above the mean on the FNE and SAD and 25 nonanxious individuals who scored one standard deviation below the mean on both of these inventories. Prose passages were created by including eight scripted events, two atypical events that were either positive or negative, and one neutral atypical event. Participants were presented with six passages corresponding to the six scenarios examined in Wenzel and Holt's (2003a) script study: (a) going to a party, (b) going on a date, (c) presenting a speech, (d) eating at a restaurant with acquaintances, (e) presenting a new idea to a supervisor, and (f) complaining to a store manager about a product. Three of the passages contained positive atypical information, and three of the passages contained negative atypical information. Participants performed a free recall task two minutes after the presentation of each passage and again after one week. Contrary to expectation, there was no evidence that scripted versus atypical information had a differential effect upon recall as a function of group in either the short- or the long-term. On the other hand, socially anxious participants were less likely than nonanxious individuals to accurately recall the gist of passages containing negative information in the immediate recall condition. In all, this study provided little evidence for the influence of maladaptive schema content on memory for threatening material in anxious individuals.

It is perplexing that socially anxious individuals do not demonstrate a clear pattern of memory biases for threat-relevant information, given that they clearly attend preferentially to stimuli that signal danger. Although the vigilance-avoidance hypotheses is a compelling argument to explain why socially anxious individuals would not demonstrate enhanced memory for threat-relevant information, it suggests that they should have difficulty retrieving these memories. A few studies indeed reported such findings (i.e., Wenzel & Holt, 2002; Wenzel et al., 2003; Wenzel et al., 2004), but the overall pattern of results is far from consistent, and the effect sizes characterizing differences between socially anxious and nonanxious groups in these studies were small. It is possible that memory biases simply are not important in maintaining symptoms of social anxiety, as the purpose of anxiety is to detect and prepare for threat in one's environment.

However, it is important to uncover the mechanism by which memory biases are observed in some studies but not in others. An alternative explanation to account for this mixed pattern of results stems from findings described by Burke and Mathews (1992), who investigated autobiographical memory biases in individuals with generalized anxiety disorder (GAD) and nonanxious individuals. After retrieving autobiographical memories, participants were instructed to choose an adjective that best described the associated mood. Later, neutral raters coded the emotional tone of participants' memories. Results indicated that, relative to nonanxious participants, participants with GAD were more likely to regard their memories as being "nervous" and less likely to regard their memories as being "pleased". However, these between-groups differences disappeared when analyses were conducted using the ratings from the neutral coders. This pattern of results raises the intriguing possibility that generally anxious participants retrieved memories that were similar to nonanxious participants but that they subsequently imposed a negative interpretation on those memories. It is possible that this mechanism is at work in socially anxious individuals, as the explicit memory studies that left the most room for interpretation (i.e., emotional faces, prose passages) were those that found memory biases in anxious participants. Below is a summary of the literature on interpretation biases associated with social anxiety and attempts in our laboratory to differentiate between memory and interpretation biases in socially anxious and nonanxious participants.

Interpretation Biases

In contrast to the literature on memory biases associated with social anxiety, there is clear evidence that socially anxious individuals interpret ambiguous information as if it were threatening. Amir, Foa, and Coles (1998) reported that social phobic participants were more likely to choose negative explanations for ambiguous social events as compared to obsessive compulsive participants and nonanxious participants, but only when they were instructed to rate the explanations that could come to their mind (versus a typical person's mind). Stopa and Clark (2000) confirmed that social phobic individuals interpret ambiguous social and evaluative information in a negative manner and also demonstrated that they catastrophize the consequences of mildly negative unambiguous social and evaluative information. Further, Roth, Antony, and Swinson (2001) examined social phobic individuals' interpretations of their own bodily sensations and found that, relative to nonanxious individuals, social phobic individuals were more likely to interpret their own anxiety symptoms as indicative of intense distress or psychiatric disturbance and were less likely to believe that others would interpret their own anxiety symptoms as being indicative of a normal physical state. Moreover, Constans, Penn, Ihen, and Hope (1999) reported that interpretation biases extend to socially anxious college students and raised the provocative notion that these biases are characterized by being less positive than interpretations of nonanxious individuals rather than more negative. Huppert, Foa, Furr, Filip, and Mathews (2003) suggested that negative and positive interpretation biases lay on separate continua, such that negative interpretation biases correlate positively with social anxiety, whereas positive interpretation biases correlate negatively with general indices of negative affect.

Brendle and Wenzel (2004) attempted to differentiate between socially anxious and nonanxious participants' memories of threat-relevant stimuli and interpretations of ambiguity associated with threat-relevant stimuli. Socially anxious ($\underline{n}$ = 54) and nonanxious ($\underline{n}$ = 58) participants read ten prose passages consisting of positive social-evaluative, negative social-evaluative, and neutral content and completed memory and interpretation tasks immediately thereafter and again after a 48-hour delay. Self-relevant passages were written in the first person, whereas other-relevant passages were written in the third person. The memory task required participants to freely recall factual details from the passages. The interpretation task, completed after the memory task, required participants to rate the likelihood of positive, negative, and neutral explanations for *the same passage details* that had been assessed in the memory task. Thus, participants in this study provided their interpretation of ambiguous events in the passages only after they had brought them to memory. It was expected that socially anxious participants would not demonstrate a memory bias for threat-relevant information, but that instead, relative to nonanxious participants, they would rate the negative interpretations as being more likely and positive interpretations as being less likely.

Results were consistent with hypotheses and provided a finer-grained illustration of interpretation biases associated with social anxiety than had been described in the literature to date. Socially anxious participants recalled a similar amount of factual details from the passages as nonanxious participants; in fact, all participants performed quite well on this cognitive task. Socially anxious participants rated the likelihood of negative interpretations higher than nonanxious participants, but particularly in the positive passages after the 48-hour delay. Moreover, socially anxious participants rated the likelihood of positive interpretations lower than nonanxious participants , but particularly in positive passages that were self-relevant. Consistent with the predictions made by Huppert et al. (2003), the finding for negative interpretations remained significant even when depressive symptomatology was controlled in subsequent analyses, but the finding for positive interpretations was not. This was the first known study to examine the course of interpretation biases over time.

Wenzel, Finstrom, Jordan, and Brendle (in press) attempted a conceptual replication of this study using positive, negative, and neutral video vignettes as stimuli rather than prose passages. Socially anxious ($\underline{n}$ = 37) and nonanxious ($\underline{n}$ = 47) viewed the videos, and similar to the procedure of Brendle and Wenzel (2004), they completed memory and interpretation tasks immediately thereafter and again after 48 hours. Instead of providing their recall of factual details from the videos, participants indicated their confidence in their recognition of central and peripheral details from the videos. Consistent with the results reported by Brendle and Wenzel, socially anxious and nonanxious participants performed similarly on the recognition task. Socially anxious participants rated negative interpretations as being more likely than nonanxious participants regardless of the valence of the video material or time period after which they completed the task. Unlike the socially anxious participants in Brendle and Wenzel's study, they did not demonstrate a bias in their ratings of the likelihood of positive interpretations for the video material. The authors noted an important different between this study and the Brendle and Wenzel study, as all of the videos depicted other individuals in the social and evaluative situations and thus were presented from an other-relevant perspective, perhaps dampening the robustness of the interpretation findings. Results from this pair of studies confirm the notion put forth by Huppert et al. (2003) that negative interpretation biases associated with social anxiety are more specific and consistent than (the lack of) positive interpretation biases and that negative interpretation biases are able to be detected across a wider range of experimental contexts.

In all, studies examining interpretation biases associated with social anxiety strongly suggest that socially anxious individuals interpret ambiguous social and evaluative situations in a biased manner. However, these biases are localized mainly to instances in which socially anxious individuals are imagining themselves, rather than others, in the social and evaluative situations. In addition to negative interpretation biases, socially anxious also are less likely than nonanxious individuals to make positive interpretations, although this pattern of cognition is more associated with indices of general distress, such as trait anxiety and depression, than social anxiety per se. Moreover, results from studies in our laboratory raise the distinct possibility that studies reporting memory biases in socially anxious samples might be confounding memory and interpretation processes and that observed results are actually due to interpretation biases rather than distortions in memory. We encourage future researchers in this area to design innovative methodologies to isolate further specific information processing biases and to uncover the sequence by which cognitive biases in early stages of processing, such as initial registration, set the context for biases to occur in later stages of processing, such as interpretation and memory.

CONCLUSION

Individuals characterized by social interaction fears struggle with a vicious cycle—they quickly detect and interpret signs of negative evaluation in their environment, and when they allocate cognitive resources to processing these signs, they make social errors because they are not engaged fully in the social or evaluative task at hand. Cognitive theories of social anxiety make contrary predictions about the direction of attentional biases. Rapee and Heimberg (1997) suggest that socially anxious individuals direct their attention toward signs of disapproval and criticism in others with whom they are interacting, whereas Clark and Wells (1995) indicate that their attention is directed away from external threat and toward their internal bodily sensations (e.g., blushing) as well as signs of problem with their own performance. Although the majority of studies indicate that socially anxious individuals are characterized by the facilitation, rather than the avoidance, of attention toward external threat, a study that examines attentional biases in the context of both external and internal threat relevant to evaluation by others would be a welcome addition to the literature.

Although the majority of observed cognitive biases associated with social anxiety are consistent with theory, surprisingly few studies have examined processing of threat-relevant information in the context of "real life" social and evaluative situations. Over a decade ago, Rapee and Lim (1992) reported that socially anxious individuals interpreted their own public speaking performance as being worse than did nonanxious individuals and that their own performance ratings were quite different than the ratings of neutral observers. Amir, McNally, Riemann, Burns, Lorenz, and Mullen (1996) demonstrated that color-naming latencies for threat-relevant single words in an emotional Stroop task were attenuated when social phobic participants anticipated giving a speech. On the other hand, Mansell and Clark (1999) found an explicit memory bias against the recall of positive self-referent words in social phobic participants *only* in a condition in which they anticipated giving a speech. Moreover, Wenzel and Holt (2003b) reported that socially anxious individuals experience interference on difficult cognitive tasks and demonstrate enhanced performance on easy cognitive tasks that are completed immediately after presenting a short speech. Thus, there is preliminary evidence state anxiety elicited by threatening social or evaluative situations elicit a pattern of information processing that is much different than is demonstrated when socially anxious individuals are presented with threat-relevant stimuli at rest. We encourage future researchers to manipulate state anxiety systematically and examine its influence upon the full range of information processing, including attention, memory, and interpretation. Moreover, a study designed to examine cognitive biases that emerge in participants' natural environments and to track their influence upon subsequent behavior would be a tremendous advance in the literature.

Despite the fact that cognitive biases associated with social interaction fears are well documented, the etiology of these information processing distortions is unknown. Only recently have cognitive biases been shown to exert a causal influence on the development of anxiety (MacLeod, Rutherford, Campbell, Ebsworthy, & Holker, 2002). However, the mechanism by which these cognitive biases come about in the first place is not well understood. Although many cognitive psychopathologists speculate that cognitive biases are facilitated by threat-relevant schemata, research from our laboratory demonstrates that threat-relevant schemata are not uniformly maladaptive, and there is no compelling evidence to conclude that these cognitive structures cause observed cognitive biases. Clinical scientists must move beyond descriptive inquiry in this area to isolate the mechanism by which these cognitive biases develop. We speculate that a combination of biological vulnerability, such as autonomic lability, and conditioned responses from early childhood experiences provide the context for at least some cognitive biases, such as initial detection of threat, to emerge.

REFERENCES

American Psychiatric Association (1994). *Diagnostic and statistical manual of mental disorders* (4th ed.). Washington, DC: Author.

Amir, N., Foa, E. B., & Coles, M. E. (1998). Automatic activation and strategic avoidance of threat-relevant information in social phobia. *Journal of Abnormal Psychology, 107,* 285-290.

Amir, N., Foa, E. B., & Coles, M. E. (2000). Implicit memory bias for threat-relevant information in individuals with generalized social phobia. *Journal of Abnormal Psychology, 109,* 713-720.

Amir, N., McNally, R. J., Riemann, B. C., Burns, J., Lorenz, M., & Mullen, J. T (1996). Suppression of the emotinal Stroop effect by increased anxiety in patients with social phobia. *Behaviour Research and Therapy, 34,* 945-948.

Asmundson, G. J. G. & Stein, M. B. (1994). Selective processing of social threat in patients and generalized social phobia: Evaluation using a dot-probe paradigm. *Journal of Anxiety Disorders, 8,* 107-117.

Barlow, D. H. (2002). *Anxiety and its disorders: The nature and treatment of anxiety and panic* (2nd ed.) New York: Guliford Press.

Beck, A. T., & Clark, D. M. (1997). An information processing model of anxiety: Automatic and strategic processes. *Behaviour Research and Therapy, 35,* 49-58.

Beck, A. T., & Emery, G. (1985). *Anxiety disorders and phobias: A cognitive perspective.* New York: Basic Books.

Becker, E. S., Roth, W. T., Andrich, M., & Margraf, J. (1999). Explicit memory in anxiety disorders. *Journal of Abnormal Psychology, 108,* 153-163.

Bower, G. H., Black, J. B., & Turner, T. J. (1979). Scripts in memory for text. *Cognitive Psychology, 11,* 177-220.

Brendle, J. R., & Wenzel, A. (2004). Differentiating between memory and interpretation biases in socially anxious and nonanxious individuals. *Behaviour Research and Therapy, 42,* 155-171.

Burke, M., & Mathews, A. (1992). Autobiographical memory and clinical anxiety. *Cognition and Emotion, 6,* 23-35.

Butler, G., & Mathews, A. (1983). Cognitive processes in anxiety. *Advances in Behaviour Research and Therapy, 5,* 51-62.

Chen, Y. P., Ehlers, A., Clark, D. M., & Mansell, W. (2002). Patients with social phobia direct their attention away from faces. *Behaviour Research and Therapy, 40,* 677-687.

Christianson, S. A. (1992). Emotional stress and eyewitness memory: A critical review. *Psychological Bulletin, 112,* 284-309.

Clark, D. M., & Wells, A. (1995). A cognitive model of social phobia: In R. G. Heimberg, M. R. Liebowitz, D. A. Hope, & F. R. Schneier (Eds.), *Social phobia: diagnosis, assessment and treatment.* New York: Guilford.

Cloitre, M., Cancienne, J., Heimberg, R. G., Holt, C. S., & Liebowitz, M. R. (1995). Memory bias does not generalize across anxiety disorders. *Behaviour Research and Therapy, 33,* 305-307.

Cohn, L. G., & Hope, D. A. (2001). Treatment of social phobia: A treatment-by-dimensions review. In S. G. Hofmann & P. M. Dibartolo (Eds.), *From social anxiety to social phobia: Multiple perspectives.* Needham Heights, MA: Allyn & Bacon.

Coles, M. E., & Heimberg, R. G. (in press). Recognition bias for critical faces in social phobia: Replication and extension. *Behaviour Research and Therapy.*

Constans, J. I., Penn, D. L., Ihen, G. H., & Hope, D. A. (1999). Interpretive biases for ambiguous stimuli in social anxiety. *Behaviour Research and Therapy, 37,* 643-651.

Crovitz, H. F., & Schiffman, H. (1974). Frequency of episodic memories as a function of their age. *Bulletin of the Psychonomic Society, 4,* 517-518.

de Ruiter, C., & Brosschot, J. F. (1994). The emotional Stroop interference in anxiety: Attentional bias or cognitive avoidance. *Behaviour Research and Therapy, 32,* 315-319.

Epstein, S. (1972). The nature of anxiety with emphasis upon its relationship to expectancy. In C. D. Spielberger (Ed.), *Anxiety: Current trends in theory and research* (Vol. 2). New York: Academic Press.

Eysenck, M. W. (1997). *Anxiety and cognition: A unified theory.* East Sussex, UK: Psychology Press.

First, M. B., Spitzer, R. L. Gibbon, M., & Williams, J. B. W. (1994). *Structured Clinical Interview for Axis I DSM-Disorders.* New York: Biometrics Research Dept.

Foa, E. B., Gilboa-Schechtman, E., Amir, N., & Freshman, M. (2000). Memory bias in generalized social phobia: Remembering negative emotional experiences. *Journal of Anxiety Disorders, 14,* 501-519.

Glass, C. R., Merluzzi, T. V., Biever, J. L., & Larsen, K. H. (1982). Cognitive assessment of social anxiety: Development and validation of a self-statement questionnaire. *Cognitive Therapy and Research, 6,* 37-55.

Graesser, A. C., Woll, S. B., Kowalski, D. J., & Smith, D. A. (1980). Memory for typical and atypical actions in scripted activities. *Journal of Experimental Psychology: Human Learning and Memory, 6,* 503-515.

Heimberg, R. G., Dodge, C. S., Hope, D. A., Zollo, L. J., & Becker, R. E. (1990). Cognitive behavioral group treatment for social phobia: Comparison with a credible placebo control. *Cognitive Therapy and Research, 14,* 1-23.

Hofmann, S. G., & Barlow, D. H. (2002). Social phobia (Social anxiety disorder). In D. H. Barlow (Ed.), *Anxiety and its disorders: The nature and treatment of anxiety and panic* (2nd ed.) New York: Guliford Press.

Holt, C. S., & Wenzel, A. (1997, November). *Toward a protocol for prototypical scripting in anxiety treatment.* Poster presented at the 31st Annual Meeting of the Association for Advancement of Behavior Therapy, Miami Beach, FL.

Hope, D. A., Rapee, R. M., Heimberg, R. G., & Dombeck, M. J. (1990). Representations of the self in social phobia: Vulnerability to social threat. *Cognitive Therapy and Research, 14,*177-189.

Huppert, J. D., Foa, E. B., Furr, J. M., Filip, J. C., & Mathews, A. (2003). Interpretation bias in social anxiety: A dimensional perspective. *Cognitive Therapy and Research, 27,* 569-577.

Kendall, P. C., & Hollon, S. D. (1989). Anxious self-talk: Development of the anxious self-statement questionnaire (ASSQ). *Cognitive Therapy and Research, 13,* 81-93.

Kessler, R. C., McGonagle, K. A., Shanyang, Z., Nelson, C. B., Hughes, M., Eshleman, S., Wittchen, H-U., & Kendler, K. S. (1994). Lifetime and 12-month prevalence of DSM-III-R psychiatric disorders in the United States. *Archives of General Psychiatry, 51,* 8-19.

Liebowitz, M. R., Gorman, J. M., Fyer, A. J., & Klein, D. F. (1985). Social phobia: Review of a neglected anxiety disorder. *Archives of General Psychiatry, 42,* 729-736.

Lundh, L. G., & Öst, L. G. (1996). Recognition bias for critical faces in social phobics. B*ehaviour Research and Therapy, 34,* 787-794.

Lundh, L. G., & Öst, L. G. (1997). Explicit and implicit memory bias in social phobia: The role of diagnostic type. *Behaviour Research and Therapy, 34,* 787-794.

MacLeod, C. (1993). Cognition in clinical psychology: Measures, methods, or models? *Behaviour Change, 10,* 169-195.

MacLeod, C., Mathews, A., & Tata, P. (1986). Attentional bias in the emotional disorders. *Journal of Abnormal Psychology, 95,* 15-20.

MacLeod, C., Rutherford, E., Campbell, L., Ebsworthy, G., & Holker, L. (2002). Selective attention and emotional vulnerability: Assessing the causal basis of their association through the experimental induction of attentional bias. *Journal of Abnormal Psychology, 111,* 107-123.

Maidenberg, E., Chen, E., Craske, M., Bohn, P., & Bytristsky, A. (1996). Specificity of attentional bias in panic disorder and social phobia. *Journal of Anxiety Disorders, 10,* 529-541.

Mansell, W., & Clark, D. M. (1999). How do I appear to others? Social anxiety and processing of the observable self. *Behaviour Research and Therapy, 37,* 419-434.

Mansell, W., Clark, D. M., Ehlers, A., & Chen, Y. P. (1999). Social anxiety and attention away from emotional faces. *Cognition and Emotion, 13,* 673-690.

Marks, M., & Hemsley, D. (1999). Retrospective versus prospective self-rating of anxiety symptoms and cognitions. *Journal of Anxiety Disorders, 13,* 463-472.

Mathews, A., & MacLeod, C. (1985). Selective processing of threat cues in anxiety states. *Behaviour Research and Therapy, 23,* 563-569.

Mathews, A., & MacLeod, C. (1986). Discrimination of threat cues without awareness in anxiety states. *Journal of Abnormal Psychology, 95,* 131-138.

Mattia, J. I., Heimberg, R. G., & Hope, D. A. (1993). The revised Stroop color-naming task in social phobics. *Behaviour Research and Therapy, 31,* 305-313.

McNally, R. J., Lasko, N. B., Macklin, M. L., & Pitman, R. K. (1995). Autobiographical memory disturbance in combat-related posttraumatic stress disorder. *Behaviour Research and Therapy, 33,* 619-630.

McNally, R. J., Litz, B. T., Prassas, A., Shin, L. M., & Weathers, F. W. (1994). Emotional priming of autobiographical memory in post-traumatic stress disorder. *Cognition and Emotion, 8,* 351-367.

Mogg, K., & Bradley, B. (2002). Selective orienting of attention to masked threat faces in social anxiety. *Behaviour Research and Therapy, 40,* 1403-1414.

Mogg, K., Mathews, A., & Weinman, J. (1987). Memory bias in clinical anxiety. *Journal of Abnormal Psychology, 96,* 94-98.

Mogg, K., Mathews, A., & Weinman, J. (1989). Selective processing of threat cues in anxiety states: A replication. *Behaviour Research and Therapy, 27,* 317-323.

Mogg, K., Philippot, P., & Bradley, B. P. (2004). Selective attention to angry faces in clinical social phobia. *Journal of Abnormal Psychology, 113,* 160-165.

Neisser, U. (1978). Anticipations, images, and introspection. *Cognition, 6,* 169-174.

Nunn, J. D., Stevenson, R. J., & Whalan, G. (1984). Selective memory effects in agoraphobicpatients. *British Journal of Clinical Psychology, 23,* 195-201.

Rapee, R. M., & Heimberg, R. G. (1997). A cognitive-behavioral model of anxiety in social phobia. *Behaviour Research and Therapy, 35,* 741–756.

Rapee, R. M., & Lim, L. (1992). Discrepancy between self- and observer ratings of performance in social phobics. *Journal of Abnormal Psychology, 101,* 728-731.

Rapee, R., M., McCallum, S. L., Melville, L. F., Ravenscroft, H., & Rodney, J. M. (1994). Memory bias in social phobia. *Behaviour Research and Therapy, 29,* 317-323.

Roediger, H. L., & McDermott, K. B. (1995). Creating false memories: Remembering words not presented in lists. *Journal of Experimental Psychology: Learning, Memory, and Cognition, 21,* 803-814.

Roth, D., Antony, M. M., & Swinson, R. P. (2001). Interpretations for anxiety symptoms in social phobia. *Behaviour Research and Therapy, 39,* 129-138.

Rubin, D. C. (1998). Beginnings of a theory of autobiographical remembering. In C. P. Thompson, D. J. Herrmann, D. Bruce, J. D. Reed, D. G. Payne, & M. P. Toglia (Eds.), *Autobiographical memory: Theoretical and applied perspectives* (pp. 47-67). Mahwah, NJ: Erlbaum.

Rubin, D. (1982). On the retention function for autobiographical memory. *Journal of Verbal Learning and Verbal Behavior, 21,* 21-38.

Rusted, J. M., & Dighton, K. (1991). Selective processing of threat-related material by spider phobics in a prose recall task. *Cognition and Emotion, 5,* 123-132.

Schank, R. C., & Abelson, R. P. (1977). *Scripts, plans, goals and understanding: An inquiry into human knowledge structures.* Oxford, England: Lawrence Erlbaum.

Stopa, L., & Clark, D. M. (1993). Cognitive processes in social phobia. *Behaviour Researchand Therapy, 31,* 255-267.

Stopa, L., & Clark, D. M. (2000). Social phobia and interpretation of social events. *Behaviour Research and Therapy, 38,* 273-283.

Watson, D., & Friend, R. (1969). Measurement of social evaluative anxiety. *Journal of Consulting and Clinical Psychology, 33,* 448-457.

Wechsler, D. (1987). *Wechsler Memory Scales-Revised Manual.* New York: The Psychological corporation.

Wenzel, A. (submitted). *Attentional disruption in the presence of negative automatic thoughts.* Manuscript submitted for publication.

Wenzel, A. (in press, a). Schema content for threat in social phobia. *Cognitive Research and Therapy.*

Wenzel, A. (in press, b). Autobiographical memory tasks in clinical research. In A. Wenzel & D. C. Rubin (Eds.), *Cognitive methods and their application to clinical research.* Washington, DC: APA Books.

Wenzel, A., & Cochran, C. K. (submitted). *Autobiographical memories prompted by automatic thoughts in panic disorder and social phobia.* Manuscript submitted for publication.

Wenzel, A., Finstrom, N., Jordan, J., & Brendle, J. R. (submitted). *Memory and interpretation of visual representations of threat in socially anxious and nonanxious individuals.* Manuscript submitted for publication.

Wenzel A., Haugen, E. N., & Schmutzer, P. A. (2003). Recall of schematic and non-schematic material related to threat in socially anxious and nonanxious individuals. *Behavioural and Cognitive Psychotherapy, 31,* 387-401.

Wenzel, A., & Holt, C. S. (2002). Memory bias against threat in social phobia. *British Journal of Clinical Psychology, 41,* 73-79.

Wenzel, A., & Holt, C. S. (2003a). Situation-specific scripts for threat in socially anxious and nonanxious individuals. *Journal of Social and Clinical Psychology, 22,* 145-168.

Wenzel, A., & Holt, C. S. (2003b). Social-evaluative threat and cognitive performance in socially anxious and nonanxious individuals. *Personality and Individual Differences, 34,* 283-294.

Wenzel, A., Jackson, L. C., & Holt, C. S. (2002). Social phobia and the recall of autobiographical memories. *Depression and Anxiety, 15,* 186-189.

Wenzel, A., Jostad, C. M., Brendle, J. R., Ferraro, F. R., & Lystad, C. (in press). An investigation of false memories in anxious and fearful individuals. *Behavioural and Cognitive Psychotherapy.*

Wenzel, A., Kerr, P., Finstrom, N., Jordan, J., & Lystad, C. M. (submitted). *A reconsideration of schema content for threat in socially anxious and nonanxious individuals.* Manuscript submitted for publication.

Wenzel, A., Werner, M. M., Cochran, C. K., & Holt, C. S. (2004). A differential pattern of autobiographical memory retrieval in social phobic and nonanxious individuals. *Behavioural and Cognitive Psychotherapy, 32,* 1-13.

Wessel, I., & Merckelbach, H. (1997). The impact of anxiety on memory for details in spider phobics. *Applied Cognitive Psychology, 11,* 223-231.

Wessel, I., & Merckelbach, H. (1998). Memory for threat-relevant and threat-irrelevant cues in spider phobics. *Cognition and Emotion, 12,* 93-104.

Wittchen, H.-U. & Beloch, E. (1996). The impact of social phobia on quality of life. *International Clinical Psychopharmacology, 11 (suppl 3),* 15-23.

Williams, M. J., & Broadbent, K. (1986). Autobiographical memory in suicide attempts. *Journal of Abnormal Psychology, 95,* 144-149.

Yiend, J., & Mathews, A. (in press). Selective attention tasks in clinical research. In A. Wenzel & D. C. Rubin (Eds.), *Cognitive methods and their application to clinical research.* Washington, DC: APA Books.

In: New Research on the Psychology of Fear
Editor: Paul L. Gower, pp. 25-41

ISBN 1-59454-334-8
© 2005 Nova Science Publishers, Inc.

Chapter 2

FOCUS OF ATTENTION AND CAUSAL ATTRIBUTIONS IN SOCIAL ANXIETY

Bethany A. Teachman[1], Sheila R. Woody[2] and Michael A. Friedman[3]*

University of Virginia[1], University of British Columbia[2],
Rutgers, The State University of New Jersey[3]

ABSTRACT

The association between self-focused attention and social anxiety is well documented, but the mediators of this relation are unknown. This experiment manipulated attentional focus from the self to a conversation partner in order to observe causal attributions of performance in an experimental social situation. Change in attentional focus was expected to evoke shifts in attributions, mirroring those documented in the actor-observer effect. Forty-two college students participated in self- and other-focused mock job interviews, and then rated the degree to which their performance had been due to themselves or to the situation. Participants attributed their behavior primarily to situational causes across all conditions. However, when self-focused, participants demonstrated an attenuation of the self-serving bias. Given that socially phobic persons typically show a reversed self-serving bias, this finding may have implications for understanding cognitive processing in social phobia.

Key words: social anxiety, self-focused attention, self-serving bias, causal attributions, actor-observer effect

Self-focus refers to the process of "selectively attending to information that originates from within and concerns the self" (Carver & Scheier, 1981, p. 34). Although self-focused attention can serve a functional or self-enhancing role (for example, self-congratulatory

---

* Department of Psychology, University of Virginia, P.O. Box 400400, Charlottesville, VA 22904-4400. Phone: 434-924-0676, Fax: 434-982-4766, E-mail: bteachman@virginia.edu.

thoughts), this inward-directed focus has more often been associated with impaired functioning among clinical populations (i.e., depression, alcoholism, and anxiety; see Ingram, 1990 for a review). Further, there is a robust association between self-focused attention and social anxiety, both on self-report (Hope, Gansler, & Heimberg, 1989; Schlenker & Leary, 1982; Woody, 1996) and information processing (Mansell, Clark, & Ehlers, 2003) measures. For example, social anxiety is positively correlated with frequency of self-relevant thoughts (Hope, Heimberg, Zollo, Nyman, & O'Brien, 1987), and these thoughts appear to occur more frequently when the individual is highly motivated to perform well, such as under conditions of social evaluation (Hope et al., 1989). Hope et al. suggest that anxious arousal induces self-focused attention, which in turn may impair task performance and increase emotional reactivity. This hypothesis is supported by findings that self-focused attention intensifies awareness of one's own affective state (Scheier & Carver, 1977; Fenigstein, 1979), may predict fears of blushing (Bögels & Lamers, 2002), and is exacerbated by arousal (Wegner & Guiliano, 1980).

Increasing evidence supports a bi-directional model of self-focused attention and social anxiety (see Spurr & Stopa, 2002; Woody & Rodriguez, 2000). Negative mood leads one to focus on the self (Salovey, 1992; Wegner & Guiliano, 1980), but self-focus can also directly increase negative affect (Woody, 1996). Specifically, manipulating focus of attention affects ratings of social anxiety, suggesting that self-focused attention plays a causal role in exacerbating social fears. Interestingly, this relation is evident among both socially phobic and normal groups. Using a contrived speech task to alter subjects' attentional locus, Woody and Rodriguez (2000) found that phobic and normal control groups responded equally to the self-focus manipulation, with each group showing anxiety-provoking effects of self-focused attention.

Many questions remain about the moderators and mediators of the association between self-focus and social anxiety. Woody and Rodriguez (2000) proposed that fear of negative evaluation was the critical moderator, on the supposition that self-focus would only increase social anxiety for those who feared the possibility of scrutiny. However, they found that neither a fear of negative evaluation nor the interaction between fear of negative evaluation and self-focused attention were significant predictors of self-reported anxiety during the task.

In a meta-analysis of the relation between self-focused attention and negative affect, Mor and Winquist (2002) found an overall moderate relation (effect size of $d = 0.51$ for correlational designs and $d = 0.41$ for experimental designs) and suggested the relation was strongest in clinical and female-dominated samples. The authors suggest this may be due to women's greater tendency to engage in particularly negative self-focus, such as during rumination (Nolen-Hoeksema, 1987). This analysis highlights moderators of the bi-directional influence of self-focus and negative affect broadly, but does not speak to the role of attentional focus in social anxiety specifically. Mor and Winquist (2002) suggest it may be important to consider the role of public and private self-focus separately. Typically, this distinction is applied to the trait form of self-focus, known as self-consciousness (Fenigstein, Scheier, & Buss, 1975), but Mor and Winquist (2002) suggest it can also distinguish among transitory states of self-focus. Public self-consciousness in this case refers to aspects of behavior that are concerned with others' impressions of oneself, while private self-consciousness reflects attention to private, autonomous goals (Carver & Scheier, 1987). Interestingly, Mor and Winquist concluded from their analysis that private self-focus was more strongly associated with depression and generalized anxiety, whereas public self-focus was more strongly associated with social anxiety[1], highlighting an important moderator of the relationship.

Several possible mediators of the connection between self-focus and social anxiety have also been examined. For example, researchers have postulated that excessive self-focused attention may prevent the individual from devoting sufficient attentional resources to social partners, thus limiting social effectiveness. The hypothesis for this mediating mechanism was based on a limited capacity model of attention (e.g., Wine, 1980). However, Woody and her colleagues (Woody, 1996; Woody, Chambless & Glass, 1997) found that self-focus did not necessarily result in diminished attention to external stimuli. This led us to consider an alternative mediator of the relationship between self-focused attention and social anxiety that would not rely on the assumption of reduced other-focused attention, but would be specific to cognitive processes active when an individual was self-focused; namely, attributions made during social interactions. The present study was designed to explore this mediator based on three converging lines of reasoning that suggest self-focused attention may result in increased internal attributions during a socially evaluative interaction.

Duval and Wicklund (1973) proposed that self-focused attention engages an aversive drive state whereby individuals are motivated to reduce the discrepancy between their present performance and a relevant standard of comparison. Carver and Scheier (1981) expanded on the Duval and Wicklund theory, suggesting that a natural consequence of this drive would be a discrepancy-reducing feedback loop. In essence, the theory states that individuals who feel they are not performing up to their own standard of comparison feel motivated to minimize the perceived performance deficit. To the extent that an individual feels incapable of reducing this discrepancy, Carver and Scheier predict an increase in negative affect, such as anxiety. Building from this model, we note that socially anxious persons, who perseverate on the prospect of social embarrassment, constantly survey their own thoughts and behaviors related to social situations. As a result, they likely become increasingly aware of their flaws (i.e., perceived performance deficit), and attribute these flaws to internal causes. Simply put, when the self is salient, it is highly accessible as a causal explanation for one's behavior (Carver & Scheier, 1981). Thus, we predict that self-focused attention will be associated with internal attributions.

A second line of related social psychology research is the actor-observer effect (Jones & Nisbett, 1972). According to this effect, actors generally attribute their own behavior to situational determinants, while observers tend to attribute the observed individual's behavior to dispositional causes. Typically, the observed individual is another person. However, in the case of self-focused attention, the actor is observing him- or herself. It is not clear whether the expected attributions under conditions of self-focus would reflect those of the actor, who would attribute mainly to the situation, or those of the observer, who would attribute mainly to the actor (in this case, the self).

Shifting attention from the social task or one's social partners to the self may accordingly shift the participant from actor to observer, which the actor-observer effect suggests would shift performance attributions. Specifically, we expect that individuals who are other-focused will make attributions about themselves like "actors," resulting in more external, situational causal explanations. On the other hand, self-focused individuals are expected to make

---

[1] Fejfar and Hoyle (2000) did find a small effect size for the relationship between private self-awareness and negative affect, but they did not evaluate studies on public self-focus.

attributions about themselves like "observers," and therefore make relatively more internal, dispositional causal explanations. This position is consistent with Clark and Wells' (1995) cognitive model of social phobia, which suggests that self-focused attention maintains social anxiety in part because it leads phobic individuals to see themselves from the perspective of an observer, viewing their appearance and performance in a distorted, negative way based on anxiety cues.

Preliminary support for the idea that socially anxious, self-focused individuals are observing themselves comes from a study by Wells, Clark, and Ahmad (1998), who asked research participants to recall anxiety-provoking situations. Wells et al. found that socially phobic participants remembered images of anxiety-provoking social events from the vantage point of an outsider, whereas normal control subjects described social events as though they saw them from their own eyes. Thus, individuals with social phobia recalled anxiety-provoking social situations as "observers," while comparison subjects recalled parallel situations as "actors." However, for memories about events other than those related to social anxiety, participants in both groups described the images from the same vantage point (as "actors"). Hackmann, Surawy, and Clark (1998) found a similar observer perspective about anxiety-provoking social situations among their participants with social phobia.

Wells and Papageorgiou (1999) replicated the finding that socially phobic participants recall social situations from an observer perspective, but interestingly, this was also true for agoraphobic participants, suggesting the phenomenon was not unique to social anxiety. Further supporting the observer-anxiety relationship, Coles, Turk, Heimberg, and Fresco (2001) found that individuals with social phobia took an observer perspective more frequently than non-anxious controls did when asked to recall high anxiety social situations. However, their study points to possible constraints of this effect because only half of their socially phobic sample took an external perspective for the high-anxiety memory, and neither the phobic nor control group took an outsider's perspective for medium- and low-anxiety memories. Coles et al. suggest that the observer perspective may be most likely for social provocations of a performance or public speaking nature.

A final phenomenon from social psychology research, the self-serving bias (see Miller & Ross, 1975), is also relevant to the interplay between attributions, self-focused attention, and social anxiety. Typically, social psychologists have found that normal individuals attribute successful outcomes to internal causes, such as skill, and failures to external causes, such as task difficulty or bad luck. However, persons with social phobia reverse this pattern in social situations, particularly when evaluative concerns are present (Arkin, Appelman, & Burger, 1980; Hope et al., 1989; Zelen, 1987); social phobics tend to blame themselves for perceived social failures and attribute their successes to external causes. Due to fear of negative evaluation from others in social situations, we propose that socially anxious individuals are hypervigilant for, and magnify the importance of, negative aspects of their performance. The combination of chiefly negative self-appraisal and the increased salience of the self (resulting from the increased self-focus in Carver and Scheier's model) likely lead individuals with social phobia to perceive abundant social failures and then to blame themselves for these perceived failures.

These three lines of reasoning converge to suggest shifting attributions may mediate the relation between self-focus and social anxiety. Indirect support for this hypothesis can be drawn from research linking attributions and attentional focus. Taylor and Fiske (1975) found that instructing a subject to focus on a particular actor (within a group) led the subject to attribute greater outcome responsibility to that actor than to others in the situation. Presumably, a similar mechanism would apply to the self, such that self-focused individuals would make more self-attributions. In addition to shifting the direction of attribution from the situation to the self, self-focused attention may shift the balance of attributions for failure and success, resulting in increased personal attributions for failure and diminished personal attributions for success in social encounters. These attributional patterns are expected to produce negative affect and undermine one's sense of confidence about social performance. The present study was designed to examine the relation between causal attributions and self-focused attention in social situations.

To examine shifts in attributions across conditions of self- and other-focused attention, participants engaged in a socially evaluative task involving a series of mock job interviews that manipulated attentional focus. Following each of two interviews, participants completed measures of internal and external causal attributions. Because previous research showed self-focused attention increases social anxiety even among unselected undergraduates (Woody & Rodriguez, 2000), this population was used in the present study. Participants were expected to make more dispositional attributions about their own behavior when in the self-focused condition and to attribute their own behavior to situational causes when in the other-focused condition. A video condition was also included in which participants viewed their own performance from the other-focused condition. Because the video shifted the participant from an other-focused "actor" to a self-focused "observer," we expected more dispositional attributions in this condition. Finally, participants were expected to show an attenuated or reversed self-serving bias, making relatively more internal attributions for their perceived negative performance outcomes when in the self- versus other-focused condition.

METHOD

Participants

In response to signs posted at the psychology department at Yale University, 46 undergraduate students agreed to complete the study in exchange for either $8 or partial course credit. Four participants were excluded either due to mechanical difficulties during the taping of the interviews or because they knew one of the confederates. The final sample of 42 had equal numbers of men and women, and the mean age was 20 years (SD = 1.30).

Measures

As a manipulation check, participants completed the Focus of Attention Questionnaire (FAQ; Chambless & Glass, 1984) immediately following each of the interview conditions. This brief scale consists of two 5-item subscales: Self-Focus, which includes monitoring of one's own internal states and behavior, and External-Focus, which evaluates attention directed toward the environment and one's social partner. The scale has demonstrated acceptable reliability and validity. See Woody (1996) and Woody, Chambless, and Glass (1997) for psychometric information and item wording.

To evaluate causal attributions following each of the interview conditions, participants rated their own performance based on 10 performance descriptors, balanced to include items with positive and negative valence. Using 7-point Likert scales, participants rated how much each descriptor (e.g., "friendly") characterized their social performance. For each of the 10 descriptor ratings, participants then used 7-point Likert scales to rate the extent to which each aspect of their performance had been due to their personality and to what extent their performance had been due to the situation. Thus, the attributions measure consisted of 10 three-part items (a descriptor rating associated with an internal and external attribution rating). The positive and negative descriptors were selected to reflect the positive goals and negative concerns regarding social performance commonly expressed by individuals with social anxiety. Positive descriptors were "friendly", "poised", "socially skilled", "successful", and "interesting." Negative descriptors were "awkward", "distant", "nervous", "boring", and "shallow."

Following each of the interview role-plays, participants completed the negative subscale of the Social-Interaction Self-Statement Test (SISST-N; Glass, Merluzzi, Biever, & Larsen, 1982). This 15-item subscale is a widely used endorsement-style cognitive assessment of negative self-statements about an immediately preceding social interaction. In addition, participants rated their anxiety level following each of the interviews on a 0-100 scale, with 100 representing the highest possible anxiety. Also using a 0-100 scale, participants rated the impression they believed they had made on the confederate, with 100 representing the best possible impression (referred to hereafter as performance impression).

Finally, participants completed two questionnaire measures commonly used to evaluate social anxiety in undergraduate samples. These measures were completed in counterbalanced order with the experimental task. The Social Avoidance and Distress scale (SAD) and the Fear of Negative Evaluation (FNE) scale are companion measures of social anxiety developed by Watson and Friend (1969) for use in undergraduate samples. The FNE is a 30-item, true-false scale that assesses how one feels about being evaluated negatively by others, and the SAD is a 28-item true-false scale that evaluates social anxiety and avoidance.

Procedure

When participants arrived at the lab, an experimenter introduced them to a study on "perception of the self and attention during social interactions, specifically during job interviews." After giving informed consent, participants engaged in two role-plays of job interviews, one in which they played the interviewer, and a second in which a confederate interviewed them. Following each interview, participants made ratings about their anxiety and performance impression during the task and completed the FAQ, SISST-N, and attribution ratings. Participants had been told earlier that the interviews would be videotaped, although they were told the taping would allow their performance "to be rated later by independent experts." Hence, participants were unaware of the final video condition where they would be asked to observe themselves and make causal attributions about their performance as the interviewer in the other-focused condition. The order of the two mock job interviews was counterbalanced across participants.

Several research assistants acted as confederates, but the confederate was always a professionally dressed young woman who was unknown to the participant. An experimenter simply introduced the confederate to the participant at the outset of each interaction, so participants were not clearly informed about whether the confederate was an assistant or another participant. The interviews lasted three minutes each and took place in the same room. In both the self-focused and other-focused interview conditions, the "interviewer" (whether it was the participant or confederate) was provided with a list of sample job interview questions (e.g., "What makes you a good candidate for this job?") and was instructed to feel free to use the sample questions or add their own. Finally, just before the interview began, the experimenter said the following:

> I ask that the interviewer please consider the candidate carefully. At the end of the study, we will be asking you to rate the job candidate's performance, suitability as a candidate, the general impression the candidate made, what you perceived their strengths and weaknesses to be, and how effectively you felt the job candidate handled the interview. Thus, we ask that you please consider their performance carefully.

The purpose of these instructions was to augment the attentional focus manipulation and to intensify the salience of the social evaluation component of the task. Specifically, when participants were in the self-focused condition (i.e. being interviewed), these instructions highlighted that the interviewer would be scrutinizing the "candidate." When participants were in the other-focused "interviewer" condition, the instructions encouraged participants to focus on the "candidate," rather than upon him- or herself. The attentional manipulation included not only the interviewer/candidate role reversal, but was also enhanced by having the self-focused "candidate" directly face a large mirror (approximately 3 feet away). Furthermore, confederates were trained in advance to ensure that the conversational focus was on the "candidate," regardless of whether the confederate or participant filled the role. Participants were allowed to be interviewed for a job of their choice; however, confederates always asked to be interviewed for the position of manager at a prestigious bank (when they were in the self-focused condition) to maximize the consistency of their performance throughout the study.

Participants were videotaped during both job interviews using a camera that was unobtrusively located on a shelf with a variety of other electrical equipment. The camera was camouflaged to discreetly tape participants in the other-focused condition without causing an undesirable increase in their self-focused attention. So, although participants had been informed during written consent that the interviews would be videotaped, they were unaware of the actual operation of the camera. This video recording was used for the third and final condition in the study. After participants had completed the self- and other-focused interview role-plays and the subsequent questionnaires, they were taken to another room to watch a videotape of their performance as an interviewer. In this video condition, participants watched (focused upon) themselves so that we could compare attributions based on literal self-observation in the video condition with those made following the actual other-focused interview. Therefore, based on the performance they observed on video, participants completed the attribution ratings and their self-reported anxious appearance and performance impression ratings a final time. The FAQ and SISST-N were not completed in this condition, since they only apply to actual interactions. Lastly, participants were fully debriefed and thanked for taking part in the study.

RESULTS

Manipulation Check

A manipulation check was conducted to ascertain that the experimental task effectively shifted focus of attention in the desired direction across the job interview conditions. A t-test of the FAQ_{self} score across conditions indicated that participants scored higher on FAQ_{self} in the self- versus other-focus interview condition (t (41) = 7.09, p < .0001, Cohen's d = .31). The comparable analysis for external focus indicated participants had significantly higher $FAQ_{external}$ scores in the other- versus self-focus interview condition (t (41) = 11.84, p < .0001, Cohen's d = .29), thus demonstrating that the job interview paradigm successfully manipulated focus of attention in the predicted directions. Shifts in attentional focus across interview conditions are depicted graphically in Figure 1.

Social Anxiety, Self-Focused Attention and Performance

As expected, the students within our sample scored within the normal range on the social anxiety measures (FNE mean = 13.47, SD = 8.03; SAD mean = 6.51, SD = 6.57), consistent with a typical distribution for undergraduate samples. Scores on the SISST-N in both the self- and other-focus conditions were also within the normal range (self-focus mean = 28.26, SD = 10.41; other-focus mean = 23.40, SD = 8.95). As expected, a repeated measures ANOVA revealed self-reported anxiety during the task was higher in the self-focused condition (F (2, 40) = 4.68, p < .02, f = .35), but there was no difference between the other-focus and video conditions (p > .05).

Self-focused attention as measured by FAQ_{self} in the self-focus condition was strongly correlated with state anxiety (r = .65, p<.0001) and the SISST-N (r = .65, p<.0001). Broader measures of social anxiety were also relatively strongly correlated with the FAQ_{self} (FNE: r = .51, p=.0005; SAD: r = .52, p=.0009). As expected, the correlation between FAQ_{self} and self-rated performance impression during the self-focus condition was negligible (r = -.13, p=.42). Thus, consistent with earlier findings (Woody, 1996), the relationship between self-focus and social anxiety was strong, but perceived performance impression was not significantly related to degree of self-focused attention. However, there was a small but significant negative correlation between the FAQ_{self} and performance valence in the self-focus condition (r = -.32, p=.04). Self-ratings of performance valence were measured by a difference score reflecting each participant's total ratings of positive descriptors minus total ratings of negative descriptors on the attributions scale. Thus, when asked directly for 0-100 ratings of their own performance quality in both of their interviews, participants rated the interviews as equivalent. Their questionnaire responses differed, however, as they rated negative adjectives as more descriptive of their performance in the self-focused condition.

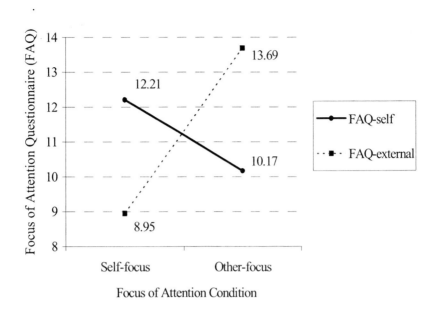

Figure 1. Manipulation check: Mean FAQ$_{self}$ and FAQ$_{external}$ scores in the Self- and Other-focus interview conditions (mean subscale score).

Causal Attributions

To characterize the general nature of participants' causal attributions during the experiment, situational and personality attributions were contrasted within each of the three conditions (self-focus, other-focus, and video). T-tests revealed that participants consistently endorsed more external than internal explanations across conditions (self-focus: t (41) = 4.24, p < .0001, d = .30; other-focus: t (41) = 6.30, p < .0001, d = .31; video: t (41) = 6.16, p < .0001, d = .33). As suggested by the relatively high values for Cohen's d, ratings for situational attributions were at least a standard deviation higher than personality attributions across all three conditions (see Table 1 for means and standard deviations).

Table 1. Causal attributions for situation versus personality within conditions

	Focus of Attention Condition					
	Self-Focus		*Other-Focus*		*Video*	
Attribution Ratings	Mean	SD	Mean	SD	Mean	SD
Performance due to situation	5.07	1.22	5.15	0.94	5.14	0.83
Performance due to personality	3.75	1.34	3.75	1.15	3.67	1.12

Note: N=42. Range is 1-7.

Planned contrasts were used to examine the hypothesis that attributions would shift across conditions to mirror the actor-observer effect. Degree of internal attributions served as the dependent variable. Difference scores were first calculated for each of the 10 performance descriptors. Recall that participants rated their performance related to each descriptor (e.g., friendly, awkward) in terms of the degree of influence from the situation and from their own personality. For each descriptor, situational ratings were subtracted from personality ratings, resulting in a difference score for which high values indicated greater internal causal attributions and low scores indicated more situational attributions. The Total Performance Attribution score was represented by the mean of the (internal – external) difference scores for all 10 performance descriptors. The Negative Performance Attribution score was calculated using the mean of (internal – external) difference scores for only the 5 negative performance descriptors. Similarly, to create the Positive Performance Attribution score, we calculated the mean of the (internal – external) difference scores for just the 5 positive performance descriptors.

In line with our hypotheses about self-focus and the actor-observer effect, we expected that participants would make more internal performance attributions when in the self- versus other-focused condition, and that attributions made in the video condition would mirror those of the self-focused condition (since subjects would again be observing themselves). Planned contrasts tested whether internal attributions (using the difference scores) would be higher for the self-focus (+1) and video (+1) conditions than they were for the other-focus (-2) condition. Contrast analyses revealed non-significant (p > .05) differences, regardless of whether Total, Negative, or Positive Performance Attributions were used. Thus, causal attributions did not shift across conditions according to predictions derived from the actor-observer effect.

To examine whether attributions differed across conditions in a manner that varied from the predicted pattern, we used a repeated measures general linear regression model with the Total Performance Attributions score as the dependent variable, and attentional focus as the within-subjects factor with three levels (self, other, and video). Additionally, to look for interaction effects, the following variables were each examined separately as continuous between-subjects factors: SAD, FNE, anxiety during the task, SISST-N, and performance impression. This set of analyses was repeated for both the Negative and Positive Performance Attribution scores. Causal attributions did not significantly differ across the attentional focus conditions and there was no significant interaction with any of the between-subjects factors. This finding was consistent for the Total, Positive, and Negative attribution scores (all ps > .05).

The analyses described above make clear that the self-focus manipulation did not cause participants to alter their global patterns of attributions across conditions. However, attributional patterns might differ depending on whether the respondent is attempting to explain a social success (positive descriptor) or a social failure (negative descriptor). Due to the effects of self-focus on social anxiety, we expected that participants might make more internal attributions about social failure when self-focused than when other-focused. This finding would suggest that self-focus might be implicated in the maladaptive reversal of the self-serving bias evidenced by individuals with social phobia.

As a preliminary step, we conducted a repeated measures ANOVA with focus condition (self and other) and valence (positive and negative) as factors. Based on our earlier analyses, we expected no main effect for focus condition. However, we did anticipate a main effect for valence representing a self-serving bias in which participants should make more internal attributions for positive (versus negative) descriptors. As predicted, there was no main effect for focus condition (F (1, 41) = .06, p > .05, f = .04), but there was a significant effect for valence (F (1, 41) = 10.29, p = .003, f = .45) along the lines predicted by the self-serving bias. The interaction term did not reach significance (F (1, 41) = 2.24, p > .05, f = .23). (However, the trend was in the right direction and given the small to moderate effect size, the failure to reach significance may have been due to limited power in the present study.)

We then conducted t-tests to contrast the causal attribution difference scores for the negative versus positive descriptors for the self- and other-focus conditions. As expected, subjects provided significantly more external explanations for negative (versus positive) aspects of their performance in the other-focused condition (t (41) = 3.57, p < .001, d = .51), but not in the self-focused condition (t (41) = 1.81, p > .05, d = .20) where they made no significant distinction. These results suggest that participants may demonstrate an attenuation of the self-serving bias under conditions of self-focused attention. See Figure 2.

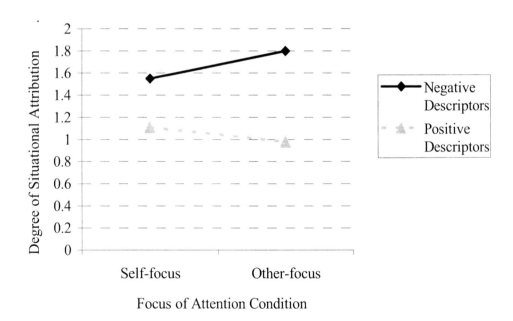

Figure 2. Attenuation of the self-serving bias: Impact of attentional focus on degree of situational attribution for positive and negative descriptors of social performance (mean item response).

DISCUSSION

The present study was designed to examine shifts in causal attributions related to self-focused attention during an evaluative social situation. Past research had demonstrated that self-focused attention actively increases social anxiety, and a shift in attributions was hypothesized to mediate this effect. Participants engaged in two mock job interviews, one in which they were self-focused and one in which they were other-focused. Global attributions were expected to shift in ways that mirrored the actor-observer effect. Thus, when participants were self-focused, they were expected to make more internal attributions because they would be focusing upon ("observing") themselves while they interacted in the social situation. In contrast, when participants were other-focused, they would only be "acting" in the situation (not observing themselves), and consequently would make more external attributions. The video condition was expected to parallel the self-focus condition since participants would then be literally observing their own social performance on screen.

Contrary to expectations, participants provided significantly more situational (versus personality) causal explanations for their social performance across all conditions, regardless of their attentional focus. However, participants' attributions for negative versus positive aspects of their social performance differed depending on whether they were in the self-focus or other-focus condition. When other-focused, participants tended to point to the situation to explain negative aspects of their performance and to take more personal credit for explaining positive aspects of their performance. This pattern follows the usual self-serving bias. However, when self-focused, participants did not make different attributions for positive versus negative aspects of their performance, suggesting an attenuation of the self-serving bias. In other words, when individuals are self-focused in a socially evaluative situation, they may not show a self-serving attributional bias, thus losing out on the confidence-boosting benefits of this bias. This finding provides preliminary evidence that self-focus may be a mediator in the process of reversing the self-serving bias for socially anxious persons and, furthermore, that even normal self-serving biases may be attenuated in socially evaluative situations if the individual is sufficiently self-focused.

Surprisingly, causal explanations did not shift along the lines predicted by the actor-observer effect. This was true for each of the attribution composite measures (total, positive, and negative), where external attributions dominated across experimental conditions. One reason why the expected shift in attributions did not occur may be that the actor-observer effect appears to be attenuated when the observer knows the observed person well (Green, Lightfoot, Bandy, & Buchanan, 1985). Observers are more likely to make dispositional attributions about strangers as opposed to individuals whose behavior they have observed across many different situations. Thus, it is possible that the actor-observer effect did not occur because participants were observing themselves, whom they presumably know very well. An alternative explanation follows from research indicating that the probability of recalling an event from the perspective of an observer increases over time (Frank & Gilovich, 1989; Nigro & Neisser, 1983). It seems plausible that the current study did not observe an effect in part because attributions from the observer perspective were examined too soon after the social event.

Additionally, the experimental task itself may have limited our ability to detect the predicted attributional shift. Because the task was novel, and the demands of the situation were clear and strong, participants' tendency to attribute their behavior primarily to the environment was appropriate. In short, the distinctiveness of the task may have led participants to make more situational attributions than they would have made under more normative social circumstances, in which expectations are often more ambiguous. Future research may thus want to address the external validity of the role-play paradigm to determine whether participants interpreted the situation in the same way as a more naturalistic interaction.

The suggestion that attentional focus may moderate the reversed self-serving bias has received little attention to date. Numerous theorists have tried to explain the phenomenon (which is not surprising given its apparent maladaptive consequences), but there has been little empirical evidence upon which to evaluate the competing explanations. Arkin et al. (1980) postulated that socially anxious persons use a "cost" orientation when under conditions of high evaluative concern, such that they believe evaluators will feel less displeased with them if they take responsibility for their perceived failure. In contrast, Hope et al. (1989) suggested a self-handicapping explanation, designed to minimize damage to self-presentational concerns and to reduce others' expectations for subsequent performances.

An intriguing study by Coles et al. (2001) found that attributions made by socially phobic participants for memories of their performance in past social situations did become more internal, stable, and global as the anxiety level of the situation increased, consistent with the reversal of the self-serving bias. Further, non-anxious control participants showed the opposite pattern, in line with the more typical self-serving bias. However, the design of their study does not permit causal inferences about the direction of the relationship between the observer perspective and attributional bias, and the authors note that low power and a restricted range on their attributions measure limited their analysis of attributional patterns in social situations. Future studies are needed to more directly address the role of self-focused attention as a mediator of the reversal process. Interestingly, self-focused attention has also been associated with depression (Greenberg, Pyszczynski, Burling & Tibbs, 1992), and depressed persons also tend to reverse the self-serving bias (e.g., see Cohen & van den Bout, 1994).

Although the results need to be replicated, this finding has implications for the treatment of individuals with social anxiety given increasing evidence that reduced self-focused attention is related to treatment gains for social phobia (Hofmann, 2000; Woody et al., 1997). The effects found in the present study were fairly small, however a number of factors argued against finding any reversal effects at all. First, the study was designed to test attributions related to the actor-observer effect, not specifically the self-serving bias. Second, using a sample of undergraduates further reduced the likelihood of finding a reversal effect in the self-serving bias. Finally, we only examined attributions that occurred during the actual interview. Anxious anticipation and self-deprecating rumination are problems that are exacerbated for socially phobic persons before and after social interactions. Quite possibly, the effects of self-focus on social anxiety (and consequent attributions) may be most devastating when individuals are either anticipating an evaluative social interaction or re-hashing a past perceived failure. Measuring the effects of self-focused attention at these additional time points may thus reveal larger attenuation effects on the self-serving bias. Therefore, although our initial findings show only a small effect size, these preliminary results suggest that further investigation of self-focus as a mediator of the reversed self-serving bias is warranted.

We are still left with the question of why self-focused attention would attenuate the self-serving bias. One possibility derives from Carver and Scheier's (1981) discrepancy-reducing feedback loop described earlier. Perhaps socially anxious individuals only get caught in the loop for negative aspects of performance because they feel least able to reduce the discrepancy between their actual and ideal performance for these negative outcomes. Positive performance descriptors may not cue the same hypervigilance for perceived negative evaluation by others (i.e. perceived failure). Therefore, only negative performance qualities would exacerbate self-focus, and make internal attributions highly accessible.

The current study has a number of limitations. First, we did not request specific details about the internal and external causal attributions to determine what aspect of the person or situation participants were using to explain their performance. Thus, we do not know whether participants' predominantly situational attributions were referring to difficulty of the task, experimental demands, or an alternative environmental variable. Understanding the nature of participants' external attributions may be particularly informative given research by Mulle and Knobe (1997) that identifies the different types of behaviors (e.g., observable, intentional) explained by actors versus observers. A further drawback of the attributions measure was that it was idiosyncratic to the task in this study, so we have no psychometric data on the scale. However, it should be noted that this limitation is typical of attributions research. Finally, given that level of anxiety shifted along with attentional focus across conditions, the specific mechanism driving the observed attenuation of the self-serving bias cannot be determined. This final point is more of an alternative explanation than a limitation of the present study, but future work will need to disentangle these competing explanations.

The results from this study have raised a number of questions for future research. Clearly, the present findings need to be replicated, ideally in a study specifically designed to investigate the roles of self-focused attention and social anxiety in the self-serving bias. Such research may benefit from using a selected sample of socially anxious or shy individuals to examine the effects of self-focused attention on attributions made in social situations with a more anxious population. If the finding is robust, it will be important to investigate the mechanisms guiding this relationship. For example, does self-focus lead to the reversal as a consequence of availability as suggested by the Carver and Scheier (1981) model, or is the process more akin to a specific deficit in processing of social information under evaluative, anxiety-provoking conditions? Additionally, future studies should address the role of depression on self-focused attention, anxiety, and attributions. This association may be especially critical given that depressed individuals also demonstrate a reversal of the self-serving bias. Understanding these relations may facilitate not only more effective treatment for social phobia, but also broaden our understanding of basic emotion pathology by highlighting how normative social processes, such as the self-serving bias, can become dysregulated.

REFERENCES

Arkin, R.M., Appelman, A.J., & Burger, J.M. (1980). Social anxiety, self-presentation, and the self-serving bias in causal attribution. *Journal of Personality and Social Psychology, 38*, 23-35.

Bögels, S. M., & Lamers, C. T. J. (2002). The causal role of self-awareness in blushing-anxious, socially-anxious and social phobics individuals. *Behaviour Research and Therapy, 40*, 1367-1384.

Carver, C.S., & Scheier, M.F. (1981). *Attention and self-regulation: A control theory approach to human behavior.* New York: Springer-Verlag.

Carver, C. S., & Scheier, M. F. (1987). The blind men and the elephant: Selective examination of the public–private literature gives rise to a faulty perception. *Journal of Personality, 55*, 525–541.

Chambless, D.L., & Glass, C.R. (1984). *The Focus of Attention Questionnaire.* Unpublished Questionnaire, American University, Washington, DC.

Clark, D. M., & Wells, A. (1995). A cognitive model of social phobia. In R.R.G. Heimberg, M. Liebowitz, D.A. Hope, & S. Scheier (Eds.), *Social phobia: diagnosis, assessment and treatment.* New York: Guilford Press.

Cohen, L., & van den Bout, J. (1994). A conceptual scheme for assessing evenhandedness and (counter) self-serving attributional biases in relation to depression. *Psychological Reports, 75*, 899-904.

Coles, M.E., Turk, C.L., Heimberg, R.G. & Fresco, D.M. (2001). Effects of varying levels of anxiety within social situations: relationship to memory perspective and attributions in social phobia. *Behaviour Research and Therapy, 39*, 651–665.

Duval, S., & Wicklund, R. (1973). Effects of objective self-awareness on attributions of causality. *Journal of Experimental Social Psychology, 9*, 17-31.

Fejfar, M. C., & Hoyle, R. H. (2000). Effects of private self-awareness on negative affect and self-referent attribution: A quantitative review. *Personality and Social Psychology Review, 4*, 132–142.

Fenigstein, A. (1979). Self-consciousness, self-attention, and social interaction. *Journal of Personality and Social Psychology, 37*, 75-86.

Fenigstein, A., Scheier, M. F., & Buss, A. H. (1975). Public and private self-consciousness: Assessment and theory. *Journal of Consulting and Clinical Psychology, 43*, 522–527.

Frank, M.G., & Gilovich, T. (1989). Effect of memory perspective on retrospective causal attributions. *Journal of Personality and Social Psychology, 57*, 399–403.

Glass, C.R., Merluzzi, T.V., Biever, J.L., & Larsen, K.H. (1982). Cognitive assessment of social anxiety: Development and validation of a self-statement questionnaire. *Cognitive Therapy and Research, 6*, 37-55.

Green, S.K., Lightfoot, M.A., Bandy, C., & Buchanan, D.R. (1985). A general model of the attribution process. *Basic & Applied Social Psychology, 6*, 159-179.

Greenberg, J., Pyszczynski, T., Burling, J., & Tibbs, K. (1992). Depression, self-focused attention, and the self-serving attributional bias. *Personality and Individual Differences, 13*, 959-965.

Hoffmann, S.G. (2000). Self-focused attention before and after treatment of social phobia. *Behaviour Research and Therapy, 38*, 1123–1132.

Hope, D.A., Gansler, D.A., & Heimberg, R.G. (1989). Attentional focus and causal attributions in social phobia: Implications from social psychology. *Clinical Psychology Review, 9*, 49-60.

Hope, D.A., Heimberg, R.G., Zollo, L.J., Nyman, D., & O'Brien, G.T. (November, 1987). *Thought-listing in the natural environment: Focus and valence of listed thoughts.*

Presented at the annual meeting of the Association for the Advancement of Behavior Therapy, Boston.

Ingram, R. (1990). Self-focused attention in clinical disorders: Review and a conceptual model. *Psychological Bulletin, 107*, 156-176.

Jones, E.E., & Nisbett, R.E. (1972). *The actor and the observer: Divergent perceptions of the causes of behavior*. Morristown, NJ: General Learning Press.

Malle, B. F., & Knobe, J. (1997). Which behaviors do people explain? A basic actor-observer asymmetry. *Journal of Personality and Social Psychology, 72*, 288-304.

Mansell, W., Clark, D. M., & Ehlers, A. (2003). Internal versus external attention in social anxiety: An investigation using a novel paradigm. *Behaviour Research and Therapy, 41*, 555-572.

Miller, D.T., & Ross, M. (1975). Self-serving biases in the attribution of causality: Fact or fiction? *Psychological Bulletin, 82*, 213-225.

Mor, N., & Winquist, J. (2002). Self-focused attention and negative affect: A meta-analysis. *Psychological Bulletin, 128*, 638-662.

Nigro, G., & Neisser, U. (1983). Point of view on personal memories. *Cognitive Psychology 15*, 467–482.

Nolen-Hoeksema, S. (1987). Sex differences in unipolar depression: Evidence and theory. *Psychological Bulletin, 101*, 259–282.

Peterson, C., Semmel, A., von Baeyer, C., Abramson, L.Y., Metalsky, G.I., & Seligman, M.E.P. (1982). The Attributional Style Questionnaire. *Cognitive Therapy and Research, 6*, 287-300.

Salovey, P. (1992). Mood-induced self-focused attention. *Journal of Personality and Social Psychology, 62*, 699-707.

Scheier, M.F., & Carver, C.S. (1977). Self-focused attention and the experience of emotion: Attraction, repulsion, elation, and depression. *Journal of Personality and Social Psychology, 35*, 625-636.

Schlenker, B., & Leary, M. (1982). Social anxiety and self-presentation: A conceptualization and model. *Psychological Bulletin, 92,* 641-669.

Spurr, J. M., & Stopa, L. (2002). Self-focused attention in social phobia and social anxiety. *Clinical Psychology Review, 22*, 947-975.

Taylor, S.E., & Fiske, S.T. (1975). Point of view and perceptions of causality. *Journal of Personality and Social Psychology, 32*, 439-445.

Turner, S.M., & Beidel, D.C. (1989). Social phobia: Clinical syndrome, diagnosis and comorbidity. *Clinical Psychology Review, 9*, 3-18.

Watson, D., & Friend, R. (1969). Measurement of social evaluative anxiety. *Journal of Consulting and Clinical Psychology, 33*, 448-457.

Wegner, D.M., & Guiliano, T. (1980). Arousal-induced attention to self. *Journal of Personality and Social Psychology, 38*, 719-726.

Wells, A., Clark, D.M., & Ahmad, S. (1998). How do I look with my mind's eye: Perspective taking in social phobic imagery. *Behaviour Research and Therapy, 36,* 631-634.

Wells, A., & Papageorgiou, C. (1999). The observer perspective: Biased imagery in social phobia, agoraphobia and blood/injury phobia. *Behaviour Research and Therapy, 37,* 653-658.

Wine, J. (1980). Cognitive-attentional theory of test anxiety. In I. Sarason (Ed.), *Test anxiety: Theory, research and application*. Hillsdale, NJ: Erlbaum.

Woody, S.R. (1996). Effects of focus of attention on social phobics' anxiety and social performance. *Journal of Abnormal Psychology, 105*, 61-69.

Woody, S.R., Chambless, D.L., & Glass, C.R. (1997). Self-focused attention in the treatment of social phobia. *Behaviour Research and Therapy, 35,* 117-129.

Woody, S.R., & Rodriguez, B.F. (2000). Self-focused attention and social anxiety in social phobics and normal controls. *Cognitive Therapy and Research, 24*, 473-488.

Zelen, S.L. (1987). Balance and reversal of actor-observer perspectives: An attributional model of pathology. *Journal of Social and Clinical Psychology, 5,* 435-451.

In: New Research on the Psychology of Fear
Editor: Paul L. Gower, pp. 43-57

ISBN 1-59454-334-8
© 2005 Nova Science Publishers, Inc.

Chapter 3

FEAR AND LEARNING

Jacklin Fisher[1] and Jan Horsfall[2]

[1]Faculty of Health Science, Australian Catholic University, Sydney, Australia,
[2]Mental Health Nurse Consultant, Sydney, Australia

ABSTRACT

This chapter explores the consequence of fear and anxiety on student learning in clinical settings. Student identified clinical incidents and their emotional corollary, particularly the emotions of fear and anxiety, provide the focus of the study. Mental health settings were selected because community attitudes towards the mentally ill frequently equate mental illness with the potential for violence, criminality and even homicide. It can be anticipated therefore that health care students undertaking clinical education in mental health settings are likely to be apprehensive and fearful and may confront considerable difficulty attempting to assimilate theory into practice in these learning environments. Data were gathered from one hundred and thirty students undertaking clinical experience in mental health settings. Two hundred and sixty critical incident reports were read and their content analyzed within three broad categories: description of incident, affect produced and effect on student learning. Immediate emotional and cognitive responses and perceived levels of fear and anxiety triggered in the students by the critical incident are reported. The impact of these emotions and cognitions was ascertained through small group debriefing and reflection exercises with the students. The findings from the study demonstrate the need for educators to integrate into the clinical curriculum learning activities aimed at assisting students manage fear and anxiety.

INTRODUCTION

Community attitudes towards the mentally ill remain negative and many people are fearful of mental illness (Bell et al, 1998; Bradshaw & Fisher, 1996; Davies, 1995; Human Rights and Equal Opportunity Commission, 1993; Perese, 1996). It is not the purpose of this chapter to explore the reasons for these negative attitudes except to say that historical notions about the causes of mental illness, and negative portrayals of the mentally ill in movies and other media images have contributed to a powerful negative stereotype that labels all mentally ill people as different and potentially dangerous. Health care students (medical, occupational therapy, social work, nursing) may also hold these negative community attitudes and their first clinical placement in a mental health setting is frequently fraught with apprehension and fear. Additionally, there are many situations in mental health settings where students may observe or become involved in incidents that challenge existing values, attitudes, and ethics. Witnessing a display of aggressive behavior in a client, the use of voluntary and involuntary treatments such as seclusion rooms, medications and electro-convulsive therapy, are likely to be confronting. Bizarre and psychotic behaviors can cause increased anxiety in the students as well as reinforce existing negative attitudes.

Assimilating, transforming and applying theoretical knowledge to professional clinical practice is the focus of student learning in clinical environments. Whilst much research acknowledges the variable nature of the clinical learning environment, and emphasizes reflection on practice to make sense of positive and negative experiences, studies that identify incidents that trigger anxiety and fear, and the consequences of these on student learning are scarce. The present research addresses these issues and elucidates the reality of student learning experience in environments where fear and anxiety are high. This chapter examines the relationship between fear and learning arising from research into 130 second-year student nurses' clinical learning experiences in urban Australian mental health settings.

LITERATURE REVIEW

Anxiety is defined as a feeling of apprehension, uneasiness, uncertainty, or dread, the source of which is often unknown or vague (Varcarolis, 2002). In contrast to the less specific precipitants of anxiety, fear is a reaction to a specific known danger. The physiological correlates of anxiety and fear are similar. Pervasive anxiety can undermine self-esteem and impact negatively on a person's daily life, whereas fear is more situation-specific and therefore transitory (Varcarolis, 2002). The term stressor pertains to environmental changes that individuals experience or perceive as challenging, threatening, or damaging to their well being (Varcarolis, 2002). Some people call stressors "stress", but technically stressors are events, experiences, or even thoughts that result in individuals stating that they "feel stressed". Hence, feeling stressed overlaps with feelings of anxiety, which is the most common response to stressors. Anxiety is commonly considered to be the most basic human emotion (Horsfall & Stuhlmiller, 2001).

Stress, anxiety and fear induce physiological, perceptual, cognitive and behavioural responses in the individual. Physiological responses are caused by excessive sympathetic nervous systems arousal and include increased heart rate, elevated blood pressure and increased rate and depth of respirations. Other immediate physiological effects include excessive perspiration and increased muscle tension. Perceptual effects range from heightened sensory awareness in mild anxiety to gross perceptual distortions in severe anxiety. Similarly, when only mildly anxious, positive cognitive changes occur including increased concentration and problem solving abilities. By contrast, difficulties in concentration and thought blocking occur when a person is extremely fearful. Behavioral changes include impaired verbal communication, such as, frequent changes of topic, rapid or loud speech, repetitive questioning, joking and wordiness in moderate anxiety, to ineffective communication arising from fear-based perceptual and cognitive distortion. Nonverbal behavioural changes include tremor, pacing and hand wringing in moderate anxiety, to panic and complete behavior disorganization such as screaming, running wildly or clinging to something or a person in extreme fear (Antai-0tong, 2003; Holmes, 2001). Clearly if anxiety or fearfulness is triggered in students these physiologic, perceptual, cognitive and behavioural responses will impact on their ability to assimilate, transform and apply theoretical knowledge to direct patient care.

Holoday-Worret (1996) considers that student fear and anxiety in mental health settings have two primary sources. These are: negative preconceptions or stereotypes about those who live with a mental illness, and self-doubt or performance inadequacy. Fears focusing on client anger or aggression commonly arise from ongoing stereotypical negative images of mentally ill people portrayed by news and entertainment media.

Other student apprehensions about clinical learning in mental health settings focus on patients and include the following: concerns about having nothing to offer distressed people; not knowing what to talk about; worry about saying the wrong thing and harming patients; and fears that clients may reject them or their attempts to help (Fontaine, 2003). Even though these concerns are couched in patient-focused language, they could equally be understood as student doubts about their skills or themselves in relation to interacting and conversing with clients in mental health facilities. These apprehensions may be realistic for many students who cannot assume they will be able to readily interact with a constructive attitude and approach, or be able to easily find the "right words". On the other hand, many patients are appreciative of a good listener and pick up cues about the students' interest in them as people (Horsfall & Stuhlmiller, 2001).

In mental health settings the apprehensions, concerns and fears of students and novice health professionals commonly correspond with those of recently diagnosed or newly admitted psychiatric clientele. Such patients may have reasonable fears about: the thoughts and feelings intrinsic to a psychotic episode; the hospital, loss of liberty and incarceration; violence at the hands of other patients; and health professionals' skills and behaviors. Furthermore, people who speak English as a second language may worry about not being understood or being prejudiced against, as well as cultural or family attributions of stigma or shame (Horsfall & Stuhlmiller, 2001). These concerns are similar to those of students new to mental health settings. Students may hold fears about: madness in general; their own coping abilities or mental health; their disapproval of psychiatric hospitals whilst having no choice about having to learn about patients with mental illness; patient violence; nurse or doctor criticism or unhelpfulness; and not being understood by clients or staff.

Perese (1996) interviewed 38 baccalaureate-nursing students to identify factors contributing to positive or negative undergraduate experiences in the clinical setting. She found the most commonly cited positive factors included staff professionalism, enthusiasm and acceptance of students, diversity of learning opportunities and direct involvement with patients. The most frequently cited negative factors or environmental stressors were related to student perceptions of staff performance. Similarly Slimmer and colleagues (1990) in a survey of 45 students found significant associations between the clinical learning site and effects on students' attitudes towards mental illness and psychiatric nursing. They found that the most important criterion to evaluate the appropriateness of a clinical learning site was the professional competency of the staff and their active support of student participation in therapeutic activities.

Stevens and Dulhunty (1992) found nursing students at the commencement of their studies held negative attitudes towards mental illness similar to those held in society. However, once in the clinical environment, active support and encouragement by staff, particularly during threatening events, positively changed their attitudes towards mental health nursing (O'Brien 1995). Similarly, greater knowledge and contact with psychiatric patients increased positive attitudes, and student confidence, and reduced fear of people with mental health problems (Ferguson & Hope, 1999; Olade,1979; Napoletano,1981; McLoughlin & Chalmers, 1991; Lam et al. 1994). Furthermore Pye & White (1996) found that placement experience in a mental health facility positively influenced undergraduate students decisions regarding a career in mental health nursing.

A number of authors suggest promoting student reflection on both positive and negative experiences in mental health settings is critical to learning, to increasing self awareness in the students, and to the successful resolution of sometimes confronting events. Pierson's (1998) literature review notes the theoretical underpinnings of reflective practice. She cites Heidegger's notion that reflection involves two modes of thought; calculative thinking defined as "a superficial level of thinking that suggests a superficial looking back at experience that is not unlike looking in a mirror" (Pierson 1998:2), and contemplative thinking involving a "spontaneous and fundamental process of exploration" (Pierson 1998:3) that requires time and cannot be forced or commanded. Heidegger believed that the integration of these two modes of thinking facilitated the development of meaning from experience. Pierson (1998:3) surmises " ...it is the integration of calculative and contemplative thinking that allows the scientist and the artist to create theories and forms that transcend present ways of thinking, doing and being". Severinsson (1998) considers that reflection increases the capacity to understand problems, for example, by reducing the theory practice gap through reflecting on the difference between how things should be done and how they are actually done in the clinical setting. Horsfall (1990) and Johns (1995) noted that it was through students reflecting on practice issues that research findings and theoretical knowledge are assimilated into nursing practice. Johns (1995:4) drew on Carper's (1978) four patterns of learning in clinical settings; "the empirical"; "the personal" involving understanding of the self in the clinical context; "the ethical" concerning the management of conflicting values and "the aesthetic" involving a synthesis of the above into the "skill of knowing, envisioning and responding to clinical situations with appropriate and skilled action". Of these four patterns, the personal, ethical, and aesthetic provide the foci most relevant to student learning in conditions where fear and anxiety in the students are triggered by environmental stressors.

METHOD

Students from a large metropolitan University in Australia participated in the study. The students undertook their mental health clinical practicum over a three-week period in a variety of settings including community mental health centres, psychiatric units attached to general hospitals and designated psychiatric hospitals. For the purposes of evaluating the clinical teaching and learning environment, the clinical teacher obtained permission from the students to collect and collate their written responses to a reflective exercise on critical clinical incidents they observed or participated in. Data was collected from a convenience sample of 130 students from a possible cohort of 248-second year students undertaking their mental health clinical. The sample was selected on the basis that they had completed their clinical experience when the project commenced.

As part of their learning activities each student was requested to outline in writing two critical incidents that they perceived were important to them in some way. The students were asked to explore each incident using the following format adapted from the work of Minghella and Benson (1995).

1. What actually happened? (the facts)
2. What did I think/feel about it at the time?
3. What do I think/feel about it now? (on reflection)
4. What did I do that I feel I could have done better/differently.
5. What did I do well?
6. Thoughts following peer reflection and debriefing.

Hour long peer reflection and debriefing sessions with small groups (eight students to one facilitator) were conducted daily or second daily during the three-week clinical placement. These sessions were aimed at developing deeper "contemplative thinking" in the student (Pierson 1998:3). During these sessions critical incidents identified by the students were discussed in a supportive environment following the format above. The impact of fear and anxiety on the learning process was determined from student written responses to this reflective exercise based on the critical clinical incidents.

Two hundred and sixty written critical incident reports were collated and analyzed to determine the environmental stressors that triggered fear and anxiety and the impact of fear and anxiety on student learning. The complexity of many of the incidents described meant it was common for each incident to evoke a range of concepts and themes. The desire to make a detailed analysis of the content meant that one incident could produce more than one theme or concept. For example a student may say she was "scared and angry" and these emotions were coded separately. Any recurring content that cast light on the questions: "What are the environmental stressors on clinical placement?" "To what degree is fear and anxiety a response to these stressors?" and "How fear and learning interact on a clinical placement" were coded.

To ensure the meanings intended by the students remained, only manifest level of content was accepted and no attempt was made to identify the latent meaning of each student response (Thomas, 1990). The original phrasing was retained as far as possible when sorting the data into thematic groups. To validate the content analysis a mental health nursing academic and the two researchers, independently analysed the thematic groupings. Minor changes were made to the groupings to accommodate variations resulting from this independent analysis. Only major findings are reported, all thematic groups with a frequency of less than 10 have been removed from the data. Thus the frequency of items in each of the three broad categories may not necessarily equate to the total number of critical incidents analyzed.

RESULTS

The analyzed data were allocated one of the following three categories: incidents identified by students; emotional responses triggered in the student by the critical incident; and feelings or thoughts after the group debriefing and reflective exercise.

Incidents Identified by Students

Three major themes were identified from student responses to the question *"What actually happened? (The facts)."* These included two hundred and ten described incidents involving an interaction with a patient; 37 described incidents involving staff members; and 37 described incidents involving treatment.

There were seven sub themes identified in incidents involving interactions with patients. These were witnessing psychotic behavior, witnessing verbal abuse by patients and threatened violence by patients. Other sub themes included: whether students felt they were therapeutic, witnessing strong emotions from the patient, invasion of student professional boundaries and witnessing actual violence by patients. The two sub themes involving staff were: witnessing uncaring/unprofessional behavior towards patients by staff and student impressed by staff competence. Incidents involving therapy treatment included three sub themes, namely administration of medication, incidents involving group therapy and incidents involving the administration of electro-convulsant therapy (ECT).

Patient focused incidents included observing psychotic behaviour or actual and threatened violence and verbal abuse by patients. Issues around violence featured in 27% of the incidents and students described psychotic behaviour in patients in 25%.

Invasion of student professional and personal boundaries, which included the patient asking personal questions, the patient attempting to become intimate with the student and sexual and racial harassment by patients, was mentioned in 7% of the critical incidents. Witnessing strong emotions from patients such as grief and fear were also mentioned in 7% of the incidents. Positive incidents such as the students being therapeutic for a client were selected in 8% of the critical incidents.

Incidents involving staff were described in 13% of the student identified critical incidents. Incidents involving staff most commonly involved the student witnessing what they stated as uncaring and unprofessional behaviour towards the patient in manner, speech and lack of attention. Seven per cent of critical incidents described witnessing uncaring/unprofessional behaviour of staff towards patients. However, in 6% of critical incidents, students described how impressed they were with staff, their attitudes of caring, and their effectiveness.

Treatment-focused incidents included giving medication 5%, group therapy 4%, and the administration of ECT 3.5%. Students noted that they wished they had more information before witnessing the administration of ECT.

Some edited common examples recorded by students in their critical incident reports are included below to illustrate the intensity of emotions, and range of environmental stressors and interpersonal experiences nursing students face when in mental health settings.

The following example was rated under the sub themes 'witnessing psychotic behavior' and 'witnessing actual violence by patient'.

A new admission was brought in by the police, very psychotic and experiencing mania. She was jumping on tables, pacing up and down, spitting, laughing to herself, trying to abscond and showing physical aggression towards staff. The staff tried to medicate her with Valium and Serenace but she threw it in their faces. Security was brought in and she was medicated through injection.

Common experiences described by students in the critical incidents were observing threatened violence, and witnessing verbal abuse. The following example encapsulates these two sub themes identified as well as the sub theme "student was impressed by staff competence".

I was sitting outside amongst the patients, when two patients started with a verbal argument. The situation quickly changed to both standing in front of each other screaming abuse at each other, raising hands as if to hit, but not actually going through with it. I felt absolutely terrified and I was shaking with fear. I thought I was going to burst into tears and at the same time helpless at not knowing how to deal with the situation. I didn't become involved; a staff member came and defused the situation. This showed me what I could have done - easy to see someone else do it!

Table 1. Critical incidents described by students

	Frequency identified	Percentage of incidents
Witnessing psychotic behaviour	72	25.4%
Witnessing verbal abuse by patients	34	11.9%
Threatened violence by patients	30	10.6%
Student felt they were therapeutic for a client	24	8.5%
Witnessing uncaring/unprofessional behavior towards patients by staff	21	7.4%
Witness strong emotions from patient eg. Grief and fear	19	6.7%
Invasion of student professional/privacy boundaries	19	6.7%
Student was impressed by staff competence	16	5.6%
Incidents involving administration of medications	15	5.3%
Witnessing actual violence by patients	12	4.2%
Incidents involving group therapy	12	4.2%
Incidents involving administration of ECT	10	3.3.5%

Emotional Response Triggered in the Student from the Critical Incident

Nine themes were identified from student responses to the question *"What did I think/feel about it at the time?"* These themes were: fear; uncomfortable/upset/concerned; shocked/surprised/amazed; pity/sadness; confused/didn't know what to do; positive feelings; anger; no feelings; embarrassment. The most common feeling described by the students was that of fear (20%), which included being, scared, frightened, anxious or nervous. Feelings of discomfort/upset/concern were also frequently mentioned (19%). Shock, surprise and amazement were mentioned by 16% of the students. The next most frequently described feelings were pity and sadness for the patient, and confusion and not knowing what to do, both comprising 10% of the student responses each. Positive feelings such as enjoyment, happiness, excitement, and pleasure made up only 8.4% of the feelings aroused in the students. Angry feelings were aroused in 6.2% of students and embarrassment was mentioned by 4.5%. Five per cent of students did not identify any feelings following the incident.

The following quotation demonstrates the intensity of emotional responses the students felt after a critical incident. In keeping with the method of identifying only manifest level of content this response was sorted into the confused/didn't know what to do thematic grouping.

I was walking down the hall and saw X sitting down by himself. I asked him how his sleep was and he said good. I didn't quite hear him so I said "pardon".
He then said "enough".
I thought he meant enough sleep, but he then said "enough I don't want to talk to you anymore."
I said "alright" and stood up to leave and walk away.
He said after me "I don't want to talk to you about how I feel, you could be my f----- daughter .... I don't like how they let young people in here to talk about that stuff".
Then I said "that's alright you don't have to talk to me if you don't want to".
I felt very very small and stupid and confused, and mumbled something about being sorry before slinking off.

For some students simply entering a psychiatric institution triggered intense feelings as demonstrated in the following quote, which was, categorize in the theme of 'fear'.

Upon arrival at the psychiatric hospital I felt overwhelmed with fear and trepidation as I entered the acute psychiatric ward...

Many incidents described by students occurred on the first day or in the first week of their clinical placement. The critical incident described below was categorized as triggering the emotions 'fear' and 'embarrassment' in the student.

I was watching one of the patients in the TV room whilst the activities were on. The nurse had asked me to keep her quiet and take her to the toilet if she needed to go. She asked to go to the toilet so I took her hand and started to walk out of the TV room with her. I felt her grip on my hand get tighter, and then she squeezed my shoulder and tried to stop me walking. She then turned me around grabbing my jumper and twisting it up. She did this roughly and became quite aggressive accusing me of robbery and murder. Whilst holding my jumper at the neck I thought she was going to hit me on the head with the tape recorder she was trying to pick up. I was extremely scared and a little embarrassed as there were quite a few people in the room doing activities at the time. Some of the nurses came up and calmed the patient down and took her to the toilet...

Table 2. Emotional response triggered in the student from critical incidents

	Frequency identified	Percentage of responses
Fear	70	19.7%
Uncomfortable/upset/concerned	66	18.6%
Shocked/surprised/amazed	57	16.1%
Pity/sadness	38	10.7%
Confused/didn't know what to do	37	10.5%
Positive feelings	30	8.5%
Anger	22	6.2%
No feelings identified by student	18	5%
Embarrassment	16	4.5%

Interaction between Fear and Learning in Clinical Settings

The majority of student responses (85%) noted that the selected incident and its emotional corollary had a negative impact on their learning experiences but that participating in small group discussions that facilitated reflection on the critical incidents assisted them to feel better and make meaning from their experiences. However there were many students for whom the reflective exercise had no effect (15%) or who felt only somewhat better; some students had quite strong, distressing reactions which were only partially resolved through educational input via the reflective exercise.

There were six thematic groupings identified from student responses to educational input via the reflective exercise. These themes were: reflective exercise helped/feels better; thinks differently about the incident/new point of view; learned something about how others might respond; reflective exercise had no effect/thinks feels the same, good to hear the experiences/feelings of peers; reflective exercise increased self awareness.

Twenty-eight per cent of the student responses included statements indicating that they 'felt better' emotionally after the reflective exercise. Twenty-seven per cent of the responses revealed that reflection and debriefing enabled them to view the incident, from different perspectives. Seventeen per cent of the student responses indicated that the reflective exercise and debriefing sessions provided opportunities to learn how other people respond to similar incidents. Fifteen per cent of students stated there was no change in their thoughts or feelings following the debriefing/reflective exercise. Others (9%) indicated it was valuable to hear the experiences and feelings of their peers, and that the reflective exercise helped to raise their self-awareness.

Two of the students' responses grouped into the 'helping/feels better' theme are presented below.

Discussing the incident made a great difference, especially getting other people's point of view on the procedure (ECT). It made me realise that there was nothing wrong with the way I reacted. In the discussion everybody told me I made the right decision and it was my way of coping. Some of the people in the group said they felt the same way I did, but attended the procedure anyway, even though they didn't want to. The discussion helped to give me closure.

After discussing it with my group I feel better as some agreed that they would have behaved in a similar way. It helped to discuss my feelings and to work through them.

The following student response was grouped into both 'helping/feels better' and 'increased self awareness'.

...As one of the clients spoke about their own issues I found myself overwhelmed and actually had to combat my emotions in an effort not to breakdown. ...after debriefing and speaking about what I had heard, I felt better and more capable of coping with my emotions. ...I felt more reassured and learned how to detach myself emotionally without losing empathy.

Table 3. Feelings/thoughts in student after educational intervention

	Frequency identified	Percentage of responses
Reflective exercise helped/feels better	83	27.9%
Thinks differently about the incident/new point of view	81	27.3%
Learned something about how others might respond	51	17.2%
Reflective exercise had no effect/ thinks feels the same	45	15.2%
Good to hear the experiences/feelings of peers	26	8.8%
Reflective exercise increased self awareness	11	3.7%

DISCUSSION

The primary goal of this study was to obtain information from students about the critical incidents they experience whilst on mental health clinical practicum, their emotional responses to these incidents and how their thoughts and feelings about the incidents interact with student learning. The findings from the data analysis of the critical incidents identified a wide range of predominantly negative environmental stressors. Significantly these stressors triggered feelings of fear, upset, and shock in the majority of students.

Twenty- seven per cent of the critical incidents involved threatened and actual violence, and verbal abuse. These descriptions included both patient assaults on staff and patient assaults on other patients. The dominance of these extreme environmental stressors in the critical incidents suggests that nursing students on mental health clinical placement fear for their personal safety and face considerable personal and professional conflict arising from their experiences in the clinical setting. It was not rare for students to be exposed to risky situations which arose from breaches of policy, for example students being asked to restrain a patient while they were being forcibly drugged; or the student being left alone with a patient whilst on walks in public places. The authors view this finding as potentially serious both in regard to the personal safety of the students and the duty of care of both the clinical setting and the students' academic institution. Violence in the workplace represents a fundamental violation of human rights. Employers and academic institutions have a responsibility for the occupational health and safety of students and employees as well as patients. Mental health settings are not exempted from occupational health and safety legislation to provide a safe and secure environment nor from criminal jurisdiction.

It is well known that both witnessing and/or experiencing episodes of violence can result in significant emotional and/or physical distress (Engel & Marsh 1986; Janoff-Bulman 1985; Holden 1985). The consequences for the students experiencing fear-inducing situations were reflected in the intensity of emotions triggered. Witnessing actual and threatened violence whilst on mental health clinical placement is likely to be the first time the student confronts the possibility of violence in their practice. The fact that a patient may respond aggressively and violently in a nursing context challenges idealistic notions that caring on the part of a nurse should be accepted and appreciated by the patient (Fisher 1998). Recent evidence suggests that violence against nurses in Australia is increasing (Poster 1996; Jackson 1998).

Over 25% of the critical incidents involved witnessing psychotic behavior in patients. This included escape attempts, catatonia, and behavioral responses to delusions, hallucinations such as shouting at visions, cowering in the corner in fear, and pacing the corridors muttering and grimacing. Deviant behavior that challenges social norms can be personally threatening through confronting strongly held values and beliefs in the student. Attempting to understand the client's perspective of reality can trigger frustration, fear and doubts about the validity of these long held values and beliefs. As a result the students' personal identity and self-esteem may be challenged triggering anxiety and confusion in the student and further affecting the ability for student learning to occur.

Unfortunately, these negative environmental stressors were not confined to incidents involving patients, but also extended to incidents involving clinical staff. There were more critical incidents that identified uncaring/unprofessional behaviour towards patients by staff than incidents complimenting staff competence. The authors believe that a number of interpretations can be taken from this finding. First, there is a possibility that the students may have misinterpreted the therapeutic role of staff in 'limit setting' and controlling problematic behaviour in patients as evidence of uncaring behaviour. Second, clinical staff working in stressful situations may, under pressure, use 'black humor' or express negative sentiments as a means of coping with that stress. The students may have interpreted these comments as indicative of negative attitudes towards patients. Third, it is possible that mental health staff have negative attitudes towards mentally ill people in some mental health clinical settings. Students who overhear negative comments or witness uncaring/unprofessional behaviour towards patients have interpreted this as unacceptable or distressing. The authors believe that it should be of serious concern to clinical staff, to consumers of mental health services, and to educators, that students so frequently identified problematic attitudes towards patients by staff.

Although not the focus of this study, these findings also provide insights into the treatment experiences of consumers and the therapeutic milieu of the clinical mental health setting. Horsfall & Stuhlmiller (2001) found the anxieties and fears of students and novice health professionals commonly paralleled those of recently diagnosed or newly admitted patients.

Given the dominance of environmental stressors identified by the students in their critical incident analysis, it is not surprising to note that the students also identified predominantly negative feelings arising from these critical incidents. Moreover a substantial majority of students described intense feelings of fear, shock or anger. Powerful feelings such as anxiety and fear will not only interfere with effective learning but also impede the ability to establish a therapeutic relationship with the client, and affect attitudes towards people with mental illness. Fear and extreme anxiety causes increased heart rate, respirations and muscle tension, perceptual distortions, difficulties in concentration, thought blocking, and impaired verbal communication skills such as repetitive questioning. Clearly if anxiety or fearfulness is triggered in students the physiologic, perceptual, cognitive, and behavioral responses identified in the literature review will impact on their learning and their ability to assimilate, transform and apply theoretical knowledge. In many instances the students felt immobilized, not knowing what they should do to resolve the situation.

Students who themselves have experienced abuse or have personal experiences with mental illness may have particular difficulty in a mental health setting (Sutherland, 1995). Unresolved fears and anxiety are likely to interfere with the learning process, preventing students from applying their theoretical knowledge to the clinical setting. They may also impact on the future career choices of these students, reducing the likelihood of a career choice in mental health nursing.

Professional learning in mental health is focused on the development of a therapeutic relationship with the mentally ill client. Knowledge that underpins the therapeutic relationship includes interpersonal and communication skills, positive attitudes and 'the humanistic approach of unconditional positive regard for the client, along with self-awareness in the student (Landeen et al.1992). Negative attitudes and feelings of fear and anxiety not only diminish effective student learning, but also the development of rapport, empathy and a therapeutic relationship with a client (Bower, Webb & Stevens, 1994; Purdon, 1992; Tierney, 1995). With the experience of such strong emotions in the student it is likely that anxiety will increase unless these feelings are directly addressed in the clinical environment. Educators therefore face considerable challenges in facilitating appropriate and rewarding learning experiences for health care students in clinical mental health settings. Teaching strategies in these settings must not only foster the integration of theory with clinical practice and the development of high level interpersonal skills, but must also focus on diminishing environmental stressors so that fear and anxiety in the student is reduced and therapeutic attitudes towards patients can develop.

The importance of the reflective exercise in reducing fear and anxiety and facilitating learning was very clearly demonstrated in this study. Eighty five per cent of students stated they had gained something out of the reflective exercise, including finding a new perspective, learning how others might respond, feeling 'better', increasing self awareness and valuing hearing the experiences and feelings of their peers. Proponents of reflective practice support this sense of gaining a new point of view from the reflective exercise (Horsfall 1990; Minghella & Benson 1995; Pierson 1998; Reynolds & Murphy, 1996; Severinsson 1998). The emergence of these positive emotions and thoughts represents a significant shift from predominantly negative emotions arising from the critical incident. This study found that daily or second daily, supervised reflection on the critical incidents in a safe environment within the clinical setting, assisted the student to resolve some of his or her own personal conflicts that arose from the critical incident thereby reducing levels of fear and anxiety, and promoting student learning and the development of positive attitudes.

LIMITATIONS

There are a number of reasons why it is necessary to be cautious in generalising too broadly from this study. Firstly, despite the written instructions to students that a critical incident need not necessarily be a negative incident, the very process of identifying something that the student considers to be critical tends to bias the student to selecting incidents that have impacted negatively. Secondly, although the authors believe the students sampled were a representative cohort of students from their particular year, not all the students were sampled, and those that were, were selected on the basis of convenience. It is possible but unlikely, that if all of the students had been sampled the findings may have been different.

CONCLUSION

This study examined the actual experience of students on mental health clinical practicum. Student descriptions of critical clinical incidents were used to identify these experiences. The content analysis of these critical incidents found that students tended to describe disturbing incidents, most commonly involving both real and threatened violence, and psychotic behaviour. The critical incidents outlined a range of very challenging situations, including ones that would be hard for anyone (e.g. walking into a patient's room and finding them in the middle of a suicide attempt) and ones which are harder for young inexperienced students than their teachers may realize. These incidents typically aroused strong, often painful emotional responses such as fear, discomfort and shock in the student. In turn these emotional responses made it difficult for the student to maintain focus on their learning tasks and hindered the ability for students to develop therapeutic relationships with clients. This study supported previous research promoting reflection and debriefing on clinical experiences as critical to the positive resolution of the critical incidents and to enhancing student learning. However, it is clear that further research is needed to explore both the relationship between fear and learning, and the impact of fear on learning in clinical settings.

The findings from this study reinforce the need for clinical staff and educators to assist the student to become aware of, process, and resolve fear, anxiety and personal conflict arising from the clinical setting. Leaving the student to resolve these feelings alone and unsupported can impede the capacity for students to achieve learning outcomes aimed towards translating theory into practice and challenge stereotypical attitudes. Successful resolution of these conflicts assists both the students and their teacher to decrease negative stereotypes of people with a mental illness, foster an understanding of themselves and the client as people with both human rights and human needs, and develop a positive outlook towards a career as a mental health professional.

REFERENCES

Antai-Otong, D. (2003). *Psychiatric Nursing Biological And Behavioral Concepts*. Thomson Delmar Learning. New York. USA.

Bell, A., Horsfall, J. & Goodin, W. (1998). The mental health nursing clinical confidence scale: a tool for measuring undergraduate learning on mental health clinical placements. *Australian and New Zealand Journal of Mental Health Nursing, 7,* 184-190.

Bower, D., Webb, A. & Stevens, D. (1994). Nursing students knowledge and anxiety about AIDS: An experiential workshop. *Journal of Nursing Education, 33,* 6, 272-276.

Bradshaw, J., & Fisher, J. (1996). My stories. An experiential learning activity for mental health settings. In *Proceedings of the first International Nursing Education Conference* p.251). Hamilton, Canada: McMaster University.

Clinton, M., & Hazelton M. (2000). Scoping mental health nursing education. *Australian and New Zealand Journal of Mental Health Nursing, 9,* 2-10.

Davies, J. (1995). Fear Busters. *Nursing Times,* 91, n.21, 46-47.

Engel, F., & Marsh, S. (1986). Helping the employee victim of violence in hospitals. *Hospital and Community Psychiatry, 37,* 2, 159-162.

Ferguson, K., & Hope, K. (1999). From novice to competent practitioner: tracking the progress of undergraduate mental health nursing students. *Journal of Advanced Nursing, 29* (3), 630-638.

Fisher, J. (1998) Violence against nurses. In Horsfall J (Ed) *Violence and Nursing.* Royal College of Nursing Australia. Canberra.

Fontaine, K.L. (2003). Introduction to mental health nursing. In Fontaine, K.L (Ed.) *Mental health nursing.* 5th edn. (pp.3-48). Upper Saddle River New Jersey: Prentice Hall.

Holden, R. (1985). Aggression against nurses'. *The Australian Nurses Journal,* 15,3,44-48.

Holmes, D. (2001). *Abnormal Psychology 4th Edition.* Allyn and Bacon. Needham Heights, MA, USA.

Holoday-Worret, P. A. (1996). Student issues regarding client and environment. In K. M. Fortinash & P. A. Holiday-Worret (Eds.) *Psychiatric-Mental Health Nursing.* (pp. 27-36). St Louis Missouri: Mosby-Year Book.

Horsfall, J. (1990). Clinical placement: prebriefing and debriefing as teaching strategies. *Australian Journal of Advanced Nursing, 8, 1, 3 - 7.*

Horsfall, J., & Stuhlmiller, C., with Champ, S. (2001). *Interpersonal Nursing For Mental Health.* New York: Springer.

Human Rights and Equal Opportunity Commission. (1993). *Human Rights and Mental Illness. Report of the National Inquiry into the Human Rights of People with Mental Illness.* Australian Government Publishing Service. Canberra.

Jackson, J (1998). Violence in the workplace. (In Horsfall J (Ed) *Violence and Nursing).* Royal College of Nursing Australia. Canberra.

Janoff-Bulman, R. (1988). The aftermath of victimisation: Rebuilding shattered assumptions. (In *Trauma and Its Wake,* ed, Figley C). Bruner/Mazel, New York.

Johns, C. (1995). The value of reflective practice for nursing. *Journal of Clinical Nursing,* 4(1) 23-30.

Lam, A., McMaster, R., & Troup, C. (1993). A pilot study: nursing students' attitudes, interest, and concerns in the mental health field. *The Australian Journal of Mental Health Nursing, 2*(6), 281-286.

Landeen, J., Byrne, C. & Brown, B. (1992). Journal keeping as an educational strategy in teaching psychiatric nursing. *Journal of Advanced Nursing.* 17, 347-355.

McLoughlin, J., & Chalmers, J. (1991). Student nurses' attitudes toward mental illness: impacr of education and exposure. *Australian Journal of Mental Health Nursing, 1* (4), 12-16.

Minghella, E., & Benson, A. (1995). Developing reflective practice in mental health nursing through critical incident analysis. *Journal of Advanced Nursing*, 21, 205-213.

Napoletano, M. (1981). Correlates of change in attitudes toward mental illness among vocational nursing students. *Psychological Reports,* 49, 147-150.

O'Brien, A. (1994). Measuring graduate attitudes to educational preparation for practice in mental health nursing. *Australian and New Zealand Journal of Mental Health Nursing,* 4, 132-142.

Olade, R. (1979). Attitudes towards mental illness: a comparison of post-basic nursing students with science students. *Journal of Advanced Nursing,* 4, 39-46.

Parkinson, F. (1997). *Critical Incident Debriefing - Understanding And Dealing With Trauma,* London, Souvenir Press.

Perese, E. (1996). Undergraduates' perceptions of their psychiatric practicum: Positive and negative factors in inpatient and community experience. *Journal of Nursing Education,* 35, 6, 281-285.

Pierson, W. (1998). Reflection and nursing education. *Journal of Advanced Nursing,* 27, 1, 165-170.

Poster, E. (1996). A multinational study of psychiatric nursing staffs' beliefs and concerns about work safety and patient assault. *Archives of Psychiatric Nursing,* 6, 365-373.

Pye, S. & Whyte, L., (1996). Factors influencing the branch choice of students in a nursing undergraduate program. *Nurse Education Today,* 16, 432-436.

Reynolds, P. & Murphy, B. (1996). Culture shock, sink or swim? The use of critical incidents to overcome barriers to deep learning. *Proceedings First International Nursing Education Conference of the Nursing Education Research Unit.* McMaster Univesity. Hamilton. Canada. p.25.

Severinsson, E. (1998). Bridging the gap between theory and practice: a supervision program for nursing students. *Journal of Advanced Nursing,* 27, 6, 1269-1277.

Slimmer, L., Wendt, A. & Martinkus, D. (1990). Effect of psychiatric clinical learning site on nursing students' attitudes toward mental illness and psychiatric nursing. *Journal of Nursing Education,* 29, 3, 127-133.

Stevens,J. & Dulhunty,G. (1992). New South Wales nursing students' attitudes towards a career in mental health, *Proceedings of the 18th National Convention of the Australian College of Mental Health Nurses, Inc,* Ballarat Victoria, 108-112.

Sutherland, J. (1995). Educational Innovations. The mental health consultation model: A conceptual framework for structuring the psychiatric nursing practicum. *Journal of Nursing Education,* 34, 3, 131 -133.

Thomas, B. (1990). *Nursing Research An Experiential Approach.* Toronto. C. V. Mosby Co.

Tierney, N. (1995). HIV/AIDS - Knowledge, attitudes, education of nurses: A review of the research. *Journal of Clinical Nursing,* 4, 1, 13-21.

Varcarolis, E. M. (2002). Understanding anxiety and anxiety defenses. In E. M. Varcarolis (Ed.) *Foundations Of Psychiatric Mental Health Nursing. A Clinical Approach.* (4th edn.), pp.282-299. Philadelphia: Saunders.

Wong, J. (1987). Towards effective clinical teaching in nursing. *Journal of Advanced Nursing,* 12, 505 - 513.

In: New Research on the Psychology of Fear
Editor: Paul L. Gower, pp. 59-89

ISBN 1-59454-334-8
© 2005 Nova Science Publishers, Inc.

Chapter 4

FEAR OF DEATH

Shulamith Kreitler

Department of Psychology, Tel-Aviv University
Psychooncology Unit, Tel Aviv Medical Center, Israel

Boswell: But is not the fear of death natural to man?
Johnson: So much so, Sir, that the whole of life is but keeping away the thoughts of it.

From *The Life of Johnson*

ABSTRACT

There may be nothing more human and ubiquitous than the fear of death. It would probably be correct to state that there is no human being who has never in his or her life experienced the fear of death, in some form, for a *given* duration of time. This statement would not be complete without the sequel which is that whatever else death may be it is first and foremost an integral part of life. These two assumptions provide a good starting point for dealing psychologically with the fear of death.

NATURE AND VARIETIES OF FEAR OF DEATH

The fear of death has several names besides fear of death, such as death anxiety, death worry, death concern, death phobia or thanatophobia, deathly fear existential anxiety. These names do not necessarily denote kinds of fear, but possibly reflect differences in the intensity of fear of death, which range from death worry to death phobia. However, the kinds of fear of death differ more in the object of fear. Kastenbaum adopts Jacques Choron's (1964) threefold analysis of the fear of death: (a) Fear of afterlife, namely, fear of what comes after death; (b) Fear of dying, namely, fear of the very event or act of stopping life; and (c) Fear of extinction, namely, of annihilation, or simply of "ceasing to be". This triadic categorization may be used in order to represent a great number of the more specific types of fear of death that have been observed in the literature or found in studies.

Thus, fear of what comes after death includes fear of punishment, of torture in hell, of suffering for one's deeds and transgressions in life, of rejection by the "authorities" in the hereafter (e.g., alienation from God), and even of facing the dead among whom there are few or many of those one is scared or does not care to meet.

Fear of dying may include fear of pain, suffering, suffocation, losing one's organs or limbs, dissociating from one's body and other events one imagines to be part of the process of "dying".

Finally, fear of extinction is the hardest fear to describe because it involves the experience or thought or conception of not-being (or being-not), of nothingness, of total and absolute negation. Kastenbaum and Aisenberg (1976, pp. 43-44) consider it to be the most characteristic and distinct type of fear of death, because all the other types of fear of death are merely fears *about* death whereas the fear of annihilation is directly and simply the only truly fear *of* death. Notably, Freud has completely contested the possibility of the unconscious to conceive of negation and hence also of death (Freud, 1957, p. 287) (viz., "our unconscious... does not know its own death").

In his intriguing history of man's obsessions and fears Wilkins (1996) cites the following five types of fears of death that have historically obsessed human beings:

(a) Fear of premature burial, i.e., of being buried alive, which may be related to agoraphobia. This fear has its origins in the unclarity of criteria for determining death, especially in past centuries. Notably, it is possible that this fear resounds at the background of the often mentioned fear of being used for organ transplantation while one is still alive.

(b) The fear of posthumous indignity, i.e., the fear of being removed from the grave by medical specialists especially anatomists eager for corpses to teach their students dissection and surgery. This fear had its origins in the absence of regulations for providing anatomy students means for studying. The fear was especially intense for Christians whose chances for resurrection were considered to be thereby diminished.

(c) Fear of bodily disintegration. Mummification, embalming and cryonics are only three example of the means applied for avoiding or delaying the bodily disintegration.

(d) Fear of being forgotten. This fear is rooted in the experience of the living that following death the memory of dead relatives and friends slowly fades away. The inscriptions in cemeteries and various commemorative rituals and objects testify to attempts to overcome this fear.

(e) Fear of an ignominious death, i.e., without honor, away from one's beloved, suffering pain, being devoid of one's cognitive abilities, etc.

Notably, at least two of these fears of death refer to the event of dying (i.e., the fears of premature burial and of ignominious death) whereas the remaining three fears refer to what comes after death. None of the fears listed by Wilkins refers to the fear of extinction per se, which raises the possibility that fears of death are shaped at least to some extent by culture.

Kastenbaum and Aisenberg (1976) amplify the list of fears of death by distinguishing between fear of one's own death and fear of the death of another person, mostly a beloved or close person.

Table 1. Meanings of fear of death

No.	Category of Response	Per Cent of Responders
1	Fear of not knowing what to do when it happens	49.45
2	Fear of the pain, the suffering at the moment of death	59.80
3	Fear of the pain and suffering for ever, after death	29.90
4	Fear of what will happen to me after I die	46.00
5	Fear of the kind of punishments I will get after I die	29.90
6	Fear of being bored, of not having enough to do, of not being occupied	9.20
7	Fear of loneliness	19.55
8	Fear of the unknown	57.50
9	Fear of losing myself, of not being myself	13.80
10	Fear of parting from the people I love	20.70
11	Fear of parting from the places I love	10.35
12	Fear of losing all the objects that are mine, that I have collected for long periods of time	16.10
13	Fear of not being able to do all the things I do or that I like doing	19.55
14	Fear of longing for eternity to get back and not being able to do it	17.25
15	Fear of losing my cognitive abilities, my memory, my ability to think	9.20
16	Fear of being stuck in a bad dream from which I can never wake up	1.15
17	Fear of dying without having exhausted all my abilities and talents	9.20
18	Fear of knowing that I have missed out on various chances I have had in life and that I will never be able to taken advantage of all the possibilities or compensate for those that I have not used	25.30
19	Fear of being buried alive	21.85
20	Fear of dying without having fulfilled my mission in life	5.75
21	Fear of dying before I had a chance to experience all I could or should have experienced	26.45
22	Fear of dying without anyone knowing that I have died	6.90
23	Fear of looking for my lost body for all eternity	3.45
24	Fear of dying before I was ready	52.90
25	Fear of being forgotten after I die	6.90
26	Fear that my death will bring about the end of all I have striven to achieve in life; it will simply die out with me	3.45
27	Fear of dying in a foreign place or land, far from the people I love	6.90
28	Fear of dying before I could provide for my children, or grandchildren	8.05
29	Fear of dying without having found out why I was born	3.45
30	Fear of dying before I could have asked for forgiveness for all the evil things I have done to others	10.35
31	Fear of being closed up in a narrow and dark hole for the whole of eternity	1.15
32	Fear of turning into nothing	6.90

Table 1. Meanings of fear of death (Continued)

No.	Category of Response	Per Cent of Responders
33	Fear of the pain of passing from here to there	17.25
34	Fear of seeing my beloved ones suffering in this world without being able to help them	13.80
35	Fear of meeting all my ancestors and all my enemies too who have died long ago	10.35
36	Fear of turning into an animal in another cycle of existence	2.30
37	Fear of meeting God	39.10
38	Fear of finding out that I was wrong all along, that I have wasted my life	5.75
39	Fear of being alone	6.90
40	**Fear of not being able to help my family if terrible things will happen to them after I die**	11.50

Note: The total of percents exceeds 100% because some respondents gave more than one response.

Despite its length, the list of fears of death is still incomplete, as indicated by the findings of a survey on the fears of death conducted with 87 participants of both genders, ranging in age from 38 to 62 years (see Table 1). There were two relevant questions: First, Have you experienced fear of death? The response options were: Yes, No, Maybe; second, What does fear of death refer to, what is fear-evoking about death – in general? For you? Whereas all participants responded positively to the first question, their responses to the second question varied a lot. These responses are listed in Table 1. They can be grouped into three clusters. One represents fears concerning the act of dying (responses 1-2, 22, 27, 33,39); a second cluster represents fears concerning the hereafter, post death (responses 3-11,19,23,25,26,31,32,34-38); and a third cluster represents fears concerning the too-early-timing of death responses 7,18,20,21,24, 28-30). The most interesting ones are the third cluster responses which represent in fact fears of life rather than of death. Notably, a great number of thinkers have noted the proximity of these two basic fears – of death and of life. One quite randomly selected quote from Ernst Becker's (1973) writings may serve as illustration: "The irony of man's condition is that the deepest need is to be free of the anxiety of death and annihilation; but it is life itself which awakens it, and so we must shrink from being fully alive".

It is of interest to note that in most cases the fear of death rests on assumptions concerning death, or for that matter life, that are treated by the person as true, despite the absence of any supporting evidence. Thus, the fear of suffering in the hereafter physically, psychologically or morally is based on the assumption that death makes no difference in the identity or existential mode of the individual, for example, the fears of being bored or lonely or longing to get back assume that the person stays after death largely the same he or she have been prior to dying. Again, the fear of dying prematurely assumes that the meaning or sense of life consists in fulfilling certain functions or attaining some specific goals in life. Other common assumptions concern the event of dying which is often conceived as painful although the evidence points to the fact that it is not necessarily so even in the case of sick people (Hinton, 1963, 1967).

DIMENSIONS OF DEATH ANXIETY

The above descriptions of the components of death anxiety clarify that death anxiety is likely to be a multidimensional construct rather than a unidimensional one as was assumed by many investigators in the early stages of research in the field. The unidimensional view is reflected in Templer's (1970) often quoted definition of death anxiety as an unpleasant emotional state precipitated by contemplation of one's own death. The complexity of death anxiety began to be revealed through the writings of Feifel (1959) who described death anxiety as consisting of surcease from pain and tribulation, reunion with one's family, loss of control, punishment and loneliness. According to Stern (1968) death anxiety consisted of a projection of actually felt annihilation of the self, fear of being immobilized, fear of suffocation and fear of vanishing into nothingness, all of which he viewed as rooted in the infant's experiences of loss of mothering. Also Lifton (1976, 1979) includes in death anxiety fear of annihilation, but in addition also fear of stasis and fear of separation. Kavanaugh (1977) focused on the fear of the process of dying, fear of one's actual death, fear of the idea of an afterlife, and the abysmal aura surrounding death.

Lonetto and Templer (1986) approached the issue of the multidimensionality of death anxiety with the methodology of empirical studies and assessment scales of death anxiety. Integrating and comparing the results of studies (e.g., Devins, 1979; Durlak & Kass, 1981-2; Lonetto, Fleming & Mercer, 1979; Nelson & Nelson, 1975) led them to the conclusion that death anxiety consists of four factors: (a) the *cognitive-affective component* that represents concern with the event of dying, fear of death, and being troubled by thoughts about death and the afterlife; (b) the component of *physical changes*, real or assumed or anticipated that accompany death or dying because of accidents, diseases, war or aging; (c) awareness of the unstoppable *flow of time* which may experientially compress the future and expand the past, evoking sadness over the rapid flow of time; and (d) fear of dying a *painful, stressful death* that may result from circumstances, such as cancer, torture or a bad accident. A study performed later (Gilliland, 1982) reached similar but not overlapping results. It showed that the four factors of death anxiety were (a) fear of death and dying, (b) thoughts and talk of death, (c) subjective proximity to death, and (d) fear of the unknown. It is evident that the first two factors correspond to the cognitive-affective factor mentioned earlier.

All of these components may be found in the writings of other investigators of fear of death, for example, cognitive-affective concerns about death and concern about physical changes were discussed by Ramos (1982) and Gilliland and Templer (1985-6); and the stress and pain of dying are reflected in the fear of catastrophic death identified by Martin (1982-3). These observations contribute to the validity of the four factors of death anxiety presented above.

The components or dimensions of death anxiety do not constitute death anxiety but enable or promote it. Lonetto and Templer (1986, p. 57) hypothesize that feelings of death anxiety arise when one or more of its components reaches a level which is critical or beyond the threshold according to personal or socially defined criteria. However, at present it is still unknown which one component or combination of components give rise to an intense fear of death and whether different components or combinations of components are associated with different experiences of fear of death.

Developmental Perspective on the Fear of Death

In order to better understand the nature of the fear of death and its origins, it would be advisable to examine the relation of the fear to the slowly developing conceptions of death in children.

Children's Conceptions of Death

There are two basic approaches to studying the construction of death in children. One approach assumes that the conception of death develops as one organized whole and is stage-bound; the other assumes that the conception of death is made up of various themes, each of which follows a separate course of development.

The first approach, which is known as the "*comprehensive stages*" approach, is based on the assumption that the child's conception of death is some kind of an integrated conceptualization that depends primarily on the child's cognitive abilities and changes in an orderly sequence. Though the rate of moving from one stage to another may differ across children, the sequence stays consistent. The developmental sequence has been described as following closely the Piagetian model. The empirical data has been collected in different countries and by means of different research tools (e.g., Anthony, 1972; Gartley & Bernasconi, 1967; Koocher, 1973; Nagy, 1948; Schilder & Wechsler, 1934; Wass, Guenther & Towry, 1979). In the sensorimotor stage of infancy (0-2 years), dominated by sensory and motor actions, babies below 6 months of age have no understanding of death because it requires the ability to grasp the constancy and identity of objects which is still missing. Hence, they react to death only as the absence of familiar persons (i.e., separation, loss), demonstrated sometimes by stranger anxiety. Toddlers identify objects but are limited by their inability to assume a frame of reference other than their own, which is living. In the preoperational stage (2-7 years) of early childhood, marked by magical thinking and egocentricity, there is no real understanding of the universality and irreversibility of death. Death is conceived as a state similar to sleep, characterized by the activities of the living, e.g., eating, going fishing. Life and consciousness are attributed to the dead. At the stage of concrete operations (7-11/12 years) of middle childhood, marked by concrete naturalistic thinking, children will personify death, often in evil images (e.g., devil, bogeyman) and will tend to regard death as punishment for evil deeds. By the age of 9 or 10 years, most children have an adult conception of death as universal, final, and irreversible, marked by a complete cessation of all biological functioning. These conceptions are further influenced by the religious conceptions of the children's culture. In the stage of formal operations (over 12 years), marked by propositional and deductive thinking, the adolescents have a good understanding of death. Hence, the possibility of non-being poses for them a great anxiety-provoking threat, which religious beliefs may mitigate to some extent.

The above presentation of stages, which the conception of death is assumed to undergo until it reaches maturity, is highly common. There are two obvious shortcomings of this approach. The first is that it is concerned mainly if not exclusively with verbal expression of concepts by the children and hence captures only partial aspects of the phenomenon, which may lead to a distorted representation of the situation. The second shortcoming is that it overlooks individual differences in the conception of death, which may lead to the expectation of consistency across children where there may be none.

The second approach, which is known as the "*specific themes*" approach, starts with identifying particular aspects of the death conception and follows their development separately. It developed mostly after the stage approach. The major most frequently examined aspects are non-functionality (i.e., death ends all life-sustaining functions), irreversibility, universality, causality (i.e., what causes death) and personal mortality. Kenyon's (2001) excellent review shows that each of the five themes develops differently and separately. For example, conceptualizing causality changes in the sense that the causes to which death is attributed shift from non-natural causes (e.g., violence, accident) in 5-6 year-olds to natural causes (e.g., illness) in 8 year-olds, to spiritual causes (e.g., invocation by God) in 11 year-olds (Reilly, Hasazi & Bond, 1983). Awareness of personal mortality follows more closely the binary developmental track: from denial in 3-4 year olds to confirmation in 8 and 11 year olds (Atwood, 1984). This suggests that there are no stages defined by a bundle of features but different developmental trajectories following individual tracks. Further, each of the themes of the death concept is affected differently by major factors, such as age, gender, cognitive ability, and culture.

The findings about the development of conceptions of death suggest that no fear of death is to be expected in children before they understand what death is and what it means. The understanding may be more complete or partial depending on the specific child but when it occurs, it may be expected to open the way to fears of death. Reports of such fears usually point to the age of 7 or 8 years as the initial phase. The children's' fears may vary in intensity and frequency and may take on different forms. Some children, for example, may be scared to fall asleep, lest they won't wake up; others may be afraid of the devil or of other fear-provoking figures that personify for them death; and still others may develop a fear of darkness, which is the state in which they believe death may overtake them. A study in which children's narratives of death were examined showed that such narratives were produced from the age of 6 years onward, but only at the age of 9 years the children responded to death with some kind of an emotional reaction (Menig-Peterson & McCabe, 1977-78).

In general, beyond the age of 7-8 years, the older the child the more fears of death are to be expected and the stronger these fears are. The fears of freshmen and sophomores were found to be higher than those of juniors and seniors in high school (Brubeck & Beer, 1992), and those of seniors higher than those of juniors (Koocher, O'Malley, Foster & Gogan, 1976).

Investigations of the correlates and determinants of death anxiety in children revealed some relations between death anxiety and religion (e.g., Jewish children tended to have higher death anxiety than Christian) (Matalon, 2000), gender (girls had more death anxiety than boys) (Brubeck & Beer, 1992), and background (African American children had higher death anxiety than White children) (Miller, 1999) but in general no relations with factors, such as exposure to violence (Miller, 1999), divorce of parents (Brubeck & Beer, 1992), or even death of a sibling (Robinson, 2001).

Parents' communications about death are an important source of information about death for many children. An interesting study (Matalon, 2000) found that parents' communications about death and children's death conceptualization, particularly the concepts of causality, irreversibility and old age, were found to be positively correlated. However, a factor that reduced parents' communication about death was found to be the parents' own death anxiety. That is, parents who are more death anxious are less effective in their communications to their children about death. Yet, notably, the parents' death anxiety and the children's death anxiety were not correlated. Another study (Miller, 1999) contributed to clarifying how the parents' death anxiety could have affected their communications about death. It showed that though children often desire to talk to their parents about death, especially children exposed to violence who are concerned about death, they often do not do so in order not to upset the important adults in their lives.

Effect of Experience on Death Conceptions

Most important is the effect of experience on the development of death concepts (Kreitler & Krivoy, 2004). Studies of children from 5 to 12 years showed that having lost a loved one through death was related to less accurate death scores (especially in regard to causality and universality) (Cotton & Range, 1990), or was not correlated with death concept scores at all (Jenkins & Cavanaugh, 1985-6; Mahon, 1993; McIntire, Angle, & Struempler,1972; Robinson, 2001). However, being oneself sick with a life-threatening disease does affect death concepts. Jay et al. (1987) found that children with cancer differed from matched healthy children in their concepts about personal mortality and death-as-justice.

Pediatric oncology patients did not necessarily have more advanced death concepts but different ones. They more often acknowledged personal mortality and less often viewed death as a punishment. Moreover, within the oncology group, those who had experienced the death of a close friend or relative had a deeper understanding of personal mortality, universality and irreversibility of death, irrespective of age. Also Clunies-Ross and Lansdown (1988) found that leukemic children (4-9 years old) did not differ from healthy children in their overall death scores, but had better understanding of the irreversibility and non-functionality of death.

It is of interest to note that independently of disease, anxiety was found to lower scores of understanding different death aspects, notably universality, irreversibility and non-functionality (Orbach et al., 1986) as well as personal mortality (Candy-Gibbs et al., 1984-5).

These findings suggest that personal experience with death in the form of a life-threatening disease like cancer may override the effects of death anxiety observed in healthy children that may cause distortions or denial. Different authors who have had therapeutic or research experience with dying children have reached the conclusion that dying children are aware of their state. Kübler-Ross, a pioneer in this domain, writes that "small children, even three- and four-year olds, can talk about their dying and are aware of their impending death" (Kübler-Ross, 1981, p. 51). Kübler-Ross (1983) believes that all terminally ill children are aware that they are dying but only those whose awareness is conscious and intellectual express it verbally whereas those whose awareness is preconscious express it symbolically. In contrast, we believe that form of expression has more to do with form of experience and habitual forms of expression by the child than with level of awareness (Kreitler, 1965).

The issue was studied from the early 50-ties, relying on clinical observations and semi-structured interviews with children and their parents (Cobbs, 1956; Richmond & Weisman, 1955; Solnit & Green, 1959), on the accounts of parents and hospital staff (Morrissey, 1963; Natterson & Knudson, 1960) and also on examining directly the terminally-ill children, for example, by means of projective techniques (Waechter, 1971, 1987). All studies showed unequivocally that children were aware of the seriousness of their condition and their impending death (Bach, 1975; Bertoia & Allen, 1988; Furth, 1988; Jampolsky & Taylor,

1978; Kübler-Ross, 1983). However, this does not necessarily indicate that their death anxiety is comparably high. AIDS-diagnosed children 4-6 years old were not found to manifest more death anxiety than healthy peers (Ireland, 1998).

The anthropologist Bluebond-Langner (1978) also found that terminally-ill children understand their prognosis and know that they will die, even if no one tells them, but in conformity with the social rules of 'mutual pretense' which they somehow surmise, they often conceal this knowledge from their own parents and the medical staff. Their fears however change in the different stages of the disease. Thus, in the first phase when the children are diagnosed and start treatments, their fears are mostly of the unknown rather than of the prognosis. In the next phase of remission, their fears subside. The fears start growing and become more focused on death after they have been through the relapse-remission cycle and have noticed the uneasy avoidance response of the adults around them. When relapse sets in with further treatments, their fear of death is manifested in planning only for very short terms and grieving about all those things of the future that they will most probably not do. When children pass to the phase of 'dying', mostly following the death of another child in the ward, all they know and have experienced about death becomes integrated into the emergent awareness of impending death. This awareness is manifested through verbal and symbolic expressions. The awareness may be accompanied by decreased communication with adults, from whom the dying children tend to hide their new awareness, and by lowered cooperation with different medical procedures that have not helped in the past. Slowly their world starts narrowing down in terms of themes, activities and interests: they play less, they move around less, and they are concerned more with death. Gradually death comes to permeate their minds and thinking.

The detailed step-by-step description provided by Bluebond-Langner demonstrates that the awareness of one's death is a slowly developing process, fed, on the one hand, by the child's personal experiences of disease and treatments, and, on the other hand, by information obtained from the adults both directly and indirectly through eavesdropping and observing their behaviors toward oneself or among themselves. However, the awareness of one's death does not necessarily spill over into a full-blown death anxiety because it may be mitigated by psychophysiological processes reflecting dying, which may be taking place at the same time, for example, a growing physical weakness, losing interest in what is going on, planning less for the future, expecting less the next day.

Reconciling the Findings on Death Concepts and Awareness of One's Death

We are confronted here with two traditions of research. Though they agree on a number of themes, there appear to be also quite large gaps between them. One source for the disparity may be traced back to the research tools used predominantly in each of these research traditions (i.e., verbal expression and questionnaires versus drawings, stories, semi-structured interviews and observations). Lonetto (1980, p. 176) has aptly summarized the situation as follows: "The evidence suggests, then, that relying solely on the terminally ill child's overt expressions of anxiety yields incomplete or misleading information". A study by Muris et al. (2002) sheds light on the importance of the tools by means of which the information is obtained. The study examined the occurrence of the following five danger and death fears from the Fear Survey Schedule for Children-Revised (FSSC-R): "Not being able to breathe",

"Being hit by a car or truck", "Falling from high places", "Bombing attacks or being invaded", and "Fire or getting burned". The participants were 102 children in the age range of 8-12 years from a regular school. Prevalence of the fears was assessed by three different methods, i.e., in line with the standard FSSC-R procedure, according to a fear list, and in terms of actual occurrence or prevalence of these fears in the past week as recorded in a diary. The results showed that these fears ranked high when using the standard FSSC-R procedure, but were considerably less common when using the fear list procedure, and least frequent, as well as least intense and least prolonged, according to the daily recordings.

However, there may be more to it. The disparities may arise out of the basic difference there may be between talking or thinking about death in general or the death of others and confronting the issue of one's own death. Kastenbaum (1992, p. 88) analyzed the presuppositions of the simple statement "I will die". It presupposes, for example, awareness of being a person with a life of one's own, of belonging to a class of beings one of whose attributes is mortality, of awaiting the certain occurrence of death at an uncertain timing, accepting the finality of the event of death as the ultimate separation of oneself from the world and from existing as a human being at least on this earth. In particular, it requires bridging the gap between what one has actually experienced of life to a hypothetical construct of life's negation, when we have absolutely nothing on which to build. To this, one should add the emotional component of sadness about not being any more, which compounds the situation further. All these play a much larger role in the fear of one's own death than in the fear of death in general.

Further evidence for the importance of the distinction between fear of one's own death and fear of the death of others, which in regard to the death of a care giver takes on the form of fear of loss and abandonment. The study showed that both fears of one's personal death as well as the death of a care-giver or loved one are evident in children and play an important role in children's inner lives, regardless of environment, age, race, religion, or experience. But the main point is that children emphasized almost entirely fear of their own death rather than fear of the death of an important other (Miller, 1999).

Assessment of Death Anxiety

There have been attempts to measure death anxiety in a variety of forms. Interviewing has been tried quite extensively (e.g., Hackett & Weisman, 1964), as well as projective techniques, such as TAT, Sentence Completion (Shrut, 1958), making up stories (McCully, 1963), and constructing images of death (Lonetto, Fleming, Gorman & Best, 1975). Due to methodological and operational difficulties, most of these approaches have been replaced by questionnaires of death anxiety. At present most of the studies of death anxiety rely on inventories. Some of the better known inventories will be mentioned here. All of them have good reliability and validity and have been applied in many studies.

The Death Anxiety Scale (DAS) (Templer, 1970): It consists of 15 items, to be responses to as "true" or "false" (e.g.,"I am very much afraid to die"). It has been translated into other languages.

Collett-Lester Fear of Death Scale (Collett & Lester, 1969): It has 36 items in a six-point response format, and four scales: fear of death of oneself, fear of death of others, fear of dying of oneself, and fear of dying of others.

Dickstein's Death Concern Scale (Dickstein, 1972). It is a 30-item scale in a four-point response format that assesses the extent to which the person contemplates death and evaluates it negatively.

Multidimensional Fear of Death Scale (Hoelter, 1979): It has 42 items, a five-point response format ("I am afraid of dying of cancer") and provides scores on eight scales: fear of the dying process, fear of the dead, fear of being destroyed, fear for significant others, fear of the unknown, fear of conscious death, fear for the body after death, fear of premature death.

Death Attitude Profile – Revised (Wong, Reker & Gesser, 1994): It has 36 items "e.g., "I look forward to life after death"), in a seven-response alternatives format, providing scores on five dimensions: Fear of death, death avoidance, neutral acceptance, approach acceptance, escape acceptance.

The Threat Index (Kreiger, Epsting, & Leitner, 1974): This instrument does not conform fully to the standard questionnaire format. The respondent is presented with triads of cards drawn from a pool of cards with death related statements and is requested to place the elements "preferred self", "self" and "my own self" on either the construct or the construct pole of each statement. The final core is the number of times "my own death" is placed on a pole different from the ones for "self" and "preferred self".

Some of the more commonly used tools for assessing death anxiety in children are the following:

Fear Survey Schedule for Children-Revised (FSSC-R) (Muris et al., 2002): The respondent is presented with different fear evoking items, including death (e.g., "Not being able to breathe", "Being hit by a car or truck", "Failing from high places", "Bombing attacks or being invaded", and "Fire or getting burned") and is requested to state their frequency.

Death narratives (Menig-Peterson & McCabe, 1977-8): The child is requested to tell a story about death. The scoring is based on content analysis that refers to the representation of death, the extent of evoked fear etc.

Death Anxiety Scale for Children (Schell & Seefeldt, 1991): It consists of 63 neutral and anxiety evoking words, including those that refer to death. The child is requested to rate the words for anxiety. The score is the mean of ratings for the words referring to death.

Children's Death Anxiety Scale (CDAS) (Robinson, 2001): A children's version of Templer's Death Anxiety Scale (DAS) was adapted for use with children.

Thematic Instrument for Measuring Death Anxiety in Children (Ireland, 1998): A projective tool, constructed along the lines of the TAT.

Some Correlates of the Fear of Death in Adults

Despite the ubiquity of death anxiety, individual differences may be expected in terms of various parameters. The most obvious ones are demographic characteristics.

Age

Studies comparing death anxiety in samples ranging in age from 18 to 61 found no differences in death anxiety between different age groups, not even when pairs of parents and their offspring were compared (Templer, Ruff, & Franks, 1971). In elderly participants (above 60 years) there is a tendency for lower death anxiety scores than in younger individuals (Quinn & Reznikoff, 1985; Schultz, 1978; Tate, 1980), except in deviant samples, such as penitentiary inmates (Templer, Barthlow, Halcomb et al., 1979), or elderly persons with insomnia (Wagner, Lorion & Shipley, 1983).

Gender

Several studies showed that females score higher on death anxiety than males (Dunagin, 1981; Litman, 1979; Lonetto, Mercer, Fleming, Bunting & Clare, 1980; Quinn & Reznikoff, 1985; Templer, Ruff & Franks, 1971).

Physical Health

Kidney dialysis patients had only an average degree of death anxiety (Lucas, 1974). Unexpectedly, terminal cancer patients had even lower death anxiety scores than individuals from the general population (Gibbs & Achterberg-Lawlis, 1978). In a sample of elderly individuals, there was a positive correlation between death anxiety and number of health problems or perceived impaired health (Neustadt, 1982; Nehrke, Morganti, Willrich & Hulicka, 1979; Tate, 1980). On the whole, it seems that sick people may be coping with their death anxiety by denial so that the relation between illness and fear of death is distorted.

Occupation

On the whole occupation does not seem to be correlated with death anxiety in any specific direction. Military officers do not differ in death anxiety from controls (Koob & Davis, 1977). Further, psychologists, psychiatrists, funeral directors and suicide experts do not differ in their death anxiety scores (Pepitone-Arreola-Rockwell, 1981). Neither were differences in death anxiety observed between medical, surgical, medical/surgical and ICU nurses (Whittenberg, 1980). Further, funeral personnel, firemen and paramedics did not differ in their death anxiety from individuals working in settings that are not death related (Latanner & Hayslip, 1984-5). It seems that dealing with death on an occupational basis does not affect death anxiety. Also the number of encounters with death in the work setting does not seem to affect death anxiety, for example in ICP nurses (Telban, 1980; Whittenberg, 1980).

However, some observations suggest the possibility that the findings showing no effect of encounters with death on death anxiety may be reflecting the final stage of some process that has been ongoing earlier. Some studies show that nurse students have higher death anxiety than other students (Ohyama, Furuta & Hatayama, 1978), that nurses with over 5 years experience had lower death anxiety than those with less experience (Whittenberg, 1980) or that hospice volunteers who worked over a year had lower death anxiety than those who left earlier (Amenta, 1984). Findings of this kind suggest hypotheses such as, individuals who deal with death occupationally are those who initially suffer from high death anxiety but the occupation with death leads to gradual lowering of the anxiety; or that occupation with death initially increases death anxiety before habituation sets in with time.

Within-Family Relations

Resemblance in death anxiety was found between husband and wife (Lucas, 1974; Koob & Davis, 1977), as well as between siblings (Kirby & Templer, 1975) and between parents and their offspring, especially of the same gender (Templer et al., 1971). Only or oldest children score higher on death anxiety than later born ones (McDonald & Carroll, 1981).

Family Status

It appears that marital status, parenthood and number of children are unrelated to death anxiety (Cole, 1978-9), but individuals who had never married may tend to higher scores than those who are or have been married (Morrison et al., 1981-2).

Socieconomic Status

It appears that income and educational level are related inversely to death anxiety (Schultz, 1978).

Religion

Comparison of death anxiety in individuals from different religions did not show any significant differences (Templer & Dotson, 1970), but individuals who are deeply involved religiously insofar as beliefs and practice are concerned score lower on death anxiety than the others (Aday, 1984-5; Templer, 1972b). Religion Jews have higher death anxiety than Christians (Matalon, 2000). However, it is only traditional religious beliefs that correlate negatively with death anxiety and not beliefs in various paranormal phenomena, extraterrestrials, extrasensory perception or witchcraft (Tobacyk, 1984).

Attitudes

It was found that death anxiety correlates negatively with attitudes reflecting acceptance of death (Flint, Gayton & Ozmon, 1983) and death transcendence in the sense of accepting one's own death without regret and calm detachment (Morgan, 1976). Death anxiety is correlated positively with dogmatism (Shepard, 1980). Death anxiety is not correlated with any specific attitude in regard to euthanasia in college students (Slezak, 1980) but is related positively to the belief in the right of people to commit suicide. Death anxiety was correlated positively with a better caring attitude toward the elderly (Minean & Brush, 1980-1).

Personality Tendencies

In college students, the MMPI showed that the high scorer on death anxiety tends to be a tense, introverted, anxious and sensitive individual, but by no means mentally disturbed. In a variety of samples, including prisoners, kidney dialysis patients and their wives and Huntington Chorea patients, it was found that high scores on death anxiety tend to be correlated positively with the MMPI scales of Depression, Psychasthenia, and Social Introversion, as well as with the anxiety scales based on the MMPI (Lucas, 1974; Gielen & Roche, 1979-1980; Templer, Barthlow, Halcomb, Ruff & Ayers, 1979).

Further, death anxiety is correlated positively with general anxiety (Gilliland, 1982; Lucas, 1974; Smith, 1977), depression (Gilliland, 1982; Ochs, 1979), and neuroticism, as assessed by Eysenck's personality inventory (Templer, 1972a). Death anxiety correlates higher with trait anxiety than with state anxiety, which indicates that death anxiety is a more stable tendency than a reaction to a specific situation. Further, it is more closely related to anxiety measures than to depression (Gilliland, 1982).

Death anxiety was found to be related positively to succorance, passivity and empathy, but negatively to endurance, aggression, assertiveness, pragmatism and exhibitionism (Thorson, 1977). Further, death anxiety was related negatively to ego strength (Templer, 1967), and interpersonal trust (Dunagin, 1981), as well as to repression tendencies (Kane &

Hogan, 1985-6). A relation was reported for death anxiety with achievement motivation but only in non-religious samples: in men inversely and in women positively (Schultz, 1978), as if immersing oneself in attaining goals helped nonreligious males to overcome death anxiety but intensified it in women perhaps by reminding them of how much they have to lose.

Notably, although death anxiety is related positively to somatization (Loewen, 1984) it is related negatively to bodily concern (Elkins & Fee, 1980).

Some studies suggest that locus of control may be associated with death anxiety. There are however findings specifying that high death anxiety is related to high external control (Litman, 1979; Sullivan, 1977) whereas others indicate that it is related to high internal control (Hunt, Lester & Ashton, 1983).

Adjustment

As could be expected, death anxiety was found to be high in individuals with poor psychological adjustment, little life satisfaction (Bolt, 1978; Sullivan, 1977), low sense of well being (Aronow, Rauchway, Peller & Devito, 1980-81), low social adequacy (Smith, 1977), few friends (Tate, 1980), and a low sense of self actualization and purpose in life (Bolt, 1978; Vargo & Batsel, 1984). Further characteristics of high scorers on death anxiety are a negative self-image, low self-esteem, low well-being, increased self-doubt, insecurity and stress-sensitivity (Neimeyer & Chapman, 1980-1981; Vargo & Black, 1984).

Addiction

Teetotalers had higher death anxiety than alcoholics who lose control (Kumar, Vaidya & Dwivedi, 1982). Although smokers did not differ from nonsmokers in death anxiety, within the group of smokers the higher the number of smoked cigarettes the higher death anxiety (Templer, 1972a). Heroin addicts do not differ from nonaddicts in death anxiety; neither do high heroin users differ from low heroin users (Katz, 1981).

Determinants of Death Anxiety

This issue may seem to some to be trivial. It is only natural that human beings should be afraid of death. It is the big unknown that plays havoc with everything they have planned and done in their life. It is often unexpected, and may be painful. In view of the facts, the question should rather be why human beings are not constantly terrified of death or rather why some human beings are not as terrified as others may be expected to be. What these questions actually suggest is that there may be deeper-lying factors that predispose human beings to greater or lesser degrees of death anxiety. We will point out factors in two domains: one set of factors consists of information processing tendencies determining identification and characterization of inputs by the individual; the other consists of beliefs reflecting deeper-lying meanings characteristic of the individual.

Fear of Death and Information Processing Tendencies

Previous studies showed that the individual's fears and anxieties depend on the manner in which the individual's information-processing system processes inputs and renders them meaningful. The most comprehensive account of these processes is provided by the psychosemantic approach, which describes how stimuli are assigned meanings (Kreitler & Kreitler, 1985b, 1990b; Kreitler, 2004b).

Meaning is defined as cognitive contents focused on a referent. The referent can be any input, such as a person, an object, a concept, an event or a situation. The cognitive contents could describe the referent in terms of its sensory qualities, structure, function, material, location, and so on. The referent and the cognitive contents together form a meaning unit which is characterized by five classes of variables:

(a) *Meaning Dimensions,* which describe the contents assigned to the referent, e.g., the function of the referent, its evaluation, its frequency, its quantity, and its sensory qualities;

(b) *Types of Relation,* which describe the relation between the referent and the contents in terms of its directness, e.g., an attributive relation, which is direct, or the comparative or metaphoric, which are mediated by other referents;

(c) *Forms of Relation,* which describe the relation between the referent and the contents in terms of formal properties, e.g., as positive or negative, total or partial, declarative or questioning;

(d) *Forms of Expression,* which describe the mode of expression of the whole unit, e.g., verbal, motional, graphic; and

(e) *Shifts of Referent,* which describe the relations between the referent of the meaning unit and the input or the previous referent, e.g., identical, opposite, partial.

These five classes of characterizations constitute together the set of meaning variables. The meaning variables represent modes of assigning meaning to inputs. Each person uses some modes more often than others. A meaning test assesses the frequency with which an individual tends to apply each meaning variable. The meaning test requests the individual to communicate the meaning of 11 stimulus words (e.g., street, bicycle). The meaning communications are analyzed into meaning units, each of which is coded in terms of the five classes of meaning variables. Summing the frequencies with which each meaning variable was used by the individual in the meaning test yields the individual's meaning profile. The meaning profile is in fact the set of frequencies with which that person tends to use each meaning variable.

The meaning profile provides information about the kind of meanings that the person tends to assign to various inputs. The meaning variables that have high frequency in the meaning profile are those that the person uses preferentially, or by default. Thus, if the meaning dimension Temporal Qualities is salient in a person's meaning profile, it is likely that the person will recall easily times and dates, will notice temporal aspects, will readily solve problems that have to do with time, and will perform well other tasks involving temporality.

Previous studies focused on identifying the meaning variables characteristic of individuals high in fear or anxiety (Kreitler & Kreitler, 1985a, 1987a, 1988; Kreitler, 2004b). Fear and anxiety were assessed by means of standard questionnaires, and the meaning assignment tendencies by means of the meaning test. The results yielded a set of meaning variables that differentiated significantly between the participants high in fear or anxiety and those low in fear or anxiety (see Table 2).

Table 2. Meaning variables correlated significantly with scales of anxiety and of fear

The scales of anxiety, fear and fear of death[a]	Meaning variables[d] correlated significantly with the scales
Anxiety scales [Fully characterizing meaning variables]	Meaning Variables Characterizing Anxiety Fully[b]: Positive Tendencies[c]: **MD: Sensory qualities experienced by referent** **MD: Feelings and emotions experienced by referent** **MD: Judgements and evaluations about referent** **MD: Judgements and evaluations held by referent** **MD: Cognitive qualities of referent** Negative Tendencies[c]: **MD: Actions by referent** **TR: Attributive: quality to substance or action to agent**
Anxiety scales [Partially characterizing meaning variables]	Meaning Variables Characterizing Anxiety Partially[b]: Largely Positive Tendencies[c]: **MD: State and possible changes in state** **MD: Locational qualities [equal pos. and neg.]** **MD: Temporal qualities** **MD: Cognitive qualities characterizing referent** **TR: Comparative: similarity** **TR: Metaphoric-symbolic: metaphor** Largely Negative Tendencies[c]: **MD: Function, purpose and role** **MD: Consequences and results** **MD: Feelings and emotions evoked by referent** **TR: Exemplifying-illustrative: exemplifying instance** **SR: Identical with input or previous referent** **Total number of meaning values**
Fear scales **[Fully characterizing meaning variables]**	Meaning Variables Characterizing Fear Fully[b]: Positive Tendencies[c]: **MD: Range of application** **MD: Size and dimensions** **MD: Locational qualities** **MD: Sensory qualities experienced by referent** **MD: Feelings and emotions experienced by referent** **MD: Feelings and emotions evoked by referent** **MD: Judgments and evaluations held by referent** **MD: Judgments and evaluations about referent** **TR: Attributive: quality to substance or action to agent** **TR: Exemplifying-illustrative: exemplifying instance** **SR: To previous meaning value** Negative Tendencies[c]: **MD: Function, purpose and role** **MD: Results and consequences** **MD: Temporal qualities**

Table 2. Continued

The scales of anxiety, fear and fear of death[a]	Meaning variables[d] correlated significantly with the scales
Fear of death	Meaning Variables Characterizing Death Anxiety: Positive Tendencies[c]: **MD: Sensory qualities experienced by referent** **MD: Feelings and emotions experienced by referent** **MD: Judgments and evaluations about referent** **MD: Judgments and evaluations held by referent** **MD: Cognitive qualities of referent** **MD: Cognitive qualities characterizing referent** **MD: State and possible changes in state** **MD: Temporal qualities** **TR: Comparative: similarity** **TR: Metaphoric-symbolic: metaphor** Negative Tendencies[c]: **MD: Function, purpose and role** **MD: Results and consequences** **TR: Attributive: quality to substance or action to agent**

[a] Anxiety scales: The Manifest Anxiety Scale (Taylor, 1953), The IPAT Anxiety Scale Questionnaire (Krug, Scheier & Cattell, 1976), The State-Trait Anxiety Inventory (STAI-2) (Spielberger, Gorsuch, Lushene & Vagg, 1977), The Self-Rating Anxiety Scale (SAS) (Zung & Cavenar, 1980), The Zuckerman Inventory of Personal Relations ZIPERS (Zuckerman, 1979), The Anxiety Test MIHALI (adapted for adults) (Ziv, Levin & Israeli, 1974), The Test Anxiety Scale (Sarason, 1978). Fear scales were those by Braun & Reynolds (1969), Geer (1965), Wolpe & Lang (1964), and two by Kreitler & Kreitler (1990b). Fear of death was assessed by the Death Anxiety Scale (Templer, 1970).

[b] The characterizing meaning variables are presented under two headings: fully and partially. "*Characterizing fully*" indicates that the listed meaning variables were correlated in the same direction in the case of all anxiety or fear scales; "*Characterizing partially*" indicates that the listed meaning variables were correlated in the same direction with only some of the examined anxiety scales or were correlated with some in one direction and with others in another direction.

[c] "Positive" tendencies denote meaning variables correlated positively with anxiety or fear; "negative" tendencies denote meaning variables correlated negatively with anxiety or fear.

[d] MD=Meaning Dimensions; TR=Types of Relation; SR=Shifts of Referent

The findings show that anxious individuals tend to focus on their own sensations, feelings and state, on evaluations and cognitions, and on temporal cues, but overlook major aspects of interpersonally-shared reality, such as action possibilities, functions and consequences. Further, their grasp of reality in general is restricted (viz., they score low on the attributive type of relation and concrete examples) and they tend to shift away from it (viz., shift away from the input) focusing rather on the metaphoric mode of experiencing, that may readily lead to a catastrophizing mood (e.g., "this is the end of the world", "My whole life is crumbling like a house of cards"). Notably, there is also evidence for narrowing down of cognitive activity (viz., lower number of meaning values).

The pattern of meaning variables corresponding to fear includes focusing on sensations, feelings and evaluations, that represent the internal sphere of experiencing, coupled with focusing on different aspects of external reality, such as locations, size, objects involved in the situation (viz. range of application), while overlooking other aspects, mainly functions, consequences and temporal cues. In general they have a good grasp of reality (viz., high scores on the attributive type of relation and concrete examples), and tend to dwell on the input and its extensions (viz., shift to previous meaning values).

Previous studies showed that changing the meaning variables of individuals in the direction indicated by the meaning pattern corresponding to anxiety increased temporarily their anxiety and reduced their level of performance on a set of logical problems, whereas changing the meaning variables in the direction away from that reflected in the meaning pattern corresponding to anxiety reduced their anxiety and raised their level of performance on logical questions (Kreitler & Kreitler, 1987a)

Comparing the patterns for anxiety and fear shows that the two patterns share the focusing on the internal sphere of experiencing emotions and sensations but differ in many other of the other characteristics of meaning assignment. There are two major differences. One difference consists in a broader-based approach to interpersonally-shared reality in the profile corresponding to fear than in the one corresponding to anxiety. This aspect may reflect the often noted definition of fear as a reaction to external specific stimuli in contrast to anxiety which is viewed as a reaction to internal non-specific stimuli (Freud 1926/1959). The other difference consists in the lower percent of negative meaning assignment tendencies in the pattern corresponding to fear (3 out of 14, 21.43%) than in the one corresponding to anxiety (8 out of 18 variables, 44.44%). Since negative tendencies involve overlooking, this difference may indicate a weaker tendency for repression in the case of fear than in the case of anxiety.

Table 2 presents also the meaning pattern corresponding to death anxiety. It is based on the results of 125 participants in the age ranges 25 to 38 years, of both genders, who completed the Death Anxiety Scale (Templer, 1970) and the Meaning Test. Comparing the meaning variables in the pattern corresponding to death anxiety with those in the patterns corresponding to anxiety and to fear shows that the pattern corresponding to death anxiety includes 12 of the 18 variables in the pattern of anxiety (66.6%) and only 6 of the 14 variables in the pattern of fear (42.8%). Notably, the pattern of death anxiety resembles the pattern of anxiety also in that it includes a positive tendency for temporality as in the anxiety pattern rather than the negative tendency for temporality as in the fear pattern. These observations support the conclusion that death anxiety consists of more components of anxiety than of fear, and may be characterized better as a variant of anxiety than as a fear.

Accordingly, the meaning variables constituting the pattern corresponding to death anxiety identifies the meaning assignment tendencies characteristically applied by individuals high in death anxiety. For example, when confronted with any stimulus they would shift away from the input as such and its properties but would focus instead on their own sensations, feelings and evaluations, as well as memories, images and thoughts about the input; further, they would overlook the regular interpersonally-shared modes of attributing qualities to the stimulus, but would rather indulge in analogies and metaphors that may readily lead to anxiety-evoking conceptualizations.

These meaning assignment tendencies become manifest in general as well as in regard to the specific stimulus or concept of death. Figure 1 presents examples of meanings assigned to death by individuals scoring high in death anxiety and Figure 2 presents the meanings assigned to death by individuals scoring low in death anxiety.

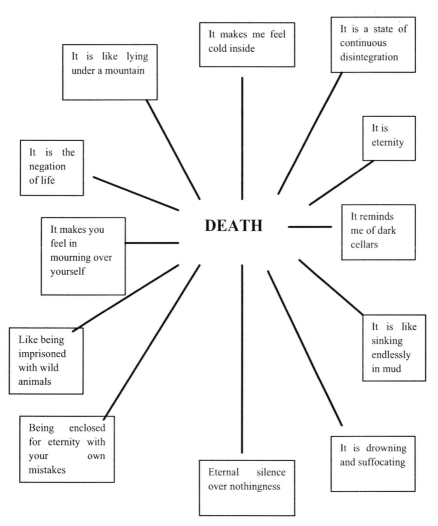

[a]Each of the meanings exemplifies one of the meaning variables constituting the pattern of meaning variables corresponding to death anxiety (see Table 2). For example, "it is eternity" is a meaning value of the meaning dimension Temporal Qualities, "it is the negation of life" is a meaning value of the meaning dimension Judgments and Evaluations about the referent.

Figure 1. Meanings assigned to death by individuals scoring high in death anxiety[a].

Fear of Death and the Individual's Beliefs

The beliefs referred to here are called "core beliefs" and are characterized by the following features:

- they represent deeper-lying meanings of the individual;

- they underlie many of the individual's beliefs in different domains, which may be derived from them;
- they do not refer specifically to any particular theme, such as death or justice;
- they are stable, contrary to many beliefs that are formed by the individual ad hoc and are transient;
- they represent basic components of the individual's world view;
- they take the form of one of four basic types of beliefs that have been defined by the cognitive orientation theory and were shown to play a basic role in guiding behavior or shaping motivational dispositions for behavior (see Table 3) (Kreitler & Kreitler, 1976, 1982, 2004a).

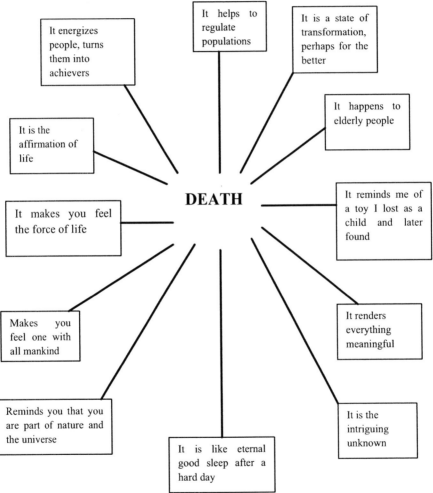

[a]Each of the meanings exemplifies one of the meaning variables constituting the pattern of meaning variables corresponding to death anxiety (see Table 2). For example, "it energizes people, turns them into achievers" is a meaning value of the meaning dimension Results and Consequences, "it is the affirmation of life" is a meaning value of the meaning dimension Judgments and Evaluations about the referent.

Figure 2. Meanings assigned to death by individuals scoring low in death anxiety[a].

Table 3. Formal structure of the four types of beliefs according to the cognitive orientation theory

Types of Beliefs	Subject of the Belief	Relation between the Subject and Predicate in the Belief	**Examples of Beliefs**
Beliefs about self	I	Existential, factual	**I rarely lie**
General beliefs (about others, reality)	Not-I	Existential, factual	**People often lie**
Beliefs about goals	I	Desired, Wished	**I want to be able never to lie**
Beliefs about rules and norms	**Not-I**	**Desirable, Deontic, Should/ought be**	**Lying should be avoided**

The individual is mostly unaware of the contents or sometimes even of the existence of the core beliefs. They can be identified by gradual step-by-step probing-by-meaning, which may start with exploring the meaning of any concept or object and delving deeper until no further elaboration of meaning is forthcoming from the individual. For example, one may start with asking an individual to communicate the meaning of "death". The response may be " the end of life"; the interviewer asks then for the meaning of "the end of life", which leads to the response "no activity can take place"; the request for the meaning of the latter, leads to the response "nothing is of any worth anymore"; and so on until the interviewee offers a response, such as "acting is the beginning and end of everything" which he or she considers as needing or enabling no further elaboration. The latter would be identified as a core belief of an individual if it is mentioned at the end-point of chains of meanings starting with various objects or concepts. Core beliefs on the social or cultural level would be beliefs identified as core beliefs in a great number of individuals in a given society or culture.

The procedure of identifying core beliefs was applied in the case of 15 individuals scoring high on death anxiety and 15 other individuals scoring low on death anxiety. In each interview the key terms that were used for starting the meaning exploration were: death, justice, happiness and art. This exploratory study led to the following preliminary list of core beliefs that appeared to characterize the high scorers on death anxiety:

1. The essence of life is activity;
2. The basic unit of existence is the individual (rather than the family, the community, the nation, etc.);
3. A person should produce things, be productive (in the sense of producing material or specific things, rather than merely be or experience or know things)
4. Life is the highest value, beyond everything else (beyond morality etc.).
5. The most important goal is preserving what is (keep change at a minimum, even at the cost of no development);
6. The most important time is the future, followed by the present and in the last rank by the past.
7. An individual is conceived as a package of potentialities for doing things and performing duties etc. An individual has not fulfilled one's task in the world if one

has not enacted all of one's potentialities. It is one's duty to enact and apply all of one's potentialities, but there is no way to know how much or how many there are.

8. One is held accountable for everything one has done in life, as well as for everything one has not done in life.

9. The responsibility lies only with the individual even though there are circumstances that may promote or hinder certain activities.

Beliefs such as those presented above are likely to predispose an individual to greater death anxiety, although they do not refer directly to anxiety or the death or to a combination of both. Thus, if a person assumes, for example, full accountability for one's deeds or misdeeds (belief no. 8), this belief promotes death anxiety regardless of whether that person is an atheist or an ardent believer in God. If that person is an atheist, the accountability will be implemented in human or social or ethical terms, whereas if the person is religious, the death anxiety will take on the form of fear of retribution or punishment in more religious terms. In either case, there will be an intense underlying death anxiety. Another example is the belief concerning the maintenance of what is (belief no. 5). Individuals who are afraid of change, of development and of transformations, tend to have stronger death anxiety than others, because in the last count death represents or introduces the biggest conceivable change into a human's existence. Finally, take the belief about the individual being the basic and ultimate unit (belief no. 2). It is evident that if an individual considers a larger unit, such as a community or nation, as basic, this belief may contribute to mitigating death anxiety because the embeddedness of the individual in the larger unit provides the potential possibility of preserving one's past attainments and continuing what one has failed or been unable to attain in the course of one's limited existence.

Notably, some of the core beliefs yielded by the preliminary study reported earlier are reminiscent of psychological theories that have dealt with the issue of death anxiety. For example, there are theories that highlight the important role of the need for self-actualization in supporting death anxiety (e.g., Maslow, 1970; Rogers, 1959). The core belief that views the human being as a package of potentialities (belief no. 7) expresses this viewpoint most closely. Another example is terror management theory (Rosenblatt, Greenberg, Solomon, Pyszezynski & Lyon, 1989) which assumes that cultural systems buffer human awareness of mortality by providing "symbolic" immortality through identification with the cultural system and "real" immortality through religion. This approach is reflected most closely in the core belief about

The basic unit of existence (belief no. 2). The special advantages of the cognitive orientation approach based on core beliefs is that it provides a broader basis for understanding death anxiety than any of the specific approaches, first, in that it grounds death anxiety in a whole set of beliefs rather than just one or two, and secondly, in that it provides a comprehensive homogenous theoretical framework for the impacts of the core beliefs rather than a variety of different theories or hypotheses.

Since core beliefs are often shared by individuals it seems likely that many of them form part of the cultural background within which many of us live and function. Some of the core beliefs in that culture promote death anxiety but others may serve to mitigate it. Different cultures and religions do it in different ways, but it is likely that they all do it, thus contributing ultimately to maintaining the delicate balance between the information that we will all die and the lust for living as long as we live, keeping death anxiety at a tolerable level.

CONCLUDING REMARKS

The presented review about the nature of death anxiety, its components and dimensions, its development, assessment, correlates and determinants shows that death anxiety is a ubiquitous component of human life and a factor that probably affects human quality of life to an appreciable degree. It has a great number of correlates and not surprisingly may play a role in different unexpected contexts, for example, as one of the themes contributing to eating disorders (Kreitler, Bachar, Canetti, Berry, & Bonne, 2003). The fact that death anxiety has so many correlates, manifestations and meanings may have led different investigators and thinkers to assume that death anxiety lies at the core of most human functioning, healthy and pathological (e.g., Becker, 1973; Sartre, 1943/1966). This assumption seems to be too far-fetched and up to now unsupported.

However, the determinants of death anxiety seem to be deeply rooted in the cognitive and emotional spheres of functioning. As shown above, death anxiety depends, on the one hand, on meaning assignment tendencies and, on the other hand, on core beliefs that underlie a great many of our beliefs that enter into a fair number of motivational dispositions. Hence, it seems unlikely any attempt at treating death anxiety or reducing it that does not deal with the deeper-lying determinants of death anxiety would be successful. Indeed, a review of several studies designed to improve coping with death anxiety have reached the conclusion that the different attempts have hardly brought any changes in death anxiety (Lonetto & Templer, 1986, p. 99). The reason is not that death anxiety is hard to change but that in order to change it, it is necessary to apply the adequate theoretical and methodological means (Kreitler & Kreitler, 1990a). Yet, before the adequate means are applied, it is necessary to deal with major issues, such as the likely side-effects of reduced death anxiety for the individual and for society, which are beyond the scope of this chapter.

REFERENCES

Aday, R. H. (1984-1985). Belief in afterlife and death anxiety: Correlates and comparisons. *Omega, 15,* 67-75.

Anthony, S. (1972). *The discovery of death in childhood and after.* New York: Basic Books.

Amenta, M. M. (1984). Death anxiety, purpose in life and duration of service in hospice volunteers. *Psychological Reports, 54,* 979-984.

Aronow, E., Rauchway, A., Peller, M., & Devito, A. (1980-81). The value of the self in relation to fear of death. *Omega, 11,* 37-44.

Atwood, V. A. (1984). Children's concepts of death: A descriptive study. *Child Study Journal, 14,* 11-29.

Bach, S. (1975). Spontaneous pictures of leukemic children as an expression of the total personality, mind and body. *Acta Paedopsychiatrica, 41,* 86-104.

Becker, E. (1973). *The denial of death.* New York: The Free Press.

Bertoia, J., & Allen, J. (1988). Counselling seriously ill children: Use of spontaneous drawings. *Elementary School Guidance and Counselling, 22,* 206-221.

Bluebond-Langner, M. (1978). *The private worlds of dying children.* Princeton, NJ: Princeton University Press.

Bolt, M. (1978). Purpose in life and death concerns. *Journal of Genetic Psychology, 132,* 159-160.

Braun, P. R., & Reynolds, D. N. (1969). A factor analysis of a 100-item fear survey inventory. *Behavior Research and Therapy, 7,* 399-402.

Brubeck, D. & Beer, J. (1992). Depression, self-esteem, suicide ideation, death anxiety, and GPA in high school students of divorced and nondivorced parents. *Psychological Reports, 71,* 755-763

Candy-Gibbs, S. E., Sharp, K. C., & Petrun, C. J. (1984-5). The effects of age, object and cultural/religious background on children's concepts of death. *Omega, 15,* 329-346.

Choron, J. (1964). *Modern man and mortality.* New York: Macmillan.

Clunies-Ross, C., & Lansdown, R. (1988). Concepts of death, illness and isolation found in children with leukemia. *Child Care, Health, and Development, 14,* 373-386.

Cobbs, B. (1956). Psychological impact of long-term illness and death of a child on the family circle. *Journal of Pediatrics, 49,* 746-751.

Cole, M. A. (1978-9). Sex an marital status differences in death anxiety. *Omega, 9,* 139-147.

Collett, L., & Lester, D. (1969). The fear of death and the fear of dying. *Journal of Psychology, 72,* 179-181.

Cotton, C. R., & Range, L. M. (1990). Children's death concepts: Relationship to cognitive functioning, age, experience with death, fear of death, and hopelessness. *Journal of Clinical Child Psychology, 19,* 123-127.

Devins, G. M. (1979) Death anxiety and voluntary passive death euthanasia. *Journal of Consulting and Clinical Psychology, 47,* 301-309.

Dickstein, L. S. (1972). Death concerns: Measurement and correlates. *Psychological Reports, 30,* 563-571.

Dunagin, J. M. (1981). *The relationship between death anxiety, interpersonal trust, and gender.* Unpublished doctoral dissertation, US International University, San Diego, CA.

Durlak, J. A. & Kass, C. A. (1981-2). Clarifying the measurement of death attitudes: A factor analytic evaluation of fifteen self-report death scales. *Omega, 12,* 129-141.

Elkins, G. R., & Fee, A. F. (1980). The relationship of physical anxiety to death anxiety and age. *Journal of Genetic Psychology, 137,* 147-148.

Feifel, H. (1976). Religious conviction and fear of death among the healthy and terminally ill. In R. Fulton (Ed.), *Death and anxiety* (pp. 131-143). Baltimore: Charles Press.

Flint, G. A., Gayton, W. F., & Ozmon, K. L. (1983). Relationship between life satisfaction and acceptance of death by elderly persons. *Psychological Reports, 53,* 290.

Freud, S. (1926/1959). Inhibitions, symptoms and anxiety. In *Standard edition of the complete psychological works Sigmund Freud* (Vol. 20). London: Hogarth Press.

Freud, S. (1957). Thoughts for the times on. war and death. In *Standard Edition,* Vol. 14, London: The Hogarth Press and the Institute of Psychoanalysis.

Furth, G. (1988). *The secret world of drawings: Healing through art.* Boston: Sigo Press.

Gartley, W., & Bernasconi, M. (1967). The concept of death in children. *Journal of Genetic Psychology, 110,* 71-85.

Geer, J. H. (1965). The development of a scale to measure fear. *Behavior Research and Therapy, 3,* 45-53.

Gibbs, H. W., & Achtenberg-Lawlis, J. (1978). Spiritual value and death anxiety: Implications for counseling with terminal cancer patients. *Journal of Counseling Psychology, 25,* 563-569.

Gielen, A. C., & Roche, K. A. (1979-80). Death anxiety and psychometric studies in Huntington's disease. *Omega, 10,* 135-145.

Gilliland, J. C. (1982). *Death anxiety: Relation to subjective state.* Unpublished doctoral dissertation, California School of Professional Psychology at Fresno.

Gillilard, J. C., & Templer, D. I. (1985-6). Relationship of death anxiety scale factors to the subjective state. *Omega, 16,* 155-167.

Hackett, T. P., & Weisman, A. D. (1964). Reactions to the imminence of death. In G. H. Grosser, H. Wechsler, & M. Greenblat (Eds.), *The threat of impending disaster: Contribution to a psychology of stress.* Cambridge, MA: MIT Press.

Hinton, J. M. (1963). The physical and mental distress of dying. *Quarterly Journal of Medicine, New Series, 32,* 1-21.

Hinton, J. (1967). *Dying.* Harmondsworth, Middlesex, England: Penguin Books.

Hoelter, J. W. (1979). Multidimensional treatment of fear of death. Journal of Consulting and Clinical Psychology, 47, 996-999.

Hollenbeck, A. R., Sussman, E. J., Nannis, E. D., Strope, B. E., Hersh, S. P., Levine, A. S., & Pizzo, A. S. (1980). Children with serious illness: Behavioral correlates of separation and isolation. *Child Psychiatry and Human Development, 11,* 3-11.

Hunt, D. M., Lester, D., & Ashton, N. (1983). Fear of death, locus of control and occupation. *Psychological Reports, 53,* 1022.

Ireland, M. (1998). Death anxiety and self-esteem in young children with AIDS: A sense of hope. *Omega, 36,* 131-145.

Jampolsky, G. G., & Taylor, P. (1978). *There is a rainbow behind every dark cloud.* Tiburon, CA: Celestial Arts.

Jay, S. M., Green, V., Jonson, S., Caldwell, S., & Nitschke, R. (1987). Differences in death concepts between children with cancer and physically healthy children. *Journal of Clinical Child Psychology, 16,* 301-306.

Jenkins, R. A., & Cavanaugh, J. C. (1985-6). Examining the relationship between the development of the concept of death and overall cognitive development. *Omega, 16,* 193-199.

Kane, A. C., & Hogan, J. D. (1985-6). Death anxiety in physicians: Defensive style, medical speciality, and exposure to death. *Omega, 16,* 11-22.

Kastenbaum, R., & Aisenberg, R. (1976). *The psychology of death* (concise edition). New York: Springer Publishing.

Katz, R. I. (1981). *Death attitudes among heroin addicts.* Unpublished doctoral dissertation, California School of Professional Psychology at Fresno.

Kavanaugh, R. E. (1977). *Facing death.* New York: Penguin Books.

Kenyon, B. L. (2001). Current research in children's conceptions of death: a critical review. *Omega, 43,* 63-91.

Kirby, M., & Templer, D. I. (1975). Death anxiety and social work students. Paper presented at the *Foundation of Thanatology Symposium* "The family and death: A social work symposium". New York, N.Y. April 12, 1975.

Koob, P. B., & Davis, S. F. (1977). Fear of death in military officers and their wives. *Psychological Reports, 40,* 261-262.

Koocher, G. P. (1973). Childhood, death, and cognitive development. *Developmental Psychology, 9,* 369-375.

Koocher, G. P., O'Malley, J. E., Foster, D., & Gogan, J. L. (1976). Death anxiety in normal children and adolescents. *Psychiatria Clinica, 9,* 220-229.

Kreiger, S., Epsting, F., & Leitner, L. M. (1974). Personal constructs, threats, and attitudes towards death. *Omega, 5,* 299-310.

Kreitler, S. (1965). *Symbolschöpfung und Symbolerfassung: Eine experimentalpsychologische Studie.* München-Basel: Reinhardt.

Kreitler, S. (2004a). The cognitive guidance of behavior. In J.T.Jost, M. R. Banaji, & D. A. Prentice (Eds.), *Perspectivism in Social Psychology: The Yin and Yang of scientific progress* (pp. 113-126). Washington, DC: American Psychological Association.

Kreitler, S. (2004b). The dynamics of fear and anxiety. In P. L. Gower (Ed.), *Psychology of fear* (pp. 1-17). New York: Nova Science Publishers.

Kreitler, S., Bachar, E., Canetti, L., Berry, E., & Bonne, O. (2003). The cognitive orientation theory of anorexia nervosa. *Journal of Clinical Psychology, 59,* 651-671.

Kreitler, H., & Kreitler, S. (1976). *Cognitive orientation and behavior.* NY: Springer.

Kreitler, H., & Kreitler, S. (1982). The theory of cognitive orientation: Widening the scope of behavior prediction. In B.A. Maher & W. A. Maher (Eds.), *Progress in experimental personality research, Vol. 11. Normal personality processes* (pp. 101-169). NY: Academic Press.

Kreitler, S., & Kreitler, H. (1984). Meaning assignment in perception. In W. D. Froehlich, G. J. W. Smith, J. G. Draguns & U. Hentschel (Eds.*), Psychological processes in cognition and personality* (pp. 173-191). Washington: Hemisphere Publishing Corp./McGraw-Hill.

Kreitler, S., & Kreitler, H. (1985a). The psychosemantic determinants of anxiety: A cognitive approach. In H. van der Ploeg, R. Schwarzer & C. D. Spielberger (Eds.)*, Advances in test anxiety research*, Vol. 4 (pp. 117-135). Lisse, The Netherlands and Hillsdale, NJ: Swets & Zeitlinger and Erlbaum.

Kreitler, S., & Kreitler, H. (1985b). The psychosemantic foundations of comprehension. *Theoretical Linguistics, 12,* 185-195.

Kreitler, S., & Kreitler, H. (1987a). Modifying anxiety by cognitive means. In R. Schwarzer, H. M. van der Ploeg & C. D. Spielberger (Eds.), *Advances in test anxiety research,* Vol. 5 (pp. 195-206). Lisse, The Netherlands and Hillsdale, NJ: Swets & Zeitlinger and Erlbaum.

Kreitler, S., & Kreitler H. (1987b). The motivational and cognitive determinants of individual planning. *Genetic, Social, and General Psychology Monographs, 113,* 81-107.

Kreitler, S., & Kreitler, H. (1988). Trauma and anxiety: The cognitive approach. *Journal of Traumatic Stress, 1,* 35-56.

Kreitler, H., & Kreitler, S. (1990a). Cognitive primacy, cognitive behavior guidance and their implications for cognitive therapy. *Journal of Cognitive Psychotherapy, 4,* 155-173.

Kreitler, S., & Kreitler, H. (1990b). *The cognitive foundations of personality traits.* NY: Plenum.

Kreitler, S., & Kriboy, E. (2004). Psychological intervention with the dying child. In Kreitler, S., & Ben-Arush, M. (Eds.), *Psychological aspects of pediatric oncology* (pp. 389-414). Chichester, England: Wiley.

Krug, S. E., Scheier, I. H., & Cattell, R. B. (1976). *Handbook for the IPAT anxiety scale.* Champaign, IL: Institute for Personality and Ability Testing.

Kübler-Ross, E. (1981). *Living with death and dying.* New York: Macmillan.

Kübler-Ross, E. (1983). *On children and death.* New York: Macmillan.

Kumar, A., Vaidya, A. K., & Dwivedi, A.V. (1982). Death anxiety as a personality dimension of alcoholics and non-alcoholics. *Psychological Reports, 51,* 634.

Latanner, B., & & Hayslip, B. (1984-5). Occupation-related differences in levels of death anxiety. *Omega, 15,* 53-66.

Lifton, R. J. (1976) The sense of immortality: On death and the continuity of life. In R. Fulton (Ed.), *Death and identity.* Bowie, MD: Charles Press.

Lifton, R. J. (1979). *The broken connection.* New York: Simon and Schuster.

Litman, J. M. (1979). *The effect of bereavement on death anxiety, manifest anxiety and locus of control.* Unpublished doctoral dissertation, University of Missouri, Hansa City.

Loewen, I. L. (1984). *Widowhood: The relationship between religious orientation and adjustment to loss of spouse.* Unpublished doctoral dissertation. California School of Professional Psychology at Fresno.

Lonetto, R. (1980). *Children's conceptions of death.* New York: Springer Publishing.

Lonetto, R., Fleming, S., Gorman, M., & Best, S. (1975). The psychology of death: A course description with some student perceptions. *Ontario Psychologist, 7,* 9-14.

Lonetto, R., Fleming, S., & Mercer, G. W. (1979). The structure of death anxiety: A factor analytic study. *Journal of Personality Assessment, 43,* 388-392.

Lonnetto, R., Mercer, G. W., Fleming, S., Bunting, B., & Clare, M. (1980). Death anxiety among university students in Northern Ireland and Canada. *Journal of Psychology, 104,* 75-82.

Lonetto, R., & Templer, D. I. (1986). *Death anxiety.* New York: Hemisphere Publishing Corporation.

Lucas, R. A. (1974). A comparative study of measures of general anxiety and death anxiety among three medical groups including patient and wife. *Omega, 5,* 233-243.

Mahon, M. (1993). Children's concept of death and sibling death of trauma. *Journal of Pediatric Nursing, 8,* 335-344.

Martin, T. O. (1982-3). Death anxiety and social desirability among nurses. *Omega, 13,* 51-58.

Maslow, A. H. (1970). *Motivation and personality* (2nd ed.). New York: Harper & Row.

Matalon, T. H. (2000). The relationship among children's conceptualization of death, parental communication about death, and parental death anxiety. Dissertation Abstracts International Section A: Humanities and Social Sciences, Vol 61(2-A): 510

McCully, R. S. (1963). Fantasy productions of children with a progressively crippling and fatal disease. *Journal of Genetic Psychology, 102,* 203-216.

McDonald, D. T., & Carroll, J. D. (1981). Three measures of death anxiety: Birth order effects and concurrent validity. *Journal of Clinical Psychology, 37,* 574-577.

McIntire, M., Angle, C., & Struempler, L. (1972). The concept of death in mid- western children and youth. *American Journal of Diseases of Children, 123,* 527-532.

Menig-Peterson, C. L., & McCabe, A. (1977-1978). Children talk about death. *Omega, 8,* 305-317

Miller, M. L. (1999). Growing up amidst violence: Death anxiety, cognitive development, and conception of death in children. *Dissertation Abstracts International: Section B: The Sciences and Engineering,* Vol 60(5-B): 2388

Minean, J. O., & Brush, L. R. (1980-1981). The correlations of attitudes towards suicide with death anxiety, religiosity, and personal closeness. *Omega, 11,* 317-324.

Morgan, D. W. (1976). Altered states variables as predictors of death anxiety. *Essence, 1,* 34-41.

Morrissey, J. R. (1963). Children's adaptations to fatal illness. *Social Work, 8,* 81-88.

Morrison, J. K., Vanderwyst, D., Cocozza, J. J., & Dowling, S. (1981-2). Death concern among mental health workers. *Omega, 12,* 189-208.

Muris, P., Merckelbach, H., Ollendick, T. H., King, N. J., Meesters, C., van Kessel,C. (2002). What is the Revised Fear Survey Schedule for Children measuring? *Behaviour Research and Therapy, 40,* 1317-1326.

Nagy, M. (1948). The child's theories concening death. *Journal of Genetic Psychology, 73,* 3-27.

Natterson, J. M., & Knudson, A. G., Jr. (1960). Observations concerning fear of death in fatally ill children and their mothers. *Psychosomatic Medicine, 22,* 456-465.

Nehrke, M. F., Morganti, J. B., Willrich, R., & Hulicka, I. M. (1979). Health status, room size, and activity level: Research in an institutional setting. *Environment and Behavior, 11,* 451-463.

Neimeyer, R. A., & Chapman, K. M. (1980-1981). Self/ideal discrepancy and fear of death: the test of an existential hypothesis. *Omega, 11,* 233-240.

Nelson, L. D., & Nelson, C. C. (1975). A factor analytic study into the multidimensionality of death anxiety. *Omega, 6,* 171-178.

Neustadt, W. E. (1982). *Death anxiety in elderly nursing home residents and amount of contact received from staff: A correlation study.* Unpublished Master's Thesis , University of Oregon, Eugene.

Ochs, C. E. (1979). *Death orientation, purpose of life, and the choice of volunteer service.* Unpublished doctoral dissertation, California School of Professional Psychology at Fresno.

Ohyama, M., Furuta, S., & Hatayama, M. (1978). Death concepts in adolescents. I. Changes of death anxiety in nursing students. *Tohoku Psychologica Folia, 37,* 25-31.

Orbach, I., Gross, Y., Glaubman, H., & Berman, D. (1986). Children's perceptions of various determinants of the death concept as a function of intelligence, age and anxiety. *Journal of Clinical Child Psychology, 15,* 120-126.

Pepitone-Arreola-Rockwell, F. (1981). Death anxiety: Comparison of psychiatrists, psychologists, suicidologists, and funeral directors. *Psychological Reports, 49,* 979-982.

Quinn, P. K., & Reznikoff, M. (1985). The relationship between death anxiety and the subjective experience of time in the elderly. *International Journal of Aging and Human Development, 21,* 197-210.

Ramos, F. R. (1982). *Personality, depression and death.* Unpublished Doctoral Thesis, University of Madrid, Madrid, Spain.

Reilly, T. P., Hasazi, J. E., & Bond, L. A. (1983). Children's concepts of death and personal mortality. *Journal of Pediatric Psychology, 8,* 21-31.

Richmond, J. B., & Weisman, H. A. (1955). Psychologic aspects of management of children with malignant disease. *American Journal of Diseases of Children, 89,* 42-47.

Robinson,Y. A. (2001). Death anxiety in children: Differences between support group bereaved and contrast group youth. *Dissertation Abstracts International: Section B: The Sciences and Engineering.* 2001, Vol 61 (12-B): 6719.

Rogers, C. R. (1959). A theory of therapy, personality, and interpersonal relationships, as developed in the client-centered framework. In S. Koch (Ed.), *Psychology: A study of a science* (Vol. 3, pp. 184-256). New York: McGraw Hill.

Rosenblatt, A., Greenberg, J., Solomon, S., Pyszezynski, T., & Lyon, D. (1989). Evidence for terror management theory: I. he effects of mortlity salience on reactions to those who violate or uphold cultural values. *Journal of Personality and Social Psychology, 57,* 681-690.

Sarason, I. G. (1978).The Test Anxiety Scale: Concept and research. In C. D. Spielberger & I. G. Sarason (Eds.), *Stress and anxiety* (Vol. 5) (pp. 193-216). Washington, DC: Hemisphere.

Sartre, J. P. (1966/1943). *Being and nothingness: An essay on phenomenological ontology.* New York: Citadel Press.

Schell, D., & Seefeldt, C. (1991). Development of a death anxiety scale for children. *Omega, 23,* 227-234.

Schilder, P., & Wechsler, D. (1934). The attitudes of children toward death. *Journal of Genetic Psychology, 45,* 406-451.

Schultz, C. M. (1978). Death anxiety reduction through the success-achievement cultural role value: A middle-class American community case study. *Journal of Psychological Anthropology, 1,* 171-188.

Shepard, S. J. (1980). A study of the relationship between dogmatism and death anxiety, both personal and anticipated from a terminally-ill person, in counselling students, nursing students, and general education students. *Dissertation Abstracts International, 41,* 1411.

Shrut, S. D. (1958). Attitudes toward old ag and death. *Mental Hygiene, 42,* 259-266.

Slezak, M. E. (1980). *Attitudes toward euthanasia as a function of death fears and demographic variables.* Unpublished doctoral dissertation, California School of Professional Psychology at Fresno.

Smith, A. H. Jr. (1977). A multivariate study of personality, situational and demographic predictors of death anxiety in college students. *Essence, 1,* 139-146.

Solnit, A. J., & Green, M. (1959). Psychologic considerations in the management of death on pediatric hospital services. *Pediatrics, 24,* 106-112.

Spielberger, C. D., Gorsuch, R. L., Lushene, R. E., & Vagg, P. R. (1977). *The state- trait anxiety inventory: Form Y.* Tampa, Fl: University of South Florida.

Stern, M. (1968). Fear of death and neurosis. Journal of the American Psychoanalytic Association, 16, 3-31.

Sullivan, W. J. (1977). *Effect of religious orientation, purpose in life and locus of control on the death anxiety of college students.* Unpublished doctoral dissertation, Fordham University, New York, NY.

Tate, L. A. (1980). *Life satisfaction and death anxiety in aged women.* Unpublished doctoral dissertation, California School of Professional Psychology at Fresno.

Taylor, J. A. (1953). A personality scale of manifest anxiety. *Journal of Abnormal and Social Psychology, 48,* 285-290.

Telban, S. G. (1980). *The relationship between death anxiety and the registered nurses' knowledge of the hospice.* Unpublished Master's Thesis, The Pennsylvania State University, University Park, PA.

Templer, D. I. (1967). *The construction and validation of a death anxiety scale.* Unpublished doctoral dissertation, University of Kentucky, Lexington, KY.

Templer, D. I. (1970). The construction and validation of a death anxiety scale. *Journal of General Psychology, 82,* 165-177.

Templer, D. I. (1972a). Death anxiety: Extroversion, neuroticism, and cigarette smoking. *Omega, 3,* 126-127.

Templer, D. I. (1972b). Death anxiety in religiously involved persons. *Psychological Reports, 31,* 361-362.

Templer, D. I., & Dotson, E. (1970). Religious correlates of death anxiety. *Psychological Reports, 26,* 895-897.

Templer, D. I., Barthlow, V. L., Halcomb, P. H., Ruff, C. F., & Ayers, J. L. (1979). The death anxiety of convicted persons. *Corrective and Social Psychiatry, 25,* 18-25.

Templer, D. I., Ruff, C. F., & Franks, C. M. (1971). Death anxiety: Age, sex, and parental resemblance in diverse populations. *Developmental Psychology, 4,* 108.

Thorson, J. A. (1977). Variations in death anxiety related to college students' sex, major field of study, and certain personality traits. *Psychological Reports, 40,* 857-858.

Tobacyk, J. (1984). Death threats, death concerns, and paranormal belief. In F. R. Epting & R. A. Neimeyer (Eds.), *Personal meanings of death* (pp. 29-38). Washington, DC: Hemisphere.

Vargo, M. E., & Batsel, W. M. (1984). Relationship between death anxiety and components of the self-actualization process. *Psychological Reports, 48,* 89-90.

Vargo, M. E., & Black, W. F. (1984). Psychosocial correlates of death anxiety in a population of medical students. *Psychological Reports, 54,* 737-738.

Waechter, E. H. (1971). Children's awareness of fatal illness. *American Journal of Nursing, 71,* 1168-1172.

Waechter, E. H. (1987). Children's reactions to fatal illness. In T. Krulik, B. Holaday & I. M. Martinson (Eds.), *The child and family facing life-threatening illness* (pp. 108-119). Philadelphia: Lippincott.

Wagner, K. D., Lorion, R. P., & Shipley, T. E. (1983). Insomnia and psychosocial crisis: Two studies of Erikson's developmental theory. *Journal of Consulting and Clinical Psychology, 51,* 595-603.

Wass, H., Guenther, Z. C., & Towry, B. J. (1979). United States and Brazilian children's concepts of death. *Death Education, 3,* 41-55.

Whittenberg, J. L. (1980). *Nurses anxiety about death and dying patients.* Unpublished Master's Thesis, University of Rochster, Rochester, NY, USA.

Wilkins, R. (1996). *Death: A history of man's obsessions and fears.* New York: Barnes and Noble.

Wolpe, J., & Lang, P. J. (1964). A fear survey schedule for use in behavior therapy. *Behavior Research and Therapy, 2,* 27-30.

Wong, P. T. P., Reker, G. T., & Gesser, G. (1994). Death Attitude Profile – Revised: A multidimensional measure of attitudes toward death. In R. A. Neimeyer (Ed.), *Death anxiety handbook* (pp. 121-148). Washington, DC: Taylor & Francis.

Ziv, A., Levin, I., & Israeli, R. (1974). *MIHALI, an anxiety test for children.* Tel-Aviv: Tel-Aviv University Publications.

Zuckerman, M. (1979). *Sensation seeking: Beyond the optimal level of arousal.* Hillsdale, NJ: Erlbaum.

Zung, W. W. K., & Cavenar, J. O., Jr. (1980). Assessment scales and techniques. In I. L. Kutash, L. B. Schlesinger & Associates (Eds.), *Handbook on stress and anxiety*. San Francisco: Jossey-Bass.

In: New Research on the Psychology of Fear
Editor: Paul L. Gower, pp. 91-103

ISBN 1-59454-334-8
© 2005 Nova Science Publishers, Inc.

Chapter 5

ORAL SURGERY APPOINTMENT ATTENDANCE: EFFECTS FROM FEARS OF DENTISTRY AND PAIN

Kevin E. Vowles[1], Daniel W. McNeil[1,2], John T. Sorrell[1], Deborah Rettig McKee[1], Michael J. Zvolensky[1], Robert W. Graves[2], Bryan D. Weaver[2] and James R. Riel[1]

West Virginia University

[1] Department of Psychology, Eberly College of Arts and Sciences, PO Box 6040, Morgantown, WV 26506, USA

[2] School of Dentistry, Robert C. Byrd Health Sciences Center, Morgantown, WV 26506, USA

ABSTRACT

Dental fears are prevalent in the general population and can have detrimental effects on dental care utilization, and subsequent oral health status. Fear of pain is an integral component in many individuals with high dental fear. The present investigation assessed how oral surgery appointment attendance rates were related to fears of dentistry and pain. Participants completed the Dental Fear Survey and Fear of Pain Questionnaire-III prior to scheduled or emergency oral surgery appointments. An oral surgery appointment attendance ratio was calculated retrospectively with data from a six-year period. Findings indicated that attendance rates were directly and negatively related to both dental fear and fear of pain. Further analyses investigated differences among three groups of patients: appointment attenders, appointment nonattenders, and individuals with emergency appointments. In general, nonattenders were more fearful than attenders; emergency patients also reported more dental fear and were older than attenders. These data indicate the importance of dental fear and fear of pain in understanding attendance behavior, and suggest that assessing these variables prospectively may aid in the identification of avoidant individuals.

Key words: Anxiety, Fear, Pain, Attendance, Adherence, Dentistry, Oral Surgery

Over the past three decades, increased attention has been focused on the role that fear and anxiety play in oral health care behaviors across the lifespan, with a consistent result being that greater dental fear is associated with poorer attendance at dental appointments, decreased compliance with treatment recommendations, and perhaps most importantly, poorer oral health status (Melamed & Fogel, 2000; Sorrell & McNeil, under review). Various models regarding the etiology of dental fear have been posited, with perhaps the most well-supported arguing that such fears likely arise from a combination of classical and operant conditioning processes, as well as modeling (Davey, 1989; de Jongh, Muris, ter Horst, & Duyx, 1995; Lautch, 1971; Lindsay & Jackson, 1993; Milgrom, Mancl, King, & Weinstein, 1995). A recent analysis underscored the importance of these conditioning experiences regardless of age of onset of dental fears (Poulton, Waldie, Thomson, & Locker, 2001). Additionally, epidemiological data suggest that dental fear is relatively widespread in the general population. Previous investigations have found that between 10% (Moore, Birn, Kirkegaard, Brodsgaard, & Sheutz, 1993) and 19% (Corah, 1988) of individuals report significant feelings of dental-specific fear, while up to 80% report dental fear of lesser severity (Pavlov, 1997), suggesting that dental fear, like other fears, is dimensional, existing along a continuum in the population (McNeil, Turk, & Ries, 1994). More importantly, studies suggest that approximately 5% of individuals are so markedly fearful regarding dental treatment that they avoid professional oral health care (de Jongh et al., 1995; Feinmann & Harrison, 1997; Litt, 1996) and these individuals also tend to experience negative psychosocial consequences associated with their fears (e.g. lower self-esteem, elevated prevalence of psychopathology; Locker, 2003). Therefore, it can be concluded that relatively high levels of dental fear are common (Melamed & Fogel, 2000), with a minority of individuals feeling significant enough fear to avoid dental appointments. Given that avoidance of dental treatment can lead to significant health care complications (Doerr, Lang, Nuyquist, & Ronis, 1998; Klepac, 1986; Schuller, Willumsen, & Holst, 2003), and even mortality in rare cases (Kloffon, 1988), the identification of this avoidant subset of dental patients is extremely important.

In addition to dental fears, it appears that fear of pain is an important variable to be assessed within dental populations. Fear of pain can be conceptualized as a negative emotional reaction to painful or potentially painful stimuli associated with significant avoidance/escape behavior, physiological arousal, and verbal reports of distress (McCracken, Zayfert, & Gross, 1992; McNeil, Au, Zvolensky, McKee, Klineberg, & Ho, 2001; McNeil & Rainwater, 1998). In fact, fear of pain has been found to be a significant predictor of dental fear above and beyond other measures of general psychological symptomology (e.g., depression, somatization, state and trait anxiety; McNeil & Berryman, 1989; McNeil et al., 2001). Based on this finding, as well as other research showing an association between elevated levels of fear of pain and distress/disability in individuals experiencing severe and persistent pain (Lethem, Slade, Troupe, & Bentley, 1983; McCracken et al., 1992; Sperry-Clark et al., 1999; Vlaeyen & Linton, 2000; Vowles & Gross, 2003), McNeil and colleagues (2001) have recommended that treatment for dental fear should focus not only on decreasing dental-related fears, but also on reducing fear of pain. This recommendation is supported by findings from a related line of research concerning prediction of dental pain in which Arntz, Van Eck, and Heijmans (1990) found that dentally anxious individuals did not experience increased pain during dental procedures, but that they experienced higher levels of fear of pain, which was theorized to contribute to inaccurate pain memories leading to avoidance behaviors.

Based on these previous investigations, it can be hypothesized that both dental fear and fear of pain contribute to avoidance behaviors in dental patients. These factors may be particularly important in the oral surgery arena, as patients are confronted both with dentistry and the possibility of pain due to surgical intervention (e.g., tooth extraction). Prior research in this general area (e.g., orofacial injury and appointment attendance) has not included fear of pain as a predictor (Brown, Shetty, Delrahim, Belin, & Leathers, 1999). The current investigation sought to refine and extend research in this area in a number of ways. First, we sought to determine if a significant relation exisisted between dental fear and adherence with scheduled appointments in an oral surgery population. The relation between fear of pain and appointment adherence also was assessed, given the previously supported relation between this construct and dental fear. Secondly, the present study sought to identify differences among qualitatively different groups of patients. We theorized that the elucidation of such differences would assist in the identification of certain demographic or psychosocial variables associated with dental attendance patterns among patients.

METHOD

Participants

Data were collected from 209 consecutive volunteer patients presenting to the outpatient Oral Surgery Clinic at the West Virginia University School of Dentistry. Patient attendance was retrospectively assessed over the preceding six calendar year period. Attended (e.g., kept) and unattended (e.g., no-showed, canceled, missed) oral surgery appointments were tallied and analyzed.

Of the total sample of 209 outpatients, there were 92 individuals (55.4% female) with scheduled appointments. On average, these patients had been scheduled for 3.0 appointments ($SD = 4.0$), and were 28.4 years old ($SD = 11.4$). Consistent with demographics of the state, as a historically isolated part of Appalachia, most were Caucasian (94.6%; 4.3% Asian American, 1.1% Hispanic), and were scheduled for a tooth extraction procedure (69.6%). The remaining individuals were seen for a consultation appointment (17.4%) or some other type of procedure (13.0%).

There were 117 individuals (60.7% female) from the total sample who did not have scheduled oral surgery appointments. These appointments were generally the result of a dental emergency; thus it was theorized that many of these patients were avoidant of dental appointments in general, and may have elevated levels of dental fear and/or fear of pain. On average, these individuals were 32.1 years old ($SD = 12.2$), with the majority (89.7%) seen for a tooth extraction. The remaining individuals were seen for consultation appointments. As was the case with those individuals who had scheduled appointments, the majority of the emergency patients were Caucasian (93.0%; 4.3% African American, 0.9% Asian American, 0.9% Native American, 0.9% Unspecified).

Measures

Dental Fear Survey (DFS)

Specific fears regarding dental situations were assessed using the 20-item DFS (Kleinknecht, Klepac, & Alexander, 1973). In addition to a total score, which ranges from 20-100, three subscale scores can be derived. These are avoidance/anticipatory fear (score range: 8-40), fear of specific dental stimuli (score range: 6-30), and physiological arousal (score range: 5-25). The DFS has been used quite extensively in research settings; its structure, reliability, and validity have been well supported (Kleinknecht & Bernstein, 1978; Kleinknecht, Thorndike, McGlynn, & Harkavy, 1984; McGlynn, McNeil, Gallagher, & Vrana, 1987)

Fear of Pain Questionnaire-III (FPQ-III)

The FPQ-III (McNeil & Rainwater, 1998), a 30-item instrument designed to assess self-reported fear across a wide variety of painful situations, was administered to all study participants. Individuals rated their fear of experiencing the pain associated with pain-related events on five-point, Likert-type scales. The FPQ-III measures fear along three dimensions: medical/dental pain, minor pain, and severe pain. A total score is available (possible total score range: 30-150), as well as scores for each subscale (possible subscale score range: 10-50). The FPQ-III has demonstrated good reliability and construct validity (Hursey & Jacks, 1992; McNeil & Rainwater; Sperry-Clark et al., 1999; Osman, Breitenstein, Barrios, Gutierrez, Kopper, 2002) and has been used previously in oral health research (e.g., McNeil et al., 2001).

Oral Surgery Appointment Attendance Ratio

As noted earlier, data regarding patients' prior attendance patterns at oral surgery appointments was collected from a computerized database at the West Virginia University School of Dentistry. Following data collection, a mathematical ratio was derived to represent the proportion of attended versus unattended appointments. The ratio was calculated by subtracting the number of unattended appointments from the number of appointments attended, and the resulting value was divided by the total number of appointments. This ratio allowed attendance to be assessed as a continuous variable with a possible range of +1.0 (indicating attendance of all scheduled oral surgery appointments) to -1.0 (indicating all scheduled oral surgery appointments were not attended). Figure 1 displays attendance frequency data for all patients who had scheduled appointments. This ratio was only derived for individuals who had scheduled appointments, and not for individuals with emergency clinic visits.

Procedure

Consecutive outpatients reporting for scheduled appointments or emergency care were informed and invited to participate at the reception window of the West Virginia University School of Dentistry Oral Surgery Clinic. Following informed consent, patients completed the

DFS and FPQ-III (in that order). Demographic and attendance data were collected from patients' records.

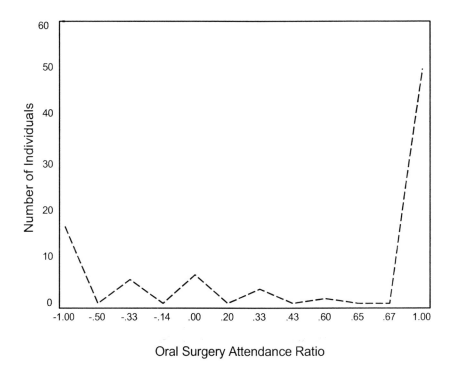

Figure 1. Frequency data for the derived oral surgery attendance ratio. Positive values indicate increasing appointment attendance; negative values indicate decreasing attendance.

RESULTS

Correlation and Regression Analyses

In order to evaluate relations among dental fear, fear of pain, and oral surgery attendance, zero order correlation coefficients were calculated for all individuals with scheduled appointments. For the purpose of these analyses, gender was coded as a binary variable. The results, presented in Table 1, indicated significant negative correlations between the oral surgery attendance ratio and total scores of both the DFS and FPQ-III, along with a number of subscales for each measure.

Table 1. Correlations Among Demographic and Self-Report Measures in Patients with Scheduled Appointments

	1	2	3	4	5	6	7	8	9	10	11
1. Attendance Ratio	--										
2. Age	-.02	--									
3. Gender	-.02	.04	--								
4. DFS – Total	-.28**	-.07	.12	--							
5. DFS – Avoid	-.27**	-.04	.16	.94***	--						
6. DFS – Physio	-.16	.03	.08	.86***	.75***	--					
7. DFS – Stimuli	-.28**	-.14	.08	.94***	.80***	.72***	--				
8. FPQ – Total	-.22*	-.20	.06	.41***	.30**	.37***	.47***	--			
9. FPQ – Med/Dent	-.22*	-.18	.08	.67***	.53***	.58***	.71***	.84***	--		
10. FPQ – Minor	-.24*	-.06	.03	.20	.14	.22*	.21*	.82***	.58***	--	
11. FPQ – Severe	-.10	-.27**	-.01	.17	.09	.12	.25*	.87***	.55***	.59***	--

Note. Gender coded such that 1=male and 2 = male; DFS – Total = Dental Fear Survey – Total Score; DFS – Avoid = Dental Fear Survey – Anticipation/Avoidance Subscale; DFS – Physio = Dental Fear Survey – Physiological Arousal Subscale; DFS – Stimuli = Dental Fear Survey – Specific Dental Stimuli; FPQ-Total = Fear of Pain Questionnaire-III – Total Score; FPQ – Med/Dent = Fear of Pain Questionnaire-III – Medical/Dental Pain Subscale; FPQ – Minor = Fear of Pain Questionnaire-III – Minor Pain Subscale; FPQ – Severe = Fear of Pain Questionnaire-III – Severe Pain Subscale.

* *p* < .05
** *p* < .01
*** *p* < .001

In order to evaluate the relative contribution of each of the self-report inventories on attendance rates among those individuals with scheduled appointments, two stepwise regression equations were calculated. With regard to the first equation, pertinent demographic variables (i.e., age and gender) were entered first and then total scores from the DFS and FPQ-III were entered in a stepwise fashion. Results indicated that only the DFS total score accounted for a significant amount of variance, $\beta = -.28$, $r^2 = .08$ ($N = 92$, $p \leq .01$) after controlling for demographic variables. The second equation also entered demographic variables first; however, subscale scores from the questionnaires, rather than total scores, were entered next. For this model, the FPQ-III Minor Pain subscale entered into the equation, $\beta = -.26$, $r^2 = .07$ ($N = 92$, $p \leq .05$), followed by the DFS Anticipation/Avoidance subscale , $\beta = -.21$; $r^2 = .11$ ($N = 92$, $p \leq .05$). Demographic variables again did not account for a significant amount of variance in attendance rates.

Analyses by Group

Three groups were identified for analysis. Visual review of the attendance ratio distribution (see Figure 1) indicated a pronounced split with regard to attendance rates among patients with scheduled appointments. Specifically, 19 individuals did not attend any appointments, 50 attended all appointments, and the remaining 23 patients had some mixture of attendance and nonattendance. Based on the conceptual classification of dental appointment attendance by Milgrom, Weinstein, and Getz (1995), we determined that consistent attenders ($n = 50$) and consistent nonattenders ($n = 19$) comprised the two most easily identifiable groups. The third group consisted of the individuals who had emergency appointments ($n = 117$). Using these individuals, analyses of variance (ANOVAs) and a chi square analysis (for the categorical gender variable) were conducted to investigate differences in dependent and demographic measures among these three groups of patients. For the ANVOVAs, Tukey's Honestly Significant Difference tests at the .05 level were conducted to follow-up significant overall differences. These analyses revealed significant between group differences in age, $F (2, 185) = 3.44$, $p \leq .05$, DFS total score, $F (2, 185) = 3.72$, $p \leq .05$, DFS Avoidance/Anticipation subscale score, $F (2, 185) = 3.51$, $p \leq .05$, DFS Specific Dental Stimuli subscale score, $F (2, 185) = 3.13$, $p \leq .05$, and FPQ-III Minor Pain subscale score, $F (2, 185) = 3.46$, $p \leq .05$. No other analyses, including the non-parametric analysis for gender, indicated significant differences, all other p's $\geq .19$. Results regarding follow-up analyses are displayed in Table 2. In general, nonattenders indicated more fear of pain and dental fear compared to the group that attended all appointments. Interestingly, individuals with emergency appointments did not differ significantly from either nonattenders or attenders on most measures. The only exceptions to this were for age and DFS total score, which were higher for individuals with emergency appointments compared to consistent attenders.

Table 2. Factorial Analyses Follow-up and Descriptive Data

	Mean (SD)		
	Consistent Attenders	Consistent Nonattenders	Emergency Appointments
Age *	28.8 (12.2) [a]	29.8 (10.6) [a,b]	32.1 (12.2) [b]
Dental Fear Survey			
Total Score *	38.7 (15.4) [a]	51.0 (19.6) [b]	45.6 (19.6) [b]
Avoidance/Anticipation *	13.1 (6.4) [a]	18.2 (8.1) [b]	15.7 (8.0) [a,b]
Physiological Arousal	9.4 (3.6)	11.1 (4.3)	10.7 (4.8)
Specific Dental Stimuli *	14.1 (6.2) [a]	18.6 (7.1) [b]	16.0 (7.3) [a,b]
Fear of Pain Questionnaire-III			
Total Score	70.9 (20.2)	79.8 (24.5)	76.6 (23.2)
Medical Pain	24.2 (8.5)	27.9 (8.0)	25.7 (9.0)
Minor Pain *	16.8 (5.3) [a]	20.9 (9.1) [b]	19.2 (6.7) [a,b]
Severe Pain	30.6 (9.5)	30.8 (12.4)	32.2 (10.4)

Note. $N = 186$.

* indicates omnibus ANOVA significant at $p \leq .05$. Means that do not share a common superscript differ on Tukey follow-up tests at $p \leq .05$.

DISCUSSION

The present study was conducted to evaluate the role of fear of pain and dental fear in attendance rates at an outpatient oral surgery clinic. Across our patient population, dental fear and fear of pain in general has a significant inverse relation with attendance rates among individuals with scheduled appointments. In addition, greater severity of specific fears of dental stimuli and equipment and anticipation of dental appointments, as well as fears of medical, dental, and minor painful experiences, were associated with lower attendance rates. To some extent, the present results replicate those of previous investigations (e.g., Kent, 1985; Schuurs, Duivenvoorden, Velze, & Verhage, 1980; 1984; ter Horst & de Wit, 1993), which have found that individuals who are more irregular and unpredictable in their attendance of dental-related appointments tend to report higher levels of fear relative to their more regularly attending counterparts. Our results, however, extend previous findings to an oral surgery population and highlight the role that fear of pain plays in appointment attendance patterns, which is consistent with more recent research indicating the importance of this construct in dental fear (e.g., McNeil et al., 2001).

The results of the second set of analyses indicated that individuals who had historically avoided all oral surgery appointments reported consistently higher levels of avoidance and anticipation of appointments, and fears of specific dental stimuli (e.g., dental equipment) than consistent attenders, with a similar but nonsignificant pattern in terms of physiological arousal. Additionally, the nonattenders had greater fears of minor pain than attenders, with a similar but nonsignificant pattern for the other FPQ-III scales. The relatively low sample size (n = 19) of the nonattender group may account for why these differences did not reach standard levels of reliability.

The emergency patients were older and had greater overall dental fear than the attenders, but did not differ significantly from them on DFS subscales or in terms of fear of pain. Their scores suggest they are like the consistent nonattenders and are perhaps "forced" into securing dental care due to pain, loss of oral function, or both.

Our findings are consistent with the ideas of Kleinknecht and Bernstein (1978), who posited that appointment adherence was the most clinically useful indicator of dental fear. They suggested that the most fearful individuals do not appear for routine oral health care, rather they show up at emergency dental clinics when discomfort levels become intolerable. It may be that clinically significant levels of dental fear led many of these individuals to delay seeking health care services until their problems required immediate and invasive (i.e., surgical) intervention. Our emergency patients also likely include some individuals who have problems in access to oral health care due to economic factors or geographic isolation in West Virginia, or those who place less value on preserving their dentition and oral health issues generally, or those for whom fear combines with these other factors.

Based on our findings, a note regarding the relation between pain and fear is necessary.

Historically, pain had been viewed a sensation resulting from tissue damage; however, this conceptualization has been found to be lacking in terms of its ability to explain why pain responsivity varies from person to person (Bocher, 1988). In addition, pain appears to be methodologically confounded with fear, in terms of self-report, physiological, and behavioral measurement (Gross & Collins, 1981; McNeil &Vowles, in press). Further, experimental investigations have indicated that painful and fearful stimuli elicit similar response patterns (McNeil & Brunetti, 1992), and that responses may be determined by the more aversive of the two type of stimuli (Vowles, McNeil, Sorrell, & Lawrence, under review). It is therefore important, in addition to evaluating pain in patients, that their fears be appropriately assessed and treated if necessary. Psychosocial interventions for high dental fear have considerable data supporting their utility and effectiveness (Gatchel, 1980; Liddell, Di Fazio, Blackwood, & Ackerman, 1994; Lindsay & Jackson, 1993; Melamed & Fogel, 2000). Given that it may be difficult to clinically determine if a patient is behaving in a distressed manner because of significant pain or significant fear, appropriate assessment is all the more necessary. The two measures utilized in the present study appear to provide appropriate screening methods for fearful patients, and may be useful to oral surgery clinics in this regard.

The present design has some inherent limitations. First, we assessed dental fear and fear of pain after patients had already established patterns of appointment attendance. Therefore, it is possible that levels of dental fear and fear of pain changed over time, and that the level indicated at assessment was not representative of the level during patients' prior appointment(s). Our results clearly indicate, however, that dental fear and fear of pain are strongly related to appointment attendance history; testing the predictive power of these measures will require other empirical designs. At the very least, these findings serve to confirm that fears of dentistry and pain are associated with a pattern of behavior. Secondly, the correlations observed between attendance rates and the utilized self-report measures were significant, but only moderate. Given that we sampled a variety of patients, however, some of whom may have cancelled appointments not due to fear, but because of some other life events (e.g., car trouble), it is noteworthy that attendance rates actually were significantly related to the measures of fear included in the present analyses.

It is important to note that the Medical/Dental Pain subscale of the FPQ-III did not enter into the regression equations while the Minor Pain subscale did so. On the surface, the

Medical/Dental Pain subscale should be more relevant to attendance behaviors at oral surgery appointments than the Minor Pain subscale. Both of these subscales were significantly correlated with the attendance ratio; however, the Minor Pain subscale was very slightly (although nonsignificantly) more highly correlated (i.e., by .02). Further, both of their subscales were significantly intercorrelated. These values suggest shared variance between these two variables that overlaps with the attendance ratio. The Minor Pain subscale's slightly greater correlation with the attendance ratio allowed it to enter first into the regression equation, thus negating the role of the Medical/Dental Pain subscale in accounting for appointment attendance rates. Based on the correlations, it can be hypothesized that both of these subscales have an important relationship to attendance rate. This finding may be somewhat specific to our sample, as the anticipated pain in oral surgery truly may be most related to the Minor pain content of the FPQ-III, more so than the diverse medical and dental contents of the Medical/Dental subscale. Relatively minor fears regarding the pain experienced in certain situations can have a broad influence on behavior, such as oral surgery appointment attendance in the case of the present sample.

In conclusion, fear of pain and dental fear both appear to be related to patient patterns of attendance at oral surgery appointments. Further, individuals who consistently do not attend these appointments display higher levels of dental fear and fear of pain compared to regular, consistent attenders. Individuals with emergency appointments, most often emergency extractions, were relatively undifferentiated from either consistent nonattenders or attenders; however, overall levels of dental fear resemble the more fearful group. Further, the emergency patients were significantly older than attenders, suggesting they may avoid oral surgery appointments for longer periods of time. The present results suggest that the two measures we utilized, the DFS and FPQ-III, may be useful in the identification of individuals who may potentially avoid oral surgery appointments. Given that appointment avoidance has been linked to a number of adverse oral health outcomes, it is important that further research refine the available methods to identify this avoidant subset of patients. These findings have implications not only for oral surgery appointments, but also for other health care appointments in which fear of pain, and fear generally, may be an issue.

AUTHOR NOTES

Correspondence regarding this article should be sent to Kevin E. Vowles (*kvowles@mix.wvu.edu*) or Daniel W. McNeil (*dmcneil@wvu.edu*), PO Box 6040, Department of Psychology and Department of Dental Practice and Rural Health, West Virginia University, Morgantown, WV 26506.

John T. Sorrell now is at the Veteran's Affairs San Diego Healthcare System, San Diego, CA. Deborah Rettig McKee now is at Webster University, Rolla, MO. Michael J. Zvolensky now is at the Department of Psychology, University of Vermont, Burlington, VT.

The authors thank Kim Capehart, Suzanne M. Lawrence, Karen Soccorsi, Carol Spearen, and J. R. Wilson for their efforts in this project.

Financial support for this research was provided in part by a grant from the West Virginia University School of Dentistry Research Fund.

REFERENCES

Arntz, A., Van Eck, M., & Heijmans, M. (1990). Predictions of dental pain: The fear of any expected evil, is worse than the evil itself. *Behaviour Research and Therapy, 28,* 29-41.

Bocher, S. (1988). *The psychology of the dentist-patient relationship.* New York; Springer-Verlag.

Brown, K. A. E., Shetty, V., Delrhim, S., Belin, T., & Leathers, R. (1999). Correlates of missed appointments in orofacial injury patients. *Oral Surgery, Oral Medicine, Oral Pathology, 87,* 405-410.

Corah, N. L. (1988). Dental anxiety: Assessment, reduction and increasing patient satisfaction. *Dental Clinics of North America, 32,* 779-790.

Davey, G. C. L. (1989). Dental phobias and anxieties: Evidence for conditioning processes in the acquisition and modulation of learned fear. *Behaviour Research and Therapy, 27,* 51-58.

Doerr, P. A., Lang, W. P., Nyquist, L. V., & Ronis, D. L. (1998). Factors associated with dental anxiety. *Journal of the American Dental Association, 129,* 1111-1119.

de Jongh, A., Muris, P., Schoenmakers, N., & ter Horst, G. (1995). Negative cognitions of dental phobics: Reliability and validity of the Dental Cognitions Questionnaire. *Behaviour Research and Therapy, 33,* 507-515.

Feinmann, C., & Harrison, S. (1997). Liaison psychiatry and psychology in dentistry. *Journal of Psychosomatic Research, 43,* 467-476.

Gatchel, R. L. (1980). Effectiveness of two procedures for reducing dental fear: Group-administered desensitization and group education and discussion. *Journal of the American Dental Association, 101,* 634-637.

Gross, R. T., & Collins, F. L. (1981). On the relationship between anxiety and pain: A methodological confounding. *Clinical Psychology Review, 1,* 375-386.

Hursey, K. G., & Jacks, S. D. (1992). Fear of pain in recurrent headache sufferers. *Headache, 32,* 283-286.

Kent, G. (1985). Cognitive processes in dental anxiety. *British Journal of Clinical Psychology, 24,* 259-264.

Klepac, R. K. (1986). Fear and avoidance of dental treatment in adults. *Annals of Behavioral Medicine, 8,* 17-22.

Kleinknecht, R. A., & Bernstein, D. A. (1978). The assessment of dental fear. *Behavior Therapy, 9,* 626-634.

Kleinknecht, R. A., Klepac, R. K., & Alexander, L. D. (1973). Origins and characteristics of fear of dentistry. *Journal of the American Dental Association, 86,* 842-848.

Kleinknecht, R. A., Thorndike, R. M., McGlynn, F. D., & Harkavy, J. (1984). Factor analysis of the Dental Fear Survey with cross-validation. *Journal of the American Dental Association, 108,* 59-61.

Kloffon, C. E. (1988). Anxiety, infection, and death. *International Journal of Psychosomatics, 35,* 61-62.

Lautch, H. (1971). Dental phobia. *British Journal of Psychiatry, 119,* 151-158.

Lethem J., Slade P. D., Troup J. D. G., Bentley G. (1983). Outline of a fear-avoidance model of exaggerated pain perception – I. *Behaviour Research and Therapy, 21,* 401-408.

Liddell, A., Di Fazio, L., Blackwood, J., & Ackerman, C. (1994). Long-term follow-up of treated dental phobics. *Behaviour Research and Therapy, 32,* 605-610.

Lindsay, S., & Jackson, C. (1993). Fear of routine dental treatment in adults: Its nature and management. *Psychology and Health, 8,* 135-153.

Litt, M. D. (1996). A model of pain and anxiety associated with acute stressors: Distress in dental procedures. *Behaviour Research and Therapy, 34,* 459-476.

Locker, D. (2003). Psychosocial consequences of dental fear and anxiety. *Community Dentistry and Oral Epidemiology, 31,* 144-151.

McCracken, L. M., Zayfert, C., & Gross, R. T. (1992). The Pain Anxiety Symptoms Scale: Development and validation of a scale to measure fear of pain. *Pain, 50,* 67-73.

McGlynn, F. D., McNeil, D. W., Gallagher, S. L., & Vrana, S. (1987). Factor structure, stability, and internal consistency of the Dental Fear Survey. *Behavioral Assessment, 9,* 57-66.

McNeil, D. W., Au, A. R., Zvolensky, M. J., McKee, D. R., Klineberg, I. J. & Ho, C. C. K. (2001). Fear of pain in orofacial pain patients. *Pain, 89,* 245-252.

McNeil, D. W., & Berryman, M. L. (1989). Components of dental fear in adults? *Behaviour Research and Therapy, 27,* 233-236.

McNeil, D. W., & Brunetti, D. G. (1992) Pain and fear: A bioinformational perspective on responsivity to imagery. *Behaviour Research and Therapy, 30,* 513-520.

McNeil, D. W., & Rainwater, A. J. (1998). Development of the Fear of Pain Questionnaire-III. *Journal of Behavioral Medicine, 21,* 389-410.

McNeil, D. W., Turk, C. L., & Ries, B. J. (1994). Anxiety and fear. In V. S. Ramachandran (Ed.), *Encyclopedia of human behavior* (Vol. 1, pp. 151-163). San Diego: Academic Press.

McNeil, D. W., & Vowles, K. E. (in press). Assessment of fear and anxiety associated with pain: Conceptualization, methods, and measures. In G. J. G. Asmundson, J. W. S. Vlaeyen, &

G. Crombez (Eds.), *Understanding and treating fear of pain.* Oxford: Oxford University Press.

Melamed, B. G., & Fogel, J. (2000). The psychologist's role in the treatment of dental problems. In D. I. Mostofsky & D. H. Barlow (Eds.) *The management of stress and anxiety in medical disorders* (pp. 268-281. Needham Heights, MA: Allyn & Bacon.

Milgrom, P., Mancl, L., King, B., & Weinstein, P. (1995). Origins of childhood fear. *Behaviour Research and Therapy, 33,* 313-319.

Milgrom, P., Weinstein, P., & Getz, T. (1995). *Treating fearful dental patients: A patient management handbook* (2nd ed.). Seattle: Continuing Dental Education, University of Washington.

Moore, R., Birn, H., Kirkegaard, E., Brodsgaard, I., & Scheutz, F. (1993). Prevalence and characteristics of dental anxiety in Danish adults. *Community Dentistry and Oral Epidemiology, 21,* 292-296.

Osman, A., Breitenstein, J. L., Barrios, F. X., Gutierrez, P. M., Kopper, B. A. (2002). The fear of Pain Questionnaire-III: Further reliability and validity with nonclinical samples. *Journal of Behavioral Medicine, 25,* 155-173.

Pavlov, C. (1997). Managing dental phobia. *Ontario Dentist, 74,* 23-27.

Poulton, R., Waldie, K. E., Thomson, W. M., & Locker, D. (2001). Determinants of early vs. late-onset dental fear in a longitudinal-epidemiological study. *Behaviour Research and Therapy, 39,* 777-785.

Schuller, A. A., Willumsen, T., & Holst, D. (2003). Are there differences in oral health and oral health behavior between individuals with high and low dental fear? *Community Dentistry and Oral Epidemiology, 31,* 116-121.

Schuurs, A. H. B., Duivenvoorden, H. J., Velzen, S. K. T., & Verhage, F. (1984). Dental Anxiety, the parental family and regularity of dental attendance. *Community Dentistry and Oral Epidemiology, 12,* 89-95.

Schuurs, A. H. B., Duivenvoorden, H. J., Velzen, S. K. T., & Verhage, F. (1980). Three factors predicting irregular versus regular dental attendance: A model fitting to empirical data. *Community Dentistry and Oral Epidemiology, 8,* 413-419.

Sorrell, J. T., & McNeil, D. W. (under review). *Fear of pain in dentistry.* Manuscript submitted for publication.

Sperry-Clark, J. A., McNeil, D. W., & Ciano-Federoff, L. (1999). Assessing chronic pain patients: The Fear of Pain Questionnaire-III. In L. VandeCreek & T. L. Jackson (Eds.), *Innovations in clinical practice: A source book* (vol. 17, pp. 293-305). Sarasota, FL: Professional Resource Press.

ter Horst, G., & de Wit, C. A. (1993). Review of behavioural research in dentistry 1987-1992: Dental anxiety, dentist-patient relationship, compliance, and dental attendance. *International Dental Journal, 43,* 265-278.

Vlaeyen, J. W., & Linton, S. J. (2000). Fear-avoidance and its consequences in chronic musculoskeletal pain: A state of the art. *Pain, 85,* 317-332.

Vowles, K. E., & Gross, R. T. (2003). Work-related beliefs about injury and physical capability for work in individuals with chronic pain. *Pain, 101,* 291-298.

Vowles, K. E., McNeil, D. W., Sorrell, J. T., & Lawrence, S. M. (under review). Which is worse, pain or fear?: Investigating the interaction between two aversive states. Manuscript submitted for publication.

In: New Research on the Psychology of Fear
Editor: Paul L. Gower, pp. 105-140

ISBN 1-59454-334-8
© 2005 Nova Science Publishers, Inc.

Chapter 6

THE TREATMENT OF DENTAL FEAR IN CHILDREN AND ADOLESCENTS – A COGNITIVE-BEHAVIOURAL APPROACH TO THE DEVELOPMENT OF COPING SKILLS AND THEIR CLINICAL APPLICATION

Helen R. Chapman[1] and Nick C. Kirby-Turner[2]

Paediatric Dentistry, Dept of Psychology, Royal Holloway, University of London, Egham, Surrey, TW20 0EX, UK[1], W Sussex Health and Social Care Trust, Princess Royal Hospital, Lewes Rd, Haywards Heath, W Sussex, RH16 4EX, UK[2]

ABSTRACT

Dental fear in children is a widespread and acknowledged problem. Much research has been conducted into aspects of dental fear such as aetiology, measurement of severity and treatment delivery, with the aim of dental fitness, rather than psychological well-being. In this very practically orientated article we hope to expound our cognitive-behavioural approach to the treatment of child dental fear which aims both to achieve dental fitness, and facilitate the development of coping strategies, thus enabling long term access to dental treatment.

1. INTRODUCTION

In this paper we aim to set out a practical guide to the treatment of dental fear in children and adolescents, referred to henceforth as 'children'. The contents have been developed over years of clinical collaboration and serve as a blueprint for clinicians wishing to collaborate in the treatment of dentally fearful children. Our approach is cognitive-behavioural and, rather than focusing simply on achieving dental fitness, aims to help children acquire adaptive coping strategies and the long-term ability to accept dental treatment in the wider clinical environment.

We have aimed to write at a practical level, both so that dentists may understand the basic psychology behind the suggestions, and that psychologists can gain a good understanding of some of the practical tasks and skills patients need to gain should they attend a psychologist directly for help.

We will start by considering clinical assessment, describing a multi-dimensional model which informs the assessment of factors predisposing, precipitating, or perpetuating dental fear. We then describe how multisystemic interventions can serve to develop coping skills and how these relate to different factors in the model. We conclude by describing how a cognitive-behavioural intervention can be illustrated in a typical fear hierarchy.

Throughout the paper examples of interventions are given with practical skills suggestions. Clinical vignettes are also used to illustrate points. (Names and details have been changed to protect patient confidentiality.) 'Care givers' are referred to as 'mothers/mummy' as, in reality, it is usually the mother who accompanies her children to the dentist.

2. ASSESSMENT

The prevalence and aetiology of dental fear in children were considered in a previous edition of this publication (Berge ten, M, 2003 pp 195-199). That paper also reviewed pen and paper assessment tools.

Clinical signs and symptoms (Kendall, P. C., 2000, pp 85-86) of fear and increased anxiety in children are apparent across Lang's 3 systems – the behavioural, the physiological and the cognitive/emotional (Lang, P. J., 1978).

Examples of behavioural manifestations include: clinging; being quiet and withdrawn and /or exhibiting fearful behaviour; "not listening"; non-compliance; physical and/or verbal hostility and aggression; fixed attention, indicating a heightened perception of threat; jittery behaviour.

Physiological indicators include: pale/cold hands; a need to use the bathroom/toilet; 'butterflies in the tummy' or stomach ache etc; headaches; sweating; feelings of suffocation/choking (exaggerated gag reflex); rapid heart rate; rapid, shallow breathing.

Examples of the cognitive/emotional manifestations include: rumination, identified as the emotion 'worry'; the intrusion of distracting thoughts, poor concentration and information processing; negative self-talk (or speech); images, the contents of which are negative and non-coping; and the emotional experience of being afraid or anxious. Crucially, anxious children often underestimate their ability to cope.

It is important to note that children have poor metacognitive skills; that is they are less able to identify and monitor their own thought processes. This applies to both the identification of 'self-talk' or the negative automatic thoughts of cognitive therapy as well as the identification of emotional states (Kagan, J., 1994, p38). In reply to questioning about what is wrong at a particular point in time, they may say, "I don't like it," or "I don't want it." The clinician must then provide a series of options (not single, closed questions) to facilitate identification of the problem. It is also important to remember to ask about images; "pictures in your head" as many will have these rather than self-talk.

As ten Berge (2003) highlighted previously, behavioural problems may reflect fearfulness, but they may also reflect non-compliance. The cognitive aspects of non-cooperation then become critical in differentiating between the two.

The other critical issue is the desynchrony of fear (Hodgson, R. & Rachman, S., 1974). Dentists tend to rely on behavioural monitoring and, in experimental settings, physiological monitoring, though there is generally a poor correlation between changes in physiological variables such as heart rate and how fearful, anxious or tense a child feels (Kagan, J., 1994, p38). It is our experience that the cognitive is the last aspect of fear to change, so a child can be 'behaving perfectly' whilst being in mental turmoil, with high levels of cognitive fear, manifesting as negative self-talk/speech which would not be apparent unless an established means of communication were established (see below).

Any treatment plan should be subject to iterative re-evlauation and modification as necessary. (Figure 1)

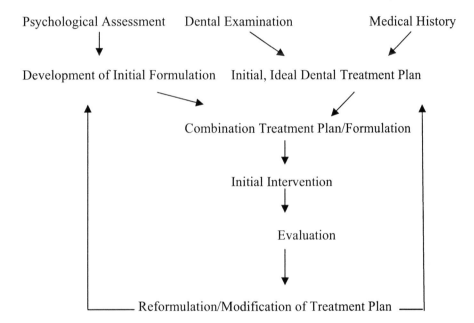

Figure 1. The iterative pattern of assessment and reformulation

2.1. The Model

The model outlined below (Figure 2) serves as a framework to guide assessment. It is based on observation of many cases. We have found it extremely useful both in making a detailed and accurate assessment of the factors influencing dental fear in the individual, and drafting an initial individualised formulation (Chapman, H. R. & Kirby-Turner, N., 1999)

We believe that there are five factors which are important in the aetiology and perpetuation of dental fear:

1. Fear of pain or its anticipation

2. A lack of trust or the fear of betrayal
3. Fear of loss of control
4. Fear of the unknown
5. Fear of intrusion/threats to self-esteem

In each domain behavioural, physiological and, crucially, cognitive factors contribute both to the development and maintenance of fear and also, conversely, to the development of coping skills.

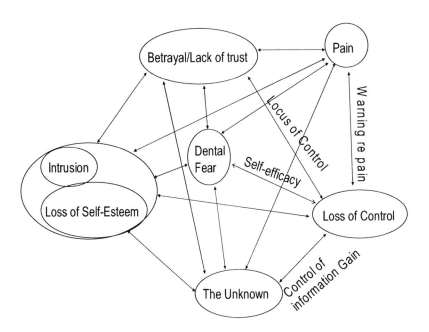

Figure 2. A proposed model of dental fear

2.1.1. Fear of Pain or its Anticipation

The link between actual or misinterpreted pain, or the anticipation of pain, and dental fear is well established (Klinberg, G., 1995; Holst, A., 1988). Unfortunately, discomfort and sometimes pain can still be a feature of dental treatment today, no matter how careful the anaesthetic technique (Matthews, R. et al., 1997). This possibility ensures that there is a genuine basis for anxiety.

The other problem is that individuals, especially children, have their feelings of pain denied. We frequently see children who report that they said that they were experiencing pain, but that the dentist ignored them and carried on. They may also have been told that they were 'being silly' or immature, thus attacking their self-esteem as well (see below).

2.1.2. Lack of Trust or Fear of Betrayal

Rotter defines trust as, "An expectancy held by an individual or a group that the word, promise, verbal or written statement of another individual or group can be relied upon." (Rotter, J. B., 1967) Thus trust is a fundamental feature of the clinical relationship, the strength of which will be reflected in the quality of patient outcome and patient satisfaction. An abuse of trust by one dentist may result in all dentists being distrusted. Distrust of medical personnel may generalise to dentists. Trust may also be learned either directly from the behaviour of parents, peers and so on, or indirectly from statements of others or observation of behaviour. It is therefore theoretically possible that children learn to trust or distrust dental or medical personnel from their parents even before they have any direct contact with such personnel (vicarious learning).

The research evidence that is available in adults suggests that trust of the dentist is an important variable in dental fear (Kvale, G., Milgrom, P., Getz, T., Weinstein, P., & Johnsen, T. B., 2004; Moore, R., Brodsgaard, I., & Birn, H., 1991) Clinical experience strongly suggests that it is important.

It is important to realise that although an individual, such as a dentist, may prove him/herself to be trustworthy, this does not automatically guarantee that trust will be given. It is up to each child to give trust to a person proven to be trustworthy. At times it will not be given.

With individuals who are extremely mistrustful, one of the great advantages of a psychologist/therapist working in partnership with a dentist is that the psychologist/therapist can fulfil the role of 'honest broker', ensuring that the dentist keeps his/her bargains with the patient.

There is a minority of children with very high fear of betrayal and high levels of treatment need, for whom no amount of 'bargain keeping' over very simple, atraumatic experiences makes any difference to their willingness to accept treatment. It is our experience that these children are 'turned around' by achieving dental fitness under general anaesthetic (or intravenous sedation for the older adolescent). It is essential to have these children back into the surgery immediately after the operative procedure to build trust, confidence and skills when there are obviously no grounds for betrayal. Unless this is undertaken, these children are likely to fall into a general anaesthetic – avoidance cycle.

Lack of trust, for some individuals, is an issue in the development of dental anxiety. It is often the direct result of intentionally or unintentionally dishonest behaviour on the part of the dentist or carer.

Patients, especially young children, may not voice these concerns directly, but will repeatedly indicate their concern by seeking reassurance. These delaying tactics can become infuriating for the busy clinician. Older children and adolescents may volunteer descriptions of experiences where their trust was abused. The betrayal may be hinted at in the history taking, which should be followed up with sensitive and direct questioning. Sometimes trust is satisfactory until more challenging treatment is reached.

2.1.3. Fear of Loss of Control

Children are used to being cared for, or controlled by, parents and those *in loci parentis*. They have an innate sense though of the boundary that defines social from personal control. While, for example, they are more or less happy to accede to parents' and teachers' requests to start or stop activities, their reaction, for example, to a request to "stop breathing", clearly demonstrates that there are limits to their compliance! Experience for children within the dental surgery parallels the example above. At the simplest level, no amount of exhortation to stop being terrified can, in itself, achieve compliance, whereas children (usually) readily accept modest demands to get in the chair and open wider.

The dental surgery might be considered to be an inappropriate setting for devolving control to children. Indeed, it is often quite difficult to ensure that they have some control when their mouths are full of dental instruments, though the importance of doing so has been recognised (Milgrom, P., Weinstein, P., & Getz, T., 1995, pp 304-305). Practical ways of achieving this are discussed below.

2.1.4. Fear of the Unknown

In anyone's eyes, a visit to the dentist may be classified as a *potentially* threatening situation. Any appraisal of the situation is going to be done from that point of view. 'Helpful' comments from the mother such as, "It won't hurt," are going to raise the possibility in the child's mind of being hurt. However, it is important to provide accurate information about possible discomfort immediately before the event. Provision of such information a long time in advance may only serve to increase fear of the unknown and the anticipation of pain. Recent functional magnetic resonance imaging (fMRI) studies in adults have shown that anticipated pain activates areas in the brain distinct from, but close to, the locations which mediated pain itself (Ploghaus, A. et al., 1999).

The poorer the quality and quantity of information provided by the dentist about the situation, the more important such misinformation from others becomes. Inadequate information also results in a reduced likelihood of the normal reactions to uncertainty and fear being overcome. The provision of a developmentally appropriate level of information, both sensory and procedural, (Cohen, F. & Lazarus, R. S., 1979) will not only reduce fear of the unknown, but also foster a sense of control as described above.

2.1.5. Fear of Intrusion

Dentistry is, by its nature, invasive. It includes X rays, fillings, extractions, but these are primarily on a physical dimension. Intrusion is more subtle. It involves impinging on the patient's personal space and into a bodily cavity; the mouth. It involves touching. And all this is only for an examination. Impinging on a patient's personal space is something that is taken for granted by professionals. They perceive this as part of their caring role, even if the patients dislike the procedure intensely.

Some children find this invasion of personal space very threatening. It may evoke withdrawal by younger children and comments, usually from older children, such as, "I don't like the thought of that thing squirting up inside my tooth.", "The bottom injection feels as if it is going down the back of my throat," "I can cope with injections anywhere else, but not in my mouth." The impact of four-handed dentistry was described by one adolescent like this, "I hate being all crowded in when you [dentist and nurse] have your eight hands in my mouth."

We have found that young children often find use of the high volume aspirator frightening because they are worried about it 'sucking them up,' especially if they have already had an experience where it has 'locked on' to buccal mucosa or floor of mouth. This fear is often made worse by referring to it as a 'hoover' or 'vacuum cleaner.' Some toddlers are actually frightened of the home cleaner (HRC's own daughter was), possibly because they fear being sucked up into it; the ultimate intrusive experience. This fear is often compounded when an enthusiastic dental nurse carries out tell-show-do (see below) and puts the end of the aspirator tip flat on the child's hand, so that it sucks and occludes on skin. We refer to our 'magic straw' and introduce humour by saying that if they are very lucky it will make rude noises like at the bottom of a drink which they get told off for making at home; they can practice this at home! We also demonstrate the aspirator sideways on the hand, squirting water from the 3-in-1 syringe across to it. We specifically point out that the nurse never lets it 'suck up bits of you.'

Intrusion may also involve a threat to self-esteem or sense of self-worth. For example the teenager who refused to attend because every visit involved perceived criticism from the dentist about how poor his diet was and how inadequate his cleaning. This is demoralising. HRC spotted a successfully desensitised 8 year old child in the shopping centre one Saturday, eating sweets. A smile and the remark, "I can see you," were the only comments made which were pertinent to the 'offence.' When a sibling attended for treatment the following week, the mother reported that her eight year old would be quite happy to have any treatment necessary, but was terrified of receiving a "good telling off."

Threat to the sense of self may be as subtle as the dentist using his/her powers of persuasion to gain compliance with a previously agreed task, which is currently being refused. For example, Hannah, a 16 year old adolescent, became anxious that HRC would persuade her to comply with previously agreed tasks. This had been successful in helping her to progress through a desensitisation package until the point was reached when she became highly anxious that HRC would be a 'snake charmer', 'manipulating' her so that she complied against her own free will. Most children would accept such persuasion as demonstrating faith in their ability to complete the task, but for Hannah, it was construed as the dentist overriding her decisional control (see below).

Fear of intrusion is the most difficult part of the model for the dentist to address.

2.1.6. Linking Constructs

The model is not static or unidirectional. The factors *seem* to be inter-related to some extent as illustrated in the last example of intrusion/decisional control.

One of the most readily identifiable links is that of 'locus of control' (Auerbach, S. M., Kendall, P. C., Cuttler, H. F., & Levitt, N. R., 1976), which links fear of the unknown with fear of loss of control. Locus of control reflects/determines the levels of information individual children need to reduce their fear of the unknown and it also determines how much control they instinctively need. 'Locus of control' may be defined as 'an expectancy that reinforcement is under one's own control.' (Rotter, J. B., 1966) This expectancy was presumed to result from generalisation of previous experiences and reinforcement of control. Locus of control may be 'internal' (coming from within the person), or 'external' (coming from outside the person). External locus of control may be sub-divided into 'fate/luck' and 'powerful others' (Figure 3). There is a continuum along the scale with very few children falling at either extreme of the scale. Individuals may have varying loci of control for differing situations, but they are unlikely to differ enormously, tending to cluster around a point on the continuum.

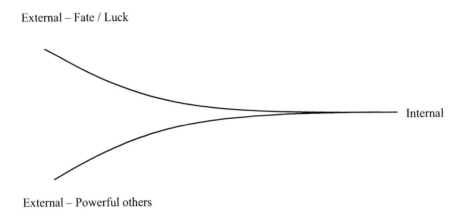

External – Fate / Luck

Internal

External – Powerful others

Figure 3. Locus of control

Children with a strong internal locus of control will want to actively participate in decision-making with regard to things such as treatment planning. They will require quite a lot of information before they take any decisions. But how much information should we give them? We have found that explicit requests to the child, "Are there any questions you want to ask?" "Is there anything else you would like to know?" will prompt questions. The child rapidly learns that s/he can ask questions until his/her need for information is satisfied. Older children with a strong internal locus of control often require detailed discussion of technical procedures and this is best facilitated by the use of sketches which have the added advantage that they may be taken away for further reference. On some occasions when the child is asked if he has any questions, the mother may interpose with a question of her own. In these circumstances we acknowledge the question, point out that it 'is the child's turn' and that we will answer any of her queries in a minute – and do.

Children with a 'powerful others' external locus of control may say, "You're the expert, Doctor; you do what you think is best" or "What do you think I should do, Mummy?" This type of child may be obviously distressed and yet fail to use the agreed stop signal. They may need to 'learn' how to use it by practising use of the signal during an atraumatic procedure such as a prophylaxis. This should involve coaching in giving a reason for the use of the stop signal.

Children with a fatalistic external locus of control will persist in ascribing their high decay rate to having "soft teeth like my mum" rather than to the constant consumption of sweets, no matter how often it is explained otherwise.

An easy way of assessing young child patients' locus of control is to offer a choice of two pairs of protective glasses to wear. Children with a strong external locus of control will not be able to choose. Forcing decision taking will result in stress. Individuals with a strong internal locus of control will be very positive in the choice. Children with an intermediate locus of control will 'not mind' (ie can't choose) between the choice of glasses, but will make the more important choice of which tooth to polish first during a prophylaxis.

Another identifiable link is that of self-efficacy – the belief that one can do something about the situation which has been found to enhanced when dental fear is treated successfully (Kent, G., 1997).

The amount of information gained and control necessary to improve self-efficacy will increase with a more internal locus of control.

2.1.7. Flexibility of the Model

This model works to explain both increases and decreases in the level of fear experienced. For example

- Fear caused by the unknown can be addressed directly by providing information (explain-show-do) – see below, (Chapman, H. R. & Kirby-Turner, N., 1999), but also indirectly by increasing perceptions of control and trust.
- Improving trust and control will reduce fear. Conversely, abuse of trust and lack of control will increase fear.
- Pain, and/or the denial of its experience will heighten fear. The provision of information about possible pain, the recognition of pain and steps taken to deal with it will reduce fear.

There are occasions when it is not possible directly to manage the important variable, for example a painful procedure such as the extirpation of a hyperaemic pulp, where total pain control is not always possible with conventional local anaesthetic procedures. By working on one or more of the other variables, it may still be possible to mitigate the situation and influence the outcome for the child for the better.

The multi-directionality of the model is particularly important when dealing with fear caused by concerns over intrusion, the factor which is the most difficult to address directly. This may be dealt with by addressing one or more of the other four factors. A sympathetic approach to the problem, coupled with a negotiated control over the intrusive procedures and a fostering of trust are the best approach. Consider, for example, the following scenario where a 14-year-old adolescent for whom the unknown, anticipated pain and intrusion were particularly important, was given significantly more control over the noxious stimulus (an inferior dental block) than dentists would normally consider giving. Heather had been seen by HRC over the course of several years, and issues of trust had been dealt with previously. She had successfully been desensitised to infiltration injections, but had to have an inferior dental block for restoration of a first permanent molar. Heather's need for detailed information meant that she demanded to know if a lower injection would be any different. HRC, feeling that to reassure her falsely that the block would be exactly the same as an infiltration would be an abuse of trust, explained very carefully that it would feel a little different. The child took this to mean that it would be painful and that topical anaesthetic would not work. (Topical anaesthetic is routinely used for inferior dental blocks with anxious patients because they expect it, having been used to its being used for previous infiltrations. Not using it generates anticipatory anxiety that the IDB will be different from an infiltration injection.) Heather also explained that she didn't like the idea of the local anaesthetic squirting into her and the idea that the needle would penetrate further than in the top jaw, having to pass through a greater depth of tissue. These were issues of intrusion. To over come the impasse which arose, Heather was given an explorer/ probe and carefully supervised while she 'prodded' the back of her mouth where the topical anaesthetic paste had been placed ready for administering the local anaesthetic. This was substituted with the anaesthetic needle by HRC and the block was duly administered. A very high degree of control had been used to circumvent the issues of intrusion and pain.

2.1.8.Contextual Variables

Co-operating with dental treatment is stressful for most children. This stress can be compounded by other stressors in the child's wider world (Kendall, P. C., 2000, p 30). These factors could include school issues (especially at exam time); peer pressure; too many activities; being tired; bereavement (relatives, friends and pets, both death and moving away, the loss of special toys); divorce; too much responsibility; physical accidents and exposure to family or community violence.

Additionally, 'squeezing in' a visit to the dentist, particularly for operative treatment and at the end of the day or during exam time, is likely to be a fraught experience.

Another issue for children as part of a family unit is competition for maternal support. Carers (usually mothers), for obvious reasons of time efficiency, like to bring all the children to the dentist together. For many children this presents no problem. For the very anxious, it may represent a significant stumbling block and provision of treatment without the presence of siblings should be negotiated.

2.1.9. Developmental Variables

It is important to consider the developmental level of the child, reflected in the changes in children's perceptions, understanding and abilities brought about by learning and maturity. It is important to remember that 'age' is judged by date of birth and maturity, not by physical size. We have been referred several children who were tall for their chronological age and, being expected to cope on the basis of size, had been overloaded by demands inappropriate to their psychological development.

Maturity will usually work in a positive direction, serving to reduce fear. The notable exceptions (Ollendick, T. H. & King, N. J., 1992) are

- fear of the unknown, which peaks at about the age of 9
- fear of bodily injury, which starts to appear at 9 years old
- fear of failure and criticism, which peaks during adolescence.

Learning, for example vicarious learning (including mothers' communication of their own dental experiences), can operate either positively or negatively, increasing or decreasing fear. It is up to the dentist to ensure that positive learning experiences are provided in the dental surgery.

To summarise, the above model serves as a conceptual tool to aid the clinician in identifying the most salient factors in each individual case of dental fear. Even relatively modest changes in building children's strengths and minimising their vulnerabilities can make considerable differences.

3. MULTISYSTEMIC APPROACHES TO THE DEVELOPMENT OF COPING SKILLS

Once an accurate and comprehensive assessment has been completed, it becomes possible to develop an intervention strategy to enhance coping.

Coping skills are the constantly changing cognitive and behavioural efforts of an individual, used to manage specific external and/or internal demands (stressors) that are appraised as taxing or exceeding the resources of a person. Coping includes all purposeful attempts to manage stress, whatever their effectiveness; that is they can be helpful or detrimental (Lazarus, R. S. & Folkman, S, 1980).

Coping skills are conscious and, in adaptive coping, are used in combination; the wider the repertoire the better. Individuals who rely on only one coping stratagem are unlikely to cope effectively.

Unfortunately, children are less able to realise that they cannot cope because of their poor meta-cognitive abilities. They are much more likely to just feel overwhelmed and burst into tears or grab the dentist's hands. In our experience, the fostering of appropriate coping skills in children not only enables them to cope with dental treatment in our clinic, but facilitates the generalisation of skills to other dental and medical settings. The portability of the skills makes this approach the most appropriate method of helping fearful children accept dental treatment.

A multisystemmic approach will involve intervention in behavioural, affective, sensory, imagery and cognitive, interpersonal and physiological domains: basic id (Lazarus, A. A., 1973).

3.1. Behavioural Interventions to Develop Coping Skills

We believe undue emphasis is placed on behavioural coping, often focussing upon deficits. As ten Berge highlighted in his review (Berge, ten M., 2003), the types of behaviour monitored may be a reflection of non-compliance as well as fear and they may fail to identify children with high levels of cognitively mediated fear. We have concerns that they tend to be a 'blunt instrument' with many of the recordable behaviours representing significant levels of fear which, in good practice, should not have been allowed to rise this high without being acknowledged and addressed; for example "white knuckles" and "patient dislodges instruments." [Melamed's Behaviour Profile Rating Scale, (Melamed, B. G., Weinstein, D., Hawes, R., & Katin-Borland, M., 1975)] It is possible that the emphasis on behaviour rating, both by independent observers and by the dentist undertaking treatment, as reviewed by ten Berge (Berge, ten M., 2003), reflects the dental profession's emphasis on completing dental treatment and rendering the patient 'dentally fit', rather than a concern for a more holistic concept of health – dental fitness together with the ability to cope confidently with dental treatment in the future.

Dentists will be all too familiar with the negative behaviours to which we refer, which include: refusal to even sit in the dental chair or open the mouth; fidgeting; gripping the arms of the dental chair; the mouth closing, tongue and cheeks 'fighting'; deliberate attempts to bite; verbal protests; grabbing or knocking away the dentist's hand or the instruments; the persistent use of social 'chit-chat' or circular questioning; leaving the dental chair or surgery/office. The ultimate behavioural control is avoidance, though most children are unable to avoid; even phobic mothers will often not allow their children to avoid.

Dentists will also be very aware of the behaviour they would like their patients to perform: sitting completely still, in the position requested for good access and visibility; maintaining a mouth that is open wide, but with the muscles of the tongue and cheeks completely relaxed for easy retraction; to maintain this position without wanting to swallow, cough, sneeze, scratch the nose or, Heaven forbid, have a rest or ask questions. If patients are this co-operative, the tendency is to concentrate on what are often highly complex and technically demanding surgical procedures using high speed rotary instruments. The good behaviour is taken for granted. Dentists will notice the mouth gradually closing through fatigue and request that it is opened wider, but are less likely to praise the wide open mouth. This is an important omission because any behaviour that is ignored is likely to extinguish (Malott, R. W. & Trojan Suarez, E. A., 2004, p 105) (see section 3.1.1).

Older children may choose to bring a lucky charm or wear a lucky piece of clothing. (We had one girl who wore Doc Martens each time she attended.) It is important, though, that other, internal attributions to success such as ability and effort are rewarded to encourage the development of self-efficacy rather than reliance on luck.

Changing diet – both snacks and drinks – can be promoted as a way of controlling caries progress, in the short-term to 'buy time' for acclimatisation to treatment and, in the longer term, to reduce disease experience. It contributes to perceived control (see Section 3.7.1.).

3.1.1. The Use of Operant Conditioning – Social Learning

Operant conditioning or social learning is a process whereby behaviours (the operants) are elicited and controlled (maintained, reinforced or extinguished) by the consequences that follow them (Kendall, P. C., 2000, pp 16-20).

The interpersonal dynamics in the dental surgery/office should be viewed as a system. Not only do behaviours from the patient provoke responses from the dental staff and parents, but the behaviour of the dental staff and parents has consequences in terms of responses from the patient. This was acknowledged by Weinstein et al in 1981 (Weinstein, P., Domoto, P., Getz, T., & Enger, R., 1981) who stated that

> 'It is our belief that successful pedodontic appointments are primarily a function of the behaviour of the dentist. Such an approach focuses on the behaviour, knowledge, and orientation of the dentist, not the child. Problematic child behaviour in the operatory is largely iatrogenic. And the majority of the problems can be either prevented or ameliorated.'

Positive Reinforcement

Positive reinforcement strengthens a behaviour and increases the likelihood of its occurring, be it positive or negative in nature (Malott, R. W. & Trojan Suarez, E. A., 2004, pp 17-19). The reinforcing reward can be attention (from another person, especially one of higher status) as well as material, such as stickers and other motivators. Behaviours that are not rewarded tend to extinguish; hence the importance of dental staff rewarding the co-operative behaviour they need to facilitate treatment.

The quietly refusing young child may be frightened or just non-compliant. There may be an established pattern of behaviour with the parent where quiet cussedness elicits a lot of coaxing from parents, and parental attention is an extremely powerful reinforcer. It is only too easy for staff to fall into a similar pattern. It may be that the child is fearful and not be capable of the meta-cognitive task of verbalising what it is that is troubling him, even with help. It is essential this distinction is established with *overtly non-traumatic* tasks, such as sitting in the dental chair. If the behaviour is apparently due to non-compliance, is very easy for staff to tell the parent that this "is naughtiness" and instantly loose parental support. We prefer to label the behaviour "stubborn," and ask if the child is stubborn at home. This is often enthusiastically endorsed by the parent. The reinforcing nature of coaxing should then be explained and the consequences of not complying (no motivator) explained. Depending on circumstances, the child can be offered the opportunity to wait in the waiting room until he changes his mind or to try again next week; but no co-operation, no motivator. It is not uncommon to see the child being torn by the desire to earn the motivator and the need to maintain a 'stance.'

A stubborn older child may be scared, but more easily identify what is troubling him. Stubbornness, particularly in adolescence, may be an indication of a power struggle between parent and child and may indicate that the young person should be seen on his own.

Appropriate Reward

Used appropriately, praise (which costs nothing) and stickers/motivators (which cost pennies/cents) are invaluable in treating children.

The worst case scenario is where every child who sets foot in the dental office is given a reward, no matter whether he had treatment, or how good he was.

In our practice, stickers are given for 'good work,' just like at school. This implies skills to be learned rather than horrors to be overcome. It also allows for the idea that you may not get a sticker every time, if you haven't worked hard.

Praise (and the use of motivators) (Brophy, J., 1981) should be contingent (that is, given at the time of the behaviour to be praised); specify the accomplishment and be spontaneous, varied and credible. It rewards specific performance, informs about the value of the skill and guides the child's understanding of his task-related behaviour. For example, "Well done, Billy! Your mouth is open really nice and wide so I can see more easily and you're sitting so still. That means I can work more easily as well and we'll be finished more quickly." This type of statement guides understanding of task-related behaviour and problem solving.

In contrast, random, unsystematic and global praise which is bland, uniform and paid with minimal attention, is not likely to be effective. An example of the latter is telling a child at the end of his treatment (and his three siblings who have sat and watched), while the dentist bends over the sink washing her hands, to go and get a sticker for being good. In this scenario, the patient does not get clear feedback on which skills were useful and the siblings have been rewarded for 'nothing,' thus devaluing the reward for the child who accepted treatment. If you would like to reward siblings for good behaviour while another is receiving treatment, have a different set of smaller, 'sitting still' stickers.

Praise used should be based on the child's own previous achievements, not on comparison and competition with others, recognising the effort and success of that particular child. This is sometimes a problem when one child in a family finds accepting treatment much harder than others and has to tackle far more and smaller steps up a fear hierarchy than the others. This usually involves receiving more praise and stickers. Again, a school analogy is useful here. Children as young as 6 or 7 usually have a good idea which math(s) set they are in and whether they find it easy or difficult. The comparison can be drawn that teachers at school will give stickers for easy sums to children who find it more difficult.

The children who don't understand about unfairness are younger toddlers. If the older child's reward is not to be devalued, a simple task should be invented for the toddler to enable a sticker to be earned. This task could be having his nose looked at with a mirror or having a ride on the dental chair on Mum's lap.

Reward structured in this way, which is focused on the child's task-relevant behaviour and attributes success to effort and ability, implies that future success can be expected. This in turn fosters endogenous attribution. Attribution of success to luck or an easy task fosters exogenous attribution and reduced self-efficacy. And, much as you have been an excellent clinician in setting a task of appropriate difficulty to enable the child to succeed, it is important that the dentist is not perceived as an external manipulator.

Negative Reinforcement

Negative reinforcement occurs when a behaviour is followed by termination of an aversive event. This increases the likelihood of the behaviour (Malott, R. W. & Trojan Suarez, E. A., 2004, pp 37-40). For example, if a child ignores being nagged to clean his teeth for long enough, the nagging will usually be abandoned. The next time he is nagged he is even more likely to ignore the exhortations.

Many interactions operate within a mutually reinforcing positive-negative reinforcement schedule. For example, the child who screams at the supermarket checkout until given sweets is positively reinforced for screaming and his mother is negatively reinforced because the screaming and all the consequent attention from other critical adults is removed. At the next shopping expedition, the child is more likely to scream and the mother more likely to give in. When giving diet advice to a mother locked into a system like this, it is always worth warning them that when they first attempt to change this system, the child is likely to scream a good deal more in a determined attempt to provoke a climb down. Capitulation at this point will result in escalation of the problem; they have to hold fast – things (the screaming) will get worse before they get better.

Some paedodontists (Thrash, W. J., Russel-Duggan, J., & Mizes, J. S., 1984) suggest using negative reinforcement as a behaviour management strategy. The argument is that if a child is showing behavioural signs of distress, for example by fidgeting, the dentist should not stop to ask what is wrong (thus negatively rewarding the child by stopping the aversive experience), or give this child a rest and positively reward him. The dentist, who no longer has to work on a non-ideal patient, who is perhaps crying, is negatively rewarded. Instead, the dentist should explain to the child that she will carry on until he is behaving appropriately and then he can earn a rest; that is, acceptable behaviour will be positively reinforced.

We would argue that there is one fundamental flaw in this – what if the child is genuinely distressed and has not been given, or is not assertive enough to use, a stop signal or does not have the metacognitive or linguistic ability to express what is wrong? How is the dentist to know that the fidgeting is because just one area of dentine is still hypersensitive, that the child needs to visit the bathroom or just needs a rest? We believe this technique should *never* be used during procedures when there is the slightest risk the child might genuinely be distressed.

Interestingly, a recent behavioural analysis of this technique (Malott, R. W. & Trojan Suarez, E. A., 2004, pp 280-282) categorises this technique as a "punishment by prevention of removal of an aversive condition" as disruption to treatment results in the failure to stop the aversive experience, whereas cooperation would have resulted in removal of the aversive condition. The very categorisation of this technique as a form of punishment calls its use into serious ethical doubt.

There are two situations in which we use this technique. The first is during overtly non-traumatic procedures, usually when introducing a prophylaxis brush on the finger. Some reluctant children accept the brush but then 'squeak' while it is in contact with them. We then tell the child that we will keep on tickling "until the little squeaky mouse goes to sleep." The second situation is during the early stages of needle desensitisation when we use it in conjunction with a SUD (subjective units of distress) scale or 'fear thermometer.' (Section 3.7)

Hand Over Mouth [Exercise] (HOM[E])

When a child suddenly becomes very distressed and disruptive, others have suggested that the dentist places her hand over the child's mouth (and sometimes obstructs the nasal airway as well) while explaining to the child that he will be released when he is quiet (or possibly anoxic).The reasoning behind this far from impressive technique is that a distressed child is not listening. If the child is not listening, the dentist should not positively reinforce this behaviour by solicitous enquiries as to what is wrong. HOME is designed to work by negatively reinforcing stopping crying by escape when appropriate behaviour is displayed.

Although this behavioural technique might serve to quiet a child, it would severely impact on cognitive mediated aspects of fearfulness, in particular by reducing trust, increasing intrusion, and removing any sense of perceived control.

A recent study of registered specialists in paediatric dentistry in the UK (Newton, J. T., Patel, H., Shah, S., & Sturmey, P., 2004) found that 59% of the respondents felt that HOM should never be used, 32% felt it should only be used with "hysterical, tantrum behaviour", 24% felt there were no psychological consequences to its use, but 51% felt, correctly in our opinion, that it would result in the child fearing dental treatment in the future. HOME has always been more popular in North America and is currently recommended for use with children who show defiant or non-co-operative behaviour (American Academy of Pediatric Dentistry, 2001).

The children who normally display the type of behaviour which would be controlled by HOME are usually under 7 years old; an age at which metacognitive skills are poor. All clinicians, no matter how skilled and experienced, will occasionally ask a patient to do more than they can cope with. It is developmentally normal for a child of this age, facing, to them, an overwhelming task, to burst into tears. Also, high levels of arousal interfere with information processing. Also known as attentional bias, raised levels of anxiety produce a narrowing of focus towards the potential threat and, as attentional processes have a limited capacity, other stimuli are relatively neglected (Rachman, S., 1998, pp 34-38), so the child probably isn't processing instructions or 'not listening.' But there is a more humane way of quietening a severely distressed young child so that they start to listen, can explain, with help, what the problem is, and treatment can be resumed. This is the 'finger on lips'. Certainly in the UK, a finger to the lips, accompanied by a 'ssssshh,' is widely used by mothers and by infant school (7 years and under) classroom teachers. Children rapidly respond to this. They can sit on the parent's or the dentist's lap while they calm down and then the problem can be addressed and treatment, even at a less demanding level resumed. Instead of being chastised for inappropriate behaviour, the severe distress experienced is acknowledged by the dentist and the child is praised for calming down, sharing the nature of the problem and being able to resume treatment. This is praised as being a 'very grown up thing' to be able to do. Encouragement to use an appropriate stop signal earlier in the distress is given.

Although most dentists would classify HOME as 'escape and reward' or negative reinforcement, we believe it, like 'milder' versions of escape and reward is being used as a punishment and has no has no place in child behaviour management.

Punishment

Other forms of punishment (an aversive event which is a consequence of behaviour) which are designed to reduce the frequency of unwanted behaviour, are smacking (something which should never feature in the surgery/office) and scolding (Thrash, W. J., Russel-Duggan, J., & Mizes, J. S., 1984). Firm 'voice control' is advocated as a means of deterring unacceptable behaviour. Although it might stop the initial behaviour, there is evidence (Melamed, B. G., 1984) that, in the absence of appropriate positive reward, disruptiveness and arousal are likely to increase during the subsequent session. There are, of course, times when a child behaves inappropriately and has to be told it is wrong, but this should be in an authoritative (not authoritarian) manner and accompanied by appropriate explanations as to why and guidance as to what a more appropriate behaviour might be.

Time Out

Time out (or response cost or penalty contingency) is the immediate termination of a positive reinforcer as a result of behaviour, resulting in a decreased frequency of that behaviour (Malott, R. W. & Trojan Suarez, E. A., 2004, pp 90-91). Hence the popular conception of the naughty little boy sitting in the corner, face to wall, though this is unlikely to be the outcome in the dental surgery. But the technique of ignoring a sibling pestering for attention while his brother is in the dental chair is an example.

Given that any behaviour that is not positively reinforced is likely to extinguish, we work on ignoring minor behavioural deficits such as wriggling and positively reinforcing appropriate behaviour – in this case sitting still.

3.2. The Impact of Mood on Coping Skills

Affect or mood will profoundly change a child's ability to cope with dental treatment.

It is possible to work co-operatively with children to enhance their sense of well-being within the bounds of normal mood, just by selecting memories and images which give them pleasure (see section 3.6).

It is also important to be alert to the possibility of clinical depression which affects between 2 and 6% of children (depending on diagnostic criteria). Children become capable of feeling depressed at about the age of six (Kendall, P. C., 2000). The frequency increases in adolescence, the rate of increase in girls exceeding that of boys. Co-morbidity of some sort is almost universal in depressed children. 75% have an anxiety disorder, 50% oppositional disorder, 30% conduct disorder and 25% substance abuse (Pearce, J., 2000). Depressed children have reduced pain and stimulus toleration (Lazarus, A. A., 1973); are likely to be tired; may neglect aspects of their self-care such as tooth brushing; and may experience an increase in appetite (American Psychiatric Association, 2000). Any consequential increase in snacking may be associated with an increase in caries rate.

On the other hand, an elevated mood (being happy, excited, having recently experienced a success) increases pain and stimulus toleration.

The practical implications for the 'normal' child are to avoid challenging dental treatment when other stressors are operating.

3.3 Sensory Factors in Developing Coping Skills

Sensation is a significant issue in dental treatment. Dentists help children to cope by aiding them modify their perception of the quality of the stimulus and by adjusting the degree or amount of the stimulus received. By encouraging small reappraisals of stimuli, we hope to avoid the ultimate in stimulus modification – avoidance.

3.3.1. Adjusting the Degree

This is done most simply by counting. Increased control is given to the child by letting him do the counting – usually on fingers as the mouth is often full! The speed of counting and the number to be reached before a rest need to be established by negotiation (and enforced; cheating results in loss of the privilege).

A simple and fun way of encouraging toddlers who are not cooperative or who have a bad gag reflex, which is often reflected in difficulties with tooth-brushing, is to get the mum to sing when cleaning the toddler's teeth. In the UK there is a song about 10 green bottles which are knocked progressively off the wall. Every time a number in the song is reached, the mother stops brushing, removes the toothbrush from the child's mouth and he has to say the number. This gives the child a rest at a known interval, enhancing a sense of control and reducing the unknown, and it is distracting. The process can start at the front of the mouth with the incisors and gradually move posteriorly as ability is fostered. This addresses any intrusive aspects of the problem. Thus much of the desensitisation is being done at home and usually readily generalises to the dental surgery. Give the mother some of your old, out of fashion stickers to cut into 4 or 6 pieces. She can then be coached about appropriately rewarding the child with a piece of 'sticker jigsaw'. Toddlers will quite happily stick these on a piece of card at random, but the slightly older child takes great pride in earning and assembling the puzzle.

Many children have problems with impression taking. This should be immediately obvious when the impression tray is tried for size. Simple distraction – wiggling toes – can be employed. If this is inadequate, a rendition of 'If you're happy and you know it' with the patient performing the hand and feet actions can be effective. These can be combined with obvious clinical 'tricks', which are pointed out to the child, to reduce the amount of time the impression is in the mouth –mixing the material with warm water; loading the tray and monitor the setting, inserting at the last minute; adding extra catalyst; using a minimally sized tray; placing a wax post dam on the upper tray. For the most severe cases, we give the child a set of trays to take home. We teach the mother how to place them and they have to practice placing the tray and keeping it in for increasing amounts of time until the setting time of the material to be used, plus a safety margin is achieved. This enhances control and reduces the perceived intrusive threat of choking. A note should be kept of progress – either a table or graph – as it is very easy to forget or discount progress.

The feelings of local anaesthetic can be introduced slowly, to accustom patients to the feelings and to stop the misinterpretation of the first 1 or 2 drops of anaesthetic as pain. (see below)

Starting restorative treatment with a small, easily accessible, quick and easy cavity, rather than a large, more clinically urgent cavity, enhances the chances of success. If a cavity is so urgent that it must be attempted first and the child's coping runs out, a glass ionomer temporary restoration may be a good compromise. If a tooth has 2 or three discrete cavities, start with this tooth, complete the cavity preparation of one cavity, check that the child can complete the second before starting that. If they cannot manage, remind them that they will have to have a local anaesthetic again, and if they still want to call a halt, accept that decision. We have found that children allowed to gradually acclimatise to sensory exposure in this way do not take advantage on future occasions and go on to become remarkably 'good' patients.

We find that many needle phobics have a distorted impression of the size of the dental needle. This appears to be for a variety of reasons

- Simple fear and focussed attention on threat will tend to magnify the perceived size
- Confusion of the metal syringe with the needle. This should improve with increasing use of single use, disposable systems
- A belief that a wide diameter venepuncture needle will be used.
- Dental nurses asking if the dentist would like a long or a short needle!

We deal with the long/short problem by training staff to ask for needle size by colour of sheath. The other problems are addressed by showing the child a short unsheathed needle, but without any delay, holding it at the bevel and pointing out that it is only this small length (1-2 mm) which goes into them – the rest is just to enable the dentist to get into those awkward little places.

3.3.2. Altering the Quality

Most clinicians who work regularly with children have their own names for the dental instruments, many of which inherently help children adjust their appraisals of the sensations associated with treatment.

Local anaesthetic makes a child's cheek, tongue and lips feel very odd – we describe it as 'fat, pins and needles and tingly, like your leg when you've sat on it for too long.' These feelings are quite disturbing for younger children, particularly if the concept has not been introduced carefully. The very young cannot carry out a cost benefit analysis and find the funny feelings difficult to make sense of 20-30 minutes or, sometimes hours, after a 10 minute filling. We have found that some young children, refusing further treatment after a first restorative visit with local anaesthetic, accept treatment happily without, and without compromise to the quality of treatment.

Once the local anaesthetic is in place, some children may have been led to expect to feel nothing. This, of course, is not accurate as vibration is a big issue and is often misinterpreted as pain. We try to pre-empt this problem with 'explain-show-do' (ESD) (Chapman, H. R. & Kirby-Turner, N., 2002). ESD is an extension of Addleston's 'tell-show-do' (TSD) – the mainstay of paediatric dental behaviour management since the 1960s (Addleston, H. K., 1959). ESD, not only shows the child the airotor and says what it is and does, (our version is that it is a whistly tooth shower that washes the dirt out of your teeth), but runs it, without a bur, in the mouth. Then the chuck can be gently run against a contra-lateral tooth and then on the LA-affected tooth to be treated. It can be pointed out that the child will still realise that the tooth is being touched and he will still be able to feel the cold water.

Similarly, when the slow handpiece is introduced, the TSD procedure of running the bur on a finger is expanded. First, the bur is run on a finger pad, where it 'tickles'. It is, after all, a 'tickling stick'. Then the bur is transferred to a fingernail, where, because it is hard it buzzes and rattles as well. Then there is the magic; the dental nurse brings a finger of the other hand up to touch the finger of the first hand and that buzzes as well! This prepares the child for the vibration passing through the mandible or right to the top of his head. Again, non-anaesthetised and anaesthetised teeth can be compared.

3.4. Relationship Factors in Developing Coping Skills

It has long been accepted that strong, accepting and nurturing relationships between adults, particularly parents, and children offer the children the secure base and an increased sense of security from which to tackle challenges and to demonstrate their capacity to be resolute (Bee, H., 1992, pp 412-434).

Behaviourally, parents can influence their children

I. as role models. This is apparent even in the 'social referencing' of infancy. Observation of very young children asked to approach a strange, noisy, potentially frightening toy or a stranger, showed much more confidence if their mothers smiled and were encouraging, rather than looking neutral or scared (Bee, H., 1992, pp 412-434). There is much evidence for the role of familial vicarious learning of dental fear within families, particularly from mothers (Berge ten, M, 2003), although Kagan (1994, pp 91-92) argues that children learn fearful behaviour from watching others, but not the fear-related physiological response. It may be that seeing and copying fearful behaviour primes development of the fear-related physiological response in minimally threatening circumstances. But, even an anxious mother can be used as a coping role model for very simple procedures in very young children.

II. by selective reward and punishment ie operant conditioning.

III. by creation of a social climate.

A healthy child-parent relationship can be very supportive even when the parent is overtly fearful. Katie was 13 when her first experience of dental treatment was to have 4 premolars/bicuspids extracted prior to orthodontic treatment. She was given a choice of local anaesthetic with or without inhalational sedation (thus enhancing control) and elected not to have sedation and to have the extractions over 2 visits. At the first visit, Katie looked a little apprehensive, but her mother looked terrified and ill. She automatically accompanied Katie into the dental surgery as she had done on all previous visits. Katie's mother became HRC's pressing clinical concern; she seemed to be on the verge of fainting. She refused the offer of a sweet drink. Concerned about the unvoiced, but all too apparent mother's threat appraisal, HRC said to Katie, "Your Mum is obviously more worried about this than you are. Would it be kinder to let her sit in the waiting room until it's all over?" (enhancing control and trust[ing her to make a decision],) Katie thought carefully before she replied, "No, I'd like her to stay." So, Katie's mother stayed and managed to remain conscious during the extractions, with which Katie coped extremely well. At the second visit, Katie's mother was considerably less apprehensive and Katie coped well once more.

The most anxious children are likely to have a parent who is reluctant to grant autonomy and is somewhat controlling (Siqueland, L., Kendall, P. C., & Steinberg, L, 1996). This becomes obvious in the surgery when the child is not given a chance to answer questions or make decisions; his mother is there first. Parents of very anxious children exacerbate the situation by encouraging problem solving in ways that are more avoidant than even the children's initial ideas (Cobham, V. E., Dadds, M. R., & Spence, S. H., 1999). This also may become apparent by suggestions of escape as soon as treatment becomes slightly challenging or repeated questions such as, "Are you *sure* you're alright?" "Are you *sure* it's not hurting?" We address this issue by pointing out, matter-of-factly, the communication options the child has been given (for example a stop signal) and that we have checked with the child who has declared himself to be fine. If we know the mother is phobic herself, we point out that her child's experiences aren't going to be the same as her own were.

We tackle, "Don't worry, she's nearly finished," as the dentist just starts drilling the access cavity by calling the mother over to look into the cavity. By pointing out the detail of where dentine is still carious and where clean, the mother can monitor the progress of cavity preparation and usually her feedback quickly becomes appropriate.

This type of comment may start before the appointment on the way to even an examination, "You will be alright, Darling, it's not going to hurt." "If you're brave, I'll buy you ….on the way home." These 'reassurances' only serve to raise the possibility of terrors to come, the child using them to construct a negative picture of what is to happen; vicarious learning can be based on indirect as well as direct messages!

The interpersonal relationships in the dental surgery are complex. In the past, much paediatric teaching has advocated splitting even very young children from their parents in order to factor them out of the interpersonal system (Wright, G. Z., Starkey, P. E., & Gardner, D. E., 1987, pp 58-75). These practices are currently much less common. In the medical field, much research has focused on coping skills training for parents and their children; involving them in their children's acute and chronic, on-going medical care and in teaching them to support them (Melnyk, B. M. & Alpert-Gillis, L. J, 1998; Grey, M. & Berry, D, 2004).

The simplest form of parent training is ESD. Parents are often tempted to interpose with information if they believe that their child is not being given enough information by the dentist. If the parent persists in giving unhelpful or untimely information, a direct request can be made by the dentist with an explanation as to why and when she is imparting information. If this does not result in co-operation, substitution by another caring adult can be tried, for example, father, a grandparent or a family friend instead of mother. An adult family friend is often an excellent substitution as they have a much lower level of emotional involvement and are in a position to support, but not be over-involved.

Lisa was eight years old when she was referred as untreatable by her family dentist who had reduced her to hysteria by picking up an explorer/probe for the first time and trying to use it without any explanation. Lisa's mother was sent from the room amid acrimonious criticism and Lisa was then humiliated by unfavourable comparison with the dentist's own 3 year old. At her first visit to HRC, Lisa had a tendency to turn to her mother for information, but Lisa was encouraged to ask the dentist questions directly (control of information gain), given a stop signal (control) and very detailed ESD (reducing the unknown) was used so that on subsequent visits this behaviour completely stopped. Lisa's self-esteem was rebuilt by overt recognition of achievement. Lisa's mother accompanied her into the surgery for restorative and orthodontic treatment and eventually multiple extractions of retained deciduous teeth without any need to 'interfere.' Lisa was a girl who needed far more than the usual amount of detailed information about procedures. In the past the appropriate source of information had been silent, so Lisa had turned to the only other available source to fill the gap; her mother.

Apart from behaviours directly relating to the acceptance of treatment, other coping strategies can be useful, for example bringing a favourite doll or teddy which can act as a security/transitional object and bring a great sense of security (see Section 3.4.) as well as acting as a 'role model', the child dressing up as the dentist. Roles are then swapped. This addresses the 'trust' and 'unknown' aspects of the dental fear model. Also, sitting the child on the dentist's or nurse's lap may be a way around intrusion; the child entering the clinician's personal space, not vice versa.

In more extreme case, where parents are critical and no family substitute is acceptable, it might be necessary to substitute another professional into the role of 'coach.' Sometimes the dental nurse can fill that role, but at others a professional perceived to be more detached such as an educational support worker, social worker or psychologist may need to fill that role.

Holding a parent's or the dental nurse/assistant's hand can also give security. It is important that any hand-holding by staff is not perceived as restraint. So, rather than an instruction to hold the nurse's hand, it is better to offer it as an option – "Ann likes having her hand held. Would you like to hold her hand?" This gives the control to the child and there is no possibility of coercion which is important if trust and an offered sense of control are not to be violated. If a sense of contact with the mother is needed, but she needs to be a little less intrusive, sitting her at the foot of the dental chair with her hand on an ankle is an ideal compromise.

3.5. Physiological Factors in the Development of Coping Skills

An anxious mood suggests that the sympathetic nervous system is already in a state of increased activity. Thus anxious children have a dysfunctional way of making sense of the world; they are more highly vigilant and have an exaggerated tendency to perceive threat. They will also have a lowered pain threshold and reduced toleration of stimuli.

Non-clinical anxiety is a feature of childhood, *from birth*. It increases towards adolescence. Anxiety disorders also increase towards adolescence. Approximately 30% of adolescents have mild symptoms of anxiety at any one time. In 5% this has a significant impact on everyday function. At least 30% of anxious children have a second anxiety disorder. There are also high rates of co-morbidity with attention deficit hyperactivity disorder (ADHD), conduct disorders, substance abuse and depression. Rates of anxiety disorders are the same in boys and girls until adolescence, when the prevalence in girls exceeds that in boys (Pearce, J., 2000 pp 47-72).

The most anxious children, who would justify a diagnosis of General Anxiety Disorder (GAD), recognise emotions but don't seem to understand how to think about emotions in order to change them. These children may well need specialist psychological help.

A child who is highly anxious may appear to be immature because significant stress may prompt reversion to the use of more basic coping strategies rather than the more sophisticated, age appropriate ones.

The main focus of many dentists' efforts to reduce their patients' level of physiological arousal to tolerable levels is pharmacological. Oral, inhalation and intravenous sedation and general anaesthetic are all widely used. This is not the forum to describe the use of these agents. They do have a use in helping children cope with more treatment than they are developmentally equipped to face, especially if the dental treatment need is urgent. For example, the 4 year old with no previous treatment experience and interproximal cavities in all 8 molars and a minimally supportive mother might do better having all the treatment carried out in one visit under general anaesthetic than face several visits with sedation. Once dentally fit, coping skills development should be begun immediately. The teenager with no previous treatment experience needing orthodontic extractions may feel happier with sedation than without.

For some patients, sedation becomes a means of avoidance and they develop a relinquished coping style, acknowledging their fear, but believing they don't have to do anything about facing up to it as they can avoid undue anxiety by the use of a dentist-administered drug. This is, perhaps, a reasonable, though not ideal, fully informed decision for adults to take; an adult can understand that they may have problems accessing dental treatment in circumstances other than from their regular practitioner. This is a treatment route not to be encouraged in children. They are not in a position to make informed long term choices. We have also found that some children treated routinely with inhalation sedation without accompanying coping skills development spiral downwards and end up in a general anaesthetic-avoidance cycle.

Thomas was a case in point. At the age of 9 he went over the handlebars of his cycle and fractured all his upper incisors at gingival level. At the age of 16, when he first attended HRC, he said that he could "still remember the 'butchery'" he received in the accident and emergency department. He became dentally phobic and was treated in a teaching department with nitrous oxide sedation. Unfortunately, no coping skills training was given in parallel and, despite receiving such high concentrations of nitrous oxide that he remembered the "room swimming," he became so anxious that he had to receive treatment under general anaesthetic. He received an annual general anaesthetic in a local facility until he decided that this could not continue for the remainder of his life and he sought treatment from HRC.

Some dentists are experimenting with aromatherapy (Lehrner, J., Ecksberger, C., Walla, P., Potsch.G., & Deecke, L., 2000). The one trial identified in the literature found that anxious female, though not the male, middle-aged adults found the scent of orange oil pleasant while at the dentist and reported lower state anxiety, a more positive mood and raised levels of calmness. The authors suggest that this is due to the sedative properties of essential orange oil, though they did not report any physiological variables. We believe these results probably have more to do with the scent disguising the typical and highly evocative smells of the dental office. As memories are contextual (Atkinson, R. L., Atkinson, R. C., Smith, E. E., & Bem, D. J, 1993 , p319), the changed olfactory environment probably triggered fewer and/or less intense memories of previous unhappy treatment experiences.

Patients often self medicate on nicotine, alcohol and illegal substances, though this is unlikely to be a problem with younger children.

3.6. The Use of Imagery in Developing Coping Skills

This category and the following one – 'cognition' - are the language based components of this multisystemic approach; they represent the 'C' in CBT (cognitive behavioural therapy). These factors have the most potential impact on aspects such as intrusion, trust, control, fear of the unknown and pain.

Distraction is the simplest form of this category and is a mainstay of the dentist's armamentarium. Techniques can be as basic as chatty conversation, which should involve the patient and not go on between surgery staff and/or the mother, literally over the patient's head. It should also not include questions which are impossible to answer with a mouth full of instruments, unless a pause is given in treatment for a reply to be heard. This is a subtle way of adjusting the degree of exposure.

Simple visual distraction can be provided by posters or TV on the ceiling. Expensive and sophisticated virtual reality systems (Frere, C. L., Crout, R., Yorty, J., & McNeil, D. W., 2001) have met with success, though we believe they fall into the category of achieving dental fitness, rather than teaching coping skills and we do wonder how well these patients would cope if forced to access standard dental treatment elsewhere or have to face medical procedures which frighten them.

The playing of music, either as background, or via headphones has been shown not to reduce anxiety (Aitken, J. C., Wilson, S., Coury, D., & Moursi.A.M., 2002; Corah, N. L., Gale, E. N., Pace, L. F., & Seyrek, S. K., 1981). This may be because speech is processed bilaterally by the primary auditory projection of the cortex (transverse gyri of Herscl) but only by the dominant side of the secondary or association area of the auditory cortex, and music is processed by the non-dominant side (Walsh, K & Darby, D, 1999, pp 184-191). So, music would not compete selectively enough with self-speech to stop the flow of automatic thoughts.

Children can simply be told to close their eyes and have a day dream, especially if a compelling, humorous story is told by the dentist or nurse while treatment is being undertaken. The advantage of story telling is that sensations of the instruments can be included in the dream. For example, the airotor can be an aeroplane.

An interesting and counter-intuitive example of this is was Daniel, an 8 year old boy who attended happily, accepted local anaesthetic and then baulked as soon as cavity preparation started. In the end we identified that he didn't like the "tickly thing [slow handpiece] in his tooth." Daniel had requested Batman dreams and HRC had told stories during visits. Having identified the vibration as the problem and, the indications being that there was a significant intrusive element to the problem, the stories were modified so that every time the slow handpiece was used, Batman® was in the Batmobile® driving past road works. Although this 'inflated' the sensation, it served to put it outside his body, thus dealing with the intrusion.

More formal visual imagery either as a restful scene, or in the form of a story, is also extremely useful. Children chose their own peaceful place or story theme, some of which may stretch the imagination of the dentist! Sometimes children cannot offer any ideas, in which case a selection of ideas should be offered. Children are encouraged to practice at home, and after the first one or two visits, they are encouraged to take over their own dreams, and generalise their use as appropriate. This enhances a sense of control and self-efficacy. We tend to use this in conjunction with behavioural muscle relaxation.

For children who don't achieve good muscular relaxation, we add on large muscle group contraction. The combination seems to be particularly effective. Clinical experience has shown that assessment of muscle tension in children should not only be based on observation of the hands, but also of the 'pulling in' of the tummy. We incorporate self-hypnosis techniques, but avoid the highly stereotyped forms of induction and deepening as many children find them 'silly' and just laugh rather than cooperate. The less formal induction procedure also fosters the concept that this is a skill they learn for themselves, not something the dentist does to them. Standard progressive muscle relaxation (PMR) with or without visual imagery can be used to good effect in children. Younger children may not consciously know what relaxed muscles feel like. In this case an old-fashioned rag doll or a 'Beany Baby'® , known as 'Floppy [Animal]' can be used for illustrative purposes.

This type of technique should not be attempted with children with very low levels of trust or an exceptionally high need for control. Children with moderate problems may effectively use these skills with their eyes open initially. Others like to open their eyes, watch an ESD explanation and be given a few seconds to regain the depth of relaxation before treatment is continued.

These skills should be used routinely with relative analgesia (inhalation sedation) so that the sedative agent can steadily be reduced, leaving the child with stand-alone coping skills.

3.7. Cognitive Factors in the Development of Coping Skills

As mentioned in the introduction, dentists tend to rely on behavioural signs of dental fearfulness. Part of the reason for this must be that we communicate our cognitive thoughts and our emotions with language – verbal or written, neither of which are easy while receiving dental treatment unless special provision is made.

3.7.1. Control

This section initially addresses the complex area of sharing control in a way which both increases coping resources and enables the dentist to complete treatment. The section then describes, in some detail, examples of numerical scaling which enable children to communicate their level of cognitive distress.

Negotiating Control in a Helpful Manner

Control is shared between the child and the dentist. It is achieved both behaviourally and cognitively. It is important to remember that the level of control offered to a child has to be developmentally appropriate. In the absence of any research data, this must be a matter of clinical judgement.

Behavioural control is achieved via stimulus modification which was discussed in Section 3.3 and via regulated administration. Regulated administration can be as simple as simply 'playing' and being allowed to handle the dental equipment. It may also be used in a more sophisticated way as a true CBT behavioural experiment, the child rating how scared they are and predicting what it will feel like etc, handling the equipment and then re-rating the actual experience.

The behavioural control every dentist knows of is the 'stop signal'. As HRC is right handed, she prefers the child to raise his left hand. This reduces the chance of being accidentally jogged. Especially if trust is an issue, the child can be told that the nurse will be looking out for the signal in case the dentist is concentrating hard and misses it. There is some evidence that introducing a stop signal for a non-stressful situation may heighten anxiety (Corah, N. L., 1973). Presumably, this is because it raises the awareness of the possibility of pain or threat. Thus, the introduction of a stop signal during a prophylaxis would be appropriate for children who were showing signs of fearfulness, but would be inappropriate for those who are obviously confident. If a stop signal is added early in the treatment hierarchy, sufficient trust must be established to allow for it to be temporarily withdrawn if fissure sealants are to be placed, especially without rubber dam.

Cognitive control is gained firstly by information gain – being allowed to ask questions, as discussed in Section 3.4., and having control of the level of informational gain; overload can be just as stressful as ignorance. A second way is using that information together with appropriate guidance to reappraise situations – using techniques such as ESD. Thirdly cognitive control is gained by being offered decisional control. Letting a four year old child choose which tooth to polish first (not whether they have the polish or not) gives them an appropriate degree of control. Six year olds are capable of deciding whether or not to have a local anaesthetic for a particular restoration, but not whether to have the restoration. Ten year olds may request that easy treatment is completed at a particular appointment because they have exams afterwards or they are not feeling well.

Perceived or experienced control is the critical factor and absolute or objective control may not be required, though the older the child, the more closely experienced control should equate to objective control until, at some individually developmentally appropriate time during adolescence, the two equate. It is the child's individual interpretation or appraisal of events which will determine how much control he experiences in a given situation (experiential control) and clinical experience suggests that this varies widely for given clinical situations.

Problems that a dentist is convinced are associated with misinterpretation of pain may be addressed by explaining the gate theory of pain. A very basic explanation which is suitable for children as young as five is as follows. "You have lots of different types of telephone wires called nerves going from your mouth to your brain (touch appropriate body parts). Some of them carry 'ouch!' messages and the others carry messages about touch (demonstrate) and hot and cold. The sleeping potion stops the ouch messages being sent, but not the touch and the hot and cold messages. So you will still know that I am touching the tooth and you will still feel the cold of the water. Your brain looks out for messages all the time. If you are convinced that it will hurt, it will. This is because if I make the ouch nerves go off to sleep and I touch you, a touch message gets sent. But your brain is looking for ouch messages and it says to itself, 'There's a message coming. It must be an ouch message.' So you go 'ouch' and it hurts, but all I did was to touch you. It's just that your brain was confused." (The language may, of course, be adjusted for older children.) If this fails to work, then active treatment should be stopped.

An appropriate level of perceived control can be highly protective in potentially traumatic situations, as illustrated by the following example. A nine year old boy, Christopher, had to have his four deciduous canines extracted for orthodontic reasons. He had experience of restorative treatment and coped well. (His older sister had had a similar procedure carried out with local analgesia (LA) and relative analgesia (RA) and coped extremely well.) Christopher elected to have LA without RA. HRC achieved a level of analgesia around the deciduous canines on the right hand side which she considered to be quite adequate, after careful testing with a probe. The sensations of pressure and 'wiggling' experienced during extractions and the noises he might hear were carefully explained. HRC placed the forceps on the upper tooth and started to apply pressure to it. Christopher put up his hand to stop the procedure; he was adamant it was hurting. More LA was administered, anaesthesia re-tested and another attempt was made. Again the child stopped the procedure. More LA was administered and further explanations of the other sensations were given, which the child seemed to be quite able to separate from pain. Again the extraction was attempted and stopped. HRC offered to abandon the procedure and to send the child for a general anaesthetic. The child refused and told HRC to continue. Despite obvious distress and repeated offers by HRC (who by this time was hoping she was successfully hiding her own distress) to discontinue, he insisted on completion of the extraction of the upper canine. No attempt was made to extract the lower canine that day. Christopher subsequently had the remaining three deciduous canines extracted under general anaesthetic. He has also returned quite happily to HRC for restorative treatment under adequate LA and was more than capable of being an excellent role model for his younger sister. He had come through a potentially very traumatic experience psychologically unscathed because he had had sufficient control over the noxious stimulus.

3.7.2. Method of Use of Visual/Verbal Analogue Scales

The use of verbal and visual analogue scales provides a clear, relatively simple way to access cognitions and to help children appraise current experience (Chapman, H. R. & Kirby-Turner, N., 2002). Although many research measures use scores of 0-8, when working clinically we use scores of 0-10. This is because children are used to being given marks out of 10 for schoolwork. Without the thermometer in front of them, some of the children find it difficult to imagine what proportion out of 8 they are experiencing. We describe '0' to the patient as, "Feeling nice and relaxed and happy, like you do curled up on the sofa at home while watching your favourite TV programme." 10 is described as, "The most scared/worried you can be, so scared/worried you want to run away" (ie panic). We then ask them, "How many out of 10 do you feel now?" Most children of six and above are capable of 'seriation' of the numbers 1 to 10 and can use this scale (Bee, H., 1992, pp 247-267). If they can't, then use the 'hands apart' form described below.

Visual or verbal analogue scales can be used flexibly to appraise general fearfulness, but may also be targeted specifically to appraise trust, sensations of pain or self-evaluation.

A Verbal Report Measure

It is self-evident that it is relatively straight forward to ask a patient to indicate on a printed sheet the level of, for example, fear they are experiencing before the commencement of active treatment, but it is difficult to complete a pen and paper measure of fear when lying in a dentist's chair. A verbal report measure or SUD (subjective units of distress) scale is thus extremely useful. It is important to monitor such levels during exposure for the following reasons:-

1. We do not wish our patients' arousal level to rise to a point that might be beyond their coping capacity and then become panicky. The fear provoked by a simple procedure such as an examination can vary significantly within an individual patient. For example, an oral examination may be comparatively easy, except for allowing the dentist to touch a particular tooth (which has been the source of acute pain during previous treatment) with a probe. A prophylaxis may be well tolerated at the front of the mouth, but prove increasing fear provoking as the brush/cup is moved posteriorly.

2. Once the exposure has been completed, it is necessary to check that the levels of arousal have fallen to a low level before the patient is allowed to leave. Leaving with high levels of arousal is more likely to be associated with high levels of arousal on return for the next visit. This is at variance with some professional practice as dentists are very keen to reward success at task completion with immediate liberation from the surgery.

3. It enhances the sense of experienced control. It thereby tends to reduce the experienced fear and hence the feelings of vulnerability because one cannot communicate with one's mouth full of dental instruments.

The 'Hands Apart Version'

Children below the age of 6, may have difficulty with the concepts of conservation of number necessary for accurate use of a numerically based fear thermometer. The 'hands apart' version is a non-verbal variation that is ideal for use with this group. It may also be very useful for very shy children who have not yet learned to trust you enough to 'open up' verbally. It is used in an identical manner to the numerical version, but the upper and lower limits are defined non-verbally. Zero is defined as hands together in front of you. The upper limit is described as arms as wide apart as you can get them. Physically demonstrate these limits and get the patient to copy you if necessary. Then ask for the current level of feeling.

Sometimes a parent or carer will report that the patient has difficulty identifying their emotions. In this case worry can be defined as 'butterflies in your tummy'. With small children you can give the tummy a small tickle to help them identify the feeling you are monitoring, but make sure you are chaperoned. You can then monitor the size of the butterflies.

Individuals, for example with hemiplegia, may have difficulty moving their own arms and hands. They can either rely on language or, if language or comprehension is problematic, you can demonstrate with your hands and then get the patient to move them to the correct distance apart.

For a patient with profound learning and physical disabilities, ask the carer to describe the patients 'yes' signal. Demonstrate the hands-apart method and then ask them to use the 'yes' signal to stop you as you slowly move your hands apart.

The Fear, Worry or Anxiety Thermometer

Children can be asked to rate their baseline level of fear and monitor rises and falls in experienced fearfulness during exposure. It is possible to expose them to *overtly non-traumatic* stimuli, for example a prophylaxis brush on a finger or a sheathed needle in the mouth, being continued until the fear level drops. More threatening procedures may have to be repeated several times in quick succession until the fear level drops.

Fear levels on the thermometer can be used in conjunction with a patient hand-up stop signal. The hand is raised when the fear gets to an agreed number. This is based on the baseline number plus 1, 2 or 3. The closer to the top of the scale, the less one can allow the fear levels to rise. When the patient's hand is raised, the procedure stops. When the patient's fear level drops back to baseline, a non-traumatic procedure is resumed. Traumatic procedures should be stopped and the patient should be carefully questioned to ascertain the cause of the problem, for example pain. Other children, often with lower absolute fear levels, may prefer to use one hand and show the number of fingers corresponding to the level of fear experienced. Another person, for example the dental nurse may need to help monitor this if the hand is out of the dentist's immediate line of vision. If there is an element of lack of trust in the fear experience, the monitoring of the signals by the nurse can be stressed, so that the patient is confident that the bargain will be adhered to.

It is important that a stop signal is not introduced too early in the fear hierarchy. Research has shown that this actually increases the level of fear because the offering of a stop signal implies that there is something to be concerned about (Corah, N. L., 1973). Thus for the 'normal' patient or the moderately fearful, this should usually be offered for restorations etc, while for the terrified, particularly if they 'choke' or are intensely distrustful, it should be offered at the beginning of treatment. It is also important to warn the patient at the beginning of technique sensitive procedures such as acid etching, that once you start, you have to finish or start all over again. If you have got this far with a relaxed, confident and competent patient, there should be no problem about acceptance of this.

The Trust Thermometer

Scaling can also be used to appraise trust. Limits are set to the thermometer with 0 being 'not believing/trusting at all' and 10 being 'completely believing/trusting'. Alternatively, 10 could be 'the dentist being very, very sneaky' and 0 being 'not sneaky at all.' Formal behavioural experiments can be used to help the child monitor his level of trust and appraise changes in trust level as a result of specific procedures. Was the information given prior to the procedure both accurate and, crucially, honest? Did the dentist keep to the agreement?

Monitoring Experienced Sensation - The 'Ouch' Thermometer

A visual/verbal analogue scale in the form of a, numerical, 'hands apart' or 'butterfly' thermometer, which is now the 'ouch' method, can all be used directly to monitor experienced levels of pain. The lower limit is described as 'completely comfortable, not knowing it's there' and the upper limit as 'the worst pain or 'ouch' you've ever had'. Young children may need help identify/ remembering this experience with prompts from a parent/carer.

The severity of the worst physical pain will vary significantly between individuals. Broken limbs (bone pain) and serious burns are often described as the most severe pain that can be experienced. A person who has experienced, say, one of these types of pain is obviously going to have a raised upper definition of pain experience. This will influence the interpretation and tolerance of all other pain-like experiences. With children, although unusual, their worst experience of pain may have been as trivial as falling over. In this case, the upper limit has to be shifted by imagining something twice or ten times as bad as that. The number of multiples will be chosen based upon the likely experience of sensation/pain to come.

Most dentists have patients whose pain thresholds go through the ceiling when touched with a prophy brush. For these patients, an expansion of their pain scale is essential for them to be able to cope with the experience of dental treatment. This is because a very low pain threshold is often linked with the misinterpretation of sensations such as the vibration of the slow hand piece as pain.

We stroke the back of the patient's hand with a finger and ask them if it is painful. The answer should be 'no', so that is defined as zero. The patient is then asked to *give themselves* a little, gentle pinch and that is defined as 'one'. A slightly harder pinch is defined as 'two' and so on until a really vicious, nail-marking *self-pinch* is defined as 'ten'. The patient is then asked to go back to the trivial sensation and redefine it in numerical terms, or, if the problem is one of misinterpretation, to redefine it as a 'funny feeling' eg vibration. If sensations are to be redefined as 'funny feelings' it is essential that there is no possibility of an element of discomfort or pain. For example, the slow handpiece should be running lightly on a restoration or the enamel of a non-pulpitic tooth.

Another common scenario is the expression of pain when the first drop of local anaesthetic takes effect. The use of topical anaesthetic, at least in the maxilla, can guarantee a pain-free passage of the needle through the mucosa. If the injection of the first drop of local anaesthetic is obviously delayed by a few seconds after the passage of the needle through the mucosa, it will be apparent whether the response is to the feelings of tingling etc of the local anaesthetic taking effect, or inadequate topical anaesthesia (which should not be a problem if anaesthesia is checked with a probe before injecting). Depending on the level of fear, trust of the dentist and cognitive ability of the patient the technique can be described

- as you are doing it
- retrospectively and the patient asked to reappraise the sensation. "Was that an ouch, or was it a 'corr'; a funny feeling?"

It is interesting that the belief that injections are painful is so widespread and strongly held that a child can be given a maxillary injection with no sign of pain or even mild discomfort, but when he is told what he has just had, says 'ow'. The advantage of the above technique for dentist-parent relations then becomes very apparent, as it is the parent who chuckles and tells the child they are a bit late with their response.

Building Self-Esteem

Visual analogue scales are also useful in developing resilience. Self-esteem is the value judgement of self against the same qualities and abilities in others or an ideal self. It usually develops after the age of seven (Bee, H., 1992, pp 384-388). In the dental surgery, self-esteem is based around the ability to accept treatment. Sometimes children, in learning skills necessary for accepting treatment, display a lack of faith in their own abilities; even when their newly acquired skill is pointed out to them and they are praised, their response is self-deprecating. Be alert to this and ask how many out of ten they would give themselves for being able to do that new, specific task. If self-esteem is poor, the answer will be a value of about five. Express surprise at the low value of the figure. Ask your dental nurse what she would award out of ten. (The answer is ten.) Award ten yourself and then ask the parent/carer what they would award. The answer should be ten or above. Then return to the child and ask what they now think they should be awarded. The child's answer should have been revised upwards, hopefully to ten. Reinforce this as the correct assessment of the child's ability. Repeat the procedure at the end of subsequent tasks/sessions. Gradually, the child should reassess his ability to cope and learn in a more positive way that will lead to increase self-esteem and self-confidence. They often become extremely accurate appraisers of their own abilities, correctly awarding themselves 9 or 9 1/2. Give feedback as to why the evaluation is correct, but remember to reinforce the good coping as well.

Other methods to bolster improved self-marking include techniques such as asking, "Who's a champ?" Prompt the reluctant to acknowledge it is him/her. This can be further reinforced by getting him to put his hands up with a positive movement (punch the air). This encourages that "Yes!" feeling we have all experienced when we have succeeded. Also, the use of multiple senses, in this case, movement, speech and hearing, promote learning.

Ultimately, it is the sense of self-achievement that will motivate your patients, especially adolescents. We should never forget that, no matter how sympathetic, kind and skilful we are as clinicians, it is our patients who have to face their fears and the ghosts of their previous experiences in order to overcome them. That takes courage.

3.7.6. How Many Thermometers and for Whom?

This scale has multiple uses and many patients have multiple problems about accepting dental treatment. For example, a patient who has experienced pain during dental treatment and has had that pain denied is likely to fear a further painful experience, mistrust dentists and have a profound sense of loss of control. In this case, start using the thermometer early in treatment to offer control, say, for requesting rests or informing when fear levels are up to an agreed level. This will foster the patient's sense of control and foster trust. Then, when potentially painful treatment is started, the control signal, used if pain is felt, should be enough. If it becomes apparent that there is a problem with a low pain threshold/confusion with stimulation, then the thermometer can be used to modify this before treatment is resumed, backed by use of the control thermometer.

The self-esteem thermometer should only be used at the end of a treatment section/session to boost self-esteem in those reluctant to take credit for their progress. Its use is best confined to children as adults may find this use patronising. As a general rule, only one form of the thermometer should be used at a time. Use of the Chapman and Kirby-Turner model of dental (Chapman, H. R. & Kirby-Turner, N., 1999) to guide dental history taking should reveal which factor is most important and thus which thermometer to use. As patient become more confident and build trust, continuous monitoring can be phased out, just leaving the patient with a simple control signal.

4. A TYPICAL FEAR HIERARCHY

In this final section we will use the example of graded exposure through a fear hierarchy to illustrate the assessment, formulation and intervention strategies described above. Graded exposure is essentially a cognitive-behavioural intervention and we use it to identify the possible import of the five factors; fear of pain, lack of trust, fear of loss of control, fear of the unknown and fear of intrusion.

We first describe a typical fear hierarchy, indicating which of the factors may be operating at each of the stages. The factors are indicated in italics in parentheses. This section is designed to demonstrate how a comprehensive assessment of the different components facilitates the development of specific coping strategies to enable a child to cope with, in this case, a phobia of needles.

A typical fear hierarchy is not difficult to construct and for many moderately fearful children, a standard fear hierarchy works as effectively as an idiosyncratic one. Many young children with little treatment experience will have insufficient knowledge to construct a hierarchy (King, N. J., Hamilton, D. I., & Ollendick, T. H., 1988, p 103).

Most dentists would order items on a fear hierarchy in this order

High demand	extractions
	Fillings
	Local anaesthetic
	Fissure sealants
	prophylaxis
	Use of probe/explorer
Low demand	mirror

Each of these stages may need to be broken down into a number of smaller steps, for example

High Demand	Look in mouth with mirror out of chair then in stationary dental chair *(unknown, trust, intrusion)*
	Look into dental surgery *(unknown, trust)*
	Look with mirror on mum's lap in waiting room *(unknown, trust, intrusion)*
Low demand	meeting on neutral territory eg waiting room *(trust, unknown)*

Below is a suggested hierarchy for needle desensitisation. A control signal, if not already introduced, will need to be introduced at stage j. A SUDs scale/thermometer may also need to be used as previously mentioned.

(a) Show syringe with sheathed needle. *(unknown, trust)*

(b) Place against cheek/and or closed lips. Patients who require more control can 'help' by handling it themselves or with you. *(unknown, trust, intrusion, control)*

(c) Place in mouth against upper incisors with sheath on. Again, the patient can help. Introduce topical anaesthetic – choice of flavour). *(unknown, trust, intrusion, control, pain)*

(d) Topical and placement of unsheathed needle in mouth or against buccal surface of upper incisor. *(unknown, trust)*

(e) As d but place needle against gum without penetration. *(unknown, trust, pain)*

(f) As e but with penetration of mucosa. *(unknown, trust, intrusion, pain)*

(g) Topical and inject two drops, then tell the child that. *(unknown, trust, intrusion, pain)*

(h) As g, but inject a bit more. *(unknown, trust, intrusion, pain)*

(i) Topical and inject at least half a cartridge and practise with airotor and slow hand piece using ESD. *(unknown, trust, intrusion, pain)*

(j) Do an upper filling (preferably a small one) as well, and/or introduce inhalational sedation. *(unknown, trust, intrusion, pain)*

(k) Transfer to inferior dental block with or without filling *(unknown, trust, intrusion, pain)*

(l) *LA and extraction (unknown, trust, intrusion, pain)*

Early stages can be run back to back with the introduction of a prophy and fissure sealing. (Seal teeth you're going to fill later if necessary, but do explain to the mother and the child what you are doing.) This gets the child used to having work done in its mouth and parents and children have something concrete to show for their efforts.

The precise nature and number of these steps will depend on the child. The pace of moving through the hierarchy is critical. Progress which is too slow is likely to stress the child (and parent) with boring underload; perceived and real lack of progress. Progress which is too rapid is stressful and distressing to child and parent. At its worst it is likely to send child and family from your office/surgery never to return. Handled sensitively, a strategic regrouping can be treated as a learning experience (see HOME, section 3.1.1. above). Any child asked to do so much that they breakdown and/or refuse to carry on, needs to be calmed and asked to complete an easier, previous task which they know they can complete. It is important for a visit to be completed on a successful note (Holst, A., 1988).

An important aspect of working up the hierarchy and keeping the child appraised of what is expected of him is to set the task for the next visit at the completion of the current one. Record it in the notes so that there are no arguments! This reduces fear of the unknown. As the child gets older, the task can be negotiated, thus improving perceived and objective control. Any questions which arise between visits can be written down (with Mum's help if necessary) and brought along. This is a useful way of forestalling unhelpful information from parents and other family members in the meantime. Often, mothers will come into the surgery and say, "Dr Chapman, Natalie wants to know…."

The importance, in the older child, of the perceived demand of tasks, which are often based on vicarious learning, cannot be over emphasised. Jill was referred at 12 years old with dental phobia. Her previous dentist had undertaken extensive restorative work of her deciduous dentition while her mother held her down. Jill successfully progressed through a treatment hierarchy and had three first molars restored under LA. Then she had to have a lower second deciduous molar extracted. Unfortunately, this was in the fourth quadrant and so the option of extraction together with restorative treatment was not possible. As Jill was briefed about the visit when the extraction was to take place, she was told that it would be simple as the tooth had absolutely no roots remaining; it would not require an IDB to extract it and she had already coped with all the difficult treatment. Her mother, who had had extensive dental treatment herself, reinforced this message. A week later, Jill sat in the waiting room terrified and sobbing; her appraisal of this was that it was having a tooth removed which was so much worse than a filling. Enough trust had been built that Jill allowed topical and the infiltration anaesthetic necessary and the tooth was 'extracted.' Jill visibly relaxed and admitted with a rueful smile and chuckle that it hadn't been nearly as bad as she had anticipated. Given the intense distress of this visit, Jill was deliberately brought back for an extra visit to have a fissure sealant, to ensure that her final experience before a break of 3 months was of very positive and confident coping.

As previously stated, children have poor metacognitive skills. Progress up the hierarchy may well reveal aspects of fear of which they had been previously 'unaware'. This should lead to continual re-evaluation and modification of the treatment plan (Figure 1) The treatment planning of children with a significant amount of dental treatment need may also require re-planning because of the improvement in skills and comprehension which are a normal part of development. Children should achieve greater insight because of this as well as because of treatment.

We also believe that the achievement of dental fitness with a practitioner skilled in these techniques does not necessarily equip a child for an immediate transfer to a general (dental) practitioner. There is increasing evidence that booster sessions and relapse prevention should be programmed in as part of CBT (Craske, M. G. & Barlow, D. H., 2001). If a child is still wary and trusts only you as a dentist, they are not going to readily transfer at the end of one course of treatment, especially if there are potentially very demanding treatments such as orthodontic extractions on the near horizon. If the child is being seen on a referral and hand on basis (as in many Community Dental Services in the UK) it is important that children and their parents understand that this is the case so as not to foster dependency. The time to hand on should be decided by a combination of clinical judgement, self-reported fear levels and prospective treatment needs and negotiation with the child and his mother.

5. SUMMARY

In this paper we have described a CBT-based model of dental fear in children which can serve to guide assessment of the nature of the individual's fear. It also serves to emphasise that dental health is not just a matter of dental fitness, but of being able to accept dental treatment in the most autonomous way possible in the future.

An intervention plan based on this model would focus on decreasing factors which increase fear and concentrate on factors which would decrease fear and increase coping.

We would expect that coping skills developed in this way would be readily generalised to other settings.

REFERENCE LIST

Addleston, H. K. (1959). Child Patient Training. *Fortnightly Review chicago Dental Society, 38,* 27.

Aitken, J. C., Wilson, S., Coury, D., & Moursi.A.M. (2002). The effect of music distraction on pain, anxiety and behavior in pediatric dental patients. *Pediatric Dentistry, 24,* 114-118.

American Academy of Pediatric Dentistry (2001). *Guidelines* Chicago: AAPD.

American Psychiatric Association (2000). *Diagnostic and Statistical Manual of Mental Disorders.* (4th (Text Revision) ed.) Washington, DC: American Psychiatric Association.

Atkinson, R. L., Atkinson, R. C., Smith, E. E., & Bem, D. J. (1993). *Introduction to Psychology*. (11th ed.) Orlando: Harcourt Brace.

Auerbach, S. M., Kendall, P. C., Cuttler, H. F., & Levitt, N. R. (1976). Anxiety, locus of control, type of preparatory information, and adjustment to dental surgery. *Journal of Consulting and Clinical Psychology, 44,* 809-818.

Bee, H. (1992). *The Developing Child*. (6th ed.) New York: Harper Collins.

Berge ten, M. (2003). Dental Fear in Children: Assessment, Prevalence and Etiology. In P.L.Gower (Ed.), *Psychology of Fear* (pp. 77-98). Hauppauge, New York: Nova Science Publishers.

Berge, t. M. (2003). Dental Fear in Children: Assessment, Prevalence and Etiology. In P.L.Gower (Ed.), *Psychology of Fear* (pp. 77-98). Hauppauge, New York: Nova Science Publishers.

Brophy, J. (1981). Teacher Praise: A functional analysis. *Review of Educational Research, 51,* 26.

Chapman, H. R. & Kirby-Turner, N. (1999). Dental fear in children - a proposed model. *British Dental Journal, 187,* 408-412.

Chapman, H. R. & Kirby-Turner, N. (2002). Visual/verbal analogue scales: examples of brief assessment methods to aid management of child and adult patients in clinical practice. *British Dental Journal, 193,* 447-450.

Cobham, V. E., Dadds, M. R., & Spence, S. H. (1999). Anxious children and their parents: What do they expect? *Journal of Clinical Child Psychology, 28,* 220-231.

Cohen, F. & Lazarus, R. S. (1979). Coping with the stress of illness. In G.C.Stone, F. Cohen, & N. Adler (Eds.), *Health Psychology* (San Fransisco: Jossey-Bass.

Corah, N. L. (1973). Affect of perceived control on stress reduction in pedodontic patients. *Journal of Dental Research, 52,* 1261-1264.

Corah, N. L., Gale, E. N., Pace, L. F., & Seyrek, S. K. (1981). Relaxation and musical programming as a means of reducing psychological stress during dental procedures. *Journal of the American Dental Association, 103,* 232-234.

Craske, M. G. & Barlow, D. H. (2001). Panic Disorder and Agoraphhobia. In D.H.Barlow (Ed.), *Clinical Handbook of Psychological Disorders* (3rd ed., pp. 1-59). New York: Guilford Press.

Frere, C. L., Crout, R., Yorty, J., & McNeil, D. W. (2001). Effects of audiovisual distraction during dental prohylaxis. *Journal of the American Dental Association, 132,* 1031-1038.

Grey, M. & Berry, D. (2004). Coping skills training and problem solving in diabetes. *Current Diabetes Reports, 4,* 126-132.

Hodgson, R. & Rachman, S. (1974). Desynchrony in measures of fear. *Behavior Research and Therapy, 12,* 319-326.

Holst, A. (1988). Behaviour management problems in child dentistry. Frequency, therapy and prediction. *Swedish Dental Journal, 54 (Suppl),* 1-155.

Kagan, J. (1994). *Galen's Prophecy: temperament in human nature*. New York: Basic Books.

Kendall, P. C. (2000). *Childhood Disorders*. Hove, UK: Psychology Press Ltd.

Kent, G. (1997). Dental Phobias. In G.Davey (Ed.), *Phobias - A Handbook of Theory, Research and Practice* (pp. 107-128). Chichester, UK: Wiley.

King, N. J., Hamilton, D. I., & Ollendick, T. H. (1988). *Children's Phobias - A Behavioural Perspective*. Chichester: Wiley.

Klinberg, G. (1995). Dental fear and behaviour management problems in children. *Swedish Dental Journal, Suppl 103,* 1-78.

Kvale, G., Milgrom, P., Getz, T., Weinstein, P., & Johnsen, T. B. (2004). Beliefs about professional ethics, dentist-patient communication, control and trust among fearful dental patients: the factor structure of the revised Dental Beliefs Survey. *Acta Odontol.Scand., 62,* 21-29.

Lang, P. J. (1978). Anxiety:Towards a psychophysiological definition. In H.S.Akishal & W. H. Webb (Eds.), *Psychiatric Diagnosis:Exploration of Biological Predictors* (New York: Spectrum Publishers.

Lazarus, A. A. (1973). Multimodal behavior therapy: treating the "basic id". *Journal of Nervous and Mental Diseases, 156,* 404-411.

Lazarus, R. S. & Folkman, S. (1980). *Stress, Appraisal, and Coping.* New York: Springer.

Lehrner, J., Ecksberger, C., Walla, P., Potsch.G., & Deecke, L. (2000). Ambient odor of orange in a dental office reduces anxiety and improves mood in female patients. *Physiology & Behavior, 71,* 83-86.

Malott, R. W. & Trojan Suarez, E. A. (2004). *Principles of Behavior.* (5th ed.) New Jersey: Prentice Hall.

Matthews, R., Ball, R., Goodley, A., Riley, C., Sanderson, S., & Singleton, E. (1997). The efficacy of local anaesthetics administered by general dental practitioners. *British Dental Journal, 182,* 175-178.

Melamed, B. G. (1984). Behavioral management in dentistry. *International Journal of Psychosomatics, 31,* 11-16.

Melamed, B. G., Weinstein, D., Hawes, R., & Katin-Borland, M. (1975). Reduction of fear-related dental management problems using filmed modeling. *Journal of the American Dental Association, 90,* 822-826.

Melnyk, B. M. & Alpert-Gillis, L. J. (1998). The COPE program: a strategy to improve outcomes of critically ill young children and their parents. *Pediatric Nursing, 24,* 521-527.

Milgrom, P., Weinstein, P., & Getz, T. (1995). *Treating Fearful Dental Patients - A Patient Management Handbook.* (2nd, revised ed.) Seattle: University of Washington.

Moore, R., Brodsgaard, I., & Birn, H. (1991). Manifestations, acquisition and diagnostic categories of dental fear in a self-referred population. *Behav.Res.Ther., 29,* 51-60.

Newton, J. T., Patel, H., Shah, S., & Sturmey, P. (2004). Attitudes towards the use of hand over mouth (HOM) and physical restraint amongst paediatric specialist practitioners in the UK. *Int.J Paediatr.Dent., 14,* 111-117.

Ollendick, T. H. & King, N. J. (1992). Fears and Phobias of Childhood. In M.Herbert (Ed.), *Clinical Child Psychology - Social Learning, Development and Behaviour* (pp. 309-330). Chichester, UK: Wiley.

Pearce, J. (2000). Emotional Disorders in Young People. In P.Aggleton, J. Hurry, & I. Warwick (Eds.), *Young People and Mental Health* (pp. 47-72). Chichester: Wiley.

Ploghaus, A., Tracey, I., Gati, J. S., Clare, S., Menon, R. S., Matthews, P. M., & Rawlins, J. N. (1999). Dissociating pain from its anticipation in the human brain. *Science, 284,* 1979-1981.

Rachman, S. (1998). *Anxiety.* Hove, UK: Psychology Press.

Rotter, J. B. (1966). Generalized expectancies for internal versus external control of reinforcement. *Psychological Monographs, 80.*

Rotter, J. B. (1967). A new scale for the measurement of interpersonal trust. *Journal of Personality, 35,* 651-665.

Siqueland, L., Kendall, P. C., & Steinberg, L. (1996). Anxiety in Children: Perceived family environments and observed family interaction style. *Journal of Clinical Child Psychology, 25,* 225-237.

Thrash, W. J., Russel-Duggan, J., & Mizes, J. S. (1984). The origin and prevention of dental fear. *Clinical preventive Dentistry, 6,* 28-32.

Walsh, K. & Darby, D. (1999). *Neuropsychology - A Clinical Approach.* (4th ed.) Edinburgh, London: Churchill Livingstone.

Weinstein, P., Domoto, P., Getz, T., & Enger, R. (1981). Reliability and validity of a measure of confidence in child behavior management. *Pediatric Dentistry, 2,* 7-9.

Wright, G. Z., Starkey, P. E., & Gardner, D. E. (1987). *Child Management in Dentistry.* Oxford, UK: John Wright & Sons.

In: New Research on the Psychology of Fear
Editor: Paul L. Gower, pp. 141-151

ISBN 1-59454-334-8
© 2005 Nova Science Publishers, Inc.

Chapter 7

THE IMPACT OF BEHAVIOURAL AND EMOTIONAL PROBLEMS IN CHILDREN'S DENTAL FEAR DEVELOPMENT

Maaike Ten Berge and Jaap S.J. Veerkamp
Academic Centre For Dentistry Amsterdam (ACTA), Dept. of Paediatric Dentistry,
University of Amsterdam, The Netherlands E-mail: m.ten.berge@acta.nl

ABSTRACT

This study was undertaken to assess the role of emotional and behavioural problems, as measured by the Child Behaviour Checklist (CBCL), in a child's dental fear development. The parents of 178 children (85 girls) referred to the Centre for Special Dental Care were asked to complete the Dental Subscale of the Children's Fear Survey Schedule (CFSS-DS) on behalf of their child, after the child's treatment at the Centre had finished. The results showed that the children's level of fear has decreased substantially after treatment at the Centre (mean 39.1 vs. 31.5, t=8.09, p=.000), but was still relatively high in comparison with children from the general Dutch child population. Fear reduction was found in all subgroups of children, with and without other problems, indicating that a structured behavioural management approach can be sufficient in reducing children's dental fear to a more controllable level. However, it was suggested that fearful children with a more complex problematic nature, in particular with internalising problems such as withdrawal and somatic complaints, might still form a risk group in daily practice. Extra attention is still needed for these children.

INTRODUCTION

Several theories on the acquisition of fears and phobias have been suggested. Rachman (1977) has proposed a three-pathway model of acquiring fear: directly through conditioning and indirectly via modelling or negative information from others. In dental research, numerous studies indeed have provided support for these pathways, in particular for the direct conditioning one (e.g., De Jongh, Muris, Ter Horst & Duyx, 1995; Liddell & Gosse, 1998; Locker, Shapiro & Liddell, 1996; Locker, Liddell, Dempster & Shapiro, 1999; Townend, Dimigen & Fung, 2000). Most of these studies have, however, been conducted retrospectively among adult patients, thus based on subjective and potentially biased reports. Child studies have resulted in more inconsistent results, and seem to indicate that Rachman's pathways do not fully explain the acquisition of dental fear in children, despite later revisions such as the latent inhibition theory (Davey, 1989; Klingberg, Berggren, Carlsson & Norén, 1995a; Milgrom, Mancl, King & Weinstein, 1995; Murray, Liddell & Donohue, 1989). Most important, the conditioning approach does not seem to account for the fact that some children became highly fearful without negative experiences or information, while other children who did undergo invasive dental treatment did not develop dental fear. Also, repeatedly parents were not able to indicate a direct cause of their child's high dental fear (Alwin, Murray & Britton 1991; Mejàre, 1989; Ten Berge, Veerkamp, Hoogstraten & Prins, 2002a).

Evidence for an additional role of temperamental factors in this process has been provided in several studies (Alwin et al., 1991; Brown, Wright & McMurray, 1986; Klingberg et al., 1995a; Klingberg & Broberg, 1998; Liddell, 1990; Williams, Murray, Lund, Harkiss & DeFranco, 1985). General fearfulness, shyness and introversion have repeatedly been associated with dental fear in children. For example, fearful children are found to have more difficulties adapting to and coping with new or unknown situations or people. Some of these studies also reported attention problems to be related to dental fear in children (see also Kindt & Van Den Hout, 1999). A study among children referred to the Centre for Special Dental Care in Amsterdam because of high dental fear indicated that these children also suffer from other emotional and behavioural problems, such as thought and attention problems, and aggressive behaviour (Ten Berge, Veerkamp, Hoogstraten & Prins, 1999a). In search for the most effective treatment method for fearful patients, treatment should therefore incorporate these different etiological and concomitant factors. That is, other problems may complicate dental treatment, which subsequently could have a less positive effect on children's fear development than in cases of simple dental fear or phobia. Thus, for children suffering from mood or conduct disorders a behaviour-based treatment program at a Centre for Special Dental Care may not suffice, these children may be in need of additional psychological treatment. Studies among adult fearful patients indeed have indicated that individuals with other psychopathological problems or anxieties may respond less favourable to an exposure-based, behavioural treatment program (e.g., Aartman, 2000; Kleinhauz, Eli, Baht & Shamay, 1992; Makkes, Schuurs, Thoden van Velzen, Duivenvoorden & Verhage, 1987). For example, Weiner & Sheehan (1990) proposed an endogenous (internal) and an exogenous (external) classification of phobic adult patients. It was suggested that the former might respond best to drug treatments while the latter may benefit more from behaviour-based therapy or treatment. Since few studies have been conducted on the potential prognostic role of other emotional or behavioural problems in children fear's development, the present study was undertaken. Its aim was to examine the effect of treatment at the Centre for Special Dental Care in Amsterdam (SBT) on the children's level of dental fear, and to assess the role of emotional and behavioural problems in this development. In addition, after treatment parents were interviewed about factors potentially responsible for changes in the children's fear level.

MATERIAL AND METHODS

Subjects

This study was conducted among 178 children (85 girls) referred to the Centre for Special Dental Care (SBT) in Amsterdam, because regular treatment by their family dentist had become impossible due to high dental fear. At this Centre, treatment generally aims at enabling children to be treated by their family-dentist again by using behavioural management techniques, sometimes combined with pharmacological agents such as nitrous oxide or propofol. This behavioural management approach is highly structured, conducted by trained dentists. Behavioural management techniques aim at behaviour modification by stepwise learning, (gradual) exposure and systematic desensitisation. Treatment takes place in absence of the child's parents, to exclude potential parental modelling influences and to allow children forming their own experiences.

At referral to the Centre, parents complete the Dutch parent's version of the Dental Subscale of the Children's Fear Survey Schedule (CFSS-DS; Cuthbert & Melamed, 1982) and of the Child Behaviour Checklist (CBCL; Achenbach, 1991), on behalf of their child. After treatment, this version of the CFSS-DS was again sent to the parents of 309 children. The parents of 223 children (response rate 72.2%) completed and returned the CFSS-DS, of which 21 had to be excluded because of other problems such as mental and physical handicaps. For another 10 questionnaires more than 4 items were missing and 14 children were treated by means of intravenous sedation, so these also had to be excluded leaving 178 questionnaires for analysis. In addition, to gain information of factors responsible for potential changes in children's fear level, interviews were held by telephone with part of the parents (n=86). All parents were well informed on the purpose of the study and all signed a consent form. The mean age of the children at time of their referral to the Centre was 6.5 years (range 4-14 years). The mean time period between pre– and post-treatment assessment was 23.6 months (range 6-42, SD 8.6). No significant difference in pre-treatment fear level was found between respondents (n=223) and non-respondents (n=86) (mean 39.0 versus 39.3, p>.05).

Measures

CFSS-DS

The CFSS-DS is a questionnaire developed to assess dental fear in children (Cuthbert & Melamed, 1982). It consists of 15 items related to different aspects of dental treatment, to be answered on a 5-point scale from 1) "not afraid at all" to 5) "very afraid". Total scores thus range from 15 to 75. Since the younger children were unable to complete the questionnaire themselves and to enable comparisons between age groups, in the present study the parents' version of the CFSS-DS was used. Research has indicated parents to be well able to assess their child's level of dental fear, and the scale was found to be reliable and valid (Klingberg, 1994; Klingberg, Berggren & Norén, 1994; Klingberg, Vannas Löfqvist & Hwang, 1995b; Milgrom, Jie, Yang & Tay, 1994; Ten Berge, Hoogstraten, Veerkamp & Prins, 1998). Cut-off scores for high dental fear have been set at scores between 38 and 42 (Chellappah, Vignesha,

Milgrom & Lo, 1990; Klingberg, 1994; Milgrom et al., 1994). A previous study among a large, representative sample of Dutch children provided two different cut-off scores: scores of 39 and higher represent high dental fear in children likely to cause problems during treatment ("clinical range"), and in addition, scores between 32 and 38 represent a so-called "borderline range" (Ten Berge, Veerkamp, Hoogstraten & Prins, 2002b). Children scoring in this "borderline range" may be fairly fearful but their behaviour during and perception of treatment may depend on circumstances or the child's temperament, or they may be at risk of developing high dental fear. Children scoring below 32 essentially are seen as non-fearful or low fearful, and in general, treatment should not be interfered with ("non-clinical range").

CBCL

The CBCL is a questionnaire developed to assess emotional and behavioural problems in children, for a period of 6 months prior to the completion of the questionnaire. The CBCL is divided into 'competence' and 'problem' scales. Since the 'competence' scales have little relevance for the investigation of different types of problem behaviour in children, in this study only the 'problem' scales were used. These problem scales consist of 118 items, which are divided over 9 problem scales: 'withdrawal' (9 items), 'somatic complaints' (9 items), 'fear/depression' (14 items), 'social problems' (8 items), 'thought problems' (7 items), 'attention problems' (11 items), 'delinquency' (13 items), 'aggression' (20 items) and 'sex problems' (6 items). The other items, not included in one of the 9 subscales, are classified as 'other problems' (11 items). These items do not form a separate scale but are included in the calculation of a "total problems" score. Each item can be scored 0 ('not true'), 1 ('somewhat or sometimes true') or 2 ('very true'); all items are summed to create an overall score. Scores on all subscales as well as a total problem score were obtained. In addition, scores for two broadband subscales, 'internalising' and 'externalising', were calculated by summing the relevant items. The 'internalising' scale consists of the items of the 'withdrawal', 'somatic complaints' and 'fear/depression' subscales and is related to internal problem behaviour. The 'externalising' scale consists of the items of the 'delinquency' and 'aggression' subscales and is related to external problem behaviour. Again, scores on all scales were classified as 'non-clinical', 'borderline' or 'clinical' according to cut-off scores suggested by Achenbach (Achenbach, 1991; Verhulst, Van Der Ende & Koot, 1996). The questionnaires were scored by computer, using the Dutch version of the CBCL-manual.

Interview

Interviews were held with the parents of 86 children (46 girls), by telephone. The aim of this interview was to retrospectively identify factors responsible for potential changes in children's level of dental fear. Therefore, the parents were asked whether their child's level of dental fear had changed in the course of treatment at the Centre, and if so, to subsequently indicate the factors responsible for this change.

Data Analysis

Total scores were calculated for the CFSS-DS pre- and post-treatment scores and for all CBCL-scales. To assess differences in pre- and post treatment CFSS-DS level, paired t-tests were performed for the total group of children, as well as for children scoring in the different cut-off ranges separately. Analyses of variance were performed to assess differences in pre- and post-treatment CFSS-DS score for high- and low CBCL-scorers separately (borderline and clinical versus non-clinical scores). To examine the role of the CBCL scales in potential fear reduction, regression analysis was performed with CFSS-DS post-treatment score as dependent variable and CFSS-DS pre-treatment score (method: enter) and the CBCL scales, the child's age and time period between pre- and post-treatment assessment (method: stepwise) as independent variables, for boys and girls separately.

Results

CFSS-DS

After treatment at the Centre, a significant reduction in mean CFSS-DS score was found for the total group (n=178: pre 39.1 versus post 31.5, t=8.09, p=.000). No significant gender differences were found in pre- or in post-treatment CFSS-DS scores (p>.05). Table 1 shows the percentages of children scoring in the severity ranges according to CFSS-DS cut-off scores, and their subsequent mean CFSS-DS scores before and after treatment at the Centre. Also, percentages of children scoring in the cut-off ranges after treatment are shown.

Table 1. Percentages of children scoring in the severity ranges according to cut-off scores, and mean CFSS-DS scores at pre- and post-treatment assessment at the Centre (n=178)

	% (n)		mean CFSS-DS		
	pre	post	pre	post	(n)
low	30.3 (54)	57.3 (102)	24.9	26.2	(54)
borderline	17.4 (31)	19.1 (34)	35.6 *	32.4	(31)
high	52.5 (93)	23.6 (42)	48.3 **	34.3	(93)

*p < .05, ** p < .01

For the total group, a significant but moderate correlation between CFSS-DS pre-treatment and post-treatment score was found (r=.37, p=.000).

CBCL

Although boys overall scored somewhat higher than girls on the CBCL-scales, these differences did not reach significance (p>.05). A substantial part of the children were found to have emotional and/or behavioural problems: 38% of the children scored in the borderline or clinical range on "total problems", 32% on "internalising" and 30% on "externalising".

Fear Reduction and CBCL Scores

Table 2 shows the mean pre- and post-treatment scores for children with high versus low CBCL scales (borderline and clinical versus non-clinical). High CBCL-scorers showed a relatively high pre-treatment CFSS-DS level compared with low CBCL scores (p<.05).

Also, a higher post-treatment fear level was found for high internalisers compared with low internalisers (p<.05). An analysis of covariance with pre-treatment CFSS-DS score included as covariate, however, showed no significant differences in post-treatment CFSS-DS score between high- and low CBCL scorers (p>.05).

Table 2. Mean pre- and post-treatment CFSS-DS scores according to severity of CBCL problems (n=165)

	borderline/clinical			non-clinical		
	pre	post	(n)	pre	post	(n)
internalising	45.1[a]	34.0[b]	(53)	36.8	30.3	(112)
externalising	42.5[a]	33.6	(49)	38.1	30.6	(116)
total problems	42.5[a]	32.6	(63)	37.5	30.8	(102)

[a] significant difference with non-clinical group pre-treatment score (ANOVA)
[b] significant difference with non-clinical group post-treatment score (ANOVA)

Regression analysis using the scores of the total group revealed no significant contribution of the CBCL-scales, the child's age and time period between pre- and post treatment assessment to the CFSS-DS post-treatment score, beside the CFSS-DS pre-treatment score (Table 3).

Table 3. Stepwise regression analysis (post-treatment CFSS-DS scores)

Variables in equation	Beta	t value	sign.	R^2 (cum.)
Total:	.387	5.35	.000	.150
CFSS-DS (pre-treatment)				
Boys:	.253	2.38	.020	.186
CFSS-DS (pre-treatment)				
age	-.356	-3.53	.001	.254
withdrawal (CBCL)	.271	2.52	.014	.308
Girls:	.344	3.22	.002	.118
CFSS-DS (pre-treatment)				

For boys, regression analysis showed CFSS-DS pre-treatment score, age and the CBCL scale "withdrawal" to be significant predictors of post-treatment CFSS-DS score (Table 3). However, this CBCL scale only contributed 6% of the variance. For girls, none of the CBCL-scales were included in the equation; only pre-treatment CFSS-DS score proved to be significant.

Interviews

Almost all parents (87%, n=75) reported their child's level of fear to have decreased after treatment; eight parents (9%) indicated no change, while three parents (4%) said they did not know. Most of the parents (84%) reporting a decrease in their child's fear indicated the treatment approach at the Centre to be the underlying cause of their child's lower level of fear. Most often, particularly taking the time and providing clear instructions and structure were thought to have had a positive effect on their child's dental fear. Also, some of the parents mentioned that being empathic though determined towards the child to have been important. Beside this structured treatment approach some parents indicated an internal change in the child to have caused the decline in dental fear such as growing older, improved coping abilities and an overall more positive emotional status (8%). Also, parents' own influence was reported to have stimulated the child. Some parents indicated that they were better able to guide their child, to be less fearful themselves and to have more confidence in dentists in general (3%). Finally, 5% of the parents were not able to indicate a specific cause of the decline in their child's fear.

DISCUSSION

The present study has shown a significant reduction in the children's level of dental fear after treatment at the Centre. This mean level of dental fear after treatment, however, still remains relatively high in comparison with children from the general Dutch child population (Ten Berge et al., 2002b). Moreover, part of the children score in the borderline range or above after treatment, indicating that a risk of interference with treatment might still exist. These children still suffer some degree of fear, but may have learned different, more effective ways of coping with dental treatment, resulting in a more controllable level of dental fear. Although a substantial part of the children in this study were found to have other emotional and behavioural problems, fear reduction seems to have taken place mostly independent of the presence of these problems. Only for boys, emotional problems (i.e., withdrawal) were found related to their dental fear development. These problems, however, only explained a small percentage of the variance implicating that this dental fear might essentially be seen and treated as a simple, isolated problem. That is, the fact that the children's dental fear did decrease independent of their other problems might indicate that a management approach based on gradual exposure and systematic desensitisation does suffice to reduce this fear to a more controllable level for most children. In other words, the importance of counter conditioning is stressed in treating high dental fear in children, regardless of its origins. Even if a child's dental fear is part of or co-exists with a more complex problematic nature or general fearfulness, it seems that the child can be taught more adequate coping strategies to deal with the situation. The importance of this management approach and the dentists' role is supported by both the present interviews and by previous research (Holst & Crossner, 1984; Holst & Ek, 1988; Ten Berge, Veerkamp & Hoogstraten, 1999b; Varpio & Wellfelt, 1991). For example, studies have indicated that the patients' subjective experience of dental treatment may be more important in the acquisition of dental fear than painful or invasive dental procedures actually performed during treatment (Ten Berge, Veerkamp & Hoogstraten,

2002a; Townend et al., 2000). It seems that the dentists' approach may not only play an important role in reducing high dental fear but might also be involved in the acquisition of this fear.

Although all subgroups showed a significant fear reduction, an interesting trend in fear development should be noted. The fear level of children with other problems was found to be significantly higher before treatment than that of children without these problems, and remained somewhat higher after treatment for children with problems of an internalising nature than for children without these problems. This might indicate that treatment at the Centre generally may have been successful in reducing the children's dental fear, but that children with more complex problems may still form a risk group for whom extra attention remains important. These children may be more susceptible to acquiring fear and may stay at risk in the long run, as also indicated in another, explorative study (Arnrup, 2003). For these children obviously subsequent dental visits are very important in their future fear development. The positive experience of children with dental treatment at the Centre needs to be continued to reinforce children's less fearful perception of the dental situation. Extra care is therefore needed when referring children back to a family dentist, also taking into account the children's alleviated but still relatively high fear level after treatment. Moreover, it may even be advisable to re-assess the child's level of fear before this intended referral and in cases of high fear to extend treatment at the Centre. Furthermore, also more attention may be needed at original referral to the Centre. That is, the fact that part of the children were rated by their parents as low fearful at referral implies that this referral may have been based on complicated dental problems or conduct disorders, but of course also dentist-related factors may have been involved (Weerheijm, Veerkamp, Groen & Zwarts, 1999).

In conclusion, treatment at the Centre did reduce children's dental fear to a more controllable level for most children. Children seem to have learned more adequate ways of coping with dental treatment by providing them with a structured setting and a behaviour-based management approach (Ten Berge et al., 1999b). It should however be noted that children with a more complex problematic nature, particularly with internalising problems, might still form a risk group. These emotional problems in children should therefore be regarded as risk factors in the acquisition of high dental fear, but possibly also in maintaining this dental fear and the subsequent risk of interference, even after treatment at a Centre for Special Dental Care or Dental Fear Clinic. Interestingly, attention problems were not found to influence children's fear development in the present study, while earlier studies have indicated that an "attentional bias" may be involved in the maintenance of fears in children (Kindt & Van den Hout, 1999). Other studies also reported a relation of child dental fear with attention problems and distractibility (Alwin et al., 1991; Liddell, 1990; Ten Berge et al., 1999a). Operationalisation of this concept may underlie this discrepancy. That is, in the present study attention problems assessed by the CBCL for the most part seem to concern behavioural aspects such as impulsivity and clumsiness, while cognitive aspects are less incorporated. Future studies should therefore further examine the potential role of "attentional bias", by using more cognitively oriented instruments. More research is also needed on the efficacy of specific treatment modes for different subgroups of children, so possibly an even greater fear reduction can be obtained after treatment. Finally, future research is needed to examine as to whether the obtained fear reduction can be maintained in the long run, also after dental treatment by a general practitioner is resumed.

REFERENCES

Aartman, I.H.A. (2000). *Treating highly anxious patients in a dental fear clinic.* PhD Thesis. University of Amsterdam, Enschede: PrintPartners Ipskamp.

Achenbach, T.M. (1991). *Manual for the Child Behavior Checklist/4-18 and 1991 profiles.* Burlington: University of Vermont.

Alwin, N.P., Murray, J.J., & Britton, P.G. (1991). An assessment of dental anxiety in children. *British Dental Journal, 171,* 201-207.

Arnrup, K. (2003). *Paediatric dentistry meets clinical child psychology: studying groups of uncooperative child dental patients.* PhD Thesis. University of Göteborg, Sweden: Kompendiet.

Berge ten, M., Hoogstraten, J., Veerkamp, J.S.J., & Prins, P.J.M. (1998). The Dental Subscale of the Children's Fear Survey Schedule: a factor analytic study in the Netherlands. *Community Dentistry and Oral Epidemiology, 26,* 340-343.

Berge ten, M., Veerkamp, J.S.J., Hoogstraten, J., & Prins, P.J.M. (1999a). Behavioural and emotional problems in children referred to a centre for special dental care. *Community Dentistry and Oral Epidemiology, 27,* 181-186.

Berge ten, M., Veerkamp, J.S.J., & Hoogstraten, J. (1999b). Dentists' behavior in response to child dental fear. *ASDC Journal of Dentistry for Children, 66,* 36-40.

Berge ten M, Veerkamp JSJ, Hoogstraten J (2002a). The etiology of childhood dental fear: the role of dental and conditioning experiences. *Journal of Anxiety Disorders, 16,* 321-329.

Berge ten, M., Veerkamp, J.S.J., Hoogstraten, J., & Prins, P.J.M. (2002b). Childhood dental fear in The Netherlands: prevalence and normative data. *Community Dentistry and Oral Epidemiology, 30,* 101-107.

Berge ten M, Veerkamp JSJ, Hoogstraten J, Prins PJM (2001). Parental beliefs on the origins of child dental fear in the Netherlands. *ASDC Journal of Dentistry for Children, 68,* 51-54.

Brown, D.F., Wright, F.A.C., & McMurray, N.E. (1986). Psychological and behavioral factors associated with dental anxiety in children. *Journal of Behavioral Medicine, 9,* 213-218.

Chellappah, N.K., Vignesha, H., Milgrom, P., & Lo, G.L. (1990). Prevalence of dental anxiety and fear in children in Singapore. *Community Dentistry and Oral Epidemiology, 18,* 269-271.

Cuthbert, M.I. & Melamed, B.G. (1982). A screening device: children at risk for dental fears and management problems. *ASDC Journal of Dentistry for Children, 49,* 432-436.

Davey, G.C.L. (1989). Dental phobias and anxieties: evidence for conditioning processes and modulation of a learned fear. *Behaviour Research and Therapy, 27,* 51-58.

Holst, A. & Crossner, C-G. (1984). Management of dental behaviour problems. A 5-year follow-up. *Swedish Dental Journal, 8,* 243-249.

Holst, A. & Ek, L. (1988). Effect of systematized "behavior shaping" on acceptance of dental treatment in children. *Community Dentistry and Oral Epidemiology, 16,* 349-355.

Jongh de, A., Muris, P., Horst ter, G., & Duyx, M.P.M.A. (1995). Acquisition and maintenance of dental anxiety: the role of conditioning experiences and cognitive factors. *Behaviour Research and Therapy, 33,* 205-210.

Kindt, M. & Hout van den, M. (1999). Anxiety and selective attention for threatening information. *Nederlands Tijdschrift voor Psychologie, 54*, 63-72.

Kleinhauz, M., Eli, I., Baht, R., & Shamay, D. (1992). Correlates of success and failure in behavior therapy for dental fear. *Journal of Dental Research, 71*, 1832-1835.

Klingberg, G. (1994). Reliability and validity of the Swedish version of the Dental Subscale of the Children's Fear Survey Schedule, CFSS-DS. *Acta Odontologica Scandinavica, 52*, 255-256.

Klingberg, G., Berggren, U., Carlsson, S.G., & Norén, J.G. (1995a). Child dental fear: cause related factors and clinical effects. *European Journal of Oral Sciences, 103*, 405-412.

Klingberg, G., Berggren, U., & Norén, J.G. (1994). Dental fear in an urban Swedish child population: prevalence and concomitant factors. *Community Dental Health, 11*, 208-214.

Klingberg, G. & Broberg, A.G. (1998). Temperament and child dental fear. *Pediatric Dentistry, 20,* 237-243.

Klingberg, G., Vannas Löfqvist, L., & Hwang, C.P. (1995b). Validity of the Children's Dental Fear Picture test (CDFP). *European Journal of Oral Sciences, 103*, 55-60.

Liddell, A. (1990). Personality characteristics versus medical and dental experiences of dentally anxious children. *Journal of Behavioral Medicine, 13*, 183-194.

Liddell, A. & Gosse, V. (1998). Characteristics of early unpleasant dental experiences. *Journal of Behavior Therapy and Experimental Psychiatry, 29*, 227-237.

Locker, D., Liddell, A., Dempster, L., & Shapiro, D. (1999). Age of onset of dental anxiety. *Journal of Dental Research, 78,* 790-796.

Locker, D., Shapiro, D., & Liddell, A. (1996). Negative dental experiences and their relationship to dental anxiety. *Community Dental Health, 13*, 86-92.

Makkes, P.C., Schuurs, A.H.B., Thoden van Velzen, S.K., Duivenvoorden, H.J., & Verhage, F. (1987). Effects of a special dental program upon extreme dental anxiety. *Community Dentistry and Oral Epidemiology, 15,* 173.

Mejàre, I., Ljungkvist, B., & Quensel, E. (1989). Pre-school children with uncooperative behaviour in the dental situation. Some characteristics and background factors. *Acta Odontologica Scandinavica, 47*, 337-345.

Milgrom, P., Jie, Z., Yang, Z., & Tay, K-M. (1994). Cross-cultural validity of a parent's version of the Dental Fear Survey Schedule for children in Chinese. *Behaviour Research and Therapy, 32,* 131-135.

Milgrom, P., Mancl, L., King, B., & Weinstein, P. (1995). Origins of childhood dental fear. *Behaviour Research and Therapy, 33*, 313-319.

Murray, P., Liddell, A., & Donohue, J. (1989). A longitudinal study of the contribution of dental experience to dental anxiety in children between 9 and 12 years of age. *Journal of Behavioral Medicine, 12*, 309-320.

Rachman, S. (1977). The conditioning theory of fear acquisition: A critical examination. *Behaviour Research and Therapy, 15,* 375-387.

Townend, E., Dimigen, G., & Fung, D. (2000). A clinical study of child dental anxiety. *Behaviour Research and Therapy, 38,* 31-46.

Varpio, M. & Wellfelt, B. (1991). Some characteristics of children with dental behaviour problems. Five year follow-up of pedodontic treatment. *Swedish Dental Journal, 15,* 85-93.

Verhulst, F.C., Ende van der, J., & Koot, H.M. (1996). *Handleiding voor de CBCL/4-18, Nederlandse versie.* Rotterdam: Sophia Kinderziekenhuis/ Academisch Ziekenhuis/ Erasmus Universiteit Rotterdam.

Weerheijm, K.L., Veerkamp, J.S.J., Groen, H.J., & Zwarts, L.M. (1999). Evaluation of the experiences of fearful children at a Special Dental Care Centre. *ASDC Journal of Dentistry for Children, 66,* 253-257.

Weiner, A.A. & Sheehan, D.J. (1990). Etiology of dental anxiety: psychological trauma or CNS chemical imbalance? *General Dentistry, 22,* 39-43.

Williams, J.M.G., Murray, J.J., Lund, C.A., Harkiss, B., & DeFranco, A. (1985). Anxiety in the child dental clinic. *Journal of Child Psychology and Psychiatry, 26,* 305-310.

In: New Research on the Psychology of Fear   ISBN 1-59454-334-8
Editor: Paul L. Gower, pp. 153-180   © 2005 Nova Science Publishers, Inc.

Chapter 8

DENTAL PHOBIA: AN OVERVIEW OF COGNITIVE BEHAVIOURAL THEORY, MODELS AND TREATMENT

Ad de Jongh[*]

Department of Social Dentistry and Public Health, Academic Centre for Dentistry
Amsterdam, University of Amsterdam, Louwesweg 1, 1066 EA Amsterdam, The
Netherlands.

Marieke Meyerink-Anderson

Mediant, Enschede, The Netherlands

ABSTRACT

Anxiety about dental treatment is a worldwide health problem of considerable significance. While 20 per cent of the population dislikes visiting the dentist to such an extent that they use dental services only when it is really necessary, approximately 5% of the population in Western countries demonstrate such an excessive and 'unreasonable' fear of dental appointments that these situations are entirely avoided.

This chapter considers the current knowledge concerning onset, theories, presentation and maintenance of the pathological form of dental anxiety, dental phobia. Particular attention is given to the behavioural model and to meaning and role of cognitive phenomena in the aetiology and maintenance of this condition. Furthermore, it includes a brief overview of effective methods and techniques that can be used for the treatment of dental phobia.

INTRODUCTION

No other state of mind is thought to be connected to the root of human agony and survival as anxiety. On the one hand, however, anxiety reactions are mostly beneficial and adaptive. For example, the unpleasantness of the anxious experience helps to identify the

[*] E-mail: info@psycho-trauma.nl

awareness of a problem, whereas a failure to recognize the experience of anxiety may leave a person unprepared for potentially aversive situations. Another function of anxiety is that it can enlist support, for example through empathy from others, thereby reassuring the anxious person in a threatening situation. On the other hand, anxiety responses can also be disruptive and maladaptive, especially when these are provoked by something that is in fact not actually dangerous.

In this respect, dental anxiety is a good example. In a study in which individuals were asked about commonly feared situations, dental anxiety ranked fifth and was reported by 20% of those questioned (Agras, Sylvester, & Oliveau, 1969). Furthermore, several studies report that more than 70% of the population is apprehensive while attending the dentist, whereas approximately 7% systematically avoid dental care because of their anxiety (e.g., Gatchell, Ingersoll, Bowman, Robertson & Walker, 1983; Stouthard & Hoogstraten, 1990). This shows that anxiety about dental treatment is a health problem of considerable significance (Berggren & Meynert, 1984; Gatchell, Ingersoll, Bowman Robertson, & Walker, 1983; Milgrom, Fiset, Melnick & Weinstein, 1988; Schuurs, Duivenvoorde, Ter Horst & De Wit, 1993; Stouthard & Hoogstraten, 1990).

PATHOLOGICAL FORMS OF DENTAL ANXIETY

Is it unreasonable to be apprehensive while anticipating dental treatment? On the one hand, even with the benefit of local anaesthesic, dentistry today still has many intrinsic, threatening aspects. A variety of dental procedures are associated with dread because they can cause pain and distress, such as root canal treatments or removal of impacted third molars. Another aspect, inherently associated with dental treatment, is that specific aspects of the dental treatment setting itself can easily lead to a sense of helplessness or powerlessness, which subsequently contributes to apprehensiveness and heightened levels of anxiety.

On the other hand, the confrontation with specific dental stimuli can lead to such high levels of disturbance that this prevents any dental treatment being carried out, or even to a situation where dental appointments are avoided entirely. This is where the normal anxiety response becomes inappropriate, irrational or problematic, particularly because this may result in a situation where the individual's health is at stake. One of the most overt indicators of pathological forms of dental anxiety is the avoidance of professional care, often expressed in a high incidence of missed or cancelled dental appointments (e.g., Kleinknecht & Bernstein, 1978).

According to the fourth edition of the Diagnostic and Statistical Manual of mental disorders (DSM-IV; American Psychiatric Association, 1994) severe dental anxiety should be considered a 'specific phobia'; that is, a "clinically significant anxiety provoked by exposure to a specific feared object or situation, often leading to avoidance behavior" (p. 393). By definition, phobic anxiety is irrational and disproportionate to the actual threat, while its' reactions such as avoidance are mainly inappropriate and counterproductive. For example, the tendency to escape an anxiety-provoking situation prevents the person from learning that this situation is not as dangerous as expected. Another important DSM-IV criterion of specific phobia is that the avoidance, anxious anticipation, or distress in the feared situations interferes significantly with the person's normal overall functioning. See Table I for the diagnostic criteria according the current DSM-IV definition of a specific phobia.

Table I. Criteria for dental phobia according DSM-IV definition

---

1. Marked and persistent fear that is excessive or unreasonable, cued by the presence or anticipation of a specific object or situation (e.g., hearing the sound of the drill, receiving an injection with local anesthesia, seeing a probe).

2. Exposure to the phobic stimulus almost invariably provokes an immediate anxiety response, which may take the form of situationally bound or situationally predisposed panic attack. Note: In children, the anxiety may be expressed by crying, tantrums, freezing or clinging.

3. The person recognizes that the fear is excessive or unreasonable. Note: In children, this feature may be absent.

4. The phobic situation(s) (e.g., dental practice) is avoided or else is endured with intense anxiety or distress.

5. The avoidance, anxious anticipation, or distress in the feared situation(s) interferes significantly with the person's normal routine, occupation, or (academic) functioning or social activities or relationships, or there is marked distress about having the phobia.

6. In individuals under 18 years, the duration is at least 6 months.

7. The anxiety, panic attacks or phobic avoidance associated with the specific object or situation are not better accounted for by another mental disorder, such as obsessive-compulsive disorder (e.g., fear of dirt – dental plaque or calculus - in someone with an obsession about contamination), post-traumatic stress disorder (e.g., avoidance of medically related stimuli associated with a medical trauma), social phobia (e.g., avoidance of social situations because of fear of embarrassment about the deteriorated state of the teeth), panic disorder (e.g., fear of panic attacks in the dental chair).

The prospect of undergoing invasive dental interventions can have a significant detrimental effect on the patient's emotional well being. Therefore, it is important to assess to what extent the dental phobic individual is able to cope with adverse or negative events, whether internal and external resources are available and what the level of motivation is for overcoming their fear as well as for undergoing dental treatment. For example, research has indicated that 50-60% of the dental phobic individuals suffer from one or more specific fears of dental procedures and dental related stimuli, while the remaining group meets the criteria of a mental disorder which may adversely impinge on the delivery of dental treatment (Roy-Byrne, Milgrom, Khoon-Mei, Weinstein & Katon, 1994).

Since additional psychological problems can limit patients' psychological resilience and coping resources, one has to establish whether the treatment - and possibly other personal or work related problems - are likely to be too demanding or overwhelming. For this reason it is important to establish whether the patient's dental phobia is the only presenting problem, or whether the patient displays intrusive and interfering psychiatric symptoms, which are manifestations of underlying emotional problems or more serious mental difficulties (e.g., psychotic, anxiety or mood disorders (Kvale, Raadal, Vika *et al.*, 2002)

Table I. Occurrence of trauma-related symptomatology as indexed by the Impact of Event Scale (IES) scores (De Jongh et al., 2003)

Item no.	Occurrence (%)			
	Not at all (0)	Rarely (1)	Sometimes (3)	Often (5)
1. I thought about it when I didn't mean to	23.5	0.6	29.4	26.5
2. I avoided letting myself get upset when I thought about it or was reminded of it	29.4	8.8	35.3	26.5
3. I tried to remove it from memory	29.4	8.8	14.7	47.1
4. I had trouble falling asleep or staying asleep, because of pictures or thoughts about it that came into my mind	38.2	20.6	32.4	8.8
5. I had waves of strong feelings about it	32.4	11.8	41.2	14.7
6. I had dreams about it	61.8	11.8	20.6	5.9
7. I stayed away from reminders of it	41.2	20.6	17.6	20.6
8. I felt as if it hadn't happened or it wasn't real	73.5	14.7	8.8	2.9
9. I tried not to talk about it	67.6	8.8	17.6	5.9
10. Pictures about it popped into my mind	35.3	20.6	29.4	14.7
11. Other things kept making me think about it	50.0	11.8	26.5	11.8
12. I was aware that I still had a lot of feelings about it, but I didn't deal with them	64.7	11.8	20.6	2.9
13. I tried not to think about it	32.4	2.9	35.3	29.4
14. Any reminder brought back feelings about	29.4	29.4	23.5	17.6
15. My feelings about it were kind of numb	67.6	17.6	8.8	5.9

One particular group of mental health problems that can cause difficulties during dental treatment are those that are the result of one or more confrontations with a traumatic stressor. These so called, post traumatic stress symptoms, have usually been described in relation to disasters, accidents, and assaults, but typical trauma-related phenomena have also been reported following a wide range of frightening medical events (Mayou & Smith, 1997). In a recent study it was found that in anticipation of dental treatment anxious individuals frequently experience intrusive memories of past painful or otherwise aversive dental treatments and other long term effects typically observed in individuals suffering from post traumatic stress disorder or PTSD (American Psychiatric Association, 1994; De Jongh, Aartman & Brand, 2003). In this study the Impact of Event Scale (IES) was used to assess the intensity of posttraumatic stress-related phenomena (Horowitz, Wilmer & Alvarez, 1979). The IES is a 15-item self-reporting questionnaire that measures two dimensions of PTSD: trauma-related intrusions (e.g., *'Pictures about it popped into my mind'*) and avoidance of the memory (e.g., *'I tried to remove it from my memory'*). The IES is one of the most widely used global self-report instruments of posttraumatic stress symptomatology (Joseph, 2000). Patients in this study were requested to keep in mind the most awful dental treatment they could remember (as described previously in the questionnaire) when scoring the IES, and to indicate how frequently the comments had been true during the past seven days. Table I shows the distribution of anxious patients across the IES items scores.

The mean score on the IES for anxious patients in this study was 25.1 (SD=18.3). Exactly half of the patients scored above the cut-off point for a clinically relevant level of trauma-related phenomena (IES score >26; Horowitz, Wilmer & Alvarez, 1979; Kleber, Brom, Defares, 1992).

Thus, it would seem that people initially classified as having a severe form of dental fear experience intrusive memories, and a tendency to avoid these memories, when they are to undergo treatment; that is, when exposure to their feared stimuli is imminent. It is noteworthy, that the level of trauma-related symptomatology found in this study was comparable with a sample of road traffic accident victims after their accident (Mayou, Ehlers & Hobbs, 2000) and a sample of residents of Lockerbie who had been exposed to the aircraft disaster in 1988 (Livingston, Livingston, Brooks & McKinlay, 1992). These findings suggest that the fear structures laid down during or following aversive experiences are activated whenever highly anxious individuals are anticipating or are being confronted with their feared stimuli. This makes them re-experience parts of their 'nightmare' and may evoke a similar perception of danger as during the original incident. In this respect, the findings provide support for the notion of a specific category of phobias, namely phobias of traumatic origin or "traumatic simple phobias" (McNally & Saigh, 1993), which have a number of commonalties with PTSD. Dental phobia may an excellent example of this.

THE ACQUISITION OF DENTAL ANXIETY: BEHAVIORAL MODEL

A valuable and most widely used model concerning the onset of clinically relevant fears and phobias has been proposed by Rachman in 1977, which is known as the 'three pathways' model of fear acquisition (Rachman, 1977; Öst & Hugdahl, 1981; Rachman, 1990). This model assumes that while some clinically relevant anxieties are acquired via observational (vicarious) learning or transmission of information, such events are seldom found in the etiology of others. For example, it has been found that phobias of the most common category of phobic fears, phobia of harmless animals (e.g., spiders, mice, bats, etc.), do not result from an experience associated with terror or pain (e.g., Davey, 1992), but appears to be related to disgust. In contrast, a wide array of studies suggest that the majority of dentally high anxious persons attribute their anxiety to traumatic experiences during previous dental treatments, while the proportions of persons ascribing the onset of their anxiety to other ways of acquisition, such as vicarious learning or information, appear to be much smaller (Bernstein, Kleinknecht & Alexander, 1979; Kleinknecht, Klepac & Alexander, 1973; Öst & Hugdahl, 1985; Moore, Brødsgaard, & Birn, 1991). These findings are also in line with the model of fear acquisition proposed by Menzies and Clarke (1995). According to these authors fears of relatively recent stimuli, for which evolution can not have directly protected the species (e.g., dental drills and hypodermic needles), have much higher conditioning rates than fears of long-standing natural dangers to the species, such as the natural environmental phobias.

Let us first briefly consider the laws that characterize classical conditioning and use Pavlov's famous experiment as an example. In this experiment a dog is brought to a soundproof laboratory. This room is arranged so that meat powder can be delivered to a dish in front of the dog, and its' salivation is recorded. A light bulb is turned on; the dog does not salivate. After a while meat powder is delivered. Since the dog is hungry it eats. While the dog eats, salivation is recorded automatically. This sequence of events is repeated a number of times. Then the experimenter turns on the light but does not deliver any meat powder the dog salivates nonetheless for it has learned to associate the light with food.

In short, the dog has been taught, or conditioned, to associate the light with food and to respond to it by salivating. This phenomenon became known as classical conditioning. As food automatically produces salvation before learning (conditioning) has occurred, it was termed an unconditioned stimulus (UCS). The response of salvation to the food was termed an unconditioned response (UCR). Before any learning had taken place the light did not elicit salvation. However, after several pairings of the light and the food, the light (the conditioned stimulus; CS) came to elicit salvation (the conditioned response; CR). In other words, the CS (light) *predicts* the occurrence of the UCS (food) for which the dogs prepares by salivation (CR).

Let us translate these experimental findings to the dental situation by pretending that I had a painful incident (UCS) while the dentist drilled a hole in one of my teeth (see Figure I). I may notice that the next time I hear the sound of the drill (CS), I will respond with anxiety. This response will occur even if drill doesn't touch the tooth. This is because I have learned to associate the sound of the drill with a fear of pain. This could become a learned (conditioned) response to a danger signal that has predictive value in a potentially harmful situation. Consequently, I may gradually learn a behavior pattern of avoiding dental treatments.

A second phenomenon that appears to play an important role in the maintenance of anxiety is known as operant conditioning. It has been found that if a particular behavior is consistently followed by a satisfying consequence or a reward such behavior is more likely to recur. Conversely, behavior which is followed by unpleasant consequences or punishment will tend to occur less frequently. Thus, if I am rewarded by the relief of anxiety each time I successfully avoid a dental treatment, my fear, and the associated avoidance behavior, could become uncontrollable. In addition, through the principle of 'generalization' my fear could carry over to similar stimuli and may ultimately include dental practices, whether dangerous or not. Eventually, even the mere word 'dentist' may become anxiety provoking. A further problem is that the tendency to escape or to avoid anxiety-provoking stimuli or situations prevents me from learning that these, in fact, may not be as dangerous as they seem.

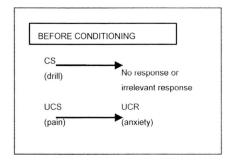

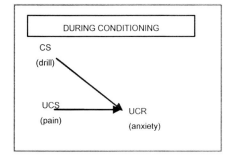

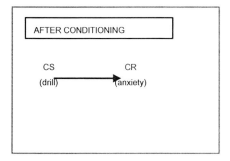

Figure 1. Classical conditioning

Indeed, the literature on anxieties and phobias suggests that the problem of clinically relevant anxiety can best be understood by the application of the principle of classical conditioning (Davey, 1987). Evidence for the contention that dental anxiety is acquired through conditioning experiences was provided by Davey (1989) and De Jongh, Muris, Ter Horst and Duyx (1995). Both studies found that the dental history of anxious patients was marked by a higher proportion of painful treatments than the history of patients who reported to feel relaxed about dental treatment. In addition, it was found that dental anxiety was related to both the extent to which earlier dental treatments are perceived as painful, and the extent to which these incidents were reported as traumatic (De Jongh *et al.*, 1995). Related to this, it was found that people who did experience traumatic, painful events, but did not acquire anxiety, reported a history of dental treatments which is characterized by a phenomenon known as 'latent inhibition' (Lubow, 1973). Latent inhibition predicts that individuals acquire dental anxiety less easily when they have received a number of relatively painless treatments prior to the conditioning event. Indeed, it was found that the anxiety level of people who had a relatively long period of painless encounters in the dental situation before they received their first painful or otherwise traumatic treatment was significantly lower than that of people who had a much shorter period between their first dental treatment and their first traumatic experience (De Jongh *et al.*, 1995).

What type of conditioning experience may cause long lasting anxiety about dental treatment? In one study among 37 highly anxious patients who attended a dental fear clinic (mean age 35.3 years, age range 16-57) four different categories of events that could explain the acquisition of their anxiety were identified (De Jongh, Aartman & Brand, 2003). A majority of the patients (56.2%) reported an event involving pain or loss of control (e.g., feeling helpless). Other categories consisted of events involving negative behavior or personality of the dentist (e.g., dentist who made belittling remarks; 28,1%), serious treatment failures (e.g., filling or extracting a healthy tooth; 6.3%) and miscellaneous (e.g., embarrassing situation; 9.4%). It was found that 86.5% of these highly anxious individuals indicated that they had experienced a horrific dental event which could explain the onset of their dental phobia. The estimated number of years ago that this event took place ranged from 0 to 43 years, with an average of 18 years (De Jongh, Aartman & Brand, 2003)

A COGNITIVE PERSPECTIVE ON THE ACQUISITION AND MAINTENANCE OF DENTAL ANXIETY

In the previous paragraph classical conditioning was proposed to explain the acquisition of anxiety as a consequence of such experiences (e.g., Lautch, 1971). According to this principle, neutral stimuli acquire painful properties and become conditioned stimuli (CS) through being paired with unconditioned stimuli (UCS) that naturally evoke anxiety. However, there are a number of the difficulties with the conditioning account of fears and phobias (e.g., Rachman, 1977). For example, many people who experience a trauma paired with a stimulus or a situation fail to develop a subsequent fear of that stimulus or situation. Another phenomenon that has raised questions about conditioning processes is that many phobic individuals appear to be unable to recall any trauma at the time their anxiety started to express itself.

Consequently, it is possible that anxiety reactions in the dental situation are the result of a more complex course of events than classical conditioning *per se*. In response to the notion that dental anxiety cannot solely be explained by traumatic conditioning experiences, a cognitive perspective on anxiety has been proposed as an additional model to explain dental patients' anxiety reactions (De Jongh, 1995). To better understand the cognitive perspective on dental anxiety, the more general aspects of the cognitive model are explained first.

According to the cognitive approach to human functioning, people are active processors of information and think, plan and make decisions on the basis of remembered information. Cognitive psychologists assert that emotional reactions, such as anxiety, often occur in response to environmental stimuli or situations, but that these reactions are influenced by individuals' interpretations of the events, rather than by the characteristics of the event itself. An essential role is attributed to the 'cognitive appraisal' of the individual: the interpretation of events and the perceived ability to deal with them (Lazarus & Folkman, 1984). These interpretations are believed to have direct and indirect effects on physiological processes, behavioral reactions, thoughts, and emotional distress. Cognitive models of emotional disorders not only encompass conscious phenomena (such as expectations, mental images, and the verbal content of one's thoughts), but also automatic or subconscious phenomena, such as the ways in which we seek, process and store information.

In the past two decades there has been increased interest in cognitive psychology and cognitive aspects of psychopathology. It is generally assumed that cognitions and cognitive processes are considered to play a role in various anxiety disorders (Beck, Emery & Greenberg, 1985; Hibbert, 1984; Ingram, 1989; Ingram & Kendall, 1987). A number of studies have investigated their significance for understanding the mechanisms underlying dental anxiety. For example, it has been found that anxiety and avoidance related to dental treatment are linked to negative expectations concerning future danger. An example of this is that fearful patients experience dental treatment as more painful than their non anxious counterparts (Wardle, 1982). Furthermore, anxious dental patients, in contrast to those showing little or no anxiety, demonstrate a tendency to strongly exaggerate the discomfort of dental treatment, expecting much more pain than they subsequently experience (Kent, 1984, Linsay, Wege & Yates, 1984; Wardle, 1984). According to Wardle (1984) the expectations of future pain and discomfort should be regarded as negative cognitions that produce anxiety.

With regard to a cognitive perspective on dental anxiety, the work of Beck and colleagues (Beck, 1976; Beck, 1991; Beck, Laude & Bohnert, 1974) is a valuable source for understanding the processes that are involved. In considering Beck's cognitive model of emotional disorders, a distinction should be made between two different levels of disturbed thinking: automatic thoughts and dysfunctional assumptions. The term negative *automatic thoughts* pertains to thoughts or images which are present in specific situations when an individual is anxious[1]. The terms *dysfunctional assumptions* and *rules* refer to general beliefs that individuals hold about the world, others or themselves. This is known as the cognitive triad. According to Beck these beliefs operate without the person's awareness and are embodied in so called *schemata*. Environmental stimuli would be selected, filtered and interpreted on the basis of these unconscious and irrational schemata (Beck, Emery & Greenberg, 1985). The common cognitive theme in beliefs and assumptions in anxiety is related to an overestimation of danger as well as an underestimation of one's coping abilities. It is assumed that once a schema is activated, it largely determines the individual's thinking and attentional activity. In practice this would mean that once anxious individuals are confronted with a threatening situation they would focus their attention to information which is consistent with their existing schemata and ignore evidence that is inconsistent with their schemata and negative expectations.

---

[1] Beck uses the word cognitions as a more technical term for automatic thoughts. Cognition as a singular noun refers to various processes in cognitive or information processing, such as perception, interpretation, and recall. Building from a detailed differentiation of various dimensions of 'cognition' (cognitive propositions, cognitive operations, cognitive products, and cognitive structures) others (Ingram & Kendall, 1987) proposed a cognitive component model of anxiety. In this model both specific critical features (schematic content and functioning, temporal distortions, and task-irrelevant thoughts), and common features (self-absorption, automatic processing, capacity limitations, and cognitive asymmetry) are described and considered as associated with anxiety.

THE NATURE AND CONTENT OF COGNITIONS RELATED TO DENTISTRY

To obtain more insight into the ways people think about frightening situations, in the 1970s, Beck and his colleagues started to explore the thoughts of anxious individuals. Research on patients suffering from generalized anxiety disorder (GAD) revealed that almost all patients, during moments of anxiety, reported ideation (images and automatic thoughts) revolving around psychological impairment or loss of control, failure and inability to cope, humiliation and rejection, physical injury, illness and death (Beck, Laude & Bohnert, 1974). Similar themes were reported by Mathews and Shaw (1977) and Butler, Gelder, Hibbert, Cullington and Klimes (1987). Relationships between thoughts and anxiety are repeatedly found, although thoughts associated with anxiety seem not always to be catastrophic in nature (e.g., Rimm, Janda, Lancaster, Nahl & Dittmar, 1977).

During the 1980s, in addressing the cognitive side of dental anxiety, the question arose whether dental patients also have negative cognitions, for instance, revolving around negative aspects of treatment. In this respect the work of Prins (1985) is particularly interesting. Prins interviewed children while they waited for treatment and as they sat in the dentist's chair, in order to obtain information on their internal dialogues. A majority of the children reported some form of self-speech. Most of the reported self talk came from the highly anxious children. Positive self-statements were found only in children with little or no anxiety. The low anxious children also showed more 'not thinking of anything' and 'neutral' thought behavior. Conversely, the highly anxious children reported self-statements indicating a preoccupation with external aversive stimuli, with the threat of pain and with escape fantasies. A relationship was found between type of self-talk (positive versus negative) and degree of anxiety. High anxiety was predominantly associated with the occurrence of negative internal self-talk.

High correlations between occurrence of negative thoughts and severity of dental anxiety appear not only to occur in children. Research among students (Kent & Gibbons, 1987) and anxious dental patients (De Jongh & Ter Horst, 1993; De Jongh, Muris, Ter Horst, Van Zuuren & de Wit, 1994) shows that high dentally anxious adults, compared with those with average or low dental anxiety, are more inclined to report thoughts indicating exaggerated or unrealistic expectations of dental treatment. It would seem that when treatment is imminent almost all patients, whether anxious or not, have negative thoughts, but highly anxious patients have a significantly greater number of such thoughts than their low-anxious counterpart (De Jongh, Muris, Ter Horst, Van Zuuren & de Wit, 1994).

With regard to the content of cognitions related to dental anxiety De Jongh and Ter Horst (1993) identified seven interpretable categories of self-statements (see Table II). They found that all patients reported thought content which in some way related to their fears, while positive self-statements were not at all present. The majority of patients (59%) reported one or more thoughts related to a sense of lack or loss of control (e.g., "I have no control over what happens"), about panicking (e.g., "I can't get away from here, I am stuck") and thoughts about choking (e.g., "I think I'm going to choke"). This category accounted for 23 percent of the total number of reported thoughts. Other thoughts referred to patients' personality (e.g., I'm just a neurotic"), catastrophic ideas about treatment (e.g., "I hope he doesn't lose control of the drill") and ideas about their teeth (e.g., "My teeth are rotten anyway"). Only a small proportion of the thoughts consisted of mental images (10%). These mental images related to being treated (e.g., images of instruments), about their teeth (e.g., images of teeth falling out) or were re-experiences of previous dental experiences (e.g., "I see a picture of a long corridor with a man in a white coat at the end of it").

Table II. Types of thoughts related to dental treatment

	% of thoughts reported	% of patients
1. Thoughts about one's own functioning (e.g., losing control, panicking, fainting)	23	59
2. Thoughts about one's own teeth	16	47
3. Thoughts about treatment, e.g., pain	14	44
4. Thoughts about one's own personality (troublesome, tense, anxious)	11	41
5. Thoughts about anxiety itself	7	26
6. Thoughts about embarrassment	5	23
7. Thoughts about the dentist	5	23
8. Mental images	9	26
9. Miscellaneous	8	29

The results of other studies underscored the qualitative difference between the thoughts of highly anxious patients and their low anxious counterparts (De Jongh, Muris, Schoenmakers & Ter Horst, 1995; De Jongh, Muris, Merckelbach & Schoenmakers, 1995). For example, while low dental anxiety patients mainly seem to be concerned with pain, the thoughts of highly dental anxious people largely pertain to worrying about possible negative outcomes of treatment in general. In other words, the quality of thinking of a highly anxious dental patient can best be characterized in terms of 'catastrophizing'; that is, the tendency "...to dwell on the worst possible outcome of any situation in which there is a possibility of an unpleasant outcome" (Beck, Emery & Greenberg, 1985, p. 33)[2]. In this respect, there are many similarities with cognitive distortions found in other types of phobias, such as spider phobia (Arntz, Lavey, van den Berg & van Rijsoort, 1993), claustrophobia (Shafran, Booth & Rachman, 1993), and in other anxiety disorders, such as panic disorder (e.g., Street, Craske & Barlow, 1989).

Although it is clear that the negative content of anxious individuals' cognitions has a predominantly anxiety-promoting character, with regard to subjects showing less anxiety it is more difficult to speculate on the role of cognitions. For instance, it is unclear whether low anxiety is more closely related to the active use of positive self-statements or to a better control of negative thinking, interrupting it or replacing it with more suitable thoughts.

---

[2] Note that there are many similarities with the work on worrying about imminent and future dangers (e.g., Tallis & Eysenck, 1994).

ESTIMATING THE PROBABILITY OF NEGATIVE DENTAL EVENTS

Even though individuals suffering from dental phobia report having thoughts indicative of negative and catastrophic happenings during treatment, this in itself seems insufficient to explain high anxiety levels, for there appear to be also anxious patients who report relatively few negative cognitions (Kent & Gibbons, 1987). Accordingly, other (cognitive) factors contribute to the maintenance and exacerbation of dental anxiety. Believability of peoples' thought content might be such a factor.

Research suggests that highly anxious individuals, compared to those low in anxiety, not only experience a higher frequency of thoughts concerning certain negative or aversive events, but also show a greater belief in their negative thoughts (De Jongh *et al.*, 1995b). Therefore, it would seem relevant to investigate whether dentally phobic individuals are inclined to exaggerate the *probability* of the occurrence of situations they fear. This was studied by Kent (1985a), who asked dental patients to describe their expectations of a forthcoming treatment. The aim was to investigate whether highly anxious patients were generally more negative, that is to say more 'catastrophic' in their assessment of the dental treatment to come - and of the complications that might arise - than patients with a low level of anxiety. It emerged that highly anxious patients indeed saw the likelihood of unpleasant events as being greater than their low anxious counterparts. This phenomenon proved to be independent of gender and of the frequency of dental attendance. These findings suggest that individuals with a dental phobia are afraid, not so much of the amount of dental work that might be required, but of the perceived probability of unpleasant consequences. In other words, dentally phobic individuals have a heightened subjective estimation of the likelihood that dreaded and unpleasant events will actually occur. This is in line with research on other anxiety disorders showing that anxious individuals generally hold unfavorable occurrences to be more likely, more negative and more threatening than do non-anxious individuals (Butler & Mathews, 1983; Kent 1985).

The pessimistic attitude of anxious patients, compared to non-anxious patients, is not only expressed in the tendency of anxious individuals to overestimate the likelihood of dreaded and unpleasant events (De Jongh *et al.*, 1995). It appears that dentally anxious individuals, compared to patients who indicate not being anxious, also believe to be less able to apply treatment strategies (relaxation and distraction) that might be helpful to cope with dental treatment, expect themselves to be more difficult to treat, and to be more nervous and helpless (De Jongh *et al.*, 1995a).

CONTROL OVER COGNITIONS

Bandura (1986) has used the term *self-efficacy* to describe individuals' perceived ability to exercise control over their own behavior. The same principle would seem to be applicable to cognitive processes.

In a study carried out by Kent and Gibbons (1987) students were presented with a number of negative thoughts and were asked to indicate how well they had been able to control these thoughts over given periods. These periods were: the week before dental treatment, the day before treatment, the morning of the actual day, on the way to the dental surgery and in the dentist's waiting room. It was found that the more imminent the treatment, the more difficult it became for the students to control the thoughts or to dismiss their negative thoughts that had been suggested to them. Highly anxious subjects indicated to have more difficulties with controlling these thoughts than did low anxious persons.

Kent (1987) also investigated whether dental patients showing high anxiety levels also felt less able to control their cognitions, their behavioral and their physiological reactions. The results indicated that this was indeed the case: highly anxious patients expected to be less able to control these reactions than did less anxious patients. Thus, besides the occurrence of negative cognitions and the appraisal of the likelihood of unpleasant occurrences, a significant role is played by the degree to which dental phobic individuals are able to keep their own negative thoughts under control.

In another study it was found that perceived cognitive control decreases with the increasing imminence of dental treatment (De Jongh, Muris, Ter Horst, Van Zuuren & De Wit, 1994). While anticipating dental treatment, highly anxious patients appear to feel less able to control their negative thoughts than their low-anxiety counterparts. A series of stepwise regression analyses revealed that both the number of negative cognitions and perceived cognitive control accounted for 75 percent of the variance in dental trait anxiety.

MEMORY

Memories are subject to change. It has been shown, for instance, that as time passes memories tend to become gradually more consistent with earlier experiences and beliefs. The way this process might work with regard to dental treatment has been described in a study by Kent (1985b). Patients were about to receive dental treatment to estimate how much pain they expected to undergo. Immediately after the treatment they were asked to describe how painful it had actually been. Three months later this was followed up with a question about how much pain they remembered having experienced at that time. Patients having little anxiety about dental treatment showed quite stable scores across all three time categories; both their predictions of future discomfort and their reports of experienced discomfort were fairly accurate. Among anxious patients, however, memories of the event differed markedly from the judgments they had expressed immediately after being treated. These memories appeared to have been gradually modified and corresponded more closely to the predictions made before treatment began.

According to Kent (1985b), these results indicate that patients' memories of dental treatments are subject to an important anxiety-preserving mechanism: the principle of 'mood-dependent recall'. Mood-dependent recall refers to the relationship between mood and memory: it holds that memories of past events become more vivid when the subject is in the same emotional mood as that which characterized the original event. Kent based this idea on research carried out by Bower (1981), who found that people in a good mood had predominantly pleasant recollections while those in a dejected mood tended to recall more unpleasant events. On the basis of his findings Bower concluded that a given state of mind raises the likelihood that the events which first generated this state of mind would be recalled. These recollections are also capable of evoking the original emotions, thereby forming a vicious cycle (see also Teasdale, 1983; Teasdale & Taylor, 1981). Kent (1989) argues that patients anxious about an imminent dental appointment are more susceptible to recollections of unpleasant and painful dental experiences than are non-anxious patients, thereby creating a vicious cycle that perpetuates anxiety.

Thus, even in case a given dental treatment is not as unpleasant as expected, the recollected discrepancy between the predicted and the experienced discomfort is available to memory only for a short time. In many cases by the time of the patient's next appointment, a few months later, anxiety has returned. Memories, instead of conforming to experiences themselves, seem to undergo a gradual modification that corresponds most to the original expectations. Moreover, due to the process of 'mood-dependent recall' people in a more despondent mood may more likely to recall other unpleasant events, which can further heighten their level of psychological distress.

The principle of mood-dependent recall would explain unexpectedly favorable event is perceived entirely differently by a highly anxious patient than by someone showing little or no anxiety. That is, the latter person is more inclined to dismiss a painful experience as non-typical, while a dentally high anxious patient regards a pain-free visit as the exception that proves the rule and is relieved at having got off so lightly. This might explain the intractability of the anxiety problem, and illustrate why, in many cases, non-traumatic treatments in themselves are not enough to dispel dental anxiety once it has developed.

FOCUS OF ATTENTION

Studies focusing on unraveling the process of anxiety have made increasing use of cognitive experimental research methods, in which cognitive processes such as attention and memory are studied by means of laboratory tasks, such as the dichotic listening task (e.g., Burgess, Jones, Robertson, Radcliffe & Emerson, 1981), the Stroop task (e.g., Mathews & MacLeod, 1986) and the probe detection task (e.g., MacLeod, Mathews & Tata, 1986). This kind of research has revealed that, in general, anxious individuals tend to direct their attention to threatening information, while non-anxious persons are inclined to move attention away from threatening material. It appears that trait anxious subjects demonstrate a selective bias, and that processing resources are preferentially allocated to emotional information. This phenomenon is described in the literature as *attentional bias* or *preattentive bias* (e.g., Eysenck, 1992). Although it has repeatedly been found that anxiety disordered patients and subjects with high levels of trait anxiety show an attentional bias when confronted with distressing stimuli, it remains unclear whether anxiety leads to a bias in attention or vice versa. Possibly, a link exists between the attentional bias phenomenon and the cognitive style people employ in order to deal with threatening information. Some interesting research was carried out in this area by Byrne (1969), who distinguished between 'repressors' and 'sensitizers'. Repressors tend to systematically avoid threatening stimuli, whereas sensitizers are inclined to seek knowledge about them (for a comparable distinction see Miller, 1989).

Since there are indications that an existing state of anxiety leads to an 'attentional bias', a selective perception of the environment which focuses on potentially distressing stimuli, it is not inconceivable that in the dental situation too, existing anxiety leads to a constant, unconscious alertness for potentially threatening stimuli. Conceivably, this would make a dentally anxious patient relatively vulnerable for 'picking-up' salient stimuli (probes, needles, drills etc.). Such a mechanism, if it exists, may contribute to the maintenance of the problem by elevating the individual's state anxiety level, which, again, may magnify a processing bias, creating a vicious cycle of anxiety and vigilance.

Similarly, at the physiological level, attention processes have been found to be capable in perpetuating and exacerbating anxiety. An explanatory model for this phenomenon has been proposed by Clark (1986). He argues that negative cognitions of people suffering from panic attacks provoke anxiety by drawing attention to certain bodily sensations (such as a rise in heart rate, breathlessness, or sweating) that, in turn, are interpreted in a catastrophic fashion. The validity of such a mechanism has been supported by other research in which medication artificially lowered the heart rate, thereby reducing dental anxiety (Liu, Milgrom & Fiset, 1991). The same might hold true for pain during treatment itself. Experimental research has indicated that in the case for fear of pain, attention is directed to the pain sensations and this actually exacerbates the pain reaction (Arntz, Dreessen & Merckelbach, 1991). These data are in accordance with the finding that pain sensations increase when a subject's attention is focused on the pain and decreases when attention is diverted elsewhere (e.g., Turk, Meichenbaum & Genest, 1983).

To date, there is still little research focusing on the role of attention processes in dental phobic individuals. However, one study investigated whether high dentally anxious individuals have an automatic inclination to direct their attention to threat-related stimuli rather than to neutral stimuli (De Jongh, Muris, Merckelbach & Ter Horst, 1995). The results showed that dental anxiety and the extent to which subjects directed their gaze to threat-related slides were not significantly correlated. Moreover, no evidence was found to support the contention that the coping styles of monitoring (i.e. seeking threat-relevant information) and blunting (i.e. avoiding threat-related information) modulate attention processes. Accordingly, the data yielded no support for a relationship between anxiety and duration of attention. Yet, it remains possible that the phenomenon of attentional bias is restricted to the early stages of the appraisal process and cannot be applied to situations in which individuals are exposed to real-life threats for a relatively long period of time. Once a person has become aware of the stimuli and has judged the severity of the threat he or she can choose to either pay more attention to it, or to avoid it (see also Muris, Merckelbach & De Jongh, 1995).

MAINTENANCE OF DENTAL ANXIETY AND AVOIDANCE

What are the mechanisms that account for the maintenance of dental phobia in the long term? Behavioral theories of anxiety disorders posit that pathological fears are acquired through classical conditioning processes, but maintained through operant conditioning (i.e., reinforcement) of avoidance behavior (Mowrer, 1960). This principle also seems to play a role in the maintenance of dental phobia. People are rewarded by the relief of anxiety if they avoid dental treatment. However, besides this, dental phobia has a number of characteristics that are rather unique and which also contribute to the maintenance of the problem. Unlike most other types of simple or specific phobias such as acrophobia or spider phobia, as a result of their inclination to avoid confrontations with dentists and other dental stimuli, individuals' health is at stake. That is, the oral health of a person who has not visited a dentist for many years is mostly in a bad state. According to Berggren (1984) this results in feelings of shame and inferiority, which would contribute to the maintenance of anxiety. Although it is likely that avoidance would result in the deteriorating of the oral state, Berggren's model does not entirely explains how feelings of shame and inferiority would cause a heightened level of dental anxiety (De Jongh, 1995).

The incorporation of cognitive factors into Berggren's model could possibly contribute to a better understanding of the mechanisms underlying dental anxiety and dental phobia. For example, people tend to evaluate the nature of a possible threat by determining the severity of the potential injury and the probability of its occurrance, while assessing their capabilities for dealing with it (Lazarus & Folkman, 1984; Beck, Emery & Greenberg, 1985). This means that if a person judges the threat of dental treatment to be low relative to his way of dealing with the situation, he or she may choose to seek treatment. Conversely, if this person judges the risk to be high relative to his coping resources, a further increase in anxiety may occur.

When dental treatment has been avoided for several years, the patient's oral health state may be in a state of neglect whereby many interventions are needed, including, extractions, endodontic interventions and surgical procedures. Most people are well aware of the poor state of their oral health. However, phobic individuals, who have long put off a visit to the dentist, tend to underestimate the health of their teeth and to overestimate the amount of dental work usually required. In addition, they are inclined to imagine catastrophic possibilities about what might go wrong during their appointment. Conceivably, the prospect of deep fillings, root canal treatments, and extractions may easily aggravate their worrying: the more treatments, the more might go wrong. This, in turn, enforces their present avoidance behaviour, thereby further aggravating the deterioration of the oral state, which in most cases has serious consequences for peoples' social life (see Figure I). Thus, dental phobics' cognitive appraisal of one's oral condition in relation to the dangers of a possible dental treatment is of considerable importance. Not only from a theoretical perspective, but also because anticipatory anxiety could maintain avoidance behavior, which greatly compromizes the health and well-being of the dental patient.

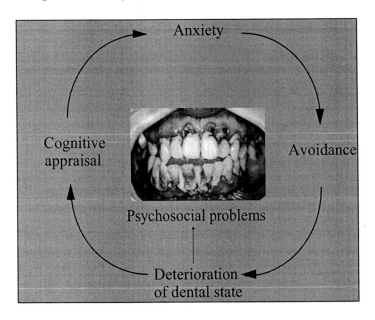

Figure I. A model of dental anxiety, incorporating the cognitive side

PHARMACOLOGICAL SUPPORT

There are a variety of ways to help the fearful patient. For example, in some countries it is possible to refer patients to dental fear clinics. Here it is determined which treatment option is most acceptable, suitable and effective for the individual patient. For example, it is generally recognized that it is important to establish a trusting relationship with the patient, and provide mental support when the patient indicates he has a hard time. Also, the provision of accurate explanations about what will happen and what type of experiences he or she might expect ('sensation information') are important interventions (De Jongh, McGoldrick, Meijerink-Anderson, in press).

In the more severe cases anxious individuals are frequently referred for pharmacological or sedation approaches, such as oral medication, nitrous oxide sedation, intravenous sedation and general anesthesia, are sometimes used to alleviate patients' apprehension. With regard to the application of inhalation sedation (nitrous oxide sedation), there is some scientific support for an anxiety reducing effect (Willumsen, Vassend & Hoffard, 2001). However, it seems that, to establish a significant level of anxiety reduction, this treatment has to be embedded in a general, anxiety management approach, including consideration for explanations, optimal predictability and control.

If necessary, a limited use of pharmacological means, for instance a prescribed pre-medication policy, can be applied to support regular dental treatment. Often this occurs by prescribing benzodiazepine (e.g., Lorazepam, Midazolam) prior to the treatment of the patient. There is evidence to suggest that the use of sedatives preceding the treatment is less effective than, for instance, the use of relaxation techniques and does not seem to reduce anxiety in the longer (Jöhren, Jackowsi & Gängler, 2000; Thom, Sartory & Jöhren, 2000). Therefore, the option for sedation should mainly be considered as a convenience to overcome the backlog of required care. Since there is little evidence that sedation alone effectively treats dental phobia, a combination of a behavioral approach with clinical expertise in this area may results in a more successful outcome in the long run (De Jongh, McGoldrick, Meijerink-Anderson, 2005). In other words, it appears to be more useful that the patient is enabled to attribute success to (active) personal coping, rather than to (passive) drug administration.

TEACHING OF COPING TECHNIQUES

With regard to the management of the dentally anxious patient an effective strategy is teaching the patient specific strategies for stress management and emotional control to be applied during dental treatment (Moses & Hollandsworth, 1985). Fortunately, many patients have learned some form of stress management skills at work or in another area of their personal life. In this respect adapting existing strategies can be a short-cut to effective patient management.

To this end, particularly the application of distraction appears to be an effective strategy. Distraction includes any technique which directs the patient's attention away from sensations or emotional reactions produced by an aversive stimulus. The principle of limited attentional capacity, which simply asserts that the conscious allocation of attention cannot be given to two competing stimuli simultaneously, predicts that expending effort on a challenging or absorbing task can consume one's attention to such an extent that there is less attention left for a possible present painful stimulus. Because of its' distracting capacity certain challenging games and exercise deserve a rightful place in the armamentarium of useful cognitive techniques for the control of pain and anxiety during dental treatment. Distraction techniques include mental exercises such as counting backwards from 1000 in 7s, remembering a favourite walk in detail and, in case of a child, by asking them to think of animals beginning with each letter of the alphabet in turn. Other examples are the instruction to concentrate on abdominal breathing, listening to favourite music, watching visual information (a poster, fish tank, television images), playing ping-pong games or solving mind games (Frere, Crout & Yorty, 2001).

Controlled studies indicate that the higher the level of attention or distraction required of the task at hand, the higher the chance of having a positive effect on the level of tension and anxiety (Corah, Gale, Pace & Seyrek, 1981; Katcher, Segal & Beck, 1984; Syrek, Corah & Pace, 1995). To this end, techniques involving visual distraction - for example paying aimed attention to a fish bowl or a poster on the ceiling, video entertainment and video games – have been found to be more effective than auditory ones (Katcher, Segal & Beck, 1984; Syrek, Corah & Pace, 1995).

Another coping method to enable the patient to deal with the stressful situation is the use of relaxation technique, such as relaxation of muscle groups, or imaginal visualisation (Lamb & Strand, 1980). This can be achieved by means of straightforward instructions via headphones (Corah, Gale & Illig, 1979), by progressively teaching the patient to relax in difficult situations (progressive relaxation; Bernstein & Carlsson, 1993) or via 'applied relaxation' (Öst, 1986). The use of applied relaxation has been found to be an effective method in the longer term (Willumsen, Vassend & Hoffard, 2001). Hypnosis is a more specialised method of relaxation and is combined with a deep form of concentration (Moore, Brødsgaard & Abrahamson, 2002). However, there are indications that the use of hypnosis is a less effective strategy for reducing anxiety in the long run than an exposure based treatment program (Moore, Abrahamson & Brødsgaard, 1996).

EXPOSURE IN VIVO

Psychotherapies involving behavioral procedures have been established as empirically supported treatments for anxiety disorders and use experimentally established learning principles to extinguish anxious responses to inappropriate feared stimuli (e.g., Chambless & Ollendick, 2001). The basic assumption in this approach is that a fear response gradually extinguishes when the provoking stimulus (CS; for instance, the sound of the drill or an injection needle) is repeatedly presented, but not followed by an aversive event (UCS), for example one involving pain. With repeated and prolonged exposure, anxiety responses gradually diminish, a process known as habituation (Wolpe, 1958).

Other theorists have postulated that the anxiety reduction seen following exposure may be explained by the disconfirming nature of the experience (Foa & Kozak, 1986). According to cognitive therapists exposure procedures can explicitly be used to test patients' predictions about how dangerous a situation is. By setting up a situation with the phobic cues present the patient can test their catastrophic beliefs and assumptions (i.e., carrying out a 'behavioral experiment'). Highly anxious individuals gain an experience in which the catastrophe they fears does not occur, thereby disconfirming their dysfunctional erroneous beliefs. This corrective information about the dangerousness of the feared situations may convincingly 'prove' that their fear is unfounded.

Systematic desensitization was the first behavioral procedure whereby a systematic and repeated exposure to fearful stimuli was used (Wolpe, 1958). During this procedure patients are firstly trained in muscular relaxation, after which patients are encouraged to gradually expose themselves to a hierarchy of fearful situations, while at the same time remaining relaxed. This procedure can be applied either individually or in a group setting (Gatchel, 1980; Moore & Brødsgaard, 1994), in imaginal (*in vitro*), with use of video confrontation (Carlson, Linde & Öhman, 1980), a computer program (Coldwell, Getz & Milgrom et al., 1998) or in real life (*in vivo*; Bernstein & Kleinknecht, 1982). Since imaginary procedures are generally found to be less effective than exposure in vivo, exposure in vivo is generally accepted as the treatment of choice (Emmelkamp, Bouman & Scholing, 1989). Also research in dental phobia has indicated that imaginal exposure has significantly less impact on avoidance behaviors, - and therefore the arrangement of dental appointments - compared to the exposure treatment with the use of video images (Moore & Brødsgaard, 1994; Hammarstrand, Berggren & Hakeberg, 1995) or exposure to real life dental situations (Bernstein & Kleinknecht, 1982). There is general consensus that systematic exposure to patients' anxiety-provoking stimuli (for instance, an injection needle or the sound of the drill) is the treatment of choice for specific fears and phobias (Moore, Brødsgaard & Abrahamson, 2002; Gauthier, Savard & Hallé, 1985; Moore, Brødsgaard & Berggren, 1991; Smith, Kroege & Lyon, 1990). However, it should be noted that there are indications that exposure therapy is less effective if it is combined with any other methods (Harrison, Berggren & Carlsson, 1989). Therefore, it is suggested that general coping strategies should be taught prior to the exposure therapy (Gauthier, Savard & Hallé, 1985).

A specific category of patients are those with a blood-injury-injection phobia who have a natural tendency to faint (Vögele, Coles, Wardle et al., 2003; De Jongh, Bongaarts & Vermeule, 1998). It is generally recommended that patients with blood-injury-injection phobia are taught a specific technique called 'applied tension' prior to exposing them to the phobic stimulus. By using this technique, whereby the muscles are tensed and the blood pressure is artificially increased, the possibility of fainting appears to be reduced (Öst, Fellenius & Sterner, 1991).

COGNITIVE INTERVENTIONS

In practice, exposure therapy is often combined with teaching the patient cognitive coping strategies, for example using pleasant and positive imagery, identifying, challenging and modifying negative and unhelpful thoughts, and replacing these with more helpful, positive and realistic thoughts or coping statements (Getka & Glass, 1992). It has also been investigated whether it is possible to influence anxious patients' irrational thinking patterns in order to alleviate dental anxiety in this way (Beck, 1976). The notion of reducing dental anxiety by modifying dysfunctional believes is supported by the strong relationship between negative beliefs and self-statements of dental phobics and their scores on measures of dental trait anxiety. Although it should be concluded that there is not enough evidence available yet to evaluate the value of cognitive therapy for dental phobia, results of an one session cognitive restructuring intervention support the notion that altering negative cognitions represents a potential change mechanism for dental anxiety (De Jongh, Muris, Ter Horst, Van Zuuren, Schoenmakers & Makkes, 1995).

In this study fifty-two patients were randomly assigned to one of three conditions: cognitive restructuring (modification of negative cognitions), provision of information (about oral health and dental treatment), and a waiting list control condition. Both interventions lasted one hour maximum. In comparison with the waiting list control condition and the information intervention condition, the cognitive intervention condition not only showed a large decrease in frequency and believability of negative cognitions, but also exhibited a clear decline in dental trait anxiety (see Figure II). Analysis at a one year follow-up demonstrated a further, drastic reduction in dental anxiety in both intervention conditions, whereas the difference among these conditions was not maintained.

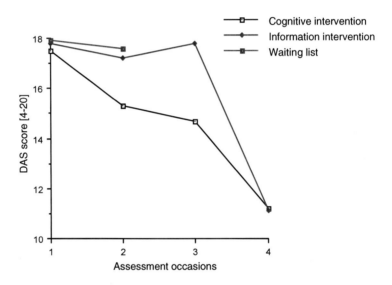

Figure II. Dental Anxiety Scale (DAS) scores for the three conditions at baseline (1), prior to the first dental appointment (2), at one month follow-up (3), and at one year follow-up (4).

The finding that in the long run both intervention groups showed a similar reduction of anxiety suggests that the exposure effects of repeated confrontations with the dental setting after the cognitive intervention 'overruled' its' initial beneficial effects. With regard to adequate psychological treatment of dental anxiety it may be most useful to apply a combination of cognitive restructuring and (gradual) exposure to anxiety-provoking situations and to maintain such a cognitive-behavioral approach over a series of visits (De Jongh et al., 1995c).

CONCLUSIONS

It has been found that aversive or otherwise extremely frightening situations serve as powerful conditioning experiences and therefore play an important role in the acquisition of dental anxiety and dental phobia. The 1980s and 1990s have seen an increasing understanding of the role of cognitive phenomena in the etiology and maintenance of phobias in general. Also with regard to the maintenance of dental phobia there is a wide array of studies supporting the usefulness of applying a cognitive approach to this condition, indicating that phobic responding may well be maintained by a network of consciously available thoughts and beliefs about the phobic stimulus and interactions with that stimulus. For example, concerning the nature and content of dental patients' thoughts it appears that dental anxiety is highly associated with a marked tendency to produce thoughts (images and self-statements) and beliefs with a negative and often unrealistic content (De Jongh, Muris, Schoenmakers & Ter Horst, 1995). It is likely that negative expectations about dental treatment, as expressed in the content of individuals' thoughts and beliefs, can give cause for anxiety, but it is also possible that dental anxiety itself prompts negative expectations of dental treatment. Possibly, both mechanisms play a role, leading to a vicious cycle of anxiety and pessimistic expectations. Various other cognitive processes, such as attention and memory processes, may exacerbate this process further.

The results from studies investigating the relationship between cognitive factors and dental anxiety led to the development of a questionnaire that assesses frequency and believability of negative cognitions (beliefs and self-statements) related to dental treatment, the Dental Cognitions Questionnaire (DCQ; De Jongh, Muris, Schoenmakers, Ter Horst, 1995). The DCQ has been found to discriminate strongly between dental phobics and non-phobic subjects, showed good internal consistency, high test-retest reliability, and satisfactory concurrent validity. Furthermore, it appears that particular combinations of DCQ items are good predictors of the experience of anxiety during treatment.

With regard to the treatment of dental phobia, training patients in the use of coping skills seem to be a sensible investment (Moses & Hollandsworth, 1985). An even more useful approach may be the application of exposure *in vivo*. Exposure has been found to be highly effective in reducing fears related to dental instruments and other dental objects. Evidence derived from clinical trials indicates that patients benefit more from such an approach compared to treatment under general anaesthetic, both in terms of completing the treatment as well as long term dental health (Aartman, De Jongh & Makkes *et al.*, 1999; De Jongh, Van der Burg & Overmeir *et al.*, 2002;).

Cognitive restructuring, if applied in a non-threatening situation, might be an useful alternative as a first step after years of avoidance of dental care and less threatening than immediate exposure to the feared stimuli. If maladaptive cognitions of patients are challenged using the Socratic dialogue and more rational ways of looking at the dental situation are generated, this can influence the severity of dental trait anxiety in a positive way (De Jongh *et al.*, 1995c). A relative new development in the field of dental anxiety is the application of Eye Movement Desensitization and Reprocessing (EMDR). EMDR has been found to be a structured, non-invasive, and time-limited treatment for trauma-related anxiety disorders, including dental phobia (De Jongh, Van den Oord & Ten Broeke, 2002; Power, McGoldrick, Brown, *et al.*, 2002). This intervention method is primarily focused on resolving the memories of events that drives current symptoms. In contrast with the learning model which proposes a strategy of gradual exposures to the feared stimuli (CS-exposure) to extinguish the fear response, the primary goal in EMDR is the processing of traumatic memories, which are thought to be impaired.

Although severe and persistent dental anxiety calls for specialized treatment, perhaps the most important condition to successfully manage the stress of anxious individuals is the behavior of the dentist. His approach should consists of the provision of trust, patience, support, reassurance, and encouragement combined with a general anxiety reducing treatment style, whereby controllability and predictability for the patient are optimized and the patient is stimulized to confront new challenges. Careful use of such an approach will not only facilitate better tolerance for an individual appointment or procedure, but will enhance patients' willingness and ability to participate enthusiastically in a lifetime of dental maintenance and care.

However, since there appear to be considerable differences in types of anxious patients (Enneking, Milgrom, Weinstein & Getz, 1992; Moore, Brødsgaard, 1995; Roy-Byrne, Milgrom, Khoon-Mei, Weinstein, & Katon, 1994) one should be cautious in considering anxious patients as a homogeneous group in terms of treatment. Accordingly, in the future more effort should be put into investigating whether it would be fruitful to use more tailored treatment approaches that fit the idiosyncrasies of the individual patient (Acierno, Hersen & Van Hasselt, 1994; De Jongh, McGoldrick & Meijerink-Anderson, 2005; Milgrom & Weinstein, 1993).

REFERENCES

Aartman, I. H. A., De Jongh, A., Makkes, P. C., & Hoogstraten, J. (1999). Treatment modalities in a dental fear clinic and the relation with general psychopathology and oral health variables. *British Dental Journal, 186*, 467-471.

Arntz, A., Dreessen L., & Merckelbach, H. (1991). Attention, not anxiety, influences pain. *Behaviour Research and Therapy, 29,* 41-50.

Acierno, R., Hersen, M., & Van Hasselt, V. B. (1994). Remedying the Achilles heel of behavior research and therapy: Prescriptive matching of intervention and psychopathology. *Journal of Behavior Therapy and Experimental Psychiatry, 25,* 179-188.

Agras, W.S., Sylvester D., & Oliveau, DC. (1969). The epidemiology of common fears and phobias. *Comprehensive Psychiatry, 10,* 151-156.

Arntz, A., Lavy, E., van den Berg, G., & van Rijsoort, S. (1993). Negative beliefs of spider phobics: A psychometric evaluation of the spider phobia beliefs questionnaire. *Advances in Behaviour Research and Therapy, 15,* 257-277.

American Psychiatric Association (1994). *Diagnostic and statistical manual of mental disorders,* (4th ed.). Washington, DC: American Psychiatric Association.

Bandura, A. (1986). *Social foundations of thought and action.* Englewood Cliffs, NJ: Prentice-Hall.

Beck, A. (1976). *Cognitive therapy and emotional disorders.* New York: International Universities Press.

Beck, A. (1991). Cognitive therapy: A 30-year retrospective. *American Psychologist, 46,* 368-375.

Beck, A. T., Emery, G., & Greenberg, R. L. (1985). *Anxiety disorders and phobias: A cognitive perspective.* New York: Basic Books.

Beck, A. T., Laude, R., & Bohnert, M. (1974). Ideational components of anxiety neurosis. *Archives of General Psychiatry, 31,* 319-325.

Berggren, U. (1984). *Dental fear and avoidance. A study of etiology, consequences and treatment.* Academic dissertation University of Göteborg.

Bernstein, D. A., & Carlson, C. R. (1993). Progressive relaxation: abbreviated methods. In P. M. Lehrer, R. L. Woolfolk (Eds.), *Principles and practice of stress management* (pp. 53-87). New York: The Guilford Press.

Bernstein, D. A, & Kleinknecht, R. A. (1982). Multiple approaches to the reduction of dental fear. *Journal of Behavior Therapy and Experimental Psychiatry, 13,* 287-292.

Bernstein, D.A., Kleinknecht, R.A., & Alexander, L.D. (1979). Antecedents of dental fear. *Journal of Public Health Dentistry, 39,* 113-124.

Bower, G. H. (1981). Mood and memory. *American Psychologist, 36,* 129-148.

Burgess, I. S., Jones, L. M., Robertson, S. A., Radcliffe, W. N., & Emerson, E. (1981). The degree of control exerted by phobic and non-phobic verbal stimuli over the recognition behaviour of phobic and non-phobic subjects. *Behaviour Research and Therapy, 19,* 233-243.

Butler, G., Gelder, M., Hibbert, G., Cullington, A., & Klimes, I. (1987). Anxiety management: Developing effective strategies. *Behaviour Research and Therapy, 25,* 6, 517-522.

Butler, G., & Mathews, A. (1983). Cognitive processes in anxiety. *Advances in Behavior Therapy, 5,* 51-62.

Byrne, D. (1969). Repression-sensitization as a dimension of personality. In B. A. Maher (Ed.), *Progress in experimental personality research. Vol I,* 169-220. New York: Academic Press.

Carlsson, S. G., Linde, A., & Öhman, A. (1980). Reduction of tension in fearful dental patients. *Journal of the American Dental Association, 101,* 638-641.

Chambless, D. L., & Ollendick, T. H. (2001). Empirically supported psychological interventions: controversies and evidence. *Annual Review of Psychology, 52,* 685-716.

Clark, D. (1986). A cognitive approach to panic. *Behavior Research and Therapy, 4,* 461-470.

Coldwell, S. E, Getz, T., & Milgrom, P. *et al.,* (1998). CARL: A LabVIEW 3 computer program for conducting exposure therapy for the treatment of dental injection fear. *Behavior Research and Therapy, 36,* 429-441.

Corah, N. L., Gale, E. N., & Illig, S. J. (1979). Psychological stress reduction during dental procedures. *Journal of Dental Research, 58,* 1347-1351.

Corah, N. L., Gale, E. N., Pace, L, F., & Seyrek, S. K. (1981). Relaxation and musical programming as means of reducing psychological stress during dental procedures. *Journal of the American Dental Association, 103,* 232-234.

Davey, G. C. L. (1987). An integration of human and animal models of Pavlovian conditioning: associations, cognitions and attributions. In G.C.L. Davey (Ed), *Cognitive Processes and Pavlovian Conditioning in Humans.* Chichester: Wiley.

Davey, G. C. L. (1989). Dental phobias and anxieties: Evidence for conditioning processes in the acquisition and modulation of a learned fear. *Behaviour Research and Therapy, 27,* 51-58.

Davey, G. C. L. (1992). Characteristics of individuals with fear of spiders. *Anxiety Research, 4,* 299-314.

De Jongh, A., & Ter Horst, G. (1993). What do anxious patients think: An exploratory investigation of anxious dental patients' thoughts. *Community Dentistry and Oral Epidemiology, 21,* 221-3.

De Jongh, A. (1995). *Dental anxiety: A cognitive perspective.* Academisch proefschrift. Universiteit van Amsterdam. Ridderkerk: Ridderprint, 1995.

De Jongh, A., Aartman, I., & Brand, N. (2003). Trauma-related symptomatology in anxious dental patients. *Community Dentistry and Oral Epidemiology, 31,* 52-58.

De Jongh, A., Bongaarts, G., Vermeule, I., Visser, K., De Vos, P., & Makkes, P. (1998). Blood-injury-injection phobia and dental phobia. *Behaviour Research and Therapy, 36,* 971-982

De Jongh, A., McGoldrick, P., Meijerink-Anderson, M. (2005). Clinical Management of Dental Anxiety: What works for whom? *International Dental Journal, 55, 73-80.*

De Jongh, A., Muris, P., Merckelbach, H., & Schoenmakers, N. (1996). Suppression of dentist related thoughts. *Behavioural and Cognitive Psychotherapy,* 24, 117-126.

De Jongh, A., Muris, P., Merckelbach, H., & Ter Horst, G. (1995). Looking at threat-relevant stimuli: The role of anxiety and coping style. *Anxiety, Stress, and Coping, 8,* 37-45.

De Jongh, A., Muris, P., Schoenmakers, N., & Ter Horst, G. (1995b). Negative cognitions of dental phobics: Reliability and validity of the Dental Cognitions Questionnaire. *Behaviour Research and Therapy, 33,* 507-515.

De Jongh, A., Muris, P., Ter Horst, G., & Duyx, M. (1995a). Acquisition and maintenance of dental anxiety: The role of aversive experiences and cognitive factors. Behaviour Research and Therapy, 33, 205-210.

De Jongh, A., Muris, P., Ter Horst, G., Van Zuuren, F. J., & De Wit, C. A. (1994). Cognitive correlates of dental anxiety. *Journal of Dental Research, 73,* 561-566.

De Jongh, A., Muris, P., Ter Horst, G., Van Zuuren, F. J., Schoenmakers, N., & Makkes, P. (1995c). One-session cognitive treatment of dental phobia: Preparing dental phobics for treatment by restructuring negative cognitions. *Behaviour Research and Therapy, 33,* 947-954.

De Jongh, A., Van der Burg, J., van Overmeir, M., Aartman, I., & van Zuuren, F.J. (2002). Trauma-related sequelae in individuals with a high level of dental anxiety: Does this Interfere with treatment outcome? *Behaviour Research and Therapy, 40,* 1017-1029.

De Jongh, A., Van den Oord, H.J.M., & Ten Broeke, E. (2002). Efficacy of Eye Movement Desensitization and Reprocessing (EMDR) in the treatment of specific phobias: Four single-case studies on dental phobia. *Journal of Clinical Psychology, 58,* 1489-1503.

Emmelkamp, P.M.G., Bouman, T.K., & Scholing, A. (1989). *Anxiety Disorders. A practitioner's guide.* Chichester: Wiley & Sons.

Enneking, D., Milgrom, D., Weinstein, P., & Getz, T. (1992). Treatment outcomes for specific subtypes of dental fear: Preliminary clinical findings. *Special Care of Dentistry, 12,* 214-218.

Eysenck, M. W. (1992). *Anxiety: The cognitive perspective.* Hillsdale, NJ: Erlbaum.

Foa, E.B., & Kozak, M.J. (1986). Emotional processing of fear: Exposure to corrective information. *Psychological Bulletin, 99*, 20-35.

Frere C. L., Crout, R., & Yorty J. et al. Effects of audiovisual distraction during dental prophylaxis. *Journal of the American Dental Association, 132*, 1031-1038.

Gatchel, R. J. (1980). Effectiveness of two procedures for reducing dental fear: group-administered desensitization and group education and discussion. *Journal of the American Dental Association, 101*, 634-637.

Gatchell, R. J., Ingersoll, B. D., Bowman, L., Robertson, M. C., & Walker, C. (1983). The prevalence of dental fear and avoidance: A recent survey study. *Journal of the American Dental Association, 107*, 609-610.

Gauthier, J., Savard, F., & Hallé, J. *et al.* (1995). Flooding and coping skills training in the management of dental fear. *Scandinavian Journal of Behaviour Therapy, 14*, 3-15.

Getka, E. J., & Glass, C. R. (1992). Behavioral and cognitive-behavioral approaches to the reduction of dental anxiety. *Behavior Therapy, 23*, 433-448.

Hammarstrand, G., Berggren, U., & Hakeberg, M. (1995). Psychophysiological therapy vs. hypnotherapy in the treatment of patients with dental phobia. *European Journal of Oral Sciences, 103*, 399-404.

Horowitz, M., Wilmer, N., & Alvarez, W. (1979). Impact of event scale: A measure of subjective stress. *Psychosomatic Medicine, 41*, 209-218.

Ingram, R. E. (1989). Unique and shared cognitive factors in social anxiety and depression: automatic thinking and self-appraisal. *Journal of Social and Clinical Psychology, 8*, 198-208.

Ingram, R. E. & Kendall, P. C. (1987). The cognitive side of anxiety. *Cognitive Therapy and Research, 11*, 523-536.

Jöhren, P., Jackowski, J., & Gängler P. et al. (2000). Fear reduction in patients with dental treatment phobia. *British Journal of Oral Maxillary Surgery, 38*, 612-616.

Joseph, S. Psychometric evaluation of Horowitz's Impact of Event Scale: A review. (2000). *Journal of Traumatic Stress, 13*, 101-113.

Katcher, A., Segal, H., & Beck, A. (1984). Comparison of contemplation and hypnosis for the reduction of anxiety and discomfort during dental surgery. *American Journal of Clinical Hypnosis, 27*, 14-21.

Kent, G. (1984). Anxiety, pain and type of dental procedure. *Behaviour Research and Therapy, 22*, 465-469.

Kent, G. (1985a). Cognitive processes in dental anxiety. *British Journal of Clinical Psychology, 24*, 259-264.

Kent, G. (1985b). Memory of dental pain. *Pain, 21*, 187-94.

Kent, G. (1987). Self-efficacious control over reported physiological, cognitive and behavioural symptoms of dental anxiety. *Behaviour Research and Therapy, 25*, 341-347.

Kent, G. (1989). Cognitive aspects of the maintenance and treatment of dental anxiety: A review. *Journal of Cognitive Psychotherapy: An international quarterly, 3*, 201-221.

Kent, G., & Gibbons, R. (1987). Self-efficacy and the control of anxious cognitions. *Journal of Behavior Therapy and Experimental Psychiatry, 18*, 33-40.

Kent, G. & Jambunathan, P. (1989). A longitudinal study of the intrusiveness of cognitions in test anxiety. Behaviour Research and Therapy, 27, 43-50.

Kleber, R. J., Brom, D., & Defares, P. B. (1992). *Coping with trauma*. Theory, prevention and treatment. Lisse: Swets & Zeitlinger.

Kleinknecht R. A., & Bernstein D. A. (1978). The assessment of dental fear. *Behavioral Therapy, 9,* 626-634.

Kleinknecht, R. A., Klepac, R. K., & Alexander L. D. (1973). Origins and characteristics of fear of dentistry. *Journal of the American Dental Association, 20,* 437-443.

Kvale, G., Raadal, M., & Vika, M., et al. (2002). Treatment of dental anxiety disorders. Outcome related to DSM-IV diagnoses. *European Journal of Oral Sciences, 110,* 69-74.

Lamb, D. H., & Strand, K. H. (1980). The effect of a brief relaxation treatment for dental anxiety on measures of state and trait anxiety. *Journal of Clinical Psychology, 36,* 270-274.

Lautch, H. (1971). Dental phobia. British Journal of Psychiatry, *119,* 151-158.

Lazarus, R. S., & Folkman, S. (1984). *Stress, appraisal, and coping.* New York: Springer Publishing.

Lindsay, S. J., Wege, P., & Yates, J. (1984). Expectations of sensations, discomfort and fear in dental treatment. *Behaviour Research and Therapy, 22,* 99-108.

Litt, M. D, Nye, C., & Shafer D. (1993). Coping with oral surgery by self-efficacy enhancement and perceptions of control. *Journal of Dental Research, 72,* 1237-1243.

Liu, H. H., Milgrom, P., & Fiset, L. (1991). Effect of a beta-adrenergic blocking agent on dental anxiety. *Journal of Dental Research, 70,* 1306-1308.

Livingston, H. M., Livingston, M. G., Brooks, D. N., & McKinlay, W. W. (1992). Elderly survivors of the Lockerbie air disaster. *International Journal of Geriatric Psychiatry, 7,* 725-729.

Lubow, R. E. (1973). Latent inhibition. *Psychological Bulletin, 79,* 398-407.

MacLeod, C., Mathews, A., & Tata, P. (1986). Attentional bias in emotional disorders. *Journal of Abnormal Psychology, 95,* 15-20.

Mathews, A., & Eysenck, M.W. (1987). Clinical anxiety and cognition. In H.J. Eysenck & I. Martin (Eds.), *Theoretical foundations of behavior therapy* (217-234). New York: Plenum Press.

Mathews, A., & MacLeod, C. (1986). Discrimination of threat cues without awareness in anxiety states. *Journal of Abnormal Psychology, 98,* 31-34.

Mathews, A., & Shaw, P. (1977). Cognitions related to anxiety, a pilot study of treatment. *Behaviour Research and Therapy, 15,* 503-505.

Mayou, R.A., Ehlers, A., & Hobbs, M. (2000). Psychological debriefing for road traffic accident victims. *British Journal of Psychiatry, 176,* 589-593.

Mayou, R.A., & Smith, K.A. (1997). Post traumatic symptoms following medical illness and treatment. *Journal of Psychosomatic Research, 43,* 121-123.

McNally, R.J., & Saigh, P.A. (1993). On the distinction between traumatic simple phobia and post-traumatic stress disorder. In J.T.R. Davidson & E.B. Foa (Eds), *Post-traumatic Stress Disorder: DSM-IV and beyond.* Washington, DC: American Psychiatric Press.

Menzies, R.G., & Clark, J.C. (1995). The etiology of phobias: a non-associative account. *Clinical Psychology Review, 16,* 337-361.

Milgrom, P., Fiset, L., Melnick, S., & Weinstein, P. (1988). The prevalence and practice management consequences of dental fear in a major U.S. city. *Journal of the American Dental Association, 116,* 641-647.

Milgrom, P., & Weinstein, P. (1993) Dental fears in general practice: New guidelines for assessment and treatment. *International Dental Journal, 43,* 288-293.

Miller, S. (1989). Cognitive informational styles in the process of coping with threat and frustration. *Advances in Behaviour Research and Therapy, 11,* 223-234

Moore, R., Abrahamson, R., & Brødsgaard, I. (1996). Hypnosis compared with group therapy and individual desensitization for dental anxiety. *European Journal of Oral Sciences, 104,* 612-618.

Moore, R., & Brødsgaard, I. (1994). Group therapy compared with individual desensitization for dental anxiety. *Community Dentistry and Oral Epidemiology, 22,* 258-262.

Moore, R., & Brødsgaard, I. (1995). Differential diagnosis of odontophobic patients using the DSM-IV. *European Journal of Oral Sciences, 103,* 121-126.

Moore, R., Brødsgaard, I., & Abrahamson, R. (2002). A 3-year comparison of dental anxiety treatment outcomes: hypnosis, group therapy, and individual desensitization vs. no specialist treatment. *European Journal of Oral Sciences, 110,* 287-295.

Moore, R., Brødsgaard, I., & Berggren, U. et al. (1991). Generalization of effects of dental fear treatment in a self-referred population of odontophobics. *Journal of Behavior Therapy and Experimental Psychiatry, 22,* 243-253.

Moore, R., Brødsgaard, I., & Birn, H. (1991). Manifestations, acquisition and diagnostic categories of dental fear in a self-referred population. *Behaviour Research and Therapy, 36:* 51-60.

Moses, A. N., & Hollandsworth, J. G. (1985). Relative effectiveness of education alone versus stress inoculation training in the treatment of dental phobia. *Behavior Therapy, 16,* 531-537.

Mowrer, O. A. (1960). *Learning theory and behavior.* New York: Wiley.

Muris., P., De Jongh, A., Van Zuuren, F. J., Ter Horst, G., Kokosky Deforchaux, Y., & Somers, P. (1995). Imposed and chosen monitoring and blunting strategies in the dental setting: Effects, self-efficacy, and coping preference. *Anxiety, Stress, and Coping, 8,* 47-59

Muris, P., Merckelbach, H., & De Jongh, A. Colour-naming of dentist-related words: Role of coping style, dental anxiety, and trait anxiety. *Personality and Individual Differences, 18,* 685-688.

Öst. L. G. (1986). Applied relaxation: description of a coping technique and review of controlled studies. *Behavior Research and Therapy, 25,* 397-409.

Öst, L. -G. & Hugdahl K. (1981). Acquisition of phobias and anxiety response patterns in clinical patients. *Behaviour Research and Therapy, 19,* 439-447.

Öst, L., & Hugdahl, K. (1985). Acquisition of blood and dental phobia and anxiety response patterns in clinical patients. *Behaviour Research and Therapy, 23:* 27-34.

Power K, McGoldrick T, Brown K, Buchanan R, Sharp D, Swanson V, & Karatzias A.A (2002). Controlled Comparison of Eye Movement Desensitization and Reprocessing versus Exposure plus Cognitive Restructuring versus Waiting List in the Treatment of Post-traumatic Stress Disorder. *Clinical Psychology and Psychotherapy, 9,* 299-318.

Prins, P. J. M. (1985). Self-speech and self-regulation of high-and low-anxious children in the dental situation: An interview study. *Behaviour Research and Therapy, 23,* 641-650.

Rachman, S. (1977). The conditioning theory of fear-acquisition: A critical examination. *Behaviour Research and Therapy, 15,* 375-387.

Rachman, S. (1990). The determinants and treatment of simple phobias. *Advances in Behaviour Research and Therapy, 12,* 1-30.

Rimm, D. C., Janda, L., Lancaster, D., Nahl, M., & Dittmar, K. (1977). An exploratory investigation of the origin and maintenance of phobias. *Behavior Research and Therapy, 15,* 231-238.

Roy-Byrne, P., Milgrom, P., Khoon-Mei, T., Weinstein, P., & Katon, W. (1994). Psychopathology and psychiatric diagnosis in subjects with dental phobia. *Journal of Anxiety Disorders, 8,* 19-31

Schuurs, A. H. B., Duivenvoorde, H. J., Thoden van Velzen, S. K., & Verhage F. (1984). Dental anxiety, the parental family and regularity of dental attendance. *Community Dentistry and Oral Epidemiology, 12,* 89-95.

Shafran, R., Booth, R., & Rachman, S. (1993). The reduction of claustrophobia- II: Cognitive analyses. *Behaviour Research and Therapy, 31,* 75-85.

Smith, T. A., Kroeger, R. F., & Lyon, H. E. *et al.* (1990). Evaluating a behavioral method to manage dental fear: A 2-year study of dental practices. *Journal of the American Dental Association, 121,* 525-530.

Stouthard, M. E. A., & Hoogstraten, J. (1990). Prevalence of dental anxiety in The Netherlands. *Community Dentistry and Oral Epidemiology, 18,* 139-142.

Street, T., Craske, M., & Barlow, D. (1989). Sensations, cognitions and the perception of cues associated with expected and unexpected panic attacks. *Behaviour Research and Therapy, 27,* 189-198.

Syrek, S. K., Corah, N. L., & Pace, L. F. (1995). Comparison of three distraction techniques in reducing stress in dental patients. *Journal of the American Dental Association, 108,* 327-9.

Teasdale, J. D. (1983). Negative thinking in depression: Cause, effect or reciprocal relationship? *Advances in Behaviour Research and Therapy, 5,* 3-25.

Teasdale, J., & Taylor, R. (1981). Induced mood and accessibility of memories. *British Journal of Clinical Psychology, 20,* 39-48.

Thom, A., Sartory, G., & Jöhren, P. (2000). Comparison between one-session psychological treatment and benzodiazepine in dental phobia. *Journal of Consulting and Clinical Psychology, 68,* 378-387.

Turk, D. C., Meichenbaum, D., & Genest, M. (1983). *Pain and behavioral medicine.* New York: Guilford Press.

Vögele, C., Coles, J., Wardle, J. *et al.* (2003). Psychophysiologic effects of applied tension on the emotional fainting response to blood and injury. *Behavior Research and Therapy, 41,* 139-155.

Wardle, J. (1982). Fear of dentistry. *British Journal of Medical Psychology, 55,* 119-126.

Wardle, J. (1984). Dental pessimism: Negative cognitions in fearful dental patients. *Behaviour Research and Therapy, 22,* 553-556.

Willumsen, T., Vassend, O., & Hoffard, A. (2001). One-year follow-up of patients treated for dental fear: Effects of cognitive therapy, applied relaxation, and nitrous oxide sedation. *Acta Odontologia Scandinavia, 59,* 335-340.

Wolpe, J. (1958). *Psychotherapy by reciprocal inhibition.* Stanford, CA: Stanford University.

In: New Research on the Psychology of Fear
Editor: Paul L. Gower, pp. 181-221

ISBN 1-59454-334-8
© 2005 Nova Science Publishers, Inc.

Chapter 9

VARIATIONS ON A THEME: THE SPECTRUM OF ANXIETY DISORDERS AND PROBLEMS WITH DSM CLASSIFICATION IN PRIMARY CARE SETTINGS

David Katerndahl

Department of Family & Community Medicine
University of Texas Health Science Center at San Antonio
Anticipated Submission Date: May 31, 2004

ABSTRACT

Although the psychiatric literature can support the splintered model of a DSM world, considerable evidence also exists in support of commonality among depressive disorders. Does this commonality of disorders also apply to the anxiety disorders? Not only do people with anxiety disorders display similar backgrounds, comorbidity, and treatment response, but similarities at both the micro- and macro- levels of the brain lead to similarities in phenomenology. Thus, the majority of anxiety disorders may represent different aspects of the same disorder. In fact, there is growing evidence for commonality between depressive and anxiety disorders. Not only do anxiety and depressive disorders frequently co-occur and their symptoms suggest a continuum, but some of these disorders have similar genetics and neurochemistry. The overlap between anxiety and depression suggests a common underlying diathesis. The unification of anxiety disorders and anxiety with depressive disorders would raise new concerns about the appropriateness of the DSM system to primary care. Not only would the appropriateness of the DSM system be compromised in primary care by patients with transient, subthreshold disorders, and distress not meeting diagnostic criteria, but if disorders are clinically indistinguishable from each other, then the DSM system would lose all relevance to primary care settings. If true, two primary clinical implications arise. First, mental health treatment is far more important than diagnosis; categorization becomes an academic exercise. Second, a new classification system for mental illness in primary care, which is dimensional, multi-axial,

---

* Department of Family and Community Medicine; University of Texas Health Science ; Center at San Antonio; 7703 Floyd Curl Drive; San Antonio, TX 78229-3900; Phone: 210-358-3885; Fax: 210-223-6940; Email: katerndahl@uthscsa.edu

reliable, and reflective of the spectrum of mental disorders seen in primary care, is needed if we are to promote a common language and conduct relevant research on mental illness in primary care settings.

The utility of the Diagnostic and Statistical Manual of Mental Disorders (DSM) classification system for mental disorders in the primary care setting has been called into question (Klinkman & Okkes, 1998). Not only are many mental disorders in primary care patients transient (Lamberts & Hofman-Okkes, 1993), but patients often present with subthreshold disorders (Sireling et al, 1985) or psychological distress alone (Coyne & Schwenk, 1997). Thus, the DSM system based on a categorical model may not capture the spectrum of mental disorders seen in primary care.

The validity of categorical models rests upon certain criteria. For categorical models to be valid, categories must have unique clinical descriptions with clear discontinuity between categories. Categories must have distinct genetic bases, pathophysiology, natural histories, and treatment responses (Lam & Stewart, 1996; Goldberg & Huxley, 1992). However, problems exist in the categories currently used in the DSM classification system when applied to primary care settings. First, the categories often do not fulfil the criteria listed above. Second, the inclusion of subthreshold syndromes often increases the validity of these systems by more accurately representing mental illness in the population and by including more of the patients that actually receive treatment (Angst et al, 1997). Finally, the overlap among disorders makes differentiation difficult.

For example, categorical modeling may not apply to depressive disorders. First, these disorders do not have unique clinical descriptions, but have similar comorbidity (Yang & Dunner, 2001; McElroy et al, 2001), family histories (Yang & Dunner, 2001), outcomes (Lyness et al, 1999; Beekman et al, 1997; Sherbourne et al, 1996; Yang & Dunner, 2001), and treatment response (de Lima et al, 1999; Szegodi et al, 1997). Although subtypes may exist (Schurhoff et al, 2000), similar neurochemical mechanisms are believed to be at work among depressive disorders (Kumar et al, 1998; Leonard & Song, 1996). This suggests a common underlying diathesis to depressive disorders. Second, subthreshold depressive syndromes are important. Evidence suggests that, just as there may be a bipolar spectrum including subthreshold bipolarity (Cassano et al, 1999a), there may be a spectrum of related forms of depression. Research observations have led to a proposed continuum of depressive symptoms. This model suggests that subthreshold depression leads to minor depression, which, in turn, leads to dysthymia. Dysthymia precedes major depression and eventually major depression with dysthymia. Thus, these depressive disorders may represent alternate forms or different symptom phases of the same underlying illness (Judd, 1997). Finally, the overlap among depressive disorders makes differentiation difficult. About half of people with major depressive disorder or recurrent brief depression have another form of depression as well. Endocrinologically, there is a continuum from borderline personality disorder to recurrent brief depression to major depression (De la Fuente et al, 2002). In addition, depressive disorders have poor stability over time (Angst et al, 2000). This explains the poor predictive validity of minor depression and depressive symptoms. Major depression can precede or develop subsequent to subthreshold forms of depression, and people can exhibit multiple forms over time (Angst & Merikangas, 1997). Thus, there is a spectrum of depressive disorders that may represent a common diathesis.

Do these similarities also apply to anxiety disorders? Do anxiety disorders represent unique processes or are they different manifestations of a common underlying pathology? Taken a step further, are anxiety and depressive disorders distinct from each other? If all affective disorders are simply different manifestations of a common underlying pathology, what then are the implications for classification of these disorders in primary care?

ARE ANXIETY DISORDERS DISTINCT ENTITIES?

In 1987, Aronson (1987) pointed out the degree of overlap between panic disorder and generalized anxiety disorder (GAD). Patients with panic disorder and GAD have more similarities than differences (Mavissakalian & Tamar, 2000). This has led people to question whether GAD and panic disorder are separate diagnoses (Massion et al, 1993). It has been speculated that panic disorder is a labile form of GAD (Koehler et al, 1988). The distinction between panic disorder and GAD is largely due to the presence of spontaneous panic attacks and the relationship with phobic avoidance.

How much overlap is there among the anxiety disorders? Are they truly distinct disorders? Using panic disorder as a focus, we will examine their overlap and separateness.

Evidence of Commonality

Comorbidity

Anxiety disorders have much in common; they are prevalent, familial, and heterogeneous (Weissman, 1988). Rarely do anxiety disorders exist alone (see Table 1). Overall, 51-91% of people with one anxiety disorder have at least one other disorder (Sanderson et al, 1990; Hunt & Andrews, 1995; Goldenberg et al, 1996). Hunt and Andrews (1995) found that 26% of people with an anxiety disorder had at least two independent disorders and 55% had at least two temporally-dependent disorders. Similarly, anxiety disorders in children (GAD, separation anxiety disorder, panic disorder, and social anxiety disorder) occur alone less than 50% of the time (Pine et al, 2000).

Specific disorders are frequently comorbid (Schweizer, 1993) (see Table 2). In panic disorder, social phobia and GAD often precede the onset of panic disorder (Argyle & Roth, 1989). In fact, GAD almost never occurs without other disorders (Carter et al, 2001; Massion et al, 1993). While 53% of people with acute stress disorder have panic attacks (Bryant & Panasetis, 2001), past posttraumatic stress disorder (PTSD) is associated with social anxiety disorder and current PTSD is associated with both social anxiety disorder and GAD (Hubbard et al, 1995). As seen in Table 2, phobias are also frequently comorbid (Argyle & Roth, 1989; Degonda & Angst, 1993; Solyom et al, 1986; Goisman et al, 1995).

Thus, not only do anxiety disorders rarely occur alone, they are often comorbid with other anxiety disorders. Are these the same disorder or are they phenomenologically distinct?

Phenomenology

Anxiety disorders are heterogeneous disorders. Yet, specific symptoms within each are responsive to treatment (Schweizer, 1993) and symptoms alone do not differentiate among the anxiety disorders (Birket-Smith et al, 1993). In fact, panic disorder, GAD, panic disorder with agoraphobia, and panic disorder with GAD are felt to represent similar phenomena (Massion et al, 1993). Spontaneous symptom attacks are seen in panic disorder, agoraphobia, social phobia, and GAD (Claycomb, 1983).

Table 1. Prevalence of "Pure" Mental Disorders

Disorder	Proportion Without Other Anxiety Disorders	Proportion Without Depression
Panic Disorder	33% - 53%	21%
Agoraphobia	32% - 43%	20%
Social Phobia	17% - 22%	7%
Generalized Anxiety Disorder	7% - 17%	4%

(Goldenberg et al, 1996; Goisman et al, 1995; Carter et al, 2001; Apfeldorf et al, 2000)

Table 2. Comorbidity Among Anxiety Disorders (%)

Comorbid Disorder	Primary Disorder			
	Panic Disorder	Agoraphobia	OCD	GAD
GAD	14-76	26	22	---
Social Phobia	11-30	20-55	7	10
Simple Phobia	7-34	26		
OCD	0-14	14	---	0
PTSD	6	9		

(Goisman et al, 1994; van Balkom et al, 2000; Apfeldorf et al, 2000; Andersch & Hanson, 1993; Solyom et al, 1986; Sanderson et al, 1990; Birchall et al, 2000)

Panic attacks differ from nonpanic symptom attacks only in intensity (Argyle & Roth, 1989). Panic attacks are felt to indicate severe psychopathology but are not limited to panic disorder or agoraphobia (Reed & Wittchen, 1998). Although the phenomenon of the panic attack is uniform within and between panic disorder patients (Katerndahl 1990; Katerndahl 1996), subtypes of panic disorder may exist based upon the predominant symptoms during attacks (Massana et al, 2001; Katerndahl et al, 1986).

The close relationship between panic disorder and agoraphobia is documented in DSM-IV. Together, panic and agoraphobia encompass the spectrum of symptoms seen in anxiety disorders. Their onset represents a discontinuity in life (Roth, 1996). Episodes of panic and anxiety seen in panic disorder and agoraphobia are similar in everything but intensity, suggesting that these are not separate diagnoses (Basoglu et al, 1992). These disorders are similar in onset, demographics, and severity, representing a uniform phenomenon (Faravelli et al, 1988). Panic and agoraphobia vary along continuous dimensions, and may be different aspects of one illness (Turner et al, 1986). Differences between panic disorder, agoraphobia, and panic disorder with agoraphobia are thus largely a matter of severity (Andrews & Slade, 2002). In addition, both social phobics and agoraphobics have a similar course and similar perspectives on anxiety-provoking social situations (Wells & Papageorgiou, 1999).

As mentioned in the previous section, the relationship between panic and GAD is unclear. However, they have similar family histories (Anderson et al, 1984), histories of separation anxiety (Raskin et al, 1982), and autonomic levels (Roth et al, 1998).

Hence, although the heterogeneity of anxiety disorders suggests that there is little relationship among them, panic disorder appears closely related to agoraphobia and possibly related to GAD. Social phobia also overlaps with agoraphobia and may be related to panic disorder.

Personality

Patients with panic disorder have a personality characterized by high anxiety and dependency (Argyle & Roth, 1989). Personality does not differentiate among anxiety disorders (Birket-Smith et al, 1993). Patients with panic disorder or agoraphobia have similar personality traits (Faravelli et al, 1988) and similar use of displacement (Pollock & Andrews, 1989). Social phobics also use displacement (Pollock & Andrews, 1989). Patients with these disorders have similar levels of intrusiveness (Antony et al, 1998) and perfectionism, but differ in social anxiety (Saboonchi et al, 1999). In addition, patients with panic disorder and those with GAD have similar personalities (Anderson et al, 1984) and patients with OCD have similar levels of intrusiveness (Antony et al, 1998). Hence, personality traits are generally similar among panic disorder, social phobia, agoraphobia, and GAD.

Genetics

Twin studies suggest that, excluding GAD, there is good concordance among anxiety disorders (Torgersen, 1983), but this concordance is not for the *same* disorder (Cohen & Biederman, 1988). Fear, anxiety, phobias, and obsessive compulsiveness are linked (Marks, 1986). Panic disorder, GAD, OCD, and phobias show familial aggregation with panic disorder, GAD, and possibly phobias, demonstrating genetic dependence (Hettema et al, 2001). Panic disorder, GAD, and PTSD show common genetic and environmental components in addition to unique components (Chantarujikapong et al, 2001). Familial analysis suggests that panic disorder and GAD are linked, and that other anxiety disorders are linked (d'Ansia, 1989).

The genetics of specific anxiety disorders are still unclear. While non-shared environment has a significant effect in the development of panic disorder and GAD (Hettema et al, 2001), duplication in Chromosome 15 is associated with familial panic disorder, social phobia, and agoraphobia (Gratacos et al, 2001). As in panic disorder, phobias are products of both inheritance and environment (Mathew et al, 2001). Experiences predispose to only one particular phobia (most important in simple phobias but least important in agoraphobia). Thus, simple phobias are a product of a moderate genetic component and a specific environmental factor. Agoraphobia and maybe social phobias are explained by a small genetic component and general environmental factors (Kendler et al, 1992). This lack of clarity may be due, in part, to misclassification (Brown, 1994).

Overall, genetics may impact both categorical disorders and dimensions such as trait anxiety, neuroticism, anxious temperament, and behavioral inhibition (Smollen & Tsuang, 1998).

Neurochemistry

In addition to genetic commonalities, anxiety disorders are related neurochemically. Catecholamines are believed to be under genetic control. Genetic polymorphism at a single locus could affect relevant enzymatic functions such as dopamine β hydrolase activity, monoamine oxidase, and COMT (Weinshilboum, 1983). Thus, the genotype may generate a continuum of risk for developing maladaptive responses and may combine with the early environment to set the threshold for activation of the autonomic system including norepinephrine in the locus ceruleus, corticotropin releasing factor (CRF), and the amygdala (Sullivan et al, 1999). Thus, anxiety disorders may be linked neurochemically.

GAD, panic disorder, and adjustment disorder with anxious mood all have high levels of methoxy-hydroxyphenylethylene glycol (MHPG) (Yamada et al, 2000) and GAD, panic disorder, separation anxiety, and social phobia are all associated with increased anxiety in response to CO2 inhalation (Pine et al, 2000). Anxiety disorders, in general, are associated with decreased sleep efficiency and REM latency (Laver & Krieg, 1992). Anatomically, the orbitofrontal cortex, the anterior insula, and the anterior cingulate are involved in a variety of anxiety disorders secondary to increased cerebral blood flow (see Table 3).

Table 3. Increased Cerebral Blood Flow In Anxiety Disorders

Area	Phobias	OCD	PTSD
Orbitofrontal Cortex	L	L,R	-
Anterior Cingulate	R	R	R
Insula	L	L	R
Anterior Temporal Cortex	R	R	R
Medial Temporal Cortex	-	-	R
Amygdala	-	-	R
Caudate	-	R	-
Thalamus	L	-	-
Visual Cortex	-	-	R
Sensorimotor Cortex	L	-	-

L = Left
R = Right
(Malizia, 1999)

In response to CO_2 inhalation, anxiety disorders are associated with autonomic reactivity in response to CO_2 (Bystritsky et al, 2000b) and CO_2-induced panic attacks are similar across disorders (Kent et al, 2001). Although people with panic disorder are more likely to exhibit panic attacks in response to 7% CO_2, hyperventilation, and lactate infusion than those with other disorders, people with any anxiety disorder clearly differ in these responses from controls (Gorman et al, 1988).

There are also neurochemical similarities between panic disorder and GAD. Comparisons show few respiratory differences between them (Wilhelm et al, 2001). Both disorders are also similar in response to caffeine in terms of anxiety levels and change in cerebral blood flow (Mathew & Wilson, 1990).

In addition, panic disorder and agoraphobia share neurochemical similarities, such as electrodermal conductance (Birket-Smith et al, 1993). Neurochemical differences between panic disorder and phobias may reflect when intense fear began. Fear earlier in childhood may produce fear of primitive features of the stimulus, which leads to sensory and emotional memories, and ultimately to panic. Fear later in childhood leads to fear of specific objects (Jacobs & Nadel, 1999).

There are also shared neurochemical characteristics between panic disorder and other anxiety disorders. Both panic disorder and PTSD respond to lactate, yohimbine, mCPP, and CCK infusions with panic attacks (Kellner & Yehuda, 1999; Jensen et al, 1998), reflecting CRF overdrive (Kellner et al, 2000). In addition, people with OCD occasionally develop panic attacks in response to lactate and yohimbine (Murphy & Pigott, 1990).

Thus, there are significant overlaps among anxiety disorders in terms of neurochemistry and neuroanatomy. Differences in clinical appearance may reflect the area of the brain associated with autonomic hyperarousal and dysfunction (Matthew et al, 2001) (see Table 4). Although there are similarities among anxiety disorders at both the micro- and macro- levels, do these similarities lead to similar treatment responses?

Table 4. Clinical Correlates Of Brain Dysfunction

Brain Region	Clinical Problem
Hippocampus, Amygdala	Anxiety, Fear
Hippocampus, Amygdala, Prefrontal Cortex	PTSD, Behavioral Inhibition
Hypothalamus, Paraventricular CRF	Comorbid Anxiety/Depression
Prefrontal Cortex, Raphe Nuclei	Social Incompetence

(Matthew et al, 2001)

Treatment Response

Although Klein and Klein (1989) contend that panic disorder is not the same as severe GAD because they differ in their treatment response, panic disorder and GAD respond similarly in many ways. Cognitive behavioral therapy (CBT) is effective in panic disorder, agoraphobia, GAD, and social phobia (Chambless & Gillis, 1993). Similarly, a meditation-based program helped patients with GAD, panic disorder, and agoraphobia (Kabat-Zinn et al, 1992). In general, anxiety disorders respond to selective serotonin reuptake inhibitors (SSRIs), tricyclic antidepressants (TCAs), and CBT.

Although placebo response rates vary across disorders, these rates overlap. Thus, response rates vary from 0-19% in OCD, 7-43% in social phobia, and 18-67% in GAD to ≥20% in panic disorder (Piercy et al, 1996; Mavissakalian et al, 1990). Hence, response rates to antidepressants, CBT, and placebos are generally similar across disorders.

Evidence Against Commonality

Despite considerable evidence in support of the commonality of anxiety disorders, evidence against commonality also exists. Neurochemically, electrodermal conductance distinguishes between panic disorder and agoraphobia on the one hand, and other anxiety disorders on the other (Birket-Smith et al, 1993). In addition, anxiety disorders differ in the patterns of increased cerebral blood flow (Malizia, 1999). Finally, although response to certain medications is similar, anxiety disorders differ in their response to buspirone and betablockers.

Looking at specific disorders, descriptive, genetic, neurobiological, and treatment studies suggest that panic disorder is a distinct entity (Breier et al, 1985, Rosenberg et al, 1991). In addition, patients with panic and agoraphobia have different demographics, onsets, cognitions, panic symptoms, and avoidances than do those with social phobia (Amies, 1983; Clum & Knowles, 1991; Reich et al, 1988). PTSD differs from panic disorder in its epidemiology, genetics, and biochemistry (Marshall et al, 2002). Unlike other anxiety disorders, OCD generally does not respond to MAOIs or benzodiazepines. In general, PTSD and OCD are considered to have little overlap with other anxiety disorders (Green et al, 1990).

Among the anxiety disorders, the strongest evidence for uniqueness, however, rests on phenomenology (Faravelli et al, 1988; Gelernter et al, 1992; Biederman et al, 2001a; Magee et al, 1996; Degonda & Angst, 1993; Noyes et al, 1992; Kopp, 1989; Anderson et al, 1984; Raskin et al, 1982; Borden & Turner, 1989; Bankier et al, 2001) and personality (Pollock & Andrews, 1989; Saboonchi et al, 1999; Kopp, 1989; Hollander et al, 1990; Ehntholt et al, 1999; Antony et al, 1998;), the weakest areas upon which to base "distinctness". Although there is some genetic (Fyer et al, 1995; Fyer et al, 1990; Noyes et al, 1992; Klein & Klein, 1989; Weissman, 1990; Weissman, 1990; Scherrer et al, 2000;) and neurochemical evidence (Rosenberg et al, 1991; Kopp, 1989; Charney et al, 1989; Noyes et al, 1992; Hollander et al, 1990; Lucey et al, 1997), the comorbidity and treatment response data for distinctness is weak.

Synthesis

Not only do people with anxiety disorders display similar backgrounds and considerable comorbidity, but most of the anxiety disorders themselves respond to the same treatments. Although genetic studies show high concordance among anxiety disorders, the genetics remains unclear. While the area of the brain responsible for key features of each disorder may differ, similarities at both the micro- and macro- levels of the brain lead to similarities in phenomenology. Thus, phobic disorders appear similar, panic disorder and GAD appear similar, and panic disorder and agoraphobia appear similar. If these links do indeed reflect commonality, then the majority of anxiety disorders, with the exception of OCD and possibly PTSD, may represent different aspects of the same disorder. A further suggestion of commonality is the observation that childhood sexual abuse is linked to panic disorder and agoraphobia (Pribor & Dinwiddie, 1992), suggesting that these disorders may represent forms of PTSD.

When two disorders are temporally separate but co-occur, they represent two independent disorders, the same disorder at two different phases, or one is misdiagnosed (Barrett, 1986). The recognition that anxiety disorders may be related is manifest in the concept of spectrum disorders. The panic-agoraphobia spectrum includes domains such as panic symptoms, anxious expectations, phobic features, and sensitivity to stress, substances, and reassurance. It is suggested that the spectrum consists of distinct disorders joined by an underlying diathesis (Cassano et al, 1997). Similarly, the obsessive-compulsive spectrum includes such disorders as OCD, body dysmorphic disorder, pathological gambling, and Tourette's syndrome. These disorders represent a spectrum from impulsivity to compulsivity and can be separated into three clusters—neurological, impulsivity, and appearance/sensation. These disorders share similar symptoms, genetics, comorbidity, onset, family history, course, and treatment response (Hollander et al, 1996).

How are anxiety disorders linked but separate? The modular model contends that certain areas of the brain are triggered in all forms of anxiety, but that specific areas are triggered in specific disorders. Thus, right hemispheric cerebral blood flow (CBF) is increased to the anterior temporal lobe and anterior cingulate gyrus in OCD, PTSD, and phobias. OCD and phobias are associated with increased CBF to the left insula while PTSD is associated with increased CBF to the right insula. However, CBF patterns for the orbitofrontal area differ among the three disorders (Malizia, 1999).

Genotype is believed to translate into a spectrum of predisposition to maladaptive responses. Coupled with the early environment, this predisposition results in varying thresholds for activation of corticotropin releasing factor (CRF) and norepinephrine (NE) in the locus ceruleus and amygdala. Stressful events and their memories can then lead to a stress response (Sullivan et al, 1999). The strength of this response is dependent upon how the stressors are perceived based on experience, information, discrimination, and interpretation. This may apply to agoraphobia, PTSD, OCD, panic disorder, and specific phobias (Davey et al et al, 1993). Gorman et al (2000) suggest that genetics leads to increased sensitivity, which results in a "fear network." This same network functions abnormally in GAD, PTSD, and social phobia. Whereas panic attacks, conditioned fear stimuli, and treatment response are similar, the parts of the fear network differ in comorbidity and the focus of CBT. These differences may account for the distinct manifestations of the specific anxiety disorders linked by a common underlying diathesis.

Conclusion

Although the psychiatric literature can support the splintered model of a DSM world, considerable evidence also exists in support of commonality among anxiety disorders. This review suggests that the state of our knowledge in this area is still limited. More primary care and community-based research is needed to focus on both the overlap and separation of these disorders. In addition, research should include treatment response when the only diagnosis is "anxiety". If unification is appropriate, two primary clinical implications arise. First, mental health treatment is far more important than diagnosis; categorization becomes an academic exercise. Second, a new classification system is needed if we are to promote a common language and conduct relevant research on anxiety disorders in primary care settings.

RELATIONSHIP BETWEEN ANXIETY AND DEPRESSIVE DISORDERS

There is also a growing concern that distinctions between anxiety disorders and depressive disorders may be artificial. As shown above, anxiety disorders have much in common. Such commonality has led to proposals of similar pathways across anxiety disorders (Davey et al, 1993) and that the same "fear network" may be at work (Gorman et al, 2000). In addition, depressive disorders may represent alternate forms or different symptom phases of the same underlying illness (Judd et al, 1987). But a larger question exists; what is the nature of mental illness in primary care? Do anxiety and depressive disorders represent unique processes or are they different manifestations of a common underlying pathology?

Evidence of Commonality

If most anxiety disorders represent different manifestations of an underlying diathesis and depressive disorders represent different manifestations of an underlying diathesis, are these diatheses interrelated? Do anxiety and depressive disorders also represent different aspects of the same illness?

There are several problems with the distinctions between anxiety and depressive disorders. First, they overlap and frequently co-occur. Second, there are no clear-cut boundaries between disorders. Third, International Classification of Diseases (ICD) and DSM systems perform poorly in terms of boundaries between categories or between illness and normalcy, robustness, stability, and meaning. Fourth, anxiety and depressive disorders have poor stability. Finally, the genetics of anxiety and depressive disorders is similar in that multiple genes play a small part in the risk of developing anxiety or depression, and that genetics is less important than environment (Goldberg & Huxley, 1992). If threshold and subthreshold anxiety and depression are related, then they either represent the same illness appearing at different times or comorbid disease represents a new disorder (Lydiard, 1991). Labeling them as distinct disorders may be a product of referral bias, psychiatry artifact, or basing classification on treatment response (Shepherd et al, 1986).

Studies in children have found that high levels of anxiety predict high levels of subsequent depression (Cole et al, 1998). This agrees with Hunt and Andrews (1995) who believe that anxiety disorders other than generalized anxiety disorder (GAD) and simple phobia are primary to depression. More specifically, panic disorder overlaps major depression (Aronson, 1987) and Breier et al (1985) suggested that they were joined by a common vulnerability. This was based on their co-occurrence, similar genetics and norepinephrine (NE) hyperactivity, and their response to antidepressants. Either one disorder leads to the other, or they share a single biology with different expressions. Diagnostic revision reflecting the relationship of depression and panic attacks may be necessary if comorbidity studies include different sources of data and if diagnostic revision leads to improved diagnostic validity (Coryell et al, 1988).

The issue of a common relationship between anxiety and depressive disorders is epitomized in the condition of mixed anxiety-depression (MAD). Studies have found that this mixed subthreshold disorder occurs with a prevalence of 1-7% in primary care settings (Tiemens et al, 1996; Zinsbarg et al, 1994; Pincus et al, 1999) and up to 11.7% in psychiatric settings (Zinsbarg et al, 1994). Although epidemiological studies suggest that MAD is associated with social and functional impairment (Zinsbarg et al, 1994; Klein, 1993), family studies have yielded contradictory results (Klein, 1993). The ICD-10 includes MAD, even though lower levels of anxiety and depression result in less distinct syndromes (Liebowitz, 1993).

Comorbidity

Anxiety and depressive disorders overlap and frequently co-occur (Angst & Merikangas, 1997; Sartorius et al, 1996). Comorbidity rates among anxiety and depressive disorders in primary care settings range from 12.7-19.2% (Ormel et al, 1991; Stein et al, 1995). This comorbidity is usually chronic (Van den Brink et al,1991). In addition, the rates of comorbid physical disorders are similar in people with anxiety disorders and those with affective disorders (see Table 5) (Wells et al, 1989).

Table 5. Prevalence of Physical Disorders In People With Anxiety Or Affective Disorders (%)

Physical Disorder	People With Affective Disorders	People With Anxiety Disorders
Chronic Lung Disease	20.4	16.6
Heart Disease	13.5	12.6
Hypertension	24.4	25.9
Arthritis	25.1	25.1

(Wells et al, 1989)

Not only do 33% of people with anxiety disorders have major depression (Nisenson et al, 1998), but specific anxiety disorders are often associated with depression (see Table 1) (Goldenberg et al, 1996; Goisman et al, 1995; Carter et al, 2001; Apfeldorf et al, 2000). Only 17% of people with any anxiety disorder are without at least one depressive disorder (Goldenberg et al, 1996). Panic disorder, GAD, and major depression overlap with 30% experiencing all three disorders (Fawcett, 1990; Stein & Uhde, 1988). Major depression is present in 27-65% of people with panic disorder (Apfeldorf et al, 2000; Birchall et al, 2000; Van Balkom et al, 2000; Goisman et al, 1994), and in 34% of those with agoraphobia (Goisman et al, 1994). Dysthymia is present in 13% of those with panic disorder (Apfeldorf et al, 2000). The link between panic and major depression is seen even in those with infrequent panic attacks (Katerndahl & Realini, 1997) and is associated with increased severity and disability (Roy-Byrne et al, 2000). GAD has been linked to major depression (Van Balkom et al, 2000) and any depressive disorder (Carter et al, 2001). Current and past depressions are also predictors of current PTSD (Hubbard et al, 1995). The strength of this comorbidity suggests limitations in classification (Kellner & Yehuda, 1999).

Similarly, 67% of people with major depression and 35% of those with subthreshold depression have an anxiety disorder (Sherbourne et al,1996). Psychiatric inpatients with affective disorders and psychosis have high comorbidity rates of panic disorder, social phobia, and OCD (Cassano et al,1999). People with major depression often develop panic disorder (44%) or GAD (62%) during their lifetime (Schulberg et al, 1995). Coryell et al (1992) noted that, although anxiety syndromes are prognostically significant during episodes of major depression, they do not imply the presence of additional disorders.

Factor analytic studies using community-based individuals support commonality. One study found two factors—an anxiety-depression factor and a substance abuse-somatization factor (Mehrabian, 2001). Krueger (1999) found that, although major depression, dysthymia, and GAD factored together as did panic disorder, agoraphobia, and simple and social phobias, a third factor (antisocial personality disorder and substance dependence) was correlated with the other two factors. Among people with panic attacks, although panic disorder and agoraphobia represent one factor, major depression, OCD, and phobias represent a second factor. GAD loaded on both factors (Katerndahl & Realini, 1997). Thus, not only do anxiety and depressive symptoms co-occur, but so do specific disorders.

Phenomenology

Phenomenologically, there is evidence of overlap among anxiety and depressive disorders. They do not differ on the severity of psychopathology (Tsuang et al,1995) and their symptoms cluster by severity rather than diagnosis. Although diagnosis influenced 6-month utilization, symptom cluster was predictive of 12-month utilization and cost (Nease et al, 1999).

Panic symptom clusters cross diagnoses (Borasso & Eaton, 1999). In addition, anxiety and depression overlap in terms of family history of anxiety, depressive, phobic, and substance use disorders (Grunhaus, 1988; Reich, 1993). Although anxiety and depressive disorders overlap in their links to childhood trauma, chronic somatic disorder, and parental psychiatric history, education is also a risk factor for anxiety disorders and comorbid anxiety-depression (De Graaf et al, 2002).

The relationships between disorders and stressors form patterns. Panic disorder, agoraphobia, social phobia, and depression show associations with childhood adversity (Brown et al, 1996) and prior trauma (Perkonigg et al, 2000). Similarly, childhood sexual abuse is a risk factor for panic disorder, agoraphobia, PTSD, and major depression (Pribor & Dinwiddie, 1992; Jumper, 1995; Rowan et al, 1994).

The relationships of symptomatology and childhood experience with anxiety and depressive disorders are unclear. Although family history overlaps, other risk factors do not. This lack of clarity may be due to confounding factors which obscure symptom patterns. First, there is a continuum of state-trait symptoms. Second, chronic conditions often display subclinical fluctuations. Finally, even after the acute episode resolves, residual symptoms often persist (Fava & Kellner, 1991).

Personality

Does personality distinguish between anxiety and depressive disorders? Looking at specific personality disorders, borderline personality disorder (BPD) is associated with a high prevalence of comorbid anxiety and depressive disorders (Zanarini et al, 1998). Comparing patients with major depression, patients with panic disorder, or patients with both disorders, the prevalences of BPD and paranoid personality are similar, but avoidant and dependent personalities are seen primarily in patients with both disorders (Alnaes & Torgersen, 1990). In addition, the levels of harm avoidance and reward dependence are similar in all three groups (Ampollini et al, 1999). Looking at vulnerabilities in patients with major depression or panic disorder, few characteristics differentiate them; only anxiety sensitivity and rumination at a lower level, and arousal and positive affect at a higher level differ (Cox et al, 2001). Overall, no significant differences in personality are seen during illness or recovery in those with panic disorder or major depression (Reich et al, 1987; Reich & Troughton, 1988).

These studies demonstrate overlap in personality when comparing anxiety and depressive disorders, particularly panic disorder and major depression. Is there an underlying genetic link between them?

Genetics

In general, genes appear to affect anxiety and depressive symptom levels nonspecifically. There is no evidence that genes affect only anxiety or only depression, but the environment has been shown to impact both (Kendler et al, 1987). It has been suggested that an underlying genetic etiology includes panic disorder, major depression, and alcoholism (Maier et al, 1993).

Panic disorder with major depression models best as a major locus rather than polygenic (Price et al, 1987). In fact, Heninger et al (1988) suggested that these disorders have a common genetic basis. Liebowitz et al (1990) felt that GAD and major depression have a shared diathesis based on family studies.

However, the relationship between panic disorder and bipolar disease is unclear. On the one hand, bipolar disease with and without panic disorder shows different genotypes (Rotondo et al, 2002). On the other hand, panic disorder and bipolar disease appear to be linked, suggesting a shared genetic etiology (MacKinnon et al, 2002). Thus, although much of the evidence suggests a genetic link between major depression and anxiety disorders, the link between bipolar disorder and panic disorder is unclear.

Neurochemistry

Our understanding of the neurochemistry of anxiety and depression has increased considerably over the past decade. While the anterior cingulate is pivotal in mood disorders, the hemispheres are also important; the right hemisphere responds to negative emotions while the left hemisphere responds to positive emotions. Panic and anxiety depend upon the fear centers in the amygdala and the memory centers in the parahippocampus. OCD is associated with increased metabolism in the medial frontal areas involved in planning.

In addition to neurotransmitters, hormones are also important in mental disorders. Glucocorticoid receptors are in high density in the hippocampus, septum, and amygdala (Fole, 1996). The HPA axis mediates the stress response; cortisol hypersecretion is linked to depression, while hyposecretion is linked to externalizing disorders. In addition, not only do adrenocorticoids trigger neurotransmitter sites (Van Bardeleben & Holsboer, 1988), but CRF interacts with specific neurotransmitters to produce anxiety and depression (Zhang & Barrett, 1990). In depression, increased CRF secretion triggers adrenocorticoids, which, in turn, decrease the negative feedback on the hippocampus. Repeated CRF administration in controls produces changes in adrenocorticoids similar to those in depression, and similar to that in panic disorder (Van Bardeleben & Holsboer, 1988). Table 6 summarizes hormonal effects in major depression, panic disorder, and PTSD. Although not identical, many of the HPA functions in panic disorder and major depression are similar (Stein & Uhde, 1988; Grunhaus, 1988).

Thus, both anxiety and depressive disorders are associated with HPA axis changes, and exhibit shared neuroanatomy and similar neurotransmitter effects.

Table 6. Hormonal Responses In PTSD, Panic Disorder, And Major Depression

	Major Depression	Panic Disorder	PTSD
ACTH			
Response To CRF	↓	↓	↓
Response To Metyrapone	↑		↑
Cortisol			
24-Hour Urine	↑		↓
Dexamethasone Suppression Test	↓	↑	↑
Circadian Cortisol	↑		↓
Glucocorticoid Receptors	↓	↑	↑
Response To Clonidine	↑N	N	
CRF			↑
CSF Concentration	↑		
CRF-ACTH Response	↓	↓	
TRH			
TSH Response	↓↑	↓↑	
Prolactin Response	↓N↑	↓	
Growth Hormone			
Response To Clonidine	↓	↓N	
REM Latency	↓	↓N	
Imipramine Binding	↓	↓N	

↑ = Increased
N = Normal
= Decreased
(Stein & Uhde, 1988; Schittecutte et al, 1988; Kellner & Yehuda, 1999)

Outcomes

Although anxiety and depressive disorders overlap in treatment response, specific disorders have specific patterns, but effective treatments have the net effect of increasing 5HT neurotransmission (Blier & de Montigny, 1999). GAD, panic disorder, and dysthymia respond similarly to TCAs, benzodiazepines, self-help programs, and cognitive behavioral therapy (Tyrer et al, 1988). In addition, panic disorder and major depression respond similarly to most treatments (Heninger et al, 1988). Even placebo response is similar in patients with anxiety and depressive disorders (Piercy et al,1996; Tyrer et al, 1988). Patients with GAD and major depression receiving behavioral therapy report concurrent decreases in both anxiety and depression no matter which disorder is the focus of therapy (Moros et al, 1993). Thus, anxiety and depressive disorders respond to similar treatments in general.

Evidence Against Commonality

Not all of the evidence supports the commonality of anxiety and depression. Coryell (1990) contends that anxiety and depression are separate entities. Familial patterns, twin studies, epidemiology, and diagnostic stability may support this. In addition, Shephard et al (Shepherd et al, 1986) contend that family history, age-of-onset, and psychiatric history discriminate between them. Among studies of specific disorders, the strongest evidence for the separation of anxiety and depressive disorders rests with neurochemical (Kellner & Yehuda, 1999; Grunhaus, 1988; Heninger et al, 1988; Fuller, 1991; Matsumoto, 1989; Kelly & Cooper, 1998; Sabelli et al, 1990) and outcomes data (Sherbourne et al, 1996; Nisenson et al, 1998; Heninger et al, 1988; Schapira et al, 1972; Kuzel, 1996; Buller et al, 1986; Van Valkenburg et al, 1984; Kerr et al, 1974; Reich, 1986; Grunhaus et al, 1986; Brown et al, 1996). The phenomenological (Fava & Kellner, 1991; Kendler et al, 1987; Blumberg & Izard, 1986; Copp et al, 1990; Bankier et al, 2001; Gurney et al, 1970; Murphy et al, 1991; Manicavasagar et al, 1998; Alnaes & Torgersen, 1989; Alnaes & Torgersen, 1990), genetic (Cohen & Biederman, 1988; Judd et al, 1987; Maier et al, 1993; Rotondo et al, 2002; d'Ansia, 1989; Weissman et al, 1993), and personality (Ampollini et al, 1999; Alnaes & Torgersen, 1989; Glyshaw et al, 1989) data only weakly support separation.

Synthesis

If anxiety and depressive disorders overlap, what are the underlying neurochemical mechanisms? From an endocrinological standpoint, increased sensitivity of the anterior pituitary and counter regulative adaptation of the adrenal cortex mean that stress leads to hypersecretion of CRF which, in turn, results in anxiety and depressive symptoms (Heim et al, 2001). From a neurotransmitter standpoint, different classes of transmitters are associated with different neurological effects. While serotonergic systems deal with adaptive responses to adverse stimuli, dopamine is important to reward systems and norepinephrine (NE) is important in attention, memory, and reinforcement (Goldberg & Huxley, 1992). In addition to endorphins, all of these transmitters modulate mood. Another way of looking at these transmitters is by the behaviors they control. Serotonin controls impulses, NE controls vigilance, and dopamine controls drives. Taken a step further, impulse and vigilance combine to lead to anxiety and irritation, while vigilance and drive combine for motivation (McNeil, 1998). This may explain the differing response patterns of SSRIs and noradrenergic drugs in different disorders (Shelton & Brown, 2001).

There is a growing recognition that anxiety and depressive disorders are not separate. This is based on clinical observation, symptom-syndrome overlap, and laboratory studies (Nemeroff, 2002). Tyrer et al (1988) proposed that anxiety and depression were on a continuum. Factor analysis of psychopathology scales failed to differentiate among them (Katerndahl & Realini, 1997). Even family studies have shown an overlap, suggesting that anxiety and depressive disorders may share a common diathesis (Weissman, 1988). Groupings based on symptoms alone suggest that there may be no formal mental disorders. While GAD-like symptoms were associated with major depression and panic-like symptoms were associated with major depression and panic disorder, anxiety-depressive symptoms were associated with poor health status and past histories of both major depression and panic disorder. Sporadic symptoms were associated with disability but no disorders (Piccinelli et al, 1999).

If we focus on panic disorder, the relationship is no more clear-cut. Both panic disorder and major depression have unique qualities, suggesting separate diatheses (Grunhaus, 1988). Depression is typically a complication of panic disorder; rarely are these disorders independent or alternate expressions of a shared diathesis (Cassano et al, 1989). Family studies suggest that while parental panic disorder is associated with panic disorder and agoraphobia, and parental depression is associated with major depression and social phobia, both are associated with separation anxiety and multiple anxiety disorders (Biederman et al, 2001). On the other hand, primary and secondary disorders are similar, suggesting that either primary disorders lead to secondary disorders with different pathophysiology or they share a common diathesis (Breier et al, 1984). Not only has a shared underlying diathesis been proposed for major depression and panic disorder (Leckman et al, 1983), but also a shared genetic vulnerability has been proposed for major depression and phobias. The same "fear network" may function abnormally in major depression, GAD, social phobia, and PTSD (Gorman et al, 2000). These disorders differ however in how environmental experiences influence them (Kendler et al, 1993).

How do we put this together? Latent trait analysis of symptoms supports either two dimensions—anxiety and depression (Goldberg & Huxley, 1992)—or three dimensions— depression, nonspecific free-floating anxiety and tension, and specific anxiety with phobic avoidance and situational anxiety (Ormel et al, 1995). These three dimensions are similar to Clark and Watson's (1991) depression, anxiety, and distress.

The anxiety-depression spectrum could represent either discrete but similar disorders or a continuum in which specific disorders represent different areas of the continuum. A shared model is most compatible with the evidence that all disorders share common features but specific disorders have additional unique features (Shelton & Brown, 2001). Using this shared model and latent trait analysis, the tripartite model was proposed. Although anxiety and depression were initially felt to represent different combinations of high negative affectivity, low positive affectivity, and physiological hyperarousal (Clark & Watson, 1991), studies have refined this model. On the one hand, factor analysis caused the original three factors of distress, somatic anxiety, and anhedonic depression to be revised. Somatic arousal and nonspecific anxiety combined into a nonspecific anxiety factor while anhedonia and nonspecific depression combined into a nonspecific depression factor. These two factors may share a common cause (Burns & Eidelson, 1998). On the other hand, Brown et al (1998) found that positive and negative affectivity could combine to produce specific anxiety and depressive disorders which, in turn, led to autonomic arousal.

Finally, the North American Primary Care Research Group's Mental Health Forum has proposed a modification in which, out of an undercurrent of distress, symptomatic peaks arise, the tips of which correspond to DSM disorders (see Figure 1). Taken a step further, the instability of disorders suggests that the specific disorder that presents in a specific patient may vary over time with its specific manifestation due to the specific stressor and the context—the Dynamic Model of Mental Illness (see Figure 2) (Katerndahl et al, 2002). Under this model, DSM disorders represent the "tip of the iceberg." Depending upon the point at which a patient is questioned, he/she may or may not meet DSM criteria for a specific disorder and that DSM classification may change depending upon when in its course it is recognized. Thus, the artificial nature of the DSM system would not accurately reflect the spectrum of mental health problems seen in primary care.

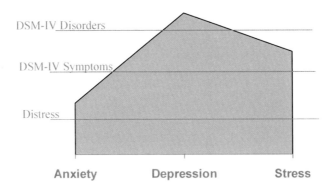

Figure 1. Model Of Mental Problem

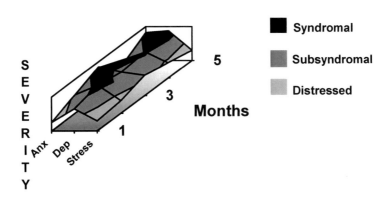

Figure 2. Dynamic Model of Mental Health Problems

Conclusion

Although the literature can support the splintered model of a DSM world, considerable evidence supports the commonality among anxiety disorders and among depressive disorders. In addition, the overlap between anxiety and depression further suggests a common underlying diathesis. This review suggests that the state of our knowledge in this area is still limited. We need more research focused on the overlap and separation among these disorders. The overlap observed raises questions about the applicability of the current DSM system to primary care settings. Either the DSM system needs revision for primary care settings or a different system is needed that reflects the reality of mental illness seen in primary care.

IMPLICATIONS FOR CLASSIFICATION OF MENTAL DISORDERS IN PRIMARY CARE

Mental disorders are common among primary care patients, but many fail to meet criteria for specific mental disorders, having subthreshold syndromes or a sense of emotional distress. Primary care physicians are trained in caring for these patients and are believed to provide cost effective care (American Academy of Family Physicians, 1995). One problem that primary care physicians face in caring for patients with psychological symptoms is the classification system used to categorize these symptoms. As presented earlier in this chapter, there is not only evidence of commonality among depressive disorders and among anxiety disorders, but between depressive and anxiety disorders as well. If the classification system used does not accurately reflect the reality of mental disorders in primary care patients, the results may be invalid research, inappropriate treatment, and inadequate provision of care.

Concerns about Current Mental Health Classification Systems

Classification facilitates research and communication among professionals, and it is useful clinically in suggesting prognosis, treatment selection, and administration of health care services (Goldberg & Huxley, 1992). However, these advantages are compromised if the system does not accurately reflect reality. There is growing concern about current mental health classifications (Klinkman & Okkes, 1998; National Institute of Mental Health, 1986). For categorical models to be valid, categories must have unique clinical descriptions with clear discontinuity between categories as well as between illness and wellness. Categories should be robust across classification systems, observers, and time. Categories should have distinct genetic bases, pathophysiology, natural histories, and treatment responses (Lam & Stewart, 1996; Goldberg & Huxley, 1992). However, categories within currently used mental health classification systems often do not fulfill these criteria. In addition, the inclusion of subthreshold syndromes often increases the validity of these systems by more accurately representing mental illness in the population and by including more of the patients that actually receive treatment (Angst et al, 1997).

The most often-used mental health classification system is the Diagnostic and Statistical Manual of Mental Disorders (DSM). The initial version of the DSM classification system was developed in 1960, primarily for research purposes (American Psychiatric Association, 1960). However, forty years and three revisions later, the DSM system is the basis for clinical diagnosis and health care delivery. Despite its hold on mental health classification, problems with the DSM system have been noted. For example, of patients with maladaptive personality problems, only 39% met criteria for an Axis II disorder (see Table 7) (Westin & Arkowitz-Westin, 1998). The convergent and discriminant validity of personality disorders is only modest (Grilo et al, 2001). For Axis I, DSM-IIIR was inadequate for patients symptomatic with both anxiety and depressive features. Creating boundaries between anxiety disorders has proven difficult. In fact, generalized anxiety disorder (GAD) was almost eliminated from DSM-IV due to its frequent comorbidity with affective disorders and concerns about its validity (Liebowitz, 1993). DSM-III criteria for panic disorder were said to be arbitrary (Aronson, 1987) and twin studies have shown a continuum of liability based on the narrowness of the definition used (Kendler et al, 2001). DSM-IIIR nosological problems have been reported in patients with panic disorder (Ciccone & Bulleltirie, 1989).

Table 7. Personality Problems Not Included In Axis II Criteria

Problem	Prevalence (%)
Intimacy	70
Anger	71
Authority	36
Shyness	35
Abandonment	60
Relationships	63
Work	31
Getting Along With People	20
Depressed	70
Anxious	59
Guilt	56
Self Esteem	69
Emotional Constriction	35
Rigidity	30
Impulsivity	29
Perfectionism	48
Devaluing Others	32

(Westen and Arkowitz-Westen, 1998)

In general, DSM symptom severity and duration criteria are considered arbitrary (Goldberg & Huxley, 1992). Kendler and Gardner's (1998) work on the DSM subthreshold-threshold boundary in major depression failed to find a discontinuity in either impairment or number of symptoms. Kessler et al (1997) confirmed this continuous increase in duration, impairment, comorbidity, and family history as the number of depressive symptoms increase. Similarly, a linear relationship was found between the number of posttraumatic stress disorder (PTSD) symptoms and the levels of impairment, comorbidity, and suicidality (Marshall et al, 2001). In fact, the prediction of major depression in twins was not dependent upon symptom number, impairment, or duration (Kendler & Gardner, 1998). No difference exists between abuse and dependence in adolescents with DSM-IV substance use disorder (Harrison & Fulkerson, 1998). In an attempt to decrease false positives, DSM-IV added a clinical significance criterion to its Axis I disorders (see Table 8). Unfortunately, this criterion often was either unnecessary or increased false negative rates. Even when needed, the addition of clinical significance could have been incorporated into the symptom criteria (Spitzer & Wakefield, 1999). Thus, the DSM system, although used widely, has several problems. In fact, the DSM system may reflect more on psychiatric culture than about the reality of mental illness in primary care (Fabrega et al, 1990). Recently, mental health providers have raised concerns about the DSM system (Helmuth, 2003). However, ICD-9 and ICHPPC-2 were no better (Jenkins et al, 1985). In addition, the hierarchical nature of ICD-10 suggests that it will be no more valid for primary care than previous classification systems (Klein & Klein, 1989).

In addition to the commonality among disorders, the dissatisfaction with the ability of the DSM system to describe mental illness in primary care settings comes from three other sources. First, the criteria-based DSM system produces a group of patients who do not quite meet diagnostic criteria (patients with subthreshold disorders). Second, there is a group of patients with psychological distress but without a mental disorder who cannot be adequately classified under the DSM system. Third, treatment recommendations based on DSM categories imply stability over time; yet, primary care patients with psychological symptoms show instability in their symptoms and diagnoses.

Table 8. Problems With DSM-IV Clinical Significance Criterion

Problem	Examples
Criterion Unnecessary	Conduct Disorder
	Selective Mutism
	Dissociative Fugue
Increased False Negative Rates	Tourette's Syndrome
	Paraphilias
	Sexual Dysfunctions
	Substance Dependence
Needed But Could Be Added To Symptom Criteria	Separation Anxiety
	Generalized Anxiety Disorder
	Posttraumatic Stress Disorder

(Spitzer and Wakefield, 1999)

Subthreshold Disorders

Primary care patients often have mild Axis I disorders or borderline disorders (Sireling et al, 1985). Subthreshold mental illness is present in 13-30% of patients (Stein et al, 1995; Karlsson et al, 1995) and is seen without a major Axis I disorder in 15% of patients (Philbrick et al, 1996).

The prevalence of subthreshold anxiety and affective disorders in primary care is presented in Table 9. In addition, community-dwelling adolescents have high rates of both subthreshold anxiety and depression (Wittchen et al, 2000). Axis I disorders are frequently associated with other subthreshold disorders (Olfson et al, 1996). In panic disorder, not only are infrequent panic attacks and limited symptom attacks common in the community (5.6% and 2.2% respectively) (Katerndahl & Realini, 1993), but also many patients are left with residual minor attacks after treatment (Schweizer et al, 1993; Liebowitz et al, 1986). Of the 13-16% of community-dwelling people reporting fearful spells, only 2-4% have recurrent panic attacks (Reed & Wittchen, 1998). In addition to the prevalence of subthreshold disorders, threshold and subthreshold disorders represent a single phenomenon. Patients with anxiety who fail to meet Axis I criteria but have mild and transient symptoms were shown to have good test-retest reliability (Fyer et al, 1989). Patients with panic symptoms do not display a threshold for classification as "panic disorder."(Eaton et al, 1994) In patients with depressive symptoms, 12% failed to meet the severity criterion for a DSM major depression diagnosis (Schulberg et al, 1995). Not only do people with major depression and subthreshold depression have similar family history for depression (Sherbourne et al, 1994), but there is also no etiologic difference between them (Ormel et al, 2001). The observation that subthreshold depression and melancholia have a common neurophysiology attests to the validity of dysthymia, subthreshold depression, and intermittent depression (Akiskal et al, 1997).

Table 9. Prevalence Of Subthreshold Mental Disorders In Primary Care

Disorder	Prevalence (%)
Anxiety Disorders	9-23
Panic Disorder	2-11
Generalized Anxiety Disorder	2-9
Obsessive Compulsive Disorder	6
Affective Disorders	5-13
Minor Depression	5-16
Recurrent Brief Depression	5-10

(Ormel et al, 1991; Olfson et al, 1996; Barrett et al, 1988; Schulberg et al, 1995; Philbrick et al, 1996; Spitzer et al, 1994; Birchall et al, 2000; Tiemens et al, 1996; Pincus et al, 1999; Carter et al, 2001)

Patients with subthreshold disorders have adverse outcomes, including increased symptomatology (Sartorius et al, 1996), health care utilization and costs (Simon et al, 1995), and impairment (Ormel et al, 1994; Tiemens et al, 1996; Spitzer et al, 1995), even across cultures (Saraceno et al, 1995). Psychological symptoms are associated with distress and utilization to a greater extent than are DSM diagnoses (Jones et al, 1987). Subthreshold anxiety is associated with disability (Olfson et al, 1996). People with subthreshold panic report more psychopathology and work disability with poorer quality of life. Panic frequency is less important than the number of symptoms (Katerndahl, 1998). Similar increases in impairment are also seen with threshold and subthreshold PTSD (Marshall et al, 2001; Zlotnick et al, 2002). Depressive disorders have a similar pattern. Not only is subthreshold depression associated with impairment (Sartorius et al, 1996; Rapaport et al, 2002), but patients with threshold and subthreshold depression may also have similar levels of disability (Ormel et al, 2001), comorbidity ((Sherbourne et al, 1994), and treatment rates (Sherbourne et al, 1994; Meredith et al, 1997). Minor depression is similar to mild major depression in terms of impairment, work disability, marital problems, and help seeking (Skodel et al, 1994). Finally, patients with either subthreshold panic disorder or major depression have increased suicide risk, and report increased symptom severity and disability (Lecrubier & Ustun, 1998).

Thus, subthreshold disorders are common and lead to impairment. There is no evidence to suggest that all subthreshold disorders are the same and, thus, they should not be lumped together under the "Anxiety NOS" rubric (Klein, 1993). But not every distressed primary care patient meets criteria for even a subthreshold disorder; some patients are simply distressed.

Psychological Distress

Although 9% of people in the community are distressed (Centers for Disease Control, 1998), the prevalence of distress in most primary care settings is 19-43% (Callahan et al, 1998; Zinsbarg et al, 1994; Tiemens et al, 1996; Robbins et al, 1994; Coyne & Schwenk, 1997; Ormel et al, 1990; van den Brink et al, 1991; Vasquez-Barquero et al, 1990; Karlsson et al, 1995). Many of these distressed primary care patients do not have a mental disorder (35-

69%) (Zinsbarg et al, 1994; Tiemens et al, 1996; Coyne et al, 1997; Ormel et al, 1990). Only 18-29% are recognized by their physician and given a diagnosis (Callahan et al, 1998; van den Brink et al, 1991), but distressed patients without a diagnosis are managed differently than non-distressed patients (Callahan et al, 1998). Referral and mental health utilization correlates with the level of distress (Simon et al, 1994).

Even without distress, primary care patients often have other psychosocial issues (Lamberts & Hofman-Okkes, 1993). Thus, using classification systems limited to diagnoses fails to reflect the reality of and morbidity due to distress, subthreshold disorders, and other non-distress psychosocial issues commonly seen in primary care. In addition, these categorical systems assume stability of the psychological conditions they include.

Instability of Symptoms and Diagnoses

Previous work suggests that distress often changes over the course of a year (Hickie et al, 1999) and symptoms often resolve after a few months (Winokur et al, 1984; Higgins, 1994; Lamberts & Hofman-Okkes, 1993). Although high levels of depression and anxiety are not stable over the short term (Barrett & Hurst, 1982), when followed over years they are generally stable (Lovibond, 1998; Watson & Walker, 1996). In fact, initial depressive symptoms correlate with symptoms after relapse (Paykel et al, 1976). Patients with a new but minor psychiatric disorders often improve within one month (Catalan et al, 1984). In primary care patients with at least one psychiatric disorder, 20% recover after three months (Ceroni et al, 1992). Diagnoses last less than four weeks 30% of the time and less than six months 65% of the time (Lamberts & Hofman-Okkes, 1993). Thus, although psychiatric symptoms may be stable over years, diagnoses are not (Degonda & Angst, 1993; Daradkeh, 1996).

Although borderline anxiety is often chronic (van den Brink et al, 1991), subthreshold panic categories have only fair-to-poor reliability (Fyer et al, 1989). One-third of anxiety disorders resolve in less than six months (van den Brink et al, 1991). However, specific anxiety disorders vary in their stability. In people with GAD symptoms, the duration criterion most often caused failure to meet DSM criteria (Carter et al, 2001). While 26% of patients with panic disorder and 23% of patients with GAD have symptom-free remissions, only 2% of agoraphobics do (Breier et al, 1988). Similarly, the levels of symptoms in patients with panic disorder and GAD often decrease over 3-4 weeks (Barrett & Hurst, 1982). Studies have found that symptom patterns vary in panic disorder (de Beurs et al, 1994), and that major and minor attacks decrease over a 4-week period with self-monitoring (de Jong & Boumon, 1995). Panic disorder remission rates are 23% at 13 weeks (Keller et al, 1994). These findings are consistent with other remission rates of 26-39% (Yonkers et al, 1998).

Depression in adolescents tends to be more stable than anxiety over a 1-year period (Wittchen et al, 2000). Although 63% of primary care patients with borderline depression improve in less than six months (van den Brink et al, 1991), Rapaport et al (2002) found that over a 4-week period, five people out of 162 with minor depression developed major depression and 14 reported resolution of their minor depression. Minor depression can be divided into episodic and chronic forms (Barrett, 1986). Depression in primary care often (47%) resolves in less than six months (van den Brink et al, 1991) and depressive symptoms tend to decrease over a 3-4 week period in both major and minor depression (Barrett & Hurst, 1982). Patients with depression report symptom-free periods (Breier et al, 1988). In a 12-year study of depressed psychiatric patients, only 27% were never asymptomatic while 59% reported a variety of levels of severity. Although they reported that 15% of their weeks were spent in major depression, 42% of their weeks were spent without symptoms (Judd et al, 1998).

Hence, although psychiatric symptoms may be stable over time, DSM disorders are not. This instability raises concerns about the validity of DSM categories if these criteria are to be used to prescribe treatment. Due to high symptom variability, it is unclear whether the number of symptoms correlates with severity; symptom persistence may be more important (Shepherd & Wilkinson, 1986). Monthly interviews of 59 primary care patients found that anxiety levels showed significant variability with 47% crossing the distressed-nondistressed threshold at least once in a 6-month period. In addition, 10% developed subthreshold criteria and 25% crossed at least one DSM threshold. Several crossed multiple times but for different disorders (Katerndahl et al, 2002). It is difficult to rationalize pharmacotherapy for what may be a transient "disorder". Coupled with the existence of distress without disorders and the prevalence of subthreshold disorders, serious concerns exist about the validity of the DSM system for primary care patients.

Limitations to the Basis for the DSM System

The applicability of the DSM system to primary care is based on problematic literature, on observations obtained in mental health settings, and on a belief in the validity of categorical descriptions. In addition to problems with confounding (Olfson et al, 1996) and controls (Allison, 1993), much of the research literature relies heavily upon patient recall. Although the stability of recall is good in patients with major depression and substance abuse, recall is poor for anxiety disorders (Fendrich et al, 1990). Even with the strongest of psychiatry-derived research, questions about the similarity of primary care and psychiatry settings pose another limitation to the applicability of the DSM system to primary care.

Experience in Primary Care Versus Psychiatric Settings

Overall, mental illness is less severe in primary care patients than in psychiatric patients, particularly in terms of symptom severity, past history, and impairment (Klinkman et al, 1997). Depressed psychiatric patients have higher levels of depressive symptomatology, higher prevalence of major depression with dysthymia, more comorbid anxiety, and poorer global functioning (Wells et al, 1995).

Less than 10% of primary care patients with mental illness have a major mental disorder needing treatment (Goldberg, 1982). Compared to the 35% of primary care patients with distress, 90% of psychiatric patients are distressed (Coyne & Schwenk, 1997). While fewer than 15% of community-dwelling people have a mental disorder, the rates in primary care and psychiatric settings are 30% and 90% respectively (Goldberg & Huxley, 1992). Primary care patients with anxiety or depressive disorders are less impaired than psychiatric patients (Zinsbarg et al, 1994; deGruy, 1996). Similar comparisons in panic disorder found similar patterns (Katerndahl & Realini, 1998).

Recognition of mental illness by primary care physicians determines the characteristics of patients referred to and seen by psychiatrists. Generalists detect 18-50% of mentally ill patients (Engel et al, 1994). Of 31% of patients with a significant mental disorder, only 3% presented with purely psychiatric symptoms (Shepherd & Wilkinson, 1986). Past history, level of distress, symptom severity, and disability are associated with increased recognition (Sartorius et al, 1996; Klinkman et al, 1997; Simon et al, 1999). Physician recognition correlates with symptoms rather than diagnosis on structured interview (Jones et al, 1987;

Robbins et al, 1994). Recognition of depression is actually better than previously thought if viewed on a severity dimension (Thompson et al, 2001). In addition to symptoms, primary care physicians attend to life events, thought, relationship, and behavioral problems, and functional status (Cole et al, 1977). Hence, primary care physicians focus more on symptoms than diagnoses.

The referral process further distorts the primary care-psychiatry differences. While both primary care physicians and psychiatrists feel that symptom severity is important in decision-making for referral, primary care physicians also feel that the diagnosis is an important factor (Farmer & Griffiths, 1992). Suicidality, hallucinations, depression, family problems, and behavior problems are also predictors of referral but somatization is not (Saraceno et al, 1995). Once referred, patients were more likely to keep their appointments with psychiatrists if they had prior mental health concerns but lacked unexplained physical symptoms (Olfson, 1991). This further distorts the applicability of psychiatry-derived observations.

The problem with psychiatrist-determined classification is that, of the 25% of primary care patients with mental illness, 40% are recognized of which 20% are referred to a mental health provider; it is upon these few patients that the classification system is largely based (Eisenberg, 1992). Hence, primary care mental illness syndromes are not the same as psychiatric mental illness syndromes (Engel et al, 1994). Therefore, DSM-IV may be inadequate for primary care settings (Barrett et al, 1988; Goldberg, 1982; Goldberg, 1992; Lamberts & Hofman-Okkes, 1993).

Dimensions Versus Categories

As DSM-IV states, "a categorical approach to classification works best when all members of a diagnostic class are homogeneous, when there are clear boundaries between classes, and when the different classes are mutually exclusive." (American Psychiatric Association, 1994) These conditions are not true for the DSM system. The diverse psychotropic applications across disorders have led to a reconceptualization of mental disorders as dimensional. In fact, different medications treat different symptom dimensions (Hollander, 1999). Personality disorders, somatization, and OCD may be amenable to dimensional description (Cloninger, 1986; Hollander, 1999; Orenstein, 1989; Pukrop, 2002). Two delusional dimensions are stable across time, stable across diagnosis, and consistent with etiologies (Appelbaum et al, 1999). The dimensionality of Axis I disorders is further supported by symptom clustering studies. Factor analysis of symptoms in adolescents with psychopathology resulted in nine factors; second order factor analysis then produced two factors (internalizing and externalizing) (Miller, 1980). Cluster analysis of anxiety and depressive symptoms led to clusters based on severity and impairment rather than diagnosis (Nease et al, 1999). Hence, it has been suggested that dimensional classification will be used to describe mental illness in primary care in the future (Shepherd & Wilkinson, 1986).

Classification in Primary Care

Although the DSM system has led to progress in our understanding of mental illness, it has had problems. A classification system based on psychiatric diagnosis provides little help to practitioners and does not account for the transient distress observed by practitioners (Goldberg, 1992). Accounting for both distress and mental illness are important for a relevant primary care system (Shepherd & Wilkinson, 1988). While severe anxiety and depressive disorders have distinct backgrounds, family histories, and natural histories in mental health settings, the less severe forms seen in primary care often overlap and may represent a common diathesis (Gelder, 1989). Most authors favor the use of multi-axial systems (Shepherd et al, 1986; Wessely et al, 1999; Guimon, 1989).

One approach to improving classification would be to revise the current DSM system. Pincus et al (1999) suggested substituting "subthreshold disorder with stressor" for adjustment disorders and possibly eliminating the "significant" stipulation used in several criteria. However, the limitations of categorical classification are clear and Aronson (1987) has recommended classification based on a combination of categories and dimensions.

A second approach would be to combine categories and dimensions. Personality assessments could be used in both categorical and dimensional classifications (Westen & Shedler, 1999). Based on predictive validity, DSM-III Axis I and II categories as well as dimensions were shown to be valid; however, adjustment and immaturity of defenses were just as valid (Valliant & Schnurr, 1988). In addition, combining personality and trait assessment with anxiety and depressive features may provide a more useful classification of anxiety disorders than the DSM-IIIR (Sanderson et al, 1990). The taxonomy needs to include subthreshold syndromes and emotional distress, recognize comorbidities, include other psychosocial factors, and incorporate the interaction between mental and physical factors (deGruy, 1996).

Finally, a dimensional system could be used. Dimensional systems may be more flexible and valid than categorical ones. Aronson (1987) suggested a 7-dimension system including anxiety, depression, phobia, hypochondriasis, obsessiveness, spontaneity, and severity. Such dimensional systems, although problematic for payers who reimburse services based on diagnoses, may better reflect the reality of mental illness. A multi-axial system that includes a dimensional approach can reflect the reality of mental illness in primary care settings. However, such a system must be able to distinguish between illness and distress (Shepherd & Wilkinson, 1986). Under a multi-axial dimensional system, management strategies would be based on patterns across dimensions.

In conclusion, there is considerable evidence for the commonality of anxiety disorders as well as the commonality between anxiety and depressive disorders. Clearly, further research is needed to deepen our understanding of mental illness and explain discrepant data supporting and refuting commonality of disorders. The applicability of the DSM system is called into question based upon the commonalities among depressive disorders and among anxiety disorders as well as between anxiety and depressive disorders, the prevalence of subthreshold disorders and distress without disorders, and the instability of diagnoses. The literature in support of the DSM system is problematic due to methodological issues and differences between patients with mental disorders in primary care versus psychiatry settings. Primary care physicians recognize these limitations and often make selective use of the DSM system. Primary care disciplines need to consider alternatives to the DSM system and work toward a new approach to classification. A new classification system for primary care is needed, which is dimensional in nature, multi-axial, reliable, and reflects the spectrum of mental disorders seen in primary care.

ACKNOWLEDGMENT

The author would like to acknowledge the editorial and technical assistance of E. Mikaila Adams in the preparation of this manuscript.

REFERENCES

AAFP Commission on Health Care Services: AAFP White Paper on the Provision of Mental Health Care Services by Family Physicians. *Am Fam Physician* 1995;51:1405-1412.

Akiskal H, Judd L, Gillin J, Lemmi H. Subthreshold depressions. *J Affect Disord* 1997; 45:53-63.

Allison D. Note on the selection of control groups and control variables in comorbidity research. *Compr Psychiatry* 1993;34:336-339.

Alnaes R, Torgersen S. Clinical differentiation between major depression only, major depression with panic disorder, and panic disorder only. *Acta Psychiatr Scand* 1989;79:370-7.

Alnaes R, Torgersen S. Parental representation in patients with major depression, anxiety disorder and mixed conditions. *Acta Psychiatr Scand* 1990;81:518-22.

Alnaes R, Torgersen S. Personality disorders among patients with major depression, anxiety disorders, and mixed conditions. *J Nerv Ment Dis* 1990;178:693-8.

American Psychiatric Association. Diagnostic and Statistical Manual of Mental Disorders. Washington, DC: *American Psychiatric Association*, 1960.

American Psychiatric Association: Diagnostic and Statistical Manual of Mental Disorders (4th ed). Washington, DC: *American Psychiatric Association*, 1994.

Amies PL, Gelder MG, Shaw PM: A comparative clinical study. *Br J Psychiatry* 1983; 142:174-179.

Ampollini P, Marchesi C, Signifredi R, et al. Temperament and personality features in patients with major depression, panic disorder, and mixed conditions. *J Affect Disord* 1999;52:203-7.

Andersch SEO, Hanson LCF: Comorbidity of panic disorder and social phobia. *Europe Journal of Psychiatry* 1993; 7:59-64.

Anderson DJ, Noyes R Jr., Crowe RR: Comparison of panic disorder and generalized anxiety disorder. 1984; 141:572-575.

Andrews G, Slade T: Agoraphobia without a history of panic disorder may be part of the panic disorder syndrome. *J Nerv Ment Dis* 2002; 190:624-30.

Angst J, Merikangas K: The depressive spectrum: diagnostic classification and course. *Journal of Affective Disorders* 1997; 45(1-2):31-39.

Angst J, Merikangas KR, Preisig M: Subthreshold syndromes of depression and anxiety in the community. *J Clin Psychiatry* 1997; 58(suppl 8)6-10.

Angst J, Sellaro R, Merikangas KR: Depressive spectrum diagnoses. *Comprehensive Psychiatry* 2000; 41(2 Suppl 1):39-47.

Antony MM, Roth D, Swinson RP, Devins GM: Illness intrusiveness in individuals with panic disorder, obsessive-compulsive disorder or social phobia. *J Nerv Ment Dis* 1998; 186:311-5.

Apfeldorf WJ, Spielman LA, Cloitre M, Heckelman L, Shear MK: Morbidity of comorbid psychiatric diagnoses in the clinical presentation of panic disorder. *Dep Anx* 2000; 12:78-84.

Appelbaum P, Robbins P, Roth L. Dimensional approach to delusions. *Am J Psychiatry* 1999;156:1938-1943.

Argyle N, Roth M: Phenomenological study of 90 patients with panic disorder. *Psychiat Develop* 1989; 3:187-209.

Aronson TA: Is panic disorder a distinct diagnostic entity? *J Nerv Ment Dis* 1987; 175:584-94.

Bankier B, Aigner M, Bach M. Alexithymia in DSM-IV disorder. *Psychosomatics* 2001;42(3):235-40.

Barrett J, Barrett J, Oxman T, Gerber P. Prevalence of psychiatric disorders in a primary care practice. *Arch Gen Psychiatry* 1988; 45:1100-1106.

Barrett J, Hurst M. Short-term symptom change in outpatient psychiatric disorders. *Arch Gen Psychiatry* 1982;39:849-854.

Barrett J: Care identification for category validation. *Compreh Psychiatry* 1986; 27(2):81-100.

Basoglu M, Marks IM, Sengun S: Prospective study of panic and anxiety in agoraphobia with panic disorder. *Br J Psychiatry* 1992; 160:57-64.

Beekman AT, Deeg DJ, Braam AW, Smit JH, Van Tilburg W: Consequences of major and minor depression in later life: a study of disability, well-being and service utilization. *Psychological Medicine* 1997; 27(6): 1397-1409.

Biederman J, Faraone SV, Hirshfeld-Becker DR, Friedman D, Robin JA, Rosenbaum JF. Patterns of psychopathology and dysfunction in high-risk children of parents with panic disorder and major depression. *Arch J Psychiatry* 2001;158:49-57.

Biederman J, Hisrhfeld-Becker DR, Rosenbaum JF, Herot C, Friedman D, Snidman N, Kogan J, Farane SV: Further evidence of association between behavioral inhibition and social anxiety in children. *Am J Psychiatry* 2001a; 158:1673-1679.

Birchall H, Brandon S, Taub N. Panic in a general practice population. *Soc Psychiatry Psychiatr Epidemiol* 2000;35:235-41.

Birket-Smith M, Hasle N, Jensen HM: Electrodermal activity in anxiety disorders. *Acta Psychaitr Scand* 1993; 88:350-355.

Blier P, de Montigny C. Serotonin and drug-induced therapeutic responses in major depression, obsessive-compulsive and panic disorders. *Neuropsychopharmacology* 1999;21:915-85.

Blumberg SH, Izard CE. Discriminating patterns of emotions in 10 and 11 year old children's anxiety and depression. *J Pers Soc Psychol* 1986;51:852-7.

Borasso G, Eaton W. Types of panic attacks and their association with psychiatric disorder and illness. *Compr Psychiatry* 1999;40:469-77.

Borden JW, Turner SM: Is panic a unique emotional experience? *Behav Res Ther* 1989; 27: 263-268.

Breier A, Charney Ds, Heninger GR. Major depression in patients with agoraphobia and panic disorder. *Arch Gen Psychiatry* 1984;41:1129-35.

Breier A, Charney DS, Heninger GR: Diagnostic validity of anxiety disorders and their relationship to depressive illness. *Am J Psychiatry* 1985; 142:787-797.

Breier A, Chavney D, Heninger G. Agoraphobia with panic attacks. *Arch Gen Psychaitry* 1988; 43:1029-1038.

Bremner JD, Narayan M, Staib LH, Southwick SM, McGlaghan T, Charney DS: Neural correlates of memories of childhood sexual abuse in women with and without posttraumatic stress disorder. *Am J Psychiatry* 156:1787-1795. 1999.

Brown C, Schulberg HC, Madonia MJ, Shear MK, Houck PR. Treatment outcomes for primary care patients with major depression and life time anxiety disorders. *Am J Psychiatry* 1996;153:1293-300.

Brown GW, Harris TO, Eales MJ. Social factors and comorbidity of depressive and anxiety disorders. *Br J Psychiatry* 1996;168(30 Suppl):50-7.

Brown TA, Chorpita BF, Barlow DH. Structural relationships among dimensions of the DSM-IV anxiety and mood disorders and dimensions of negative affect, positive affect, and autonomic arousal. *J Abnorm Psychol* 1998;107:179-92.

Bryant RA, Panasetis P: Panic symptoms during trauma and acute stress disorder. *Behav Res Ther* 2001; 39:961-966.

Buller R, Maier W, Benkert O. Clinical subtypes in panic disorder. *J Affect Disord* 1986;11:105-14.

Burns DD, Eidelson RJ. Why are depression and anxiety correlated? *J Consult Clin Psychol* 1998;66:461-73.

Bystritsky A, Croske M, Maidenberg E, Vapnik T, Shapiro D: Autonomic reactivity of panic patients during a CO_2 inhalation procedure. *Dep Anx* 2000b; 11:15-26.

Callahan E, Jaen C, Crabtree B, Zyzanski S, Goodwin M, Stange K. Impact of recent emotional distress and diagnosis of depression or anxiety on the physician-patient encounter in family practice. *J Fam Pract* 1998;46:410-418.

Carter RM, Wittchan HU, Pfister H, Kessler RC. One-year prevalence of subthreshold and threshold DSM-IV generalized anxiety disorder in a nationally representative sample. *Dep Anx* 2001;13:78-88.

Cassano GB, Dell'Osso L, Frank E, Miniati M, Fagiolini A, Shear K, Pini S, Maser J: Bipolar Spectrum. *J Affect Disord* 1999a; 54:319-328.

Cassano GB, Michelini S, Shear MK, Coli E, Maser JD, Frank E: The panic-agoraphobia spectrum. *Am J Psychiatry* 1997; 154(6 Festschrift suppl):27-38.

Cassano GB, Perugi G, Musetti L, Akiskal HS. The nature of depression presenting concomitantly with panic disorder. *Compr Psychiatry* 1989;30:473-82.

Cassano GB, Pini S, Saettoni M, Dell'Osso L. Multiple anxiety disorder comorbidity in patients with mood spectrum disorders with psychotic features. *Am J Psychiatry* 1999;156:474-6.

Catalan J, Gath D, Edwards G, Ennis J. Effects of non-prescribing of anxiolytic in general practice. *Br J Psychiatry* 1984;44:593-602.

Centers for Disease Control: Self-reported frequent mental distress among adults-United States, 1993-1996. *MMWR* 1998;47(16):325-330.

Ceroni G, Ceroni F, Bivi R. DSM-III mental disorders in general medical sector. *Soc Psychiatry Psychiatr Epidemiol* 1992;27:234-241.

Chambless DL, Gillis MN: Cognitive therapy of anxiety disorders. *J consult Clin Psychol* 1993; 61:248-260.

Chantarujikapong SI, Scherrer JF, Xian H, Eisen SA, Lyons MJ, Goldberg J, Tsuang M, True WR: Twin study of gereralized anxiety disorder symptoms panic disorder symptoms and post-traumatic stress disorder in men. *Psychiatry Res* 2001; 103:133-145.

Charney DS, Woods SW, Heninger GR: Noradrenergic function in Generalized Anxiety Disorder. *Psychiat Res* 1989; 27: 173-182.

Ciccone P, Bellettirie G. Patient with panic disorder eventuating in psychosis. *Psychiatr J Univ Ottawa* 1989;14:478-480.

Clark LA, Watson D. Tripatite model of anxiety and depression. *J Abnorm Psychol* 1991;100:316-36.

Claycomb JB: Endogenous anxiety. *J Clin Psychiatry* 1983; 44(8, Sec 2):19-22.

Cloninger C.Unified biosocial theory of personality and its role in the development of anxiety status. *Psychiatr Develop* 1986;3:167-226.

Clum GA, Knowles SL: Why do some people with panic disorder become avoidant? A review. *Clin Psychol Rev* 1991; 11:295-313.

Cohen LS, Biederman J: Further evidence for an association between affective disorders and anxiety disorders. *J Clin Psychiatry* 1988; 49:-313-316.

Cole DA, Peeke LG, Martin JM, Truglio R, Seroczynaki AD. Longitudinal look at the relation between depression and anxiety in children and adolescents. *J Consult Clin Psychol* 1998;66:451-60.

Cole W, Baker R, Twersky R. Classification and coding of psychosocial problems in family medicine. *J Fam Pract* 1977;4:85-89.

Copp JE, Schwiderski VE, Robinson DS. Sympton comorbidity in anxiety and depressive disorders. *J Clin Psychopharmacol* 1990;10:525-60.

Coryell W, Endicett J, Andreasen NC, et al. Depression and panic attacks. *Am J Psychiatry* 1988;145:293-300.

Coryell W, Endicott J, Winokur G. Anxiety syndromes as epiphenomenon of primary major depression. *Am J Psychiatry* 1992;149:100-7.

Coryell W. Anxiety secondary to depression. Psychiatr *Clin North Am* 1990;13:685-98.

Cottraux J, Gebuhrer L, Bardi R, Betuel H: HLA system and panic attack. *Biol Psychiatry* 1989; 25:505-508.

Cox BJ, Enns MW, Walker JF, Kjernisted K, Pidlubny SR. Psychological vulnerabilities in patients with major depression vs. panic disorder. *Behav Res Ther* 2001;39:567-73.

Coyne JC, Schwenk TL: Relationship of distress to mood disturbance in primary care and psychiatric populations..*J Consult Clin Psychol* 1997; 65:167-168.

Crowe RR, Goedker R, Samuelson S, Wilson R, Nelson J, Noyes R Jr: Genomewide survey of panic disorder. *Am J Med Genetics* (Neuropsychiatric Genetics) 2001; 150:105-109.

Crowe RR, Noyes R Jr, Samuelson S, Wesner R, Wilson R: Close linkage between panic disorder and alpha-haptoglobin excluded in 10 families. *Arch Gen Psychiatry* 1990; 47:377-80.

Crowe RR, Noyes R. Jr., Wilson AF, Elston RC, Ward LJ: Linkage study of panic disorder. *Arch Gen Psychiatry* 1987; 44:933-937.

d'Ansia GID. Familial analysis of panic disorder and agoraphobia. *J Affect Disord* 1989;17:1-8.

Daradkeh TK: Stability of psychiatric diagnoses in clinical practice. *Intl J Soc Psychiatry* 1996; 42:207-12.

Davey GCL, de Jong PJ, Tallis F: UCS inflation in the aetiology of a variety of anxiety disorders. *Behav Res Ther* 1993; 31:495-498.

De Beurs E, Garssen B, Buikhuisen M, Lange A, Van Balkom A, Van Dyck R. Continuous monitoring of panic. *Acta Psychaitr Scand* 1994;90:38-45.

De Graaf R, Bijl RV, Smit F, Vollebergh WAM, Spijker J. Risk factors for 12-month comorbidity of mood, anxiety, and substance use disorders. *Am J Psychiatry* 2002;159:620-9.

De Jong G, Bouman T. *Panic disorder J Anxiety Disord* 1995;9:185-199.

De la Fuente JM, Bobes J, Vizuete C, Mendlewicz J: Biological nature of depressive symptoms in borderline personality disorder. *J Psychiatr Res* 2002; 36:137-45.

De Lima MS, Hotoph M, Wessely S: The efficacy of drug treatments for dysthymia: a systematic review and meta-analysis. *Psychological Medicine* 1999; 29(6):1273-1289.

Degonda M, Angst J: Zurich study. *Eur Arch Psychiatry Clin Neurosci* 1993; 243:95-102.

DeGruy F. Mental health care in the primary care setting. In: Institute of Medicine Committee on the Future of Primary Care: Primary Care: America's Health in a New Era. Washington D.C.: *National Academy Press*, 1996.

Eaton W, Kessler R, Wittchen H, Magee W. Panic and panic disorder in the United States. *Am J Psychiatry* 1994;151:413-420.

Ehntholt KA, Salkovskis PM, Rimes KA: Obsession compulsive disorder, anxiety disorders and self-esteem. *Behav Res Ther* 1999; 37:771-781.

Eisenberg L. Treating depression and anxiety in primary care (ed.) *N Engl J Med* 1992;326: 1080-1083.

Engel C, Kroenke K, Katon W. Mental health services in army primary care. *Military Med* 1994;159:203-209.

Fabrega H Jr., Ahn C, Boster J, Mezzich J. DSM III as a systemic culture pattern. *J Psychaitr Res* 1990;24:139-154.

Faravelli C, Pallanti S, Frassine R, Albanesi G, Degl Innocenti BG: Panic attacks with and without agoraphobia. *Psychopathology* 1988; 21:51-56.

Farmer A, Giffiths H. Labeling and illness in primary care. *Psychol Med* 1992;22:717-723.

Fava GA, Kellner R. Prodronal symptoms in affective disorders. *Am J Psychiatry* 1991;148:823-30.

Fawcett J. Targeting treatment in patients with mixed symptoms of anxiety and depression. *J Clin Psychiatry* 1990;51:11(Suppl):40-3.

Fendrich M, Weissman M, Warner V, Mufson L. Two-year recall of lifetime diagnosis in offspring at high an low risk for major depression. *Arch Gen Psychiatry* 1990;47:1121-1127.

Fole SE. Recent developments in anxiety, stress, and depression. *Pharmacol Biochem Behav* 1996;54:3-12.

Fuller RW. Role of serotonin in therapy of depression and related disorders. *J Clin Psychiatry* 1991;52(Suppl):52-7.

Fyer A, Mannuzza S, Martin L, Gallops M, Endicatt J, Schleyer B, et al. Reliability of anxiety assessment. *Arch Gen Psychiatry* 1989;46:1102-1110.

Fyer AJ, Mannuzza S, Chapman TF, Martin LY, Klein DF: Specificity in familial aggregation of phobic disorders. *Arch Gen Psychiatry* 1995; 52:564-573.

Fyer AJ, Mannuzza S, Gallops MS, Martin LY, Aaronson C, Gorman JM, Liebowitz MK, Klein DF: Familial transmission of simple phobias and fears. *Arch Gen Psychiatry* 1990; 47:252-256.

Gelder M. Classification of anxiety disorders. *Br J Psychiatry Suppl* 1989;154(suppl 4):28-32.

Gelder MG: Panic disorder (ed): *Psychol Med* 1989; 19:277-283.

Gelernter CS, Stein MB, Tancer ME, Uhde TW: Examination of syndromal validity and diagnostic subtypes in social phobia and panic disorder. *J Clin Psychiatry* 1992; 53:23-27.

Glyshaw K, Cohen LH, Towbes LC. Coping strategies and psychological distress. *Am J Community Psychol* 1989;17:607-23.

Goddard AW, Mason GF, Almai A, Rothman DL, Behan KL, Petroff OAC, Charney DS, Krystal JH: Reductions in occipital cortex GABA levels in panic disorders detected with H-magnetic reschance spectroscopy. *Arch Gen Psychiatry* 2001; 58:556-567.

Goisman RM, Goldenberg I, Vasile RG, Keller MB: Comorbidity of anxiety disorders in a muticenter anxiety study. *Compreh Psychaitry* 1995; 36:303-311.

Goisman RM, Warshaw MG, Peterson LG, Rogers MP, Coneo P, Hunt MF, Tomlin-Albanese JM, Kazim A, Gollan JK, Epstein-Kaye T, Reich JH, Keller MB: Panic agoraphobia and panic disorder with agoraphobia. *J Nerv Ment Dis* 1994; 182:72-79.

Goldberg D, Huxley P. Common Mental Disorders. New York, NY: Tavistock; 1992.

Goldberg D. Classification of psychological distress for use in primary care settings. *Soc Sci Med* 1992;35:189-193.

Goldberg D. Concept of a psychiatric "case" in general practice. *Soc Psychiatry* 1982;17:61-65.

Goldenberg IM, White K, Yonkers K, Reich J, Warshaw MG, Goisman RM, Keller MB: Infrequency of "pure culture" diagnosis among the anxiety disorders. *J Clin Psychiatry* 1996; 57:528-533.

Gorman JM, Fyer MR, Goetz R, Askanazi J, Liebowitz MR, Fyer AJ, Kinney J, Klein DF: Ventilatory physiology of patients with panic disorder. *Arch Gen Psychiatry* 1988; 45:31-39.

Gorman JM, Kent JM, Sullivan GM, Coplan JD: Neuro-anatomical hypothesis of panic disorder, revised. *Am J Psychiatry* 2000; 157:493-505.

Gratacos M, Nadal M, Martin-Santos R, Pujana MA, Gago J, Peral B, Armengol L, Ponsa I, Miro R, Bulbena A, Estivill X: A Polymorphic genomic duplication on human chromosome 15 is a susceptibility factor for panic and phobic disorder. *Cell* 2001; 106:367-379.

Green BL, Grace MC, Lindy JD, Gleser GC, Leonard A: Risk factors for PTSD and other diagnosis in a general sample of Vietnam veterans. *Am J Psychiatry* 1990; 147:729-733.

Grilo C, McGlashan T, Morey L, Gunderson J, Skodol A, Tracie S, et al. Internal consistency intercriterion overlap and diagnostic efficiency of criteria sets for DSM-IV Schizotypal, borderline, avoidant and obsessive-compulsive personality disorders. *Acta Psyciatr Scand* 2001;104:264-272.

Grunhaus L, Rabin D, Greden JF. Simultaneous panic and depressive disorders. *J Clin Psychiatry* 1986;47:4-7.

Grunhaus L. Clinical and psychobiological characteristics of simultaneous panic disorder and major depression. *Am J Psychiatry* 1988;145:1214-21.

Guimon J. Biases of psychiatric diagnosis. Br J Psychiatry Suppl1989;154(suppl 4):33-37.

Gurney C, Roth M, Garside RF. Use of statistical techniques in classifications of affective disorders. *Proc R Soc Med* 1970;63:232-5.

Harrison P, Fulkerson J, TJ. DSM-IV substance use disorder criteria for adolescents. *Am J Psychiatry* 1998;155:486-492.

Heim C, Newport DJ, Bonsall R, Miller AH, Nemeroff CB. Altered pituitary-adrenal axis responses to provocative challenge tests in adult survivors of childhood abuse. *Am J Psychiatry* 2001;158:575-81.

Helmuth L: In sickness or in health? *Science* 2003; 302:808-10.

Heninger GR, Charney DS, Price LH. Noradrenergic and serotonergic receptor system function in panic disorder and depression. *Acta Psychiatr Scand* 1988;77(341 Suppl):138-50.

Hettema JM, Neale MC, Kendler KS: Review and meta-analysis of the genetic epidemiology of anxiety disorders. *Am J Psychiatry* 2001; 158:1568-1578.

Hickie I, Koschera A, Hadzi-Pavlovio D, Bennett B, Lloyd A. Temporal stability and comorbidity of prolonged fatigue. *Psychol Med* 1999;29:885-861.

Higgins E. Review of unrecognized mental illness in primary care. *Arch Fam Med* 1994; 3:908-917.

Hollander E, Kwon JH, Stein DJ, Broatch J, Rowland CT, Himelein CA: Obsessive-compulsive and spectrum disorder. *J Clin Psychiatry* 1996; 57(suppl 8):3-6.

Hollander E, Schiffman E, Cohen B, et al: Signs of central nervous system dysfunction in OCD. *Arch Gen Psychiatry* 1990; 47:27-32.

Hollander E. Managing aggressive behavior in patients with obsessive-compulsive disorder and borderline personality disorder. *J Clin Psychiatry* 1999;60(suppl 15):38-44.

Hubbard J, Realmuto GM, Northwood AK, Musten AS: Comorbidity of psychiatric diagnosis with posttraumatic stress disorder in survivors of childhood trauma. *J Am Acad Child Adolesc Psychiatry* 1995; 34:1167-1173.

Hunt C, Andrews G. Comorbidity in the anxiety disorders. *J Psychiatr Res* 1995;29:467-80.

Jacobs WJ, Nadel L: The first panic attack. *Canad J Exp Psychology* 1999; 53:92-107.

Jenkins R, Smeeton N, Marinker M, Shepherd M. Study of the classification of mental ill-health in general practice. *Psychol Med* 1985;15:403-409.

Jensen CF, Peskind ER, Kelller TW, McFall ME, Raskind MA: Comparison of sodium lactate-induced panic symptoms between panic disorder and posttraumatic stress disorder. *Dep Anx* 1998; 7:122-125.

Jones L, Badger L, Ficken R, Leoper J, Anderson R. Inside the hidden mental network. *Gen Hosp Psychiatry* 1987;9:287-293.

Judd FK, Burrow GD, Hay DA. Panic disorder. *Aust N Z J Psychiatry* 1987;21:197-208.

Judd L, Akiskal H, Maser J, Zeller P, Endicott J, Covyell W, et al. Prospective 12-year study of subsyndromal and syndromal depressive symptoms in unipolor major depressive disorders. *Arch Gen Psychiatry* 1998;55:694-700.

Judd LL: Pleomorphic expressions of unipolar depressive disease. *J Affect Dis* 1997; 45:109-116.

Jumper SA. Meta-analysis of the relationship of child sexual abuse to adult psychological adjustment. *Child Abuse Negl* 1995;19:715-28.

Kabat-Zinn J, Massion AO, Kristeller J, Peterson LG, Fletcher KE, Pbert L, Lenderking WR, Santorelli SF: Effectiveness of a meditation-based stress reduction program in the treatment of anxiety disorders. *Am J Pscychiatry* 1992; 149:936-943.

Karlsson H, Lehtinen V, Joukamaa M. Psychiatric morbidity among frequent attends patients in primary care. *Gen Hosp Psychiatry* 1995;17:19-25.

Katerndahl D, Amodei N, Larme A, Palmer R. Stability of psychiatric symptoms in primary care. *Silver Spring, MD: Agency for Healthcare Research and Quality*, NTIS #PB2002-108254, 2002.

Katerndahl D, Realini J. Lifetime prevalence of panic states. *Am J Psychiatry* 1993;150:246-9.

Katerndahl D, Realini JP. Patients with panic attacks seeking care from family physicians compared with those seeking care from psychiatrists. *J Nerv Ment Dis* 1998;186:249-50.

Katerndahl DA, Gabel LL, Monk JS: Comparative Symptomatology of Phobic and Nonphobic Panic Attacks. *Fam Pract Res* J, 6:106-13, 1986.

Katerndahl DA, Realini JP. Comorbid psychiatric disorders in subjects with panic attacks. *J Nerv Ment Dis* 1997;185(11):669-74.

Katerndahl DA: Intrapatient Agreement In Phenomenology of Panic Attacks" *Psychol Rep* 79:219-224, 1996.

Katerndahl DA: Panic is Panic: The Homogeneity of the Panic Attack Experience. *Fam Pract Res J,* 9:147-55, 1990.

Keller M, Yonkers K, Warshaw M, Pratt L, Gollan J, Massion A, et al. Remission and relapse in subjects' with panic disorder and panic with agoraphobia. *J Nerv Ment Dis* 1994;182:290-296.

Kellner M, Wiedemann K, Yassouridis A, Levengood R, Guo LS, Holsboer F, Yehuda R: Behavioral and endocrine response to cholecystokinin tetrapeptide in patients with posttraumatic stress disorder. *Biol Psychiat* 2000; 47:107-111.

Kellner M, Yehuda R. Do panic disorder and posttraumatic stress disorder share a common psychoneuroendocrinology? *Psychoneuroendocrinology* 1999;24:485-504.

Kelly CB, Cooper SJ. Plasma nor-epinephrine response to a cold pressure test in subtypes of depressive illness. *Psychiatry Res* 1998;81:39-50.

Kendler K, Gardner C. Bounderies of major depression. Am J Psychiatry 1998;155:172-177.

Kendler K, Neale MC, Kessler RC, Health AC, Eaves LJ. Major depression and phobias. *Psychol Med* 1993;23:361-71.

Kendler KS, Garder CG, Prescott CA: Panic syndromes in a population-based sample of male and female twins. *Psychol Med* 2001; 31:989-1000.

Kendler KS, Health AC, Martin NG, Eaves LJ. Symptoms of anxiety and symptoms of depression. *Arch Gen Psychiatry* 1987;44:451-7.

Kendler KS, Neale MC, Kessler RC, Heath AC, Eaves LJ: Genetic epidemiology of phobias in women. *Arch Gen Psychiatry* 1992; 49:273-281.

Kendler R, Gardner C, Prescott C. Panic syndromes in a population-based sample of male and female twins. *Psychol Med* 2001;31:989-1000.

Kent JM, Pupp LA, Martinez JM, Brown ST, Coplan JD, Klein DF, Gorman JM: Specificity of panic response to CO_2 inhalation in panic disorder. *Am J Psychiatry* 2001; 158: 58-67.

Kerr TA, Roth M, Schapira K. Prediction of outcome in anxiety states and depressive illnesses. *Br J Psychiatry* 1974;124:125-33.

Kessler R, Zhao S, Blazer D, Swartz M. Prevalence, correlates, and course of minor depression and major depression in the national comorbidity survey. *J Affect Disord* 1997;45:19-30.

Klein D, Klein H. Utility of the panic disorder concept. *Eur Arch Psychiatry Clin Neurosci* 1989; 238:268-279.

Klein D. Mixed anxiety depression. *L'Encephale* 1993;19:493-495.

Klinkman M, Schwenk T, Coyne J. Depression in primary care-more like asthma than appendicitis. *Canad J Psychiatry* 1997;42:966-973.

Klinkman MS, Oakes I: Mental health problems in primary care. *J Fam Practice* 1998; 47:379-384.

Koehler K, Vartzopoulos D, Ebel H: Relationship of panic attacks to autonomically labile generalized anxiety. *Compreh Psychiat* 1988; 29:91-97.

Kopp MS: Psychophysiological characteristics of anxiety patients and controls. *Psychother Psychosom* 1989; 52:74-79.

Krueger RF. Structure of common mental disorders. *Arch Gen Psychiatry* 1999;56:921-6.

Kumar A, Jin Z, Bilker W, Udupa J, Gottlieb G: Late-onset minor and major depression: early evidence for common neuroanatomical substrates detected by using MRI. *Proceedings of the National Academy of Sciences of the United States of America* 1998; 95(13):7654-7658.

Kuzel RJ. Treating comorbid depression and anxiety. *J Fam Pract* 1996;43(Suppl):545-53.

Lam RW, Stewart JN: Validity of atypical depression in DSM-IV. *Compreh Psychaitry* 1996; 37:375-383.

Lamberts H, Hofmans-Okkes IM: Classification of psychological and social problems in general practice. *Huisartsen Wetenschap* 1993; 36:5-13.

Lanius RA, Williamson PC, Densmore M, Boksman K, Gupta MA, Neufold RW, Gati JS, Menon RS: Neural correlates of traumatic memories in posttraumatic stress disorder. *Am J Psychaitry* 2001; 158:1920-1922.

Laver CJ, Krieg JC: Sleep electroencephalographic patterns and cranial competed tomography in anxiety disorders. *Compreh Psychiatry* 1992; 33:213-219.

Leckman JF, Weissman MM, Merikangas KR, Pauls DL, Prusoff BA. Panic disorder and major depression. *Arch Gen Psychiatry* 1983;40:1055-60.

Lecrubier Y, Ustun T. Panic and depression. *Int Clin Psychopharmacol* 1998;13(suppl 4):S7-11.

Leonard BE, Song CAI: Stress and the immune system. *Pharmacol Biochem Behav* 1996; 54:299-303.

Liebowitz M, Fyer A, Gorman J, Campeas R, Levin A, Davies S, et al. Alprazolam in the treatment of panic disorders. *J Clin Psychopharmacol* 1986;6:13-20.

Liebowitz MR, Hollander E, Schneier F, et al. Anxiety and depression. *J Clin Psychophamacol* 1990;0:61S-6S.

Liebowitz MR. Functional classification of anxiety-panic. *Int Clin Psychopharm*acol 1993;8(1 Suppl):47-52.

Lovibond P. Long-term stability of depression, anxiety and stress syndromes. *J Abnorm Psychol* 1998;107:520-526.

Lucey JV, Costa DC, Busatto G, Pilowsky LS, Marks IM, Ell PJ, Kerwin RW: Caudate regional cerebral blood flow in obsessive –compulsive disorder, panic disorder and health controls on single photoenissin conpitensed tonography. *Psychiatr Res* 1997; 74:25-33.

Lydiard RB. Coexisting depression and anxiety. *J Clin Psychiatry* 1991;51(6 Suppl):48-54.

Lyness JM, King DA, Cox C, Yoediono Z, Caine ED: The importance of subsyndromal depression in older primary care patients: prevalence and associated functional disability. *Journal of the American Geriatrics Society* 1999; 47(6):647-652.

MacKinnon DF, Zandi PP, Cooper J, et al. Comorbid bipolar disorder and panic disorder in families with a high prevalence of bipolar disorder. *Am J Psychiatry* 2002;159:30-5.

Magee WJ, Eaton WW, Wittchen HU, McGozagle KA, Kessler RC: Agoraphobia, simple phobia and social phobia in the National comorbidity study. *Arch Gen Psychiatry* 1996; 53:159-168.

Maier W, Lichtermann D, Minges J, Oehrlein A, Franke P. Controlled family study in panic disorder. *J Psychiatr Res* 1993;27(1 Suppl)79-87.

Malizia AL: What do brain imaging studies tell us about anxiety disorders? *J Psychopharmacol* 1999; 13:372-378.

Manicavasagar V, Silove D, Hadzi-Pavlovic D. Subpopulations of early separtion anxiety. *J Affect Disord* 1998;48:181-90.

Marks IM: Genetics of fear and anxiety disorders. *Br J Psychiatry* 1986; 149:406-418.

Marshall R, Olfson M, Hellman F, Blanco C, Guardico M, Struening E. Comorbidity, impairment and suicidality in subthreshold PTSD. *Am J Psychiatry* 2001; 158:1467-1473.

Marshall RD, Blanco C, Printz D, Liebowitz MR, Klein DF, Coplan J: Pilot study of noradrenergic and HPA axis functioning in PTSD vs. panic disorder. *Psychiatry Res* 2002; 110:219-30.

Massana J, Risueño JAL, Masana G, Marcos T, Gonzalez L, Otero A: Subtyping of panic disorders patients with bradycardic. *Eur Psychiatry* 2001, 16:109-114.

Massion AO, Warshaw MG, Keller MB: Quality of life and psychiatric morbidity in panic disorder and generalized anxiety disorders. *Am J Psychiatry* 1993; 150:600-607.

Mathew RJ, Wilson WH, Blazer DG, George LK: Psychiatric disorders in adult children of alcoholics. *Am J Psychiatry* 1993; 150:793-800.

Mathew RJ, Wilson WH: Behavioral and cerebrovascular effects of caffine in patients with anxiety disorders. *Acta Psychiatr Scand* 1990; 82:17-22.

Matsumoto RR. GABA receptors. *Brain Res* 1989;14:203-25.

Matthew SJ, Coplan JD, Gorman JM: Neurobiological mechanisms of social anxiety disorder. *Am J Psychiatry* 2001; 158:1558-1567.

Mavissakalian MR, Jones B, Olson S: Absence of placebo response in obsessive-compulsive disorder. *J Nerv Ment Dis* 1990; 178:268-270.

Mavissakalian MR, Tamar N: Generalized anxiety disorder versus panic disorder. *Compreh Psychiatry* 2000; 41:253-258.

McElroy SL, Altshuler LL, Suppes T, Keck PE Jr., Frye MA, Denicoff KD, Nolen WA, Kupka RW, Leverich GS, Rochussen JR, Ruch AJ, Post RM: Axis I psychiatric comorbidity and it relationship to historical illness variables in 288 patients with bipolar disorder. *Am J Psychiatry* 2001; 158:420-426.

McNeil R. Toward a greater understanding of depressive illness. *Fam Doctor* 1998;10:13-5.

Mehrabian A. General relative among drug use, alcohol use and major indexes of psychopathology. *J Psychol* 2001;135:71-86.

Meredith L, Sherbourne C, Jarkson C, Camp P, Wells K. Treatment typically provided for comorbid anxiety disorders. *Arch Fam Med* 1997;6:231-237.

Miller L. Dimensions of adolescent psychopathology. *J Abnorm Child Psychol* 1980;8:161-173.

Moros K, Telfer LA, Barlow DH. Efficacy and specific effects data on new treatments. *J Consult Clin Psychol* 1993;61:412-20.

Murphy DL, Pigott TA: Comparative examination of a role for serotonin in obsessive-compulsive disorder, panic disorder, and anxiety. *J Clin Psychiatry* 1990; 51(4 suppl):53-58.

Murphy JM, Olivier DC, Monson RR, Subol AM, Federman B, Leighton AH. Depression and anxiety in relations in relating to social status. *Arch Gen Psychiatry* 1991;48:223-9.

National Institute of Mental Health. Series DN No. 7, Overview of Mental Health Practices in Primary Care Settings, With Recommendations for Further Research, by Wilkinson G. DHHS Pub. No. (ADM) 86-1467. Washington, DC: Supt. Of Docs, Us Govt. Print. Off., 1986.

Nease D, Volk R, Cass A. Investigation of a severity based classification of mood and anxiety symptoms in primary care patients. *J Am Board Fam Pract* 1999;12:21-31.

Nease DE Jr., Volk RJ, Cass AR. Does the severity of mood and anxiety symptoms predict health care utilization? *J Fam Pract* 1999;48:769-77.

Nemeroff CB. Comorbidity of mood and anxiety disorders (ed.) *Am J Psychiatry* 2002;159:3-4.

Nisenson LG, Pepper CM, Schwenk TL, Coyne JC. Nature and prevalence of anxiety disorders in primary care. *Gen Hosp Psychiatry* 1998;20:21-8.

Noyes R Jr., Woodman C, Garvey MJ, Cook BL, Suelzer M, Clanoy J, Anderson DJ: Generalized anxiety disorder vs. panic disorder. *J Nerv Ment Dis* 1992; 180:369-379.

Olfson M, Broadhead W, Weissman M, Leon A, Farber L, Hoven C, et al. Subthreshold psychiatric symptoms in a primary care group practice. *Arch Gen Psychiatry* 1996;53:880-886.

Olfson M. Primary care patients who refuse specialized mental health services. *Arch Intern Med* 1991;151:239-132.

Orenstein H. Briquet's syndrome in association with depression and panic. *Am J Psychiatry* 1989;146:334-338.

Ormel J, Koeter MWJ, Van den Brink W, Van de Willige G. Recognition management, and course of anxiety and depression in general practice. *Arch Gen Psychiatry* 1991;48:700-6.

Ormel J, Oldehinkel A, Brilman E. Interplay and etiological continuity of neuroticism, difficulties, and life events in the etiology of major and subsyndromal first and recurrent depressive episodes in later life. *Am J Psychiatry* 2001;158:885-891.

Ormel J, Oldehinkel AJ, Goldberg DP, Hodiamont PPG, Wilmink FW, Bridges K. Structure of common psychiatric symptoms. *Psychol Med* 1995;36:521-30.

Ormel J, van den Brink W, Koeter M, Giel R, Van Der Meer K, Van De Willige G, et al. Recognition, management and outcome of psychological disorders in primary care. *Psychol Med* 1990;20:909-923.

Ormel J, Von Korff M, Ustun B, Pini S, Korten A, Oldehinkel T. Common mental disorders and disability across cultures. *JAMA* 1994;272:1741-1748.

Pauls DL, Bucher KD, Crowe RR, Noyes R Jr.: Genetic study of panic disorder pedigrees. *Am J Hum Genet* 1980; 32:639-644.

Paykel E, Prusoff B, Tanner J. Temporal stability of symptom patterns in depression. *Br J Psychiatry* 1976;128:369-374.

Perkonigg A, Kessler RC, Storz S, Wittchen HU. Traumatic events and post-traumatic stress disorder in the community. *Acta Psychiatr Scand* 2000;101:46-59.

Philbrick J, Connelly J, Woffand A. Prevalence of mental disorders in rural office practice. J *Gen Intern Med* 1996;11:9-15.

Piccinelli M, Rucci P, Ustun B, Simon G. Typological of anxiety depression and somatization symptoms among primary care attenders with no formal mental disorder. *Psychol Med* 1999;29:677-88.

Piercy MA, Sramek JJ, Kurtz NM, Cutler NR: Placebo response in anxiety disorder. *Arch Pharmacotherapy* 1996; 30:1013-1019.

Pincus HA, Davis WW, McQueen LE. 'Subthreshold' mental disorders: a review and synthesis of studies on minor depression and other 'brand names'. *Br J Psychiatry* 1999;174:288-96.

Pine DS, Klein RG, Coplan JD, Papp LA, Haren CW, Martinez J, Kovalenko P, Mandell DJ, Moreau D, Klein DF, Gorman JM: Differential carbon dioxide sensitivity in childhood anxiety disorders and non ill comparison group. *Arch Gen Psychiatry* 2000; 57:960-967.

Pollock C, Andrews G: Defense styles associated with specific anxiety disorders. *Am J Psychiatry* 1989; 146:1500-1502.

Pribor EF, Dinwiddie SH: Psychiatric correlates of incest in childhood. *Am J Psychiatry* 1992; 149:52-6.

Price RA, Kidd KK, Weissman MM. Early onset (under Age 30 Years) and panic disorder as markers for etidogic homogeneity in major depression. *Arch Gen Psychiatry* 1987;44:434-40.

Pukrop R: Dimensional personality profiles of borderline personality disorder in comparison with other personality disorders and healthy controls. *J Person Dis* 2002; 16:135-47.

Rapaport M, Judd L, Schettler P, Yonkers K, Thase M, Kupfer D, et al. Descriptive analysis of minor depression. *Am J Psychiatry* 2002;159:637-43.

Raskin M, Peeke HVS, Dickman W, Pinsker H: Panic and generalized anxiety disorders. *Arch Gen Psychiatry* 1982; 39:687-689.

Reed V, Wittchen HU: DSM-IV panic attacks and panic disorder in a community sample of adolescents and young adults. *J Psychiat Res* 1998; 32:335-345.

Reich J, Noyes R Jr., Hirschfeld R, Coryell W, O'Gorman T. State and personality in depressed and panic patients. *Am J Psychiatry* 1987;144:181-7.

Reich J, Noyes R, Yates W: Anxiety symptoms distinguishing social phobia from panic and generalized anxiety disorders. *J Nerv Ment Dis* 1988; 176:510-513.

Reich J, Troughton E. Comparison of DSM III personality disorders in recovered depressed and panic disorder patients. *J Nerv Ment Dis* 1988;176:300-4.

Reich J. Distinguishing mixed anxiety/depression from anxiety and depression groups using the family history method. *Compr Psychiatry* 1993;34:285-90.

Reich J. Epidemiology of anxiety. *New Direct Ment H Serv* 1986(winter);32:11-30.

Rickels K, Ryan MA: What is generalized anxiety disorder? *J Clin Psychiatry* 2001; 62(suppl 11):4-12.

Robbins J, Kirmayer L, Cathebras P, Yaffe M, Dworking M. Physician characteristics and the recognition of depression and anxiety in primary care. *Med Care* 1994;32:795-812.

Rosenberg R, Ottosson JO, Beach P, Mellergard M, Rosenberg NK: Validation criteria for panic disorder as a nosological entity. *Acta Psychiatr Scand* 1991; (suppl)365:7-17.

Roth M: Panic-agoraphobia syndrome. *Am J Pschiatry* 1996; 153:111-124.

Roth WT, Wilhelm FH, Trabert W: Voluntary breath holding in panic and generalized anxiety disorders. *Psychosom Med* 1998; 60:671-679.

Rotondo A, Mazzanti C, Dell'Osso L, et al. Catechol O-Methyl transferase, serotonin transporter, and tryptophan hydrolase gene polymorphisms in bipolar disorder patients with and without comorbid panic disorder. *Am J Psychiatry* 2002;159:23-9.

Rowan AB, Foy DW, Rodriguez N, Ryan S. Posttraumatic stress disorder in a clinical sample of adults sexually abused as children. *Child Abuse Negl* 1994;18:51-61.

Roy-Bryne PP, Staug P, Wittchen HU, Ustun B, Watters EE, Kessler RC. Lifetime panic-depression comorbidity in the National Comorbidity Survey. *Br J Psychiatry* 2000;176:229-35.

Sabelli HC, Javaid JI, Fawcett J, Kravitz HM, Wynn P. Urinary phenylacetic acid in panic disorder with and without depression. *Acta Psychiatr Scand* 1990;82:14-6.

Saboonchi F, Lundh LG, Ost LG: Perfectionism and self-consciousness in social phobia and panic disorder with agoraphobia. *Behav Res Ther* 1999; 37:799-808.

Sanderson WC, Di Nardo PA, Rapee RM, Barlow DH: Syndrome comorbidity in patients diagnosed with a DSM-III-R anxiety disorder. *J Abn Psychol* 1990; 99:308-312.

Saraceno B, Terzian E, Barguero F, Tognoni G. Mental health care in the primary health care setting. Health Policy Planning 1995;10(2):133-143.

Sartorius N, Ustun TB Lecruber Y, Wittchen HU. Depression comorbid with anxiety. *Br J Psychiatry* 1996;30(Suppl):38-43.

Schapira K, Roth M, Kerr TA, Gurney C. Prognosis of affective disorders. *Br J Psychiatry* 1972;121:175-81.

Scherrer JF, True WR, Xian H, Lyons MJ, Eisen SA, Goldberg J, Lin N, Tsuang MT: Evidence for genetic influences common and specific to symptoms of generalized anxiety and panic. *J Affect Dis* 2000; 57:25-35.

Schittecutte M, Charles G, Depauw Y, Mesters P, Wilmotte J. Growth hormone response to clonidine in panic disorder patients. *Psychiatry Res* 1988;23:147-51.

Schulberg H, Madonia M, Block M, Coulehan J, Scott C, Rodriguez E, et al. Major depression in primary care practice. *Psychosomatics* 1995;36:129-137.

Schurhoff F, Bellivier F, Jouvent R, Mouren-Siméoni MC, Bouvard M, Allialaire JF, Leboyer M: Early and late onset bipolar disorders. *J Affect Dis* 2000; 58:215-221.

Schweizer E, Rickels K, Weiss S, Zavodnick S. Maintenance drug treatment of panic disorder. *Arch Gen Psychiatry* 1993;50:51-60.

Schweizer E: Problems investigating efficacy in anxiety states. *Intl Clin Psychopharm* 1993; 8 suppl. 2: 57-61.

Shelton RC, Brown LL. Mechanisms of action in the treatment of anxiety. *J Clin Psychiary* 2001;62(12 Suppl):10-5.

Shepherd M, Wilkinson G, Williams P (eds). Mental Illness in Primary Care Settings. New York, NY: *Tavistock;* 1986.

Shepherd M, Wilkinson G. Primary care as the middle ground for psychiatric epidemiology (ed). *Psychol Med* 1988;18:263-267.

Sherbourne C, Wells K, Hays R, Rogers W, Burnam M, Judd L. Subthreshold depression and depressive disorder. *Am J Psychiatry* 1994;151:1777-1784.

Sherbourne CD, Wells KB, Meredith LS, Jackson CA, Camp P: Comorbid anxiety disorder and the functioning and well-being of chronically ill patients of general medical providers. *Arch Gen Psychiatry* 1996; 53:889-895.

Simon G, Goldberg D, Tiemens B, Ustua T. Outcomes of recognized and unrecongnized depression in an international primary care study. *Gen Hosp Psychiatry* 1999;21:97-105.

Simon G, Ormel J, VonKorff M, Barlow W. Health care costs associated with depressive and anxiety disorders in primary care. *Am J Psychiatry* 1995;152:352-357.

Simon G, Von Korff M, Durham M. Predictions of outpatient mental health utilization by primary care patients in a health maintenance organization. *Am J Psychiatry* 1994;151:908-913.

Sireling LI, Paykel ES, Freeling P, Rao BM, Patel SP: Depression in general practice. *Br J Psychiatry* 1985; 147:113-119.

Skodel A, Schwartz S, Dohrenwend B, Levav I, Shrout P. Minor depression in a cohort of young adults in Israel. *Arch Gen Psychiatry* 1994;51:542-551.

Smollen JW, Tsuang MT: Panic and phobic anxiety . *Am J Psychiatry* 1998; 155:1152-1162.

Solyom L, Ledwidge B, Solyom C: Delineating social phobia. *Br J Psychiatry* 1986; 149:464-70.

Spitzer R, Kroenke K, Linzer M, Hahn S, Williams J, deGruy FV III, et al. Health-related quality of life in primary care patients with mental disorders. *JAMA* 1995;274:1511-1517.

Spitzer RL, Williams JBW, Kroenke K, Linzer M, deGruy FV, Hahn SR, Broday D, Johnson JG: Utility of a new procedure for diagnosing mental disorders in primary care. *JAMA* 1994; 272:1749-1756.

Spitzer R, Wakefield J. DSM-IV diagnostic criterion for clinical significance. *Am J Psychiatry* 1999;156:1856-1864.

Stein MB, Kirk P, Prabho V, Grott M, Terepa M. Mixed anxiety-depression in a primary care clinic. *J Affect Disord* 1995;34:79-84.

Stein MB, Uhde TW. Panic Disorder and major depression. *Psychiatr Clin North Am* 1988;11:441-61.

Sullivan GM, Coplan JD, Kent JM, Gorman JM: Noradrenergic system in pathological anxiety. *Bio Psychiatry* 1999; 46:1205-1218.

Szegodi A, Wetzel H, Angersbach D, Philipp M, Benkert O: Response to treatment in minor and major depression: results of a double-blind comparative study with paraxetine and maprotiline. *Journal of Affective Disorders* 1997; 45(3):167-178.

Thompson C, Ostler K, Pereler R, Raker N, Kinmonth A. Dimensional perspective on the recognition of depressive symptoms in primary care. *Br J Psychiatry* 2001;179:317-323.

Tiemens BG, Ormel J, Simon GE. Occurrence, recognition and outcome of psychological disorders in primary care. *Am J Psychiatry* 1996;153:636-44.

Torgersen S: Genetic factors in anxiety disorders. *Arch Gen Psychiatry* 1983; 40:1085-1089.

Tsuang D, Cowley D, Ries R, Dunner DL, Roy-Byrue PP. Effects of substance use disorder on the clinical presentation of anxiety and depression in an outpatient psychiatric clinic. *J Clin Psychiatry* 1995,56:549-55.

Turner SM, Williams SL, Beidel DC, Mezzich JE: Panic disorder and agoraphobia with panic attacks. *J Abnorm Psychol* 1986; 95:384-388.

Tyrer P, Murphy S, Kingdon D, et al. Nottingham study of neurotic disorder. *Lancet* 1988;8605:235-40.

Valliant G, Schnurr P. What is a case? *Arch Gen Psychiatry* 1988;45:313-319.

Van Balkom AJLM, Beekman ATF, de Beurs E, Deeg DJH, van Dyck R, van Tilburg W: Comorbidity of the anxiety disorders in a community-based older population in the Netherlands. *Acta Psychiatr Scand* 2000; 101:37-45.

Van Bardeleben V, Holsboer F. Human corticotropin releasing hormone. *Prog Neuropsychopharmacol Biol Psychiatry* 1988;12:5165-87.

Van den Brink W, Leenstra A, Ormel J, Van de Willige G. Mental health intervention programs in primary care. *J Affect Disord* 1991;21:273-284.

Van den Hauvel OA, van de Wetering BJM, Veltman DJ, Pauls DL: Genetic studies of panic disorder. *J Clin Psychiatry* 2000; 61:756-766.

Van Valkenburg C, Akiskal HS, Puzantian V, Rosenthal T. Anxious depressions. *J Affect Disord* 1984;6:67-82.

Vasquez-Barguero J, Wilkinson G, Williams P, Diez-Manrique JF, Rena C. Mental health and medical consultation in primary care settings. *Psychol Med* 1990;20:681-694.

Verburg C, Griez E, Meijer J: 35% carbon dioxide challenge in simple phobias. *Acta Psychiatr Scand* 1994; 90:420-423.

Watson D,Walker L. Long-term stability and predictive validity of trait measures of affect. *J Pers Soc Psychol* 1996;70:567-577.

Weinshilboum RM: Biochemical genetics of catecholamines in humans. *Mayo Clin Proc* 1983; 58:319-330.

Weissman MM, Fyer AJ, Haghighi F, HeimanG, Deng Z, Hen R, Hodge SE, Knowles JA: Potential panic disorder syndrome. *Am J Med Genetics* 2000; 96:24-35.

Weissman MM, Wickramaratne P, Adams PB, et al. Relationship between panic disorder and major depression. *Arch Gen Psychiatry* 1993;50:767-80.

Weissman MM: Epidemiology of anxiety disorders. *J Psychiatr Res* 1988; 22(suppl 1):99-114.

Weissman MM: Panic and generalized anxiety. *J Psychiat Res* 1990; 24(suppl 2):157-162.

Wells A, Papageorgiou C: Observe perspective. *Behav Res Ther* 1999; 37:653-658.

Wells K, Burnam A, Camp P. Severity of depression in prepaid and fee-for-service general medical and mental health specialty practices. *Med Care* 1995;33:350-364.

Wells KB, Golding JM, Burnam MA. Chronic medical conditions in a sample of the general population with anxiety, affective and substance use disorders. *Am J Psychiatry* 1989;146:1440-6.

Wessely S, Nimnuan C, Sharpe M. Functional somatic syndromes. *Lancet* 1999;354:936-939.

Westen D, Arkowitz-Westen L. Limitations of Axis II in diagnosing personality pathology in clinical practice. *Am J Psychiatry* 1998;155:1767-1771.

Westen D, Shedler J. Revising and assessing Axis II. *Am J Psychiatry* 1999;156:258-272.

Wilhelm FH, Trabert W Rothe WT: Physiologic instability in panic disorder and generalized anxiety disorder. *Biol Psychiatry* 2001; 49:596-605.

Winokur A, Winokur D, Rickels K, Cox D. Symptoms of emotional distress in a family planning services. *Br J Psychiatry* 1984;144:395-399.

Wittchen H, Lieb R, Pfisteo H, Schusten P. Waxing and warning of mental disorders. *Compr Psychiatry* 2000;41(suppl 1):122-132.

Yamada S, Yamauchi K, Yajima J, Hisadomi S, Maeda H, Toyomosu K, Tamaka M: Saliva level of free 3-methoxy 4-hydroxyphenylglycol (MHPG) as a biological index of anxiety disorders. *Psychiat Res* 2000; 93:27-23.

Yang T, Dunner DL: Differential subtyping of depression. *Dep Anx* 2001; 13:11-7.

Yonkers K, Zlotnick C, Allsworth J. Is the course of panic disorder the same in women and men? *Am J Psychiatry* 1998;155: 596-602.

Zanarini MC, Frankerburg FR, Dubo ED, et al. Axis I comorbidity of borderline personality disorder. *Am J Psychiatry* 1998;155:1733-9.

Zhang L, Barrett JE. Interactions of corticotropin releasing factor with antidepressant and anxiolytic drugs. *Biol Psychiatry* 1990;27:953-67.

Zinsbarg R, Barlow D, Liebowitz M, Street L, Broadhead E, Katon W, et al. DSM-IV field trail for mixed anxiety-depression. *Am J Psychiatry* 1994;151: 1153-1162.

Zlotnick C, Franklin CL, Zimmerman M: Does "subthreshold" posttraumatic stress disorder have any clinical relevance? *Compreh Psychiatry* 2002; 43:413-9.

INDEX

A

ability to think, 61
abuse, 48, 49, 52, 54, 109, 113, 199, 212
acceptance, 45, 69, 71, 82, 125, 132, 149
accountability, 80
achievement, 72, 87, 125, 134, 137
acid, 132, 218
acrophobia, 167
activation, ix, 1, 8, 12, 14, 18, 186, 189
activity level, 86
acute stress, 102, 183, 208
adaptation, 195
ADHD, 125
adjustment, 72, 85, 138, 186, 205, 212
adolescence, 114, 117, 120, 125, 129
adolescent(s), 64, 84, 86, 105, 109, 110, 111, 113, 125, 134, 199, 200, 202, 204, 209, 212, 216, 217
adults, 66, 67, 75, 101, 102, 109, 110, 118, 123, 126, 134, 162, 208, 218
affect, x, 5, 6, 13, 14, 16, 26, 27, 29, 39, 40, 43, 54, 66, 70, 186, 192, 193, 208, 220
affective disorder, 183, 191, 198, 200, 209, 210, 212, 218
age, 19, 29, 62, 63, 64, 65, 66, 68, 69, 76, 82, 86, 92, 97, 114, 119, 120, 126, 131, 133, 143, 145, 146, 150, 160, 195
aggression, 45, 71, 106
aggressive behavior, 44, 142, 212
AIDS, 56, 57, 67, 83
alcohol, 127, 215
alcoholics, 72, 85, 215
alcoholism, 26, 193
alertness, 166
alienation, 60
alternative(s), 7, 15, 27, 36, 38, 69, 173, 205
ambiguity, 16
ambiguous events, 16

ambiguous stimuli, 3, 19
American Psychiatric Association, 18, 121, 137, 154, 156, 174, 198, 204, 206
American Psychological Association, 84
amygdala, 186, 189, 193
analyses of variance (ANOVA), 32, 34, 97, 98, 146
anger, 6, 45, 49, 54
anorexia nervosa, 84
antidepressants, 187, 190
antisocial personality disorder, 191
anxiety, ix, x, xi, 1, 2, 3, 4, 5, 6, 7, 8, 9, 10, 11, 14, 15, 16, 17, 18, 19, 20, 21, 22, 23, 25, 26, 27, 28, 29, 30, 32, 34, 36, 37, 38, 39, 40, 41, 43, 44, 45, 46, 47, 53, 54, 55, 56, 57, 59, 62, 63, 64, 65, 66, 67, 68, 69, 70, 71, 72, 73, 74, 75, 76, 77, 78, 79, 80, 81, 82, 83, 84, 85, 86, 87, 88, 89, 92, 101, 102, 103, 106, 108, 109, 113, 119, 120, 125, 126, 127, 129, 137, 139, 149, 150, 151, 153, 154, 155, 157, 158, 159, 160, 161, 162, 163, 164, 165, 166, 167, 168, 169, 170, 171, 172, 173, 174, 175, 176, 177, 178, 179, 180, 181, 183, 184, 185, 186, 187, 188, 189, 190, 191, 192, 193, 194, 195, 196, 197, 198, 200, 201, 202, 203, 204, 205, 206, 207, 208, 209, 210, 211, 212, 213, 214, 215, 216, 217, 218, 219, 220, 221
anxiety disorder(s), xi, 11, 19, 20, 120, 125, 161, 163, 164, 166, 167, 170, 173, 178, 181, 183, 184, 185, 186, 187, 188, 189, 190, 191, 192, 193, 196, 197, 198, 202, 203, 205, 206, 207, 208, 209, 210, 211, 212, 213, 214, 215, 216, 217, 218, 219, 220
anxious mood, 125, 186
appetite, 121
appraisals, 122
argument, 15, 49, 118
arousal, 2, 26, 44, 88, 119, 120, 131, 192, 196, 208
assertiveness, 71

assessment, 19, 20, 30, 39, 63, 81, 99, 101, 106, 107, 115, 128, 134, 135, 137, 138, 143, 145, 146, 149, 164, 178, 205, 210
assessment tools, 106
association, ix, 21, 25, 26, 38, 92, 127, 207, 209, 216
asthma, 214
asymmetry, 40, 161
attention, ix, xi, 2, 3, 4, 7, 8, 9, 12, 17, 18, 19, 21, 23, 25, 26, 27, 28, 29, 30, 31, 32, 35, 36, 37, 38, 39, 40, 41, 48, 92, 106, 116, 117, 118, 120, 122, 125, 141, 142, 144, 148, 153, 161, 166, 167, 169, 170, 173, 195
attentional bias, ix, 1, 3, 7, 8, 9, 10, 11, 12, 17, 21, 119, 148, 166, 167
attitudes, x, 4, 43, 45, 46, 48, 53, 54, 55, 56, 57, 71, 82, 83, 84, 85, 87, 88
attribution, 29, 30, 31, 34, 35, 36, 39, 40, 118
auditory cortex, 127
Australia, 43, 46, 53, 56
autobiographical memory, 12, 13, 15, 21, 22, 23
automatic processing, 161
autonomy, 124
avoidance, 2, 7, 11, 13, 15, 17, 18, 20, 30, 67, 69, 92, 93, 94, 98, 100, 101, 103, 109, 116, 121, 126, 154, 155, 157, 158, 161, 167, 168, 171, 173, 175, 177, 183, 192, 196
avoidance behavior, 92, 93, 154, 158, 167, 168, 171
awareness, 5, 21, 26, 44, 46, 51, 52, 54, 63, 66, 67, 68, 80, 88, 129, 154, 161, 178

B

Beck Depression Inventory, 9
behavior(s), ix, x, 3, 6, 18, 25, 26, 27, 29, 36, 37, 38, 40, 44, 45, 48, 49, 53, 67, 78, 84, 88, 91, 92, 99, 100, 103, 137, 139, 140, 149, 150, 158, 160, 162, 164, 174, 178, 179, 195, 204
behavior therapy, 88, 139, 150, 178
behavioral medicine, 180
behavioral problems, 204
beneficial effect, 172
bias, x, 3, 7, 10, 11, 12, 14, 16, 17, 18, 19, 20, 21, 22, 25, 28, 29, 34, 35, 36, 37, 38, 39, 55, 148, 166, 167, 178, 190
biology, 190
bipolar disorder, 193, 215, 218
birth, 114, 125
blocking, 44, 54, 178
blood flow, 186, 187, 189, 214
blood pressure, 44, 171
body, ix, 60, 61, 69, 81, 127, 129, 188
borderline personality disorder, 182, 192, 210, 212, 217, 221

boys, 65, 120, 125, 145, 146, 147
brain, xi, 110, 129, 181, 187, 188, 189, 215

C

Canada, 56, 57, 85
cancer, 63, 66, 69, 70, 82, 83
case study, 87
categorization, xi, 59, 181, 189
causal, ix, 8, 18, 21, 25, 26, 27, 29, 30, 33, 34, 35, 36, 37, 38, 39
causal attribution, ix, 25, 29, 30, 33, 34, 35, 36, 38, 39
causality, 39, 40, 65, 66
central nervous system, 212
childhood, 18, 64, 81, 102, 125, 149, 150, 187, 188, 192, 208, 212, 217
children, x, xi, 61, 64, 65, 66, 67, 68, 69, 70, 71, 81, 82, 83, 85, 86, 87, 88, 105, 106, 108, 109, 110, 111, 112, 114, 115, 116, 117, 118, 119, 120, 121, 122, 123, 124, 125, 126, 127, 128, 129, 130, 131, 132, 133, 134, 135, 136, 137, 138, 139, 141, 142, 143, 144, 145, 146, 147, 148, 149, 150, 151, 155, 162, 179, 183, 190, 207, 209, 215, 218
classical conditioning, 158, 159, 160, 167
classroom, 119
clients, 45, 52, 55
clinical assessment, 106
clinical depression, 120
clinical disorders, 40
clinical psychology, 20
closure, 52
clusters, 62, 188, 192, 204
coding, 6, 13, 209
coercion, 125
cognition(s), ix, x, 1, 2, 13, 17, 20, 21, 43, 75, 84, 101, 130, 161, 162, 163, 164, 165, 167, 172, 173, 175, 176, 177, 178, 180, 188
cognitive ability(ies), 60, 61, 64, 65, 115, 133
cognitive activity, 75
cognitive biases, ix, 1, 3, 4, 5, 8, 9, 17, 18
cognitive development, 83, 85
cognitive functioning, 82
cognitive performance, 22
cognitive perspective, 2, 19, 160, 161, 175, 176
cognitive process(es), x, 25, 27, 161, 164, 166, 173
cognitive psychology, 2, 4, 5, 14, 161
cognitive research, 14
cognitive style, 166
cognitive tasks, 9, 18
cognitive therapists, 170
cognitive therapy, 84, 106, 172, 180
cohort, 47, 55, 219

college students, ix, 16, 25, 71, 87, 88
communication, 44, 54, 65, 67, 85, 107, 114, 124,
    139, 198
communication skills, 54
community, x, 43, 44, 46, 56, 57, 79, 80, 87, 102,
    103, 114, 137, 149, 150, 176, 179, 180, 181, 189,
    191, 200, 201, 203, 206, 211, 217, 220
competence, 46, 48, 49, 53
competition, 114, 117
complex, xi, 2, 13, 116, 124, 128, 141, 147, 148, 160
complexity, 47, 63
comprehension, 84, 131, 137
computer, 9, 13, 144, 171, 175
concept, 47, 65, 66, 73, 76, 79, 82, 83, 85, 86, 115,
    122, 128, 148, 188, 214
conceptions, 64, 65, 83, 85
conceptual model, 40
conditioned stimulus, 158
conditioning, 92, 101, 116, 141, 147, 149, 150, 158,
    159, 160, 173, 176, 179
conduct, xii, 120, 125, 142, 148, 182, 189
conduct disorders, 125, 142, 148
confidence, 5, 16, 29, 36, 46, 56, 109, 123, 140, 147
conflict(s), ix, 52, 54, 55
conformity, 67
confrontation, 154, 171
confusion, 50, 53, 134
conscious awareness, 9
consciousness, 26, 39, 64
consequence(s), x, 15, 27, 37, 38, 43, 44, 53, 74, 75,
    76, 92, 102, 103, 116, 117, 119, 120, 158, 160,
    164, 168, 175, 178
conservation, 131
construct validity, 94
construction, 64, 87, 88
consumption, 112
context(s), 3, 4, 17, 18, 46, 53, 81, 196
contingency, 120
continuity, 85, 216
control, 13, 20, 26, 28, 37, 39, 63, 72, 108, 110, 111,
    112, 113, 116, 121, 123, 125, 127, 128, 129, 130,
    131, 134, 135, 136, 139, 160, 162, 163, 164, 165,
    169, 170, 172, 175, 177, 186, 195, 206
control condition, 172
control group, 26, 28, 206
cooperation, 67, 107, 119
coping, xi, 45, 52, 53, 70, 81, 105, 106, 108, 115,
    122, 123, 124, 125, 126, 127, 128, 131, 134, 135,
    137, 142, 147, 148, 155, 161, 167, 168, 169, 170,
    171, 173, 176, 177, 178, 179
coping strategies, xi, 105, 125, 126, 135, 147, 171
core, 69, 77, 79, 80, 81, 94
correlation, 32, 86, 95, 100, 107, 145

correlation coefficients, 95
cortex, 127, 186, 195
cortisol, 193
counseling, 82
criterion, 45, 154, 199, 200, 202, 219
criticism, 3, 5, 17, 45, 111, 114, 125
cross-validation, 101
crying, 118, 119, 155
cues, 3, 6, 12, 13, 21, 23, 28, 45, 75, 76, 170, 178,
    180
cultural values, 87
culture(s), 60, 64, 65, 79, 80, 199, 201, 210, 211, 216
curriculum, x, 43

D

damage, 37, 99
dangerousness, 171
data collection, 94
decision, 5, 51, 112, 122, 124, 126, 204
decision-making, 112, 204
definition, 63, 76, 132, 139, 154, 155, 199
delusions, 53, 207
demand characteristic, 4
demographic characteristics, 69
denial, 65, 66, 70, 81, 113
dependent variable(s), 9, 34, 145
depression, xi, 17, 26, 37, 38, 39, 40, 71, 86, 92, 125,
    177, 180, 181, 182, 190, 191, 192, 193, 194, 195,
    196, 197, 199, 200, 201, 202, 204, 205, 206, 207,
    208, 209, 210, 212, 213, 214, 215, 216, 217, 218,
    219, 220, 221
depressive, xi, 16, 181, 182, 183, 189, 190, 191, 192,
    193, 194, 195, 196, 197, 198, 199, 200, 202, 203,
    204, 205, 206, 207, 208, 209, 210, 211, 212, 213,
    215, 216, 218, 219
depressive symptomatology, 16, 203
depressive symptoms, 182, 191, 195, 199, 200, 202,
    204, 210, 212, 219
desire, 47, 66, 117
detachment, 71
deviation, 14
diagnoses, 178, 183, 184, 192, 200, 201, 202, 204,
    205, 206, 207, 209
Diagnostic and Statistical Manual of Mental
    Disorders (DSM), viii, xi, 1, 2, 5, 20, 137, 154,
    155, 178, 179, 181, 182, 184, 189, 190, 196, 197,
    198, 199, 200, 201, 202, 203, 204, 205, 206, 207,
    208, 210, 211, 212, 214, 217, 218, 219, 221
diagnostic criteria, xi, 120, 155, 181, 200
dialogue, 173

differences, x, 5, 13, 15, 34, 40, 59, 69, 70, 71, 76, 82, 85, 91, 93, 97, 98, 103, 114, 145, 146, 174, 183, 186, 189, 192, 204, 205
differentiation, 161, 182, 206
dimensionality, 204
dimensions, 5, 6, 13, 19, 63, 69, 74, 81, 94, 157, 161, 184, 185, 196, 204, 205, 208
directionality, 113
disability(ies), 92, 131, 191, 195, 201, 203, 207, 215, 216
discrimination, 21, 178, 189
disease, 66, 67, 83, 85, 86, 116, 190, 193, 212
disgust, 157
displacement, 185
dissatisfaction, 200
distress, xi, 1, 2, 11, 16, 17, 53, 83, 92, 118, 119, 120, 128, 130, 136, 154, 155, 166, 181, 182, 196, 200, 201, 202, 203, 204, 205, 208, 209, 211
distribution, 6, 32, 97, 157
diversity, 45
divorce, 65, 114
dominance, 52, 53
dopamine, 186, 195
double-blind, 219
drive, 27, 195
drug(s), 126, 142, 169, 195, 207, 210, 215, 218, 221
drug use, 215
DSM-III, 20, 198, 205, 208, 218
DSM-IV, 1, 2, 5, 154, 155, 178, 179, 184, 198, 199, 200, 204, 207, 208, 211, 212, 214, 217, 219, 221

E

earth, 68
eating, 4, 14, 64, 81, 111
eating disorders, 81
education, x, 43, 56, 57, 87, 101, 177, 179, 192
effective, xi, 38, 54, 57, 65, 117, 121, 128, 142, 147, 153, 169, 170, 171, 173, 175, 187, 194, 198
efficiency, 114, 186, 211
ego strength, 71
elaboration, 9, 79
elderly, 69, 70, 71, 82, 86
emergence, 54
emotion(s), x, 2, 4, 38, 40, 43, 44, 47, 48, 49, 50, 52, 53, 54, 74, 75, 76, 106, 126, 128, 131, 165, 207
emotional disorders, 21, 161, 174, 178
emotional distress, 160, 198, 205, 208, 220
emotional experiences, 20
emotional information, 166
emotional reactions, 160, 169
emotional responses, 48, 50, 52, 55
emotional state(s), 63, 106

empathy, 52, 54, 71, 154
empirical studies, 3, 4, 63
encoding, 12, 14
endorphins, 195
England, 22, 83, 84
English, 45
enthusiasm, 45
environment, 9, 11, 15, 17, 29, 37, 39, 46, 47, 53, 54, 56, 68, 105, 126, 166, 185, 186, 189, 190, 193
environmental change, 44
environmental factors, 185
environmental stimuli, 160
epinephrine, 213
episodic, 19, 202
ethics, 44, 139
Europe, 206
euthanasia, 71, 82, 87
evaluation, 2, 3, 4, 17, 26, 28, 38, 73, 74, 75, 76, 82, 134, 137, 174, 177
everyday life, 12
evil, 61, 64, 101
evolution, 158
exercise, xi, 6, 47, 48, 51, 52, 54, 164, 170, 181, 189
expectation(s), 4, 11, 12, 14, 36, 37, 65, 161, 162, 164, 166, 173, 188
experiment, ix, 4, 8, 25, 33, 128, 158
experimental condition, 36
experimental design, 12, 26
expertise, 169
explicit memory, 10, 11, 12, 15, 18
expression, 64, 66, 67, 73, 81, 133
external locus of control, 112
external validity, 37
externalizing disorders, 193
extinction, 59, 60

F

facial expressions, 8
factor(s), 2, 34, 37, 45, 57, 63, 65, 72, 83, 93, 99, 101, 102, 103, 106, 107, 108, 111, 113, 114, 127, 134, 135, 137, 142, 143, 144, 148, 149, 150, 164, 168, 173, 176, 177, 191, 192, 195, 196, 204, 205, 208, 210, 211, 219
factor analysis, 82, 196, 204
failure, 29, 34, 35, 37, 38, 114, 119, 150, 154, 162, 202
faith, 111, 133
family(ies), 45, 62, 63, 79, 82, 83, 88, 103, 114, 117, 123, 124, 125, 136, 140, 143, 148, 180, 182, 185, 188, 190, 192, 193, 195, 199, 200, 204, 208, 209, 213, 215, 217, 220
family environment, 140

family members, 136

fatigue, 116, 212

fear(s), ix, x, xi, 1, 2, 4, 5, 7, 8, 17, 18, 26, 28, 43, 44, 45, 46, 47, 48, 49, 50, 52, 53, 54, 55, 59, 60, 61, 62, 63, 64, 65, 67, 68, 69, 70, 72, 73, 74, 75, 76, 80, 81, 82, 84, 86, 87, 88, 91, 92, 93, 94, 95, 97, 98, 99, 100, 101, 102, 103, 105, 106, 107, 108, 109, 110, 111, 113, 114, 115, 117, 119, 122, 123, 125, 126, 127, 130, 131, 132, 133, 134, 135, 136, 137, 138, 139, 140, 141, 142, 143, 144, 145, 146, 147, 148, 149, 150, 153, 155, 157, 158, 160, 162, 164, 167, 169, 170, 171, 173, 174, 175, 176, 177, 178, 179, 180, 187, 189, 193, 196, 211, 215

fear response, 170, 174

feedback, 27, 38, 117, 124, 134, 193

feelings, ix, 44, 45, 48, 49, 50, 51, 52, 53, 54, 55, 63, 75, 76, 92, 106, 108, 122, 131, 133, 156, 167

female(s), 26, 70, 93, 126, 139, 213

focusing, 36, 45, 75, 76, 105, 166, 167

forgiveness, 61

free recall, 12, 14

free will, 111

frequency, 2, 26, 47, 65, 69, 73, 94, 120, 164, 172, 173, 201

Freud, Sigmund, 60, 76, 82

friends, 60, 72, 114

frontal, 193

frustration, 53, 179

functional, 25, 110, 138, 190, 204, 215

functional analysis, 138

functioning, 26, 64, 81, 155, 160, 161, 163, 203, 215, 219

G

gambling, 188

gender, 65, 70, 82, 95, 97, 145, 164

gender differences, 145

generalisation, 111, 115

generalized anxiety disorder, 11, 15, 162, 183, 190, 198, 206, 208, 215, 217, 218, 220

genes, 190, 193

genetics, xi, 181, 185, 188, 189, 190, 220

genotype, 186

gestures, 3

girls, xi, 65, 120, 125, 141, 143, 144, 145, 146

God, 60, 62, 65, 80

GPA, 82

grief, 48

group therapy, 48, 49, 179

grouping, 50

H

habituation, 70, 170

hallucinations, 53, 204

happiness, 50, 79

harm, 192

hate, 110

health care, x, 43, 54, 92, 99, 100, 198, 201, 210, 216, 218

health problems, 46, 70, 214

health services, 53, 210

health status, x, 91, 92, 195

helplessness, 154

heroin, 72, 83

heterogeneity, 185

high school, 65, 82

hippocampus, 193

homicide, x, 43

homogeneity, 217

hopelessness, 82

hormones, 193

hospice, 70, 81, 87

hostility, 106

HPA axis, 193, 215

human behavior, 39, 102

human brain, 139

human nature, 138

human rights, 53, 55

husband, 70

hyperactivity, 125, 190

hypnosis, 128, 170, 177, 179

hypnotherapy, 177

hypochondriasis, 205

hypothesis, 11, 13, 26, 27, 28, 34, 86, 211

I

iatrogenic, 116

ID, 37, 115, 139

identification, x, 72, 80, 91, 92, 93, 100, 106, 207

identity, 62, 64, 85

idiosyncratic, 14, 38, 135

imagery, 40, 102, 115, 127, 128, 171

imagination, 127

immortality, 80, 85

immune system, 214

implicit memory, 10, 20

impulsivity, 148, 188, 199

incarceration, 45

inclusion, 182, 198

income, 71

independent variable, 145

indices, 16, 17
indirect effect, 160
individual differences, 22, 39, 65, 69, 179
induction, 21, 128
inferences, 37
inferiority, 168
influence, 9, 13, 15, 18, 26, 34, 100, 113, 123, 132, 147, 148, 171, 173, 196
information processing, 6, 7, 9, 11, 17, 18, 19, 26, 72, 106, 119, 161
inhibition, 159, 178, 180, 185, 207
injury, 40, 93, 101, 103, 114, 162, 168, 171, 176, 180
inmates, 70
inputs, 72, 73
insight, 137, 162
insomnia, 70
integration, 46, 54, 175
intelligence, 86
intensity, 48, 50, 53, 59, 65, 157, 184
interaction, 2, 3, 26, 27, 31, 34, 35, 37, 48, 103, 140, 205
interaction effects, 34
interference, 1, 7, 18, 20, 147, 148
internal change, 147
internal consistency, 102, 173
internal locus of control, 112, 113
internalizing, 204
International Classification of Diseases (ICD), 190, 199
interpersonal relationships, 87, 124
interpersonal skills, 54
interpretation, 3, 9, 15, 16, 17, 18, 19, 22, 129, 132, 160, 161, 189
intervention(s), 52, 84, 93, 99, 106, 115, 134, 137, 155, 168, 169, 172, 173, 174, 175, 220
interview, 1, 11, 29, 30, 31, 32, 33, 37, 79, 144, 179, 203
introspection, 21
introversion, 142
intrusions, 157
investment, 173
Ireland, 67, 69, 83, 85

J

Jordan, 6, 16, 22, 23
justice, 66, 78, 79

K

Kentucky, 87

knowledge, xi, 5, 6, 22, 44, 45, 46, 54, 56, 67, 87, 116, 135, 153, 166, 189, 197

L

lack of control, 113
language, xii, 45, 127, 128, 129, 131, 182, 189
latency, 13, 186
latent inhibition, 142
later life, 207, 216
laughing, 49
lead, xi, 28, 38, 64, 75, 76, 92, 134, 137, 154, 181, 187, 188, 189, 195, 196, 201
learning, x, 11, 43, 44, 45, 46, 47, 51, 52, 53, 54, 55, 56, 57, 109, 114, 123, 124, 131, 133, 134, 136, 143, 154, 157, 158, 170, 174
learning activity, 56
learning environment, x, 43, 44, 46
learning outcomes, 55
learning skills, 133
left hemisphere, 193
liberation, 131
life satisfaction, 72, 82
lifespan, 92
light, ix, 11, 12, 47, 67, 158
likelihood, 16, 17, 37, 54, 110, 116, 118, 164, 165
location, 7, 73
locus of control, 72, 83, 85, 87, 111, 112, 138
loneliness, 61, 63
longitudinal study, 150, 177
long-term memory, 14
love, 61
low risk, 210
lying, 72, 77, 81, 130

M

magnetic resonance imaging (MRI), 110, 214
major depression, 182, 190, 191, 192, 193, 194, 195, 196, 199, 200, 201, 202, 203, 206, 207, 208, 209, 210, 211, 213, 214, 217, 219, 220
maladaptive, ix, 1, 3, 4, 5, 6, 8, 9, 15, 18, 34, 37, 154, 173, 186, 189, 198
male, 12, 96, 126, 213
management, xi, 46, 86, 87, 102, 118, 120, 123, 138, 139, 140, 141, 143, 147, 148, 149, 169, 175, 177, 178, 205, 216
mania, 49
manipulation, 26, 29, 31, 32, 34
marital status, 71, 82
matching, 174
maternal support, 114

mean, xi, 14, 29, 32, 33, 34, 35, 69, 113, 141, 143,
    145, 146, 147, 156, 157, 160, 161, 195
meanings, 9, 47, 72, 73, 76, 77, 78, 79, 81, 88
measurement, x, 82, 99, 105, 140
medication, 48, 167, 169
memory, ix, 1, 3, 4, 9, 10, 11, 12, 13, 14, 15, 16, 17,
    18, 19, 21, 22, 23, 28, 39, 60, 61, 156, 157, 165,
    166, 173, 175, 193, 195
memory biases, ix, 1, 3, 10, 15, 17
memory performance, 10, 14
memory processes, 173
memory retrieval, 12
mental disorder, xi, 1, 18, 154, 155, 174, 182, 184,
    193, 195, 198, 200, 201, 203, 204, 205, 208, 211,
    214, 216, 217, 219, 220
mental health, x, xi, 2, 43, 44, 45, 46, 47, 48, 52, 53,
    54, 55, 56, 57, 86, 156, 181, 189, 196, 198, 199,
    202, 203, 204, 216, 219, 220
mental health professionals, 2
mental illness, x, xi, 43, 45, 46, 54, 55, 57, 181, 182,
    189, 197, 198, 199, 200, 203, 204, 205, 212
mental image(s), 3, 12, 161, 163
mental representation, 3
meta-analysis, 26, 40, 210, 212
metaphor, 74, 75
methodology, ix, 1, 4, 5, 63
Miami, 20
Missouri, 56, 85
mode, 9, 62, 73, 75
modeling, 92, 139, 141, 143, 182
models, ix, 1, 3, 4, 20, 92, 123, 160, 175, 182, 193,
    198
moderators, 26
mood, 15, 26, 75, 120, 121, 139, 142, 155, 165, 166,
    180, 193, 195, 208, 209, 210, 216
mood disorder(s), 155, 193, 208
morality, 79
morbidity, 120, 125, 202, 213
mortality, 65, 66, 68, 80, 82, 86, 92
mothers, 86, 106, 114, 116, 119, 123, 136
motivation, 72, 155, 195
multidimensional, 63, 88
multiples, 132
murder, 50
muscle relaxation, 128
muscles, 116, 128, 171
music, 12, 127, 137, 170

N

natural, 18, 27, 39, 59, 65, 72, 158, 171, 182, 198,
    204
needs, 55, 118, 125, 136, 137, 148, 197, 205

negative affectivity, 196
negative attitudes, 43, 46, 53
negative emotions, 54, 193
negative experiences, 44, 46, 142
negative outcomes, 38, 163
negative reinforcement, 118, 120
negative valence, 30
neglect, 121, 168
negotiation, 121, 137
Netherlands, 84, 141, 149, 153, 180, 220
neuroticism, 71, 88, 185, 216
neurotransmitter(s), 193, 195
neutral, 7, 8, 9, 10, 11, 12, 13, 14, 15, 16, 18, 69,
    123, 135, 160, 167
neutral stimulus, 7
nicotine, 127
noise, 10
non-verbal, 131
norepinephrine, 186, 189, 190, 195
normal children, 84
nurses, 50, 53, 56, 57, 70, 85, 122

O

observations, 63, 66, 67, 70, 76, 182, 203, 204
obsessive-compulsive disorder, 155, 206, 212, 215,
    216
occipital cortex, 211
omission, 116
operant conditioning, 92, 123, 158, 167
organization, 219
overload, 129

P

panic attack, 2, 155, 167, 180, 183, 184, 186, 187,
    189, 190, 191, 200, 207, 208, 209, 212, 213, 214,
    217, 219
panic disorder, 21, 22, 155, 163, 183, 184, 185, 186,
    187, 188, 189, 190, 191, 192, 193, 194, 195, 196,
    198, 200, 201, 202, 203, 206, 207, 208, 209, 210,
    211, 212, 213, 214, 215, 216, 217, 218, 220, 221
parental support, 117
parents, xi, 65, 66, 67, 69, 70, 82, 109, 116, 117,
    123, 124, 125, 136, 137, 138, 139, 141, 142, 143,
    144, 147, 148, 207
partnership, 109
passive, 82, 169
pathways, 141, 189
Pavlovian conditioning, 175
peers, 51, 52, 54, 67, 109
perceived control, 116, 119, 129, 138

perception(s), 2, 30, 39, 40, 45, 57, 71, 84, 85, 86, 101, 106, 113, 114, 121, 144, 148, 157, 161, 166, 178, 180
perceptions of control, 113, 178
perceptual, 44, 54
perfectionism, 185
performance, ix, 2, 3, 6, 7, 8, 9, 12, 17, 18, 21, 25, 26, 27, 28, 29, 30, 31, 32, 34, 35, 36, 37, 38, 41, 45, 76, 117
performance ratings, 18
personal control, 109
personal identity, 53
personal life, 169
personality, 30, 33, 34, 36, 71, 81, 84, 85, 87, 88, 160, 162, 163, 175, 185, 188, 192, 195, 198, 205, 206, 209, 211, 217, 220
personality disorder(s), 192, 198, 211, 217
personality research, 84, 175
personality trait(s), 84, 88, 185
perspective, 4, 14, 17, 20, 28, 36, 37, 39, 40, 53, 54, 102, 160, 168, 219, 220
persuasion, 111
pessimism, 180
phenomenology, xi, 181, 188
phobia(s), x, xi, 1, 2, 5, 7, 8, 10, 11, 12, 13, 18, 19, 20, 21, 22, 23, 25, 28, 34, 37, 38, 39, 40, 41, 59, 101, 102, 135, 136, 141, 142, 149, 153, 154, 155, 157, 159, 160, 163, 164, 167, 168, 169, 171, 172, 173, 174, 175, 176, 177, 178, 179, 180, 183, 184, 185, 186, 187, 188, 189, 190, 191, 192, 196, 205, 206, 211, 213, 215, 217, 218, 219, 220
phobic stimulus, 155, 171, 173
physical aggression, 49
physiological arousal, 92, 94, 98, 126
physiological correlates, 44
placebo, 20, 187, 194, 215
planning, 67, 84, 112, 137, 193, 220
pleasure, 50, 120
police, 49
population, x, xi, 1, 29, 38, 70, 88, 91, 92, 93, 98, 139, 141, 147, 150, 153, 154, 179, 182, 198, 207, 213, 220
positive correlation, 70
positive emotions, 54, 193
positive mood, 126
post-traumatic stress disorder (PTSD), 21, 155, 156, 157, 178, 183, 184, 185, 186, 187, 188, 189, 191, 192, 193, 194, 196, 199, 201, 209, 211, 215, 217
power, 35, 37, 99, 117
PP, 215, 218, 219
pragmatism, 71
predictability, 169, 174
prediction, 84, 92, 138, 199

predictive validity, 182, 205, 220
predictors, 26, 86, 87, 146, 173, 191, 204
preference, 179
prejudiced, 45
premature death, 69
preoperational stage, 64
pressure, 53, 114, 130, 213
priming, 10, 21
principle, 158, 159, 160, 164, 165, 166, 167, 169
prisoners, 71
probability, 36, 164, 168
problem solving, 44, 117, 124, 138
professionalism, 45
program, 57, 139, 142, 150, 170, 171, 175, 187, 213
programming, 138, 175
provision, 110, 206
psychiatric diagnosis, 180, 204, 212
psychiatric disorders, 20, 202, 207, 213
psychiatric hospitals, 45, 46
psychiatric institution, 50
psychiatric morbidity, 215
psychiatric patients, 46, 202, 203
psychiatrist, 204
psychological development, 114
psychological problems, 155
psychological stress, 138, 175
psychological well-being, x, 105
psychopathology, 3, 92, 161, 174, 184, 192, 195, 201, 204, 207, 215, 216
psychosis, 191, 209
psychosocial factors, 205
punishment, 60, 63, 64, 66, 80, 118, 120, 123, 158

Q

quality of life, 23, 81, 201, 219
questioning, 45, 54, 73, 106, 109, 116

R

racial, 48
range, 9, 17, 18, 32, 37, 44, 47, 48, 52, 55, 59, 68, 76, 94, 143, 145, 147, 156, 160, 190
rational, 173
reaction time, 9
reading, 8
reality, 44, 53, 75, 76, 79, 106, 127, 197, 198, 199, 202, 205
reasoning, 8, 27, 28, 119
recall, 10, 11, 12, 13, 14, 16, 18, 22, 23, 28, 73, 160, 161, 165, 166, 203, 210
recalling, 11, 36

receptors, 193, 215
recognition, 12, 16, 113, 125, 175, 188, 195, 203, 217, 219
recognition test, 12
reconcile, 8
recovery, 192
reflection, x, 43, 44, 46, 47, 51, 54, 55, 115
regression, 34, 97, 99, 145, 146, 165
regression analysis(es), 145, 146, 165
reinforcement, 111, 116, 118, 139, 167, 195
relationship(s), ix, 2, 20, 27, 28, 32, 37, 38, 39, 44, 54, 55, 82, 83, 85, 86, 87, 100, 101, 103, 109, 123, 150, 155, 162, 165, 167, 169, 171, 173, 180, 183, 184, 185, 190, 192, 193, 196, 199, 204, 207, 208, 212, 215
relatives, 60, 114
relaxation, 128, 164, 169, 170, 171, 175, 178, 179, 180
reliability, 13, 29, 68, 94, 98, 102, 202
religion, 65, 68, 80
religiosity, 85
religious, 64, 71, 72, 80, 82, 85, 87
REM, 186, 194
remembering, 22, 132, 170
replication, 16, 21
repression, 71, 76
resilience, 133, 155
resolution, 46, 55, 202
response, xi, 2, 7, 8, 12, 29, 35, 44, 47, 50, 51, 52, 62, 67, 68, 69, 79, 99, 120, 123, 133, 143, 149, 154, 155, 158, 160, 179, 180, 181, 182, 186, 187, 188, 189, 190, 193, 194, 195, 213, 215, 217, 218
response format, 68, 69
responsibility, 5, 29, 37, 53, 80, 114
retention, 14, 22
retention interval, 14
retribution, 80
retrieval, 5, 14, 23
reunion, 63
reward, 116, 117, 118, 120, 123, 131, 158, 192, 195
right hemisphere, 193
risk, xi, 118, 141, 144, 147, 148, 149, 168, 186, 190, 192, 201, 207
risk factor(s), 148, 192
robustness, 17, 190

S

sadness, 49, 51, 63, 68
safety, 52, 57, 121
satisfaction, 87, 101, 109
scaling, 128
schema, ix, 1, 3, 4, 5, 6, 8, 14, 15, 23, 161

school, 68, 114, 117, 119, 150
scientific progress, 84
second order, 204
selecting, 55, 120
selection, 127, 198, 206
selective attention, 150
self, ix, 2, 4, 5, 6, 16, 18, 20, 21, 25, 26, 27, 28, 29, 30, 31, 32, 33, 34, 35, 36, 37, 38, 39, 40, 44, 45, 46, 51, 52, 53, 54, 63, 69, 72, 79, 80, 81, 82, 83, 88, 92, 94, 97, 99, 106, 107, 108, 111, 113, 116, 118, 121, 125, 127, 128, 130, 133, 134, 137, 139, 157, 161, 162, 163, 164, 171, 173, 177, 178, 179, 194, 202, 210, 218
self-actualization, 80, 88
self-awareness, 4, 27, 39, 51, 54
self-confidence, 134
self-consciousness, 26, 39, 218
self-doubt, 45, 72
self-efficacy, 113, 116, 118, 128, 164, 178, 179
self-esteem, 44, 53, 72, 82, 83, 92, 108, 111, 125, 133, 134, 210
self-evaluation, 130
self-image, 72
self-monitoring, 202
self-observation, 31
self-presentation, 37, 38, 40
self-regulation, 39, 179
self-relevant, 16, 26
self-reports, 4
self-schemata, 6
self-worth, 111
sensation(s), ix, 16, 17, 75, 76, 99, 122, 127, 130, 132, 133, 167, 169, 178, 188
sensitivity, 72, 188, 189, 192, 195, 217
sensitization, 175
separateness, 183
septum, 193
series, ix, 1, 10, 12, 14, 29, 106, 165, 172
serotonin, 187, 210, 216, 218
severity, x, 92, 98, 105, 132, 145, 146, 162, 167, 168, 173, 184, 191, 192, 199, 200, 201, 202, 203, 204, 205, 216
sexual, 48, 188, 192, 208, 212
sexual abuse, 188, 192, 208, 212
shame, 45, 167
shaping, 78, 149
sharing, 120, 128
siblings, 70, 114, 117
signals, 132
Singapore, 149
situation, ix, 2, 4, 25, 27, 29, 30, 33, 34, 36, 37, 38, 44, 49, 54, 64, 67, 68, 71, 73, 76, 110, 113, 119,

124, 129, 147, 148, 150, 154, 155, 158, 159, 160, 161, 163, 166, 168, 170, 173, 179
skill, 28, 46, 117, 128, 133
smoking, 88
social activities, 155
social anxiety, vii, 25, 32
social desirability, 4, 85
social evaluation, 26, 31
social events, 15, 22, 28
social interaction(s), 2, 4, 8, 17, 18, 27, 30, 37, 39
social learning, 116
social life, 168
social norms, 53
social problems, 144, 214
social psychology, 27, 28, 39
social rules, 67
social situations, 3, 27, 28, 29, 37, 38, 39, 155, 184
social status, 216
somatization, 72, 92, 191, 204, 217
speech, 1, 4, 5, 11, 14, 18, 26, 45, 48, 106, 107, 127, 134, 162, 179
speed, 116, 121
spontaneity, 205
stability, 102, 182, 190, 195, 200, 202, 203, 212, 214, 217, 220
stages, 13, 17, 63, 64, 65, 67, 119, 135, 136, 167
standard deviation, 14, 33
statistics, 5
stereotype, 44
stereotypes, 45, 55
stimuli, 7, 8, 9, 10, 11, 12, 13, 14, 15, 16, 18, 27, 73, 76, 92, 94, 98, 99, 119, 121, 125, 131, 154, 155, 157, 158, 160, 161, 162, 166, 167, 169, 170, 171, 173, 175, 176, 189, 195
stress, 19, 21, 44, 53, 63, 72, 83, 89, 102, 112, 114, 115, 126, 136, 138, 156, 169, 174, 175, 177, 179, 180, 183, 188, 189, 193, 195, 199, 208, 210, 212, 213, 214, 218, 221
stressor, 44, 156, 196, 205
stroke, 133
students, x, 2, 29, 32, 43, 44, 45, 46, 47, 48, 49, 50, 51, 52, 53, 54, 55, 56, 57, 60, 70, 82, 83, 86, 87, 88, 162, 164
subjective experience, 86, 147
substance abuse, 120, 125, 191, 203
substance use, 192, 199, 210, 212, 219, 220
suicide, 23, 55, 70, 71, 82, 85, 201
surprise, 49, 133
Sweden, 149
sympathetic nervous system, 44, 125
symptomology, 92
symptoms, xi, 15, 16, 21, 22, 82, 106, 125, 155, 156, 174, 177, 178, 181, 182, 183, 184, 188, 192, 195,

196, 198, 199, 200, 201, 202, 203, 204, 208, 209, 210, 212, 213, 216, 217, 218

T

task difficulty, 28
taxonomy, 205
temperament, 138, 144, 185
temporal, 73, 75, 76, 161, 189
temporal lobe, 189
tension, 44, 54, 128, 170, 175, 180, 196
terror management theory, 80, 87
terrorism, ix
test-retest reliability, 173, 200
theory, x, 9, 18, 20, 22, 27, 39, 40, 43, 46, 54, 55, 57, 78, 79, 84, 87, 88, 129, 142, 150, 179, 209
therapy, 2, 19, 20, 21, 22, 39, 40, 41, 44, 48, 82, 86, 87, 88, 101, 102, 103, 127, 138, 142, 149, 150, 171, 174, 175, 176, 177, 178, 179, 180, 187, 194, 208, 210
thinking, 46, 47, 64, 67, 68, 161, 162, 163, 171, 177, 180
threat, ix, 1, 2, 3, 4, 5, 6, 7, 8, 9, 10, 11, 12, 13, 14, 15, 16, 17, 18, 19, 20, 21, 22, 23, 64, 83, 106, 111, 119, 122, 124, 125, 129, 154, 162, 167, 168, 176, 178, 179
threatened violence, 48, 49, 53, 55
threshold(s), 63, 125, 133, 134, 186, 189, 190, 199, 200, 201, 203, 208
torture, 60, 63
toys, 114
traditional, 71
training, 122, 124, 126, 138, 173, 177, 179
trait anxiety, 17, 71, 87, 92, 165, 166, 172, 173, 178, 179, 185
traits, 185
transcendence, 71
transformations, 80
transgressions, 60
trauma, 85, 151, 153, 155, 156, 157, 160, 173, 177, 192, 208, 212
traumatic experiences, 157
treatments, 44, 67, 137, 142, 154, 156, 157, 158, 159, 165, 166, 168, 170, 188, 194, 210, 216
triggers, 193
trust, 71, 82, 108, 109, 113, 119, 124, 125, 127, 128, 129, 130, 131, 132, 133, 134, 135, 136, 139, 140, 174
twins, 199, 213

U

uncertainty, 44, 110
unconditional positive regard, 54
unconditioned response, 158
unconscious, 60, 161, 166
universality, 64, 65, 66
university students, 85

V

vacuum, 110
valence, 17, 32, 34, 39
validation, 20, 39, 87, 88, 102, 207
validity, 8, 29, 53, 63, 68, 85, 94, 101, 102, 140, 150, 167, 173, 176, 182, 190, 198, 201, 203, 207, 211
values, 33, 34, 44, 46, 53, 74, 75, 76, 95, 100
variability, 203
variable, 11, 38, 44, 73, 92, 94, 95, 97, 109, 113
variance, 97, 100, 131, 145, 146, 147, 165
variation, 131
victimisation, 56
victims, 157, 178
Vietnam, 211

violence, x, 43, 45, 48, 49, 52, 53, 56, 65, 66, 85, 114
vision, 132
voice, 12, 13, 109, 120
vulnerability, 2, 6, 18, 21, 131, 190, 196

W

war, 63, 82
well-being, 72, 120, 168, 207, 219
wellness, 198
withdrawal, xi, 110, 141, 146, 147
wives, 71, 83
women, 29, 72, 87, 208, 213, 221
words, 3, 7, 8, 9, 10, 11, 12, 13, 18, 22, 25, 36, 45, 69, 73, 91, 147, 158, 163, 164, 169, 179
workers, 86
workplace, 52, 56
worry, 2, 45, 59, 124, 131
writing, 47

Y

young adults, 217, 219